OPERATING IN EMERGING MARKETS

A GUIDE TO MANAGEMENT
AND
STRATEGY IN THE NEW INTERNATIONAL ECONOMY

Luciano Ciravegna
Robert Fitzgerald
Sumit Kundu

© 2014 by Luciano Ciravegna, Robert Fitzgerald, and Sumit Kundu
Publishing as FT Press
Upper Saddle River, New Jersey 07458

FT Press offers excellent discounts on this book when ordered in quantity for bulk purchases or special sales. For more information, please contact U.S. Corporate and Government Sales, 1-800-382-3419, corpsales@pearsontechgroup.com.
For sales outside the U.S., please contact International Sales at international@pearsoned.com.

Printed in the United States of America

First Printing August 2013

ISBN-10: 0-13-298338-9
ISBN-13: 978-0-13-298338-9

Pearson Education LTD.
Pearson Education Australia PTY, Limited.
Pearson Education Singapore, Pte. Ltd.
Pearson Education Asia, Ltd.
Pearson Education Canada, Ltd.

Pearson Educación de Mexico, S.A. de C.V.
Pearson Education—Japan
Pearson Education Malaysia, Pte. Ltd.

Library of Congress Control Number: 2013941690

Vice President, Publisher
Tim Moore

Associate Publisher and Director of Marketing
Amy Neidlinger

Executive Editor
Jeanne Glasser

Operations Specialist
Jodi Kemper

Marketing Manager
Lisa Loftus

Cover Designer
Alan Clements

Managing Editor
Kristy Hart

Project Editor
Elaine Wiley

Copy Editor
Bart Reed

Proofreader
Sarah Kearns

Indexer
Lisa Stumpf

Senior Compositor
Gloria Schurick

Manufacturing Buyer
Dan Uhrig

Dedicated to our families and to all the people who helped us.

Contents

---

[*] Ying Liu (MBA, University of Connecticut) is a doctoral candidate in Management and International Business at Business School, Florida International University. She has an MBA degree in Operations and Information Management from University of Connecticut. Her current research interests include global strategy and international business of firms in emerging economies, inter-firm cooperation and competition, and corporate governance.

Foreword

When the history of the late 20th and early 21st centuries is written by future generations, all the wars, terrorist incidents, and political upheavals will be reduced to a passing mention or a footnote. But one salient fact will be recorded—the emergence of 80 percent of the world's population from poverty to a middle class status, from ignorance to enlightenment, and the transformation of their somnolent, regulated markets into economic dynamism.

It will be remembered as the great rebalancing. As recently as the year 2000, emerging countries, despite comprising over three-quarters of the world's population, had only a 40 percent share of world GDP. A mere 10 years later, this share had grown to 49 percent, and is on its way to 60 percent by 2025. Emerging market companies, long reduced to playing a servile role as low-margin commodity exporters or mere assemblers of gadgets and toys, are now beginning to climb both ends of the "smiling curve" (a term popularized by Stan Shih, former CEO of Acer to suggest greater value capture in the R&D and brand portions of the value chain). Twenty-five years ago, almost no one in the West had heard of Lenovo, LG, Haier, Embraer, and Concha y Toro. Yet today, their research skills and brands out-innovate and outmaneuver the old champions like Apple, Electrolux, and Microsoft. Companies based in the BRICs punch above their weight class in global competition—as they indeed have to, because they are relatively new to international business, and their home base is still institutionally weak.

No manager should be let loose in international competition, no student of business should be given a diploma, no CEOs should cocoon themselves in the relative serenity of their advanced home nation without an exposure to the conditions, economies, business practices, and requirements of doing business in emerging countries. A tsunami of opportunities, with heady currents, awaits there.

Professor Farok J. Contractor
Rutgers Business School

Acknowledgments

We wish to thank all the people who helped us through this project, in particular the entrepreneurs, managers, and workers who have been kind enough to share their experiences with us. We found amazing people in emerging markets, people who opened their doors to us, told us their stories, and, in short, helped us see a broader, certainly more complex and exciting picture of the realities in which they live and work. We thank all of them; this book would have been impossible without their help and generosity. We also owe a great deal to Susanna Siddiqui, who did an amazing job at integrating our work and improving its style and narrative. Thanks also to Melina, for her help in collecting and assembling data for the project.

—The authors

I owe special acknowledgments to several people, including my dad. The idea for this project initially developed through conversations I had with him during our walks through the countryside—and he believed in this work long before I did. I also wish to thank my wife, Sara, for supporting me throughout the project and especially in its most stressful moments; my mum and brother; Susanna; Sara Roberts; and my friends in Costa Rica, the UK, Italy, Brazil, Hong Kong, Nicaragua, Chile, Peru, the Czech Republic, and many other places. Thank you all.

—Luciano Ciravegna

My thanks, for many reasons, to Christina and Izabelle.

—Robert Fitzgerald

I would like to thank my former mentor late Professor John Dunning and Professor Farok J. Contractor, who supported me every step of the way in my professional development. Over the years my doctoral students have been an excellent pool with which to work and have stimulating intellectual conversations on new research projects. Their continuous encouragement and friendship made a profound impact on my career, and I dedicate this book to them.

—Sumit Kundu

About the Authors

Dr. Luciano Ciravegna is an Associate Professor in Strategy and International Business (University of London, INCAE). His research interests include regional and global internationalization strategies, international entrepreneurship, and the impact of multinational companies on the countries where they invest. His focus is on emerging markets and emerging markets' businesses. His work has been published in several peer-reviewed journals, including the *Journal of International Business Studies,* the *Journal of Development Studies,* the *International Journal of Operations Management,* and the *Journal of Business Research.* He has worked on research, consulting, and policy advisory projects in Argentina, Brazil, China, Chile, Colombia, Costa Rica, the Czech Republic, El Salvador, Guatemala, Honduras, Hong Kong, Italy, Nicaragua, Peru, and the UK. His background includes a BSc at the London School of Economics, an MPhil at the University of Oxford, St. Antony's College, and a PhD at the London School of Economics. He is an alumnus of the United World College and a fellow of the Centro Studi D'Agliano.

Dr. Robert Fitzgerald is a Reader in Business History and International Management at the Royal Holloway School of Management, University of London, specializing in business history, comparative management, international business, and the economies of the Asia Pacific and Japan. He has written on human resource management and labor, business cultures, economic development, marketing and consumption, and business organization, often from an international and comparative perspective, and has recently completed a book on the rise of the multinational enterprise from the nineteenth to the twenty-first century.

Dr. Sumit K. Kundu is a Professor and James K. Batten Eminent Scholar Chair in International Business at the College of Business Administration at Florida International University. He has published several articles in prestigious journals—namely, *Journal of International Business Studies, Journal of Management Studies, Management International Review, Journal of World Business, Journal of International Management, Journal of International Marketing, Journal of Business Research, Journal of Business Ethics, Journal of World Business, Journal of International Management, Leadership Quarterly,* and *Journal of Small Business Economics.* He has served as a chair and member on ten dissertation committees. Dr. Kundu has presented numerous papers at the Academy of International Business, Academy of Management, and Strategic Management Society conferences. He served as the track chair for the AIB annual conference in Stockholm, Sweden in July 2004; Milan, Italy in June 2008; San Diego, California in

June 2009; and Nagoya, Japan in June 2011. Dr. Kundu organized the Junior Faculty Consortium at the annual Academy of International Business 2006 conference in Beijing, China and the Doctoral Consortium at the annual Academy of International Business 2012 conference in Washington, DC. He has also served as the president and program chair for the Midwest Academy of International Business Conference in 2003 and 2002. He has worked for several global companies, such as Boeing, MasterCard International, Ingersoll-Rand, and Novartis, to name a few.

Emerging Markets, BRICS, N11, and Civets

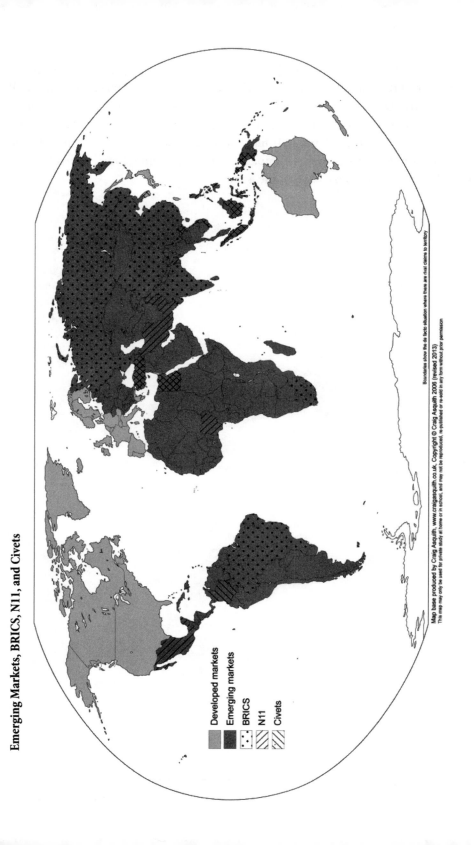

Developed markets

Emerging markets

BRICS

N11

Civets

Map base produced by Craig Asquith, www.craigasquith.co.uk. Copyright © Craig Asquith 2006 (revised 2013)
This map may only be used for private study at home or in school, and may not be reproduced, re-published, re-sold in any form without prior permission

Boundaries show the de facto situation where there are rival claims to territory

Introduction

Emerging Markets and the New International Economy

T he dawn of new the millennium heralded a new era where emerging markets assert themselves as the new driving force of the world economy. An era where the United States still maintains its leading economic and military position in the world while Europe's economic power—a legacy of its imperial past and leading role in the industrial revolution—gradually wanes. The axes of the world economy are changing in irreversible ways. Year by year, developed economies account for a lower proportion of the wealth, consumption, investment, trade, and technology generated in the world. The rise of emerging markets—their emergence after more than 200 years of being relatively minor players in the global economy—is causing one of the most significant shifts in the global economic and geopolitical structure since the beginning of the industrial revolution. This shift is less sudden and less immediately visible than spectacular political changes, such as the fall of the Soviet Union. And yet, it is altering the way in which we see the world: the markets most coveted by consumer goods producers and investors, the companies that conquer their respective industries and become global leaders, the cities and landscapes that are changing fastest. This shift is generating new business opportunities, supporting a new breed of competitive multinational companies based in emerging markets, and forcing established global leaders to adapt their strategies or face an inevitable decline.

Financial investors have been quick to spot the trend, developing a variety of instruments designed to capture higher returns from these fast-growing markets. Goldman Sachs led the trend, back in 2001, and much before anyone predicted the financial crisis of 2008, pointing to the BRICS and then in 2005 to the N11 as locations for new investment opportunities (for more information on the BRICS, N11, and Civets, please see the Appendix). Management books and business guides have been less quick to adapt—the vast majority of texts covering the subject of emerging markets have been written by finance experts, targeting mainly a finance-oriented readership (Moebius, 2012; O'Neill, 2011; Sharma, 2012; Van Agtmael, 2007). In spite of the effort of authors such as Khanna and Palepu (2010), academics have been slow in developing new models, strategies, and theories aimed at the thousands of companies, managers, and entrepreneurs interested in running non-financial operations in emerging markets. Business schools and management departments across the world continue to rely on texts, theories, and case studies written with a strong developed economy-centric mindset, suited to training students for a world where companies had U.S., Europe, and Japan divisions, and the rest of the world was often bundled together as "the rest." The world has changed, however, and for the better.

Between 2008 and 2013, emerging markets have contributed to approximately 80% of the world's economic growth, while unemployment, public debt, and recession have continued to dominate the economic and political discourse in Europe, the U.S., and Japan. Emerging markets own the majority of the world's natural resources, ranging from fertile land to minerals and oil. They have accumulated almost 80% of the world's foreign exchange reserves and are contributing to a rising share of global trade and investment. Some of the most prestigious developed economy firms, such as Land Rover, Arcelor, and Volvo, survive thanks to emerging market investors. Others, such as Nestlé, McDonald's, and General Electric, are betting heavily on emerging markets for their future growth. Meanwhile, companies based in emerging markets have become global leaders in almost every sector, ranging from baked products to smartphones, oil, gas, solar panels, telecommunication equipment, personal computers, refrigerators, airlines, and commercial ports. All of these factors give much visibility in the media to the shift in the balance of economic power between developed and emerging economies.

For decades, the big question for multilateral organizations, such as the UN and World Bank, for policy makers and academics has been why other economies have failed to catch up with the "Triad" (the U.S., Western Europe, and Japan). Since 2009, the world has awoken to the fact that emerging economies actually are catching up—and fast. Old industrial powers such as the UK and France are becoming less and less important in the global economy, while China, Russia, Brazil, Indonesia, Vietnam, Turkey, and other emerging markets continue to expand. The U.S. remains the largest economy in the world, but it has been struggling to recover from the 2008 crisis. Japan has lost its second position to China, an incumbent that prior to the 2000s had a smaller total GDP than Italy despite its population being about 20 times larger. It may soon appear anachronistic to catalogue the UK, France, and Italy among the world's economic powers. And it may soon be obvious that all the world's largest economies, with the exceptions of the U.S., Japan, and Germany, will be emerging markets. As of 2013, the rest of the world, the South, or the Third World, as these countries were rather disparagingly referred to for many years, already generates a higher share of global wealth than the developed world. Emerging markets already account for the vast majority of the world's population and land mass. What is surprising is that for many years, they only contributed to a minor share of the world economy.

The shift has been occurring for several years now. Having an "emerging markets" strategy has become a priority, not a luxury. In this book, we discuss the implications for managers and companies, providing a guide to different types of emerging markets and examining the risks related to operating in these environments. One of the most important take-outs of this book is that emerging markets have not "emerged" yet. They continue to be affected by poverty, inequality, and infrastructural deficiencies. Many are ruled by authoritarian regimes, armed violence and endemic corruption are more widespread and have more nefarious consequences than in developed economies, and large shares of their populations still have poor access to health, shelter, and education. This means, in spite of their current popularity and positive economic performance, most people in emerging markets live shorter lives, earn less, and have a less comfortable existence than in developed economies. It is precisely because of these reasons that emerging markets will continue to generate important business opportunities in the future. In most fields, ranging from infrastructure to banking services, there is a long way to go before these markets come close to reaching the levels of saturation we see in richer economies. And, as we illustrate in the second part of this book, there is no shortage of opportunities to develop businesses that generate healthy profits. For companies and managers interested in having a wider impact, we explore opportunities to achieve healthy profits while also directly improving the quality of life of the citizens in emerging markets citizens.

Emerging markets have by no means solved all their structural problems, but their general condition has been improving at a remarkable rate, which seems to have unsettled a long established assumption about their status of "periphery." Millions of people in Asia, Latin America, and Africa have seen some improvement in their living conditions; every year they earn more, spend more, and acquire access to new goods and services that improve their standards of living further. It is this accelerating change that has shifted the axes of the world economy, generating unprecedented business opportunities. Change also causes disruption, forcing people to acquire new skills and migrate, in line with Shumpeter's description of "creative destruction." The transformation of economies can disrupt the lives of those reliant on traditional sectors and ways of working, such as those in small-scale agriculture, and can draw large numbers into urbanizing or industrializing areas to exist in insanitary slums. Growth, while bringing benefits to many, can likewise push significant sections of the population into poverty, making them losers in the battle for scarce resources, including, in known cases, access to drinkable water. Economic change can bring with it the danger of rising social tensions or conflict between ethnic groups. Yet, it means by definition unleashing a country's productive potential and the opportunity to invest and profit, and thus contributing to local economic and social development in the long term. We have written this book to aid those who are willing to take a leading attitude and drive creation and to inspire those who are desperately trying to avoid some of the inevitable, destructive aspects of change, to stop clinging on to old ideas and strategies that are no longer relevant when faced with the shifts we have described.

In the year 2012, amid the untangling of the Euro crisis, some articles we submitted to refereed academic journals were rejected because fresh empirical information about business in emerging markets was deemed to be irrelevant, and insufficient for advancing the theory. The suggestions we received hinted, much to our surprise, that theory had to be advanced from a Europe- or U.S.-centric perspective. Our misadventures in the academic publishing arena illustrate the need for a change in mindset to a perspective where emerging markets cease to be an afterthought, something exotic but rather secondary, and acquire the more central status they deserve to have in the theory and practice of management. The presumption that good ideas, innovative products, and creative strategies are only the realm of the Triad is not only unacceptable because of its pejorative attitude to emerging markets, it is also becoming obsolete. Only the companies, entrepreneurs, and strategists that take this into account will make it as leaders in this new global context.

We believe that preparing the leaders of tomorrow is perhaps the most important mission of good universities and business schools. We realize that many of the theories we and our colleagues teach fail to take into account the structural features that make emerging markets different, losing much of their appeal to students eager to understand the current economic order. This is why we have decided to offer a comprehensive account of emerging markets that can complement more conventional material and provide a useful guide to business in emerging markets.

After extensive reading of publications on the topic of management in emerging markets, we were left with the clear idea, shared by our publisher, that a new approach is needed, one that takes emerging markets as its specific focus (Cavusgil, Ghauri, and Akcal, 2012; Guillen and Garcia-Canal, 2012; *Harvard Business Review*, 2011). We thus decided to start from scratch with this book rather than recycling old material and adding emerging markets as an afterthought or a modification of old models. Our objective is to provide the reader with a good basic understanding of emerging markets and a tool to help in the development of suitable operational strategies for those looking to locate businesses there. To do this, we have been engaged in a four-year-long journey that started in the theoretical realm, discussing what was missing in the international business and strategy fields, and involved hundreds of trips to interview managers and entrepreneurs working in countries in Asia, Latin America, and Africa to establish what was happening in the real world.

Our fieldwork, though tiring and time consuming, was very refreshing. We found that where the theory was lacking, practitioners were already putting into practice innovative solutions. As always, theory had not yet caught up with real life. Following the fieldwork, we sat together and discussed the topic extensively. We identified three main conceptual blocs, which form the three parts of this book. First, we identify the structural features that distinguish emerging markets from developed economies, explaining their common characteristics and also factors that vary strongly from country to country. Second, we propose an analytical method to develop emerging market strategies. Third, we discuss how emerging markets have changed our discipline, introducing new types of firms and making older theories obsolete. The aim of these three conceptual blocks is not only to inform our readers about emerging markets, but also to equip them with a set of flexible strategic tools that they can apply to their own cases.

More and more knowledge will be generated from and about emerging markets. This book is only a first step in a long path toward thoroughly examining and discussing how emerging markets affect management theory and practice. Nonetheless, we do hope that it will provide students and managers interested in emerging markets with an improved understanding of these economies. The book also contains some useful tools and exercises to help managers identify opportunities and risks and formulate strategies.

The term "emerging markets" may soon go out of fashion, just like "less developed" and "periphery" did in the past (see the Appendix, "From Third World to Emerging Markets: Definitions, Contents, and Meanings"). But emerging markets are here to stay—their economic and geopolitical importance is anchored in structural trends that will not be reversed. Many of them may never fully emerge, but most are likely to continue on a positive evolutionary path, generating more wealth, reducing poverty within their borders, and developing endogenous skills and capabilities. The characteristics of these economies are changing, though notably not necessarily in ways that make them more similar to developed economies. They are growing and evolving in their own way, and by doing so are affecting the very nature of international business and management. This book is a guide to management in this new era. Marcos Hashimoto, a Brazilian management professor and friend of ours, once told us "Brazil is not for beginners." We agree and extend the logic to argue throughout the book that emerging markets in general are not for beginners—they are exciting but difficult, at times dangerous, and often frustrating. Most significantly, they are different. Hopefully, we can provide a useful companion on your journey of developing emerging market strategies.

Globalization, the Financial Crisis, and the Rise of Emerging Markets

At the beginning of the 1990s, the U.S. and its allies cheered the end of communism, imagining a world where capitalism, now unchallenged by other systems, would lead to unlimited prosperity. Fukuyama (2006), a famous political scientist, promptly declared "the end of history," hinting that the world's economic, political, and social systems had moved away from the dramatic imbalances and rapid changes that characterized the twentieth century to a more linear evolutionary path toward economic liberalism and political democracy. The early cheerleaders of these trends thought that through financial liberalization, privatization, and market deregulation, the U.S. and Europe would continue to expand and, by doing so, drive global economic growth, which in turn would also benefit emerging markets as a side effect. The financial crisis of 2008 shook all assumptions about the robustness of their economic growth. How did the crisis unfold and how were emerging markets affected?

Since the 1990s, rich economies, primarily the U.S., Western Europe, and Japan, have established a multitude of bilateral free trade agreements. They have encouraged (or pushed, depending on your perspective) other countries to sign up to multilateral agreements, such as the WTO. Meanwhile, European countries have engaged in one of the most ambitious multinational and intercultural integration projects in history, strengthening the economic union between the founding economies and integrating the countries of Eastern Europe immediately after they emerged from communism. They also introduced a common currency, the Euro, which was quickly adopted by all of the major European economies but the UK. Advances in the information and telecommunications industry, notably the diffusion of Internet connectivity and the associated advantages, have opened up new frontiers for business by lowering the cost and time needed to transmit information, including virtual money, across organizational and spatial borders. It seemed for a time that political and technological barriers to trade and economic growth were being broken down and a new era of peace and prosperity had arrived.

U.S. policy makers, unexpectedly freed of the USSR, their political, ideological, and military counter-ego, began to set ever more optimistic and ambitious objectives. Western European policy makers also rode the wave of optimism—they committed to integrating countries that had just come out of several decades of authoritarian government and centralized economic planning. The European Union, it was envisaged, would become a giant, multinational, multiethnic, multi-religious federal entity. The Euro was pushed through, despite the diversity of economic structures and the lack of agreement over fiscal policy, exit mechanisms, and ways to ensure rules compliances by member countries—the thinking at the time was that surely confronted by such an ambitious and ideal project, local politics would certainly converge and act for the common good.

Meanwhile, Japan, the poster child of development economists, a country that had become the envy of the West and the benchmark for all Asian countries, entered into a period of crisis and economic stagnation that has already lasted over 20 years. Because Japan's achievements had been outstanding, growth was expected to return, but, mysteriously, it did not. On the contrary, it was Japan's economic malaise that spread to the U.S. and Europe. Japan was the first developed economy to stall. While Japan stagnated, other economies in Asia, ranging from South Korea to Thailand and Malaysia, continued to grow at a very fast pace up to 1999, when speculation and a stock market boom turned into a widespread regional crisis. Unlike Japan, these countries rebounded fast, diversifying their productive structure and attracting more foreign investment, though in a more controlled and pragmatic manner than in the pre-1999 years. During that same period, China provided the most dramatic example of economic transformation since the development of the U.S.—it went through over 20 years of continuous economic growth, developing its infrastructure, generating one of the world's largest markets, creating export-intensive and low-cost manufacturing, and pulling hundreds of millions out of poverty.

Asia, the most populous and fastest-growing region of the world since the 1970s, anticipated the changes that were to occur at the global level (Hobday, 2003). Japan, the region's most developed and advanced economy, an inspiration for policy makers and management gurus alike, stood still while its poorer neighbors raced ahead. During the 1990–2010 period, China, India, Brazil, Turkey, Vietnam, Thailand, Indonesia, Mexico, Colombia, Ghana, Uganda, and Poland, among others, entered into a long period of sustained economic growth, which, despite temporary crises, transformed their economic and social structures, as well as their weight in the world economy. Remarkably, up to 2008–2009, the economic and political elites of the Triad did not take much notice of this dramatic structural change. Throughout most of the 1990s and 2000s, the Japanese stagnation was discussed mainly as an aberration, not as a warning sign. Policy makers in the U.S. and Europe were too preoccupied with liberalizing finance and providing access to cheap credit to sustain domestic consumption. Statistics seemed to justify these policies—inflation was low, GDP growth was positive, and productivity was improving. Real estate and finance booms especially benefited the rich but also provided funds for charities and governments, ensuring that the model was scarcely criticized or even discussed.

As the finance and real estate boom came to its moment of truth in 2007, the West entered a period of economic crisis that revealed all of the structural problems it had tried so hard to hide. It became evident that it was impossible to continue boosting domestic consumption by extending credit and maintaining low interest rates—in many economies, notably the U.S., household indebtedness was already reaching worrying levels. The real estate boom, which had contributed to economic growth and generated many jobs, had gone bust, leaving a long stream of bankruptcies, dispossessions, and idle construction workers. Aging populations, especially in Japan and Europe, mean that a shrinking number of workers have to generate enough wealth to care for a rising number of older people who are no longer in the workplace. The growing macroeconomic imbalances of most rich economies, especially fiscal deficits, public debt, and trade deficits, have become a primary cause of concern. In spite of technological progress, most developed economies have reached a point where they find it very difficult to achieve any economic growth. Emerging markets, by contrast, benefit from younger populations, unsaturated markets, and great scope to catch up and converge with richer economies.

The crisis has had dramatic consequences for business. Up to 2008, American, Japanese, and European companies focused mainly on the Triad, investing millions of dollars studying the sophisticated Triad consumer and trying to anticipate or determine the latest trends. As consumers passed from acquiring their first car, fridge, and TV, to substituting their TV for the fifth time, putting one in their child's bedroom, and buying their third video game console, they also became more difficult to lure. Triad companies segmented the market, creating ever new product niches. They have made cars safer, faster, and more comfortable, filling them with all sorts of amenities and gadgets. They have experimented with advertising techniques, hiring stars to promote the virtues of their products, and making adverts so costly and complex they are equivalent to short movies. They have sold safety, comfort, speed, eco-credentials, and friendliness in struggling to "build" brands that could command loyalty from such difficult consumers. In short, consumer companies invested in R&D and attempted to come out with ever more advanced inventions, some of which were fantastically successful (for example, the DVD), others irrelevant (the Minidisc). They competed fiercely to capture a share of demand, becoming more diversified and sophisticated. And yet consumers are now less likely to be loyal. Indeed, they defect easily to other brands, happy to have the growing availability and choice of products. They will complain and return any item with a defect, and delay their consumption until the next model comes out, and are ever more informed by means of the Web and other sources.

The vast investments that Triad companies undertook to sell a few hundred thousand additional fridges or cameras in Europe or the U.S. did not pay off. In 2008, the crisis hit. Negative trends were about to get much worse—and to stay that way. Meanwhile, good news came from unexpected places, such as Brazil, Turkey, Indonesia, and Vietnam. Finally, after decades of recovery, growth, stabilization, and painful reforms, emerging markets got the attention of economic and political observers. Investing in emerging markets, selling in these markets, and mastering the art of operating in them was not a sideshow or a curiosity anymore—it became necessary for American, European, and Japanese companies to survive. Large firms, such as Procter and Gamble and Unilever, which had long-standing experience of selling in very diverse markets, have benefitted. Companies from emerging markets have benefitted, too. Being based in fast-growing economies has provided them with the resources to expand internationally, develop new competencies, and build their brands. Firms that have traditionally focused on developed markets, such as Mazda among car makers or Barilla among food companies, have suffered.

Structure of the Book

Since the crisis of 2008, internationalizing to emerging markets has become a priority for U.S., European, and Japanese companies. Nonetheless, most of them continue to operate with a "developed world" mentality—they first address developed markets and *then* adapt strategies and products to suit emerging markets. This often leads them to underestimate the difficulties and risks of managing a business in contexts that are fundamentally different from those of developed economies. Succeeding in emerging markets entails accepting that they are different, and that a retooling of business models, products, and strategies in ways that can best exploit these differences is needed. This book provides a step-by-step guide to business and strategy in emerging markets. It is structured in three parts: The first part sets the stage for our analysis. It discusses the main features of emerging markets that companies and managers should examine to improve their chance of being successful in these economies, framing them in a theoretical and historical context. The second part provides a set of analytical tools to support the development of emerging-market strategies. The final part of the book examines the empirical and theoretical implications of the rise of emerging-market multinational companies, explaining their main features and their internationalization. Some of our chapters, such as Chapters 2, 3, and 9, are more theoretical. Others, such as Chapters 4, 5, 6, and 7, are more practical and strategic in nature. We believe that the combination of empirical, theoretical, and strategic insights of the book make it interesting and hopefully useful for different types of readers and for different types of purposes. We structured it in a flexible manner, so that readers can choose whether to read the whole content in a sequential way, read the chapters in a different sequence, or pick and choose the topics they wish to spend time focusing on.

In Chapter 1, "What Are Emerging Markets?," we "open the black box" of emerging markets and their most important characteristics and the different ways in which they have been defined. We explain the dimensions in which emerging markets differ from developed economies and point out their relevance for business. In particular, we examine the obstacles that make operating a business in emerging markets more difficult and often more costly. The chapter introduces the topic in a structured way for students, managers, and entrepreneurs who are not familiar with the complex and highly diverse world of emerging markets.

Chapter 2, "Markets and Institutions," provides a theoretical background for the book, examining some key concepts related to the generation of wealth in different economies. It traces the evolution of markets and institutions through ancient history, demonstrating how these differ across societal and cultural contexts. It is an important corollary for readers who lack an economics or political science background and are interested in finding out more about markets, trade, and economic growth.

Debates over the causes and implications of the rise of emerging markets normally overlook the earlier history of multinationals, predominantly from European and other industrialized countries, which invested in developing and underdeveloped territories, mostly in the southern hemisphere. Chapter 3, "A Historical Perspective," addresses this neglect, looking at two distinctive periods of the global economy: 1850–1914 and 1948–1980. The chapter is aimed at students and practitioners interested in acquiring a historical perspective of internationalization toward emerging markets and the challenges it poses for business.

In the second part of the book, we develop our conceptual model, which is structured in four steps: the identification of the "Determinants of Attractiveness," the analysis of Four Dimensions, the examination of risk and development of risk-management strategies, and, finally, the structuring of strategies to target different segments of emerging-market clients. In Chapter 4, "The Determinants of Attractiveness and the Four Dimensions," we discuss the first two steps of the model. First, we explain how to use the Determinants of Attractiveness as part of a structured effort to identify the reasons why it may be attractive to do business in a given market. Next, we explain how to examine the context where a business may operate by looking at the Four Dimensions: geography, population, business environment, and economic performance. We provide a set of analytical tools to help readers go through the steps of the model, collecting information and putting together its different aspects.

In Chapter 5, "Managing Risk," we discuss the risks of operating in emerging markets and ways in which they can be managed. We explain the different aspects and effects of risk, and provide a tool to examine risk that focuses on two dimensions—the extent to which risk can be predicted, and the extent to which it is general or specific to the business we intend to operate. We explain how this information can be combined with the analysis of the Four Dimensions to develop the background information needed to formulate successful emerging markets strategies.

The next two chapters are aimed at students, scholars, and practitioners interested in businesses that sell to clients based in emerging markets. Chapter 6, "Targeting Emerging Market Clients I: The Rich and the Middle Classes," discusses strategies to target rich, upper-middle class, and new middle class consumers. It illustrates how these groups of consumers differ from each other and the extent to which targeting them entails emulating strategies experimented in developed economies. Chapter 7, "Targeting Emerging Market Clients II: Strategies for the Base of the Pyramid," examines consumers at the "base of the pyramid," which make up the majority of the populations of emerging economies, discussing different strategies to target these consumers in ways that generate profits but also contribute to improving their livelihoods.

The third part of the book discusses how emerging markets are changing the theory and practice of international management. Chapter 8, "Multinationals Based in Emerging Markets: Features and Strategies," looks at how companies based in emerging markets differ from firms based in developed economies and how they have conquered leading positions in many industries. Chapter 9, "The Internationalization of Emerging Market MNEs: A Critical Examination of International Business Theories," discusses how international business theory can explain the global expansion of multinational enterprises based in emerging markets, anchoring the information presented in Chapter 8 in a structured theoretical framework. The Appendix gives a brief account of the definitions that have been used through history to categorize economies according to their various features.

References

Cavusgil, S. T., Ghauri, P. N., and Akcal, A. A. (2012). *Doing Business in Emerging Markets*. London, SAGE Publications Limited.

Guillen, M.F. and E. Garcia-Canal (2012). *Emerging Markets Rule: Growth Strategies of the New Global Giants*. New York, McGraw-Hill.

Khanna, T., and Palepu, K. G. (2010). *Winning in Emerging Markets: A Roadmap for Strategy and Execution*. Cambridge, Massachusetts, Harvard Business School Press.

Harvard Business Review (2011). *Harvard Business Review on Thriving in Emerging Markets*. Cambridge, Massachusetts, Harvard Business School Press.

Magnus, G. (2010). *Uprising: Will Emerging Markets Shape or Shake the World Economy.* Chichester, UK, Wiley. Mobius, M. (2012). *The Little Book of Emerging Markets: How to Make Money in the World's Fastest Growing Markets* (Vol. 35). Singapore, John Wiley & Sons.

O'Neill, J. (2011). *The Growth Map. Economic Opportunity in the BRICs and Beyond.* London, Penguin Books.

Pacek, N. and Thorniley, D. (2007). *Emerging Markets: Lessons for Business Success and the Outlook for Different Markets* (Vol. 18). New York, Bloomberg Press.

Sharma, R. (2012). *Breakout Nations: In Pursuit of the Next Economic Miracles.* London, Penguin Books.

Van Agtmael, A. (2007). *The Emerging Markets Century: How a New Breed of World-class Companies Is Overtaking the World.* London, Simon and Schuster.

PART I

Opening the Black Box of Emerging Markets

Between the year 2000 and 2013, and especially after the economic downturn of 2008–2009, emerging markets acquired popularity at an impressive speed. They became one of the "hottest" subjects for consulting companies, news reports, and conferences. Developed economies' governments rushed to send diplomatic missions to the largest emerging economies, attempting to secure trade deals and support national business interests. Businesses began to formulate new strategies, incorporating these economies as a major concern in their future plans. Every major company based in developed economies is either already operating, or trying to operate, in emerging markets. Hedge funds focusing on "emerging markets" are proliferating and new "emerging market" divisions are being opened in large corporations. Nonetheless, as we discussed in the Introduction, emerging markets remain a complex and under-studied phenomenon, especially from the perspective of international business. In this part of the book, we try to open up the black-box term "emerging markets," outline the main features of emerging markets, and lay the basis for the following parts of the book, which provide the tools to develop emerging-market strategies.

Chapter 1, "What Are Emerging Markets?," discusses the different potential interpretations of the term "emerging markets." Drawing from development studies, international business, and economic history, it identifies features that distinguish emerging markets from developed economies, especially those characteristics that have direct implications for business. Our discussion starts with economic dimensions—in particular, indicators of wealth creation, such as gross domestic product, and of macroeconomic stability, such as inflation. Next, we examine how political stability affects the business environment, and we discuss the role of income inequality, demography, and consumption. Finally, we look at infrastructure and market institutions.

Chapter 2, "Markets and Institutions," and Chapter 3, "A Historical Perspective," provide a theoretical and historical background for the rest of the book. In Chapter 2, we examine some of the key concepts that are often used to discuss emerging markets and their economic performance, such as institution, market, and trade. By looking at ancient history, we provide the reader with an idea of the mechanisms through which wealth is created and business environments develop, offering opportunities and challenges for private firms. Chapter 3 examines multinational companies and their investments in emerging markets from a historical perspective. It looks at the internationalization of early multinational firms searching for natural resources between 1850 and 1914, discussing how their business activities often became intertwined with the European powers' imperial projects. It then examines the internationalization activities of Triad-based companies during the 1948–1980 period, discussing the reasons why they focused mainly on developed as opposed to emerging economies.

1

What Are Emerging Markets?

Emerging, Developing, Catching Up

*T*he term *"emerging markets" is at the very least confusing. It indicates markets that are growing, which, thanks to their positive economic performance, may "emerge" and become richer. In the gloom of the current economic downturn, this is how businessmen in Europe, the U.S., and Japan see most other markets. Hundreds of hours of contact and discussion with managers of leading multinational companies have shown us that the term "emerging markets" does not have a hard and fast definition. It is commonly used to refer to economies that are outside North America, Japan, and Western Europe, without necessarily implying that they are growing (which, in many cases, they are). One could object that the "every country but the Triad" emerging market definition is too broad to be useful. It also makes it difficult to categorize countries such as South Korea, Israel, Taiwan, Australia, New Zealand, Hong Kong, and Singapore, which are more similar to Triad countries in terms of wealth and sophistication of the economy but are located elsewhere. Other emerging markets, such as Qatar and the United Arab Emirates, are also difficult to categorize because they have high incomes, but their economies have yet to reach the level of diversification of Taiwan or Singapore.*

But the term does highlight that changes are taking place, and many economies that had an almost pariah status in international markets are becoming more and more palatable for Triad businesses. It also points to a shift in the spatial equilibrium of global production, away from Europe and North America, and toward Asia, Latin America, and Africa. To simplify our discussion, the term "Triad" is used in the book to refer to North America, Western Europe, and Japan, whereas terms including "developed economies" and "rich economies" refer to the U.S., Canada, Western Europe, Japan, Australia, New Zealand, South Korea, Taiwan, Hong Kong, and Israel. The terms "emerging markets," "developing economies," and "emerging economies" refer to all other countries (for more information on different definitions of emerging markets, see the Appendix). Not all of the countries we define as "emerging" have been actually growing during the 2010–2013 period. Egypt and

Syria, among others, are actually going through an economic crisis. However, like other emerging markets, they have plenty of scope to develop, or to "emerge." That is, they share a young population, unsaturated markets, and the potential to become more productive.

The connotation "emerging" calls the attention to the potential of these markets, which contrasts with the already mature state of the Triad economies that concentrated the vast majority of the world's wealth between 1950 and 1990. The sort of thinking behind this draws on one of the key tenets of economic history—that economic growth is cyclical, and that it is possible for countries to "catch up" with their richer counterparts. Great Britain started the Industrial Revolution, generating ingenious new ways of accumulating capital and wealth. It became the "manufacturing workshop" of the world. Yet, its dominance lasted less than 100 years. Toward the end of the nineteenth century, Germany and the U.S. were already matching or overtaking Great Britain in several key manufacturing sectors, such as steel and precision machinery. The U.S., a largely agricultural society, quickly became the world's industrial power, while Germany consolidated its position as the leading economy in Europe. Japan and Italy achieved a transformation from densely populated agricultural economies that sent millions of hungry migrants to the Americas and Australia, to being respectively the second largest economy in the world and the second largest manufacturing producer in Europe.

Economies such as Germany, and later Italy and Japan, were characterized by having smaller economies and also lower per-capita incomes than the dominating economic powers (first Great Britain, then the U.S.). They also had a less sophisticated productive structure, a less skilled workforce, and, last but not least, lower standards of living. Their inhabitants were poorer, less educated and lived shorter lives. Yet, at some point, due to factors that we discuss throughout the book, their rates of economic growth accelerated, and they "caught up" gradually with the leading economies. Although it is naive to assume that all countries will eventually and automatically catch up and become rich, several economies do have the potential to close the gap that separates them from the rich Triad. Many, such as Thailand and Malaysia, have been quietly "catching up" for decades. Others, such as Vietnam, started "catching up" more recently and are still very poor—yet they are changing at breathtaking speed. The counter-argument also holds—most economies that do catch up go through several years of accelerated economic growth and transformation, and they then slow down once they reach levels of average per capita income that are close to those of Western Europe or the U.S. Economies that are less "rich" have more potential to go through the sort of "catching up" and development of their markets that justifies the label of "emerging market."

If we label those markets that have average incomes considerably lower than those of Western Europe, North America, and Japan as "emerging markets," we quickly realize that these now so-fashionable economies have been historically labeled with a range of less positive phrases: "the Third World," "the poor," "the South," "the less developed," and, perhaps most similar to emerging, "developing." Emerging economies are the poor economies of the world. They include countries where a large share of the population is still very poor but that are growing fast, such as Vietnam, and have economies that are not so poor but are currently failing to grow, such as Egypt. Leaving aside political correctness for a moment, the very fact that they are poor provides them with their potential for improvement: they have a great many potential workers to be trained, many potential consumers to be lured by old and new products, many markets that have been left under-developed and isolated due to infrastructural and institutional deficiencies, and an impressive wealth of under-exploited natural resources.

The most important Triad companies, from Coca-Cola and Nestlé to Toyota, developed when Triad economies were growing. They fostered and simultaneously benefitted from the advent of mass production and mass consumption. The transformation that occurred in the U.S., Europe, and Japan is now occurring in emerging markets, to different extents, and at different speeds. It has already created new champions, such as the Chinese white good producer Haier. It will continue to provide the market space to develop new products, services, and business models. The companies at the forefront of this global societal change will not only contribute to it, they will become world leaders in their field. It is, however, a much more difficult game than it may at first sight seem, for, as we will illustrate throughout this book, emerging markets are a completely different ballgame to Triad economies.

Economic Performance, GDP, and Emerging Markets

The size of an economy is generally measured using the gross domestic product (GDP), an aggregated indicator of the wealth generated in an economy by both local and foreign organizations. Year-to-year changes in GDP are often dubbed "GDP growth." Notably, it is called GDP growth even when performance is negative, leading to such confusing economic jargon as "GDP growth was negative." GDP growth is one of the most common indicators measuring the economic performance of a given country, region, or city. Another common indicator is GDP growth divided by population, referred to as "GDP per capita or per head," which provides a more accurate picture, especially for countries where the population grows fast. For a more detailed explanation of the different methods of measuring economic performance and wealth, see Box 1.1.

Box 1.1: Measuring the Value of Economic Activity

Indicators to measure and compare aggregate economic activity are relatively new. It was only after the end of the Second World War that national accounts systems, which consist in the implementation of consistent accounting techniques for measuring economic activity, became widespread across the world (Blanchard, 2006; pp. 24–47). **Gross domestic product (GDP)** is one of the best known indicators, measuring the size of an economy, or, when used on a per-capita basis, measuring the average wealth of a population. GDP is the monetary value of the sum of all economic activities that take place in a country during a given period of time (Dornbusch and Fischer, 1987; pp. 31–67). GDP can be estimated using current prices or using constant prices. This explains the difference between nominal GDP and real GDP. The first is calculated at current prices (i.e., the prices reported in the economy at the time of calculation); meanwhile, real GDP is estimated using a set of constant prices, making it a better indicator of production in terms of inter-temporal comparisons, because it eliminates the effect of price changes (Mankiw, 2006; pp. 63–98). Another possible variation for the calculation of GDP is the adjustment for purchasing power parity (PPP), which reflects the value of goods of services that a given unit of currency can effectively buy in different economies. Converting the value added of production from different countries using a particular currency can lead to inaccurate data, because in all countries the prices of many goods, mainly non-tradable, are not correctly reflected in the exchange rates. The PPP technique was developed in order to avoid erroneous perceptions derived from the problem of exchange rates. GDP at PPP consists of calculating GDP based on international prices, constructed from averages of the prices that goods and services have in different countries (Ray, 1998; 5–43). **Gross national product (GNP)** differs from GDP because it estimates production or income generated only by the "national" citizens and organizations. In other words, GDP focuses on the location of economic activities, whereas GNP focuses on ownership. GNP includes income earned abroad by nationals and neglects income derived by foreigners and foreign companies in the economy. **Gross national income (GNI)** is "the sum of value added by all resident producers plus any product taxes (less subsidies) not included in the valuation of output plus net receipts of primary income (compensation of employees and property income) from abroad" (The World Bank, accessed on 4/25/2013 at http://data.worldbank.org/indicator/NY.GNP.PCAP.PP.CD).

The main problem with qualifying emerging markets on the basis of their aggregate economic performance is that economic performance tends to be highly variable, hard to predict, and difficult to measure. Moreover, not all the economies outside the Triad are growing—just like not all the Triad economies are stalling. Germany, for example, performed remarkably well throughout the 2000s. Egypt and El Salvador, on the other hand, did not grow much during the same period. Among "well performing" emerging markets, average rates of economic growth differ starkly. Within Latin America, economies growing at 5–6%, such as Colombia and Peru between 2006 and 2012, are considered to be performing well. The Chinese government worries when growth slows down to 8–9% per year. Vietnam and Indonesia have also grown fast for several years—in their economies a slowdown to 5% GDP growth would feel like a mini economic crisis. So, what is the threshold of growth above which an economy should be considered emerging? And what about economies such as Singapore, Israel, Hong Kong, Taiwan, and South Korea? They were significantly poorer and less sophisticated than the Triad economies in the 1970s. Yet, by 2012 their average income per head had converged toward Western European levels and their economic structure has become very sophisticated as they have specialized in electronic manufacturing, software, and, in the case of South Korea, several other fields, including shipping and transport equipment. Their rates of growth have slowed down as they have become richer, though they continue to outperform Triad countries. Are they emerging markets? If we use a taxonomy based on income or indicators of development, such as poverty rates and life expectancy, they should not be counted as such. If we look at economic growth, they could be considered as such, though it is unclear for how much longer. An easy and practical solution is to see these economies as emerging markets that have already emerged, or as exceptionally performing emerging economies.

Relying on current economic performance as an indicator of whether an economy is emerging is also made complex by the variability of GDP growth through the years. A large share of economies outside the Triad are affected by violent fluctuations in their economic performance. They may grow faster, but when they enter a crisis, they tend to do so in a dramatic manner. Argentina, for example, stagnated between 1998 and 2001, losing about 30% of the value of its GDP between 2000 and 2001 (Ciravegna, 2002). Yet, between 2002 and 2010, it rebounded very fast, growing on average more than 6% per year. Thus, Argentina in the 1980s: stagnating. Argentina between 1991 and 1998: emerging. Between 1998 and 2002: collapsing. Between 2002 and 2010: emerging. If we summarize how Argentina's economy has evolved since the 1980s, we see violent fluctuations in its GDP as well as an overall modest improvement in economic performance in 30 years as opposed to the fast growth that its most positive years would suggest. Emerging markets, and especially countries in Africa and Latin America, are often ruled by governments that pursue short-term popularity through pro-cyclical policies: they cut spending during economic downturns and increase it during economic booms. These factors exacerbate the cyclicality of economic performance, boosting growth in good times and depressing it during crises.

Developing economies tend to be characterized by more creative, or experimental, economic policy making. Such creativity explains why Brazil subsidized bio fuels for decades despite low oil prices, and can now claim to be the most competitive bio fuel producer in the world. Creativity, especially when managed by governments with nationalist and socialists tendencies, such as that of Venezuela under Hugo Chavez, can also generate perverse outcomes, such as hyperinflation, exchange controls, defaults, and other forms of economic instability.

Several non-Triad countries, ranging from Chile to Mongolia, are net exporters of commodities—grain, soy, minerals, oil, gas, and coffee. Their economic performance is also strongly affected by commodity prices, a factor they have no control over. Commodity prices, the variability of economic policies, and their tendency to be pro-cyclical mean that non-Triad economies tend to have less stable and less predictable GDP growth than Triad economies. Depending on the period analyzed, they may appear to be "emerging" or "stalling." During the 1980s, when commodity prices stalled, reaching historical lows, countries such as Peru and Nigeria, which rely on the export of minerals and oil, respectively, failed to grow. Since the 1990s, commodity prices have risen exponentially (largely because of demand from fast-growing emerging markets such as China and India). It is not a coincidence that several emerging markets rich in resources have been growing faster than they were in the past. What is important for business is that their economic performance as measured by GDP may be strongly influenced by the price of the products they export. Should prices decline again, as they did during the 1980s, commodity exporters would also struggle to grow.

An interesting case illustrating such fluctuations is Brazil, one of the largest emerging economies, one of the BRICS, and the economic giant of Latin America. Throughout its history, Brazil has repeatedly been considered both as a leading emerging economy and as an economic basket case. Between 1950 and 1973, Brazil went through its "economic miracle"—it transformed from an agricultural economy into the industrial powerhouse of Latin America. Through protectionism and state dirigisme, directed by a sequence of military juntas, Brazil developed a transport equipment industry, an electronic industry, an aerospace and weapons industry, and steel and construction industries, as well as built the Trans-Amazonic highway, which, as Brazilians like to boast, can be seen from the moon. It seemed that its form of state-centered capitalism and technocratic authoritarianism were superior to both capitalist democracies and communism. Yet, the Brazilian development model was highly reliant on cheap imported oil, machinery inputs, and debt financing at zero or negative interest rates. By 1982, as both oil prices and interest rates rose, Brazil, at the time a net oil importer, went through a difficult period of economic rebalancing, inflation, and debt restructuring—its image among investors and Triad policy makers changed from that of a regional economic champion, albeit not a very democratic one, to that of an economic failed state in need of serious reform to its polity, economy, and society.

Throughout the 1980s, Brazil (in fact, all of Latin America) went through "the lost decade"—ten years of stagnating economic performance. In the 1990s, these economies began to recover, and by the 2000s, most of them were growing fast. Once again, Brazil has become the Latin American leader, a huge economy, rich in resources and capable of exporting not only commodities but also complex engineering products such as airplanes and underwater drilling technology. The example of Brazil reinforces the idea that even when emerging economies are indeed emerging, growth can be temporary and cyclical. It can quickly halt, become negative, and then resume. In summary, current economic growth is not necessarily a good indicator of whether or not an economy is emerging, especially because it can be caused by factors that are unrelated to the structure of the economy, such as commodity prices.

Financial Markets and Macroeconomic Stability

In the previous section, we claimed that emerging markets tend to be more "creative" in their economic policy making and that they experiment more. Very few emerging markets, for example, are part of strict binding monetary agreements such as the Euro, which strongly circumscribe the ability to increase interest rates or expand the money supply. And no emerging market has a currency used as a key global means of transaction as the British pound sterling used to be before the Second World War and the U.S. dollar continues to be. They thus have more policy space to pursue creative solutions to promote economic growth and development.

Several emerging markets, including Argentina, Malaysia, and China, are more closed to international trade and investment than the average developed economy. Their currencies are not traded in international financial markets. Foreign investors cannot freely trade assets denominated in their currencies. Foreign control over their banks is regulated. And many of their largest, stock-market-listed firms are partly or fully owned by the state. Policy changes do not have an immediate effect on their stock markets or the value of their currencies. There has been much debate about whether the Chinese currency is undervalued, with some U.S. politicians accusing China of keeping the value of the Yuan low in order to boost China's export competitiveness. If China had a floating currency like the U.S. dollar or the Euro, such discussions would be meaningless— the value of the Yuan would be determined by demand and supply in the international money market, which in turn would be dependent on demand for Chinese made goods. The current situation might stir anti-Chinese sentiment and suspicions of unfair trade practices, but it allows the Chinese government to manage its monetary policy, and hence domestic prices, with more freedom.

✳ The fact that emerging markets tend to have financial (and monetary) markets that are more closed shields them from market pressures. As the 2008 financial crisis illustrated, this can be a very positive feature. It also has its downfalls. Being more protected from market pressures, emerging markets can push unsustainable economic policies for longer—for example, importing more than they export and borrowing more than they can repay. Governments that have a short-term perspective, or are simply corrupt and inefficient, often try "buying" the support of different groups in the economy by increasing salaries, lowering taxation, and starting new infrastructure projects. International markets generally notice when this is happening in an emerging market only when it has reached enormous proportions. A notable example of this occurred in Zimbabwe when inflation reached over 13 billion percent per month in 2008.

Printing money to fund public works is a common tool for populist policy makers to "buy" constituencies. It leads to inflation and to a devaluation of the currency vis-à-vis other currencies. In economies that depend strongly on imports, devaluation of the currency causes a rise in average prices, which unsurprisingly generates discontent. Since the mid 2000s, the governments of both Venezuela and Argentina have been sustaining high levels of public spending through expansionary monetary policy. To limit the effects on food prices, they fixed these prices, forcing producers to sell even at a loss. In most developed economies, there are regulations limiting a governments' ability to fix prices. And most importantly, being open markets, any governmental attempt to do so would cause investors to leave and companies to relocate. In Argentina and Venezuela, the reaction of international financial markets does not matter because they are not open markets in any case. Local producers reacted by simply refusing to sell, creating scarcity in spite of the abundance of fertile land and labor in both countries. Meanwhile, a parallel black market for food items boomed. The result of this is that the official prices that the Venezuelan and Argentinean governments declare diverge dramatically from the prices that citizens tend to pay for goods. Real inflation rates are thus higher than those officially declared.

The same applies for currencies. Venezuela imports everything but oil. The large state-owned companies have a big incentive to keep the currency at a high value so that they can import their inputs more cheaply. As the government prints money, the value of the Venezuelan currency should fall in international markets—more of it is available while demand for it remains stable. This would create a rise in the prices of imported goods, which include food, telephones, air conditioning units, most consumption items, and the inputs used by state-owned corporations, such as oil extraction machinery. To avoid this consequence, the government fixed the value of the currency. It controls the exchange rate and limits the transactions that each citizen can make in a foreign currency, including for travel. Again, as a result, there is a divergence between the value of the currency in the official market and the value that it sells for in informal markets. In other words, given that it is hard to get access to dollars, the average Venezuelan is willing to pay far more to get dollars than the exchange rate their government establishes. To sum up, more policy space means governments can reverse their policies more often and invent new measures, such as introducing new currencies, defaulting on debt, and closing international money exchanges. And this leads to a higher unpredictability of the macroeconomic indicators of emerging markets.

Though not all emerging markets are as closed and macroeconomically unstable as Venezuela, they tend in general to be less predictable than developed economies. Even in the post-financial-crisis context, emerging markets continue to remain more vulnerable to irresponsible policy making and price fluctuations. There are different types of shocks that can be caused by financial and macroeconomic variables: debt crises (default on public or external debt), banking crises (bank runs, banks becoming insolvent and defaulting, possible bailouts to avoid isolated instances becoming a systemic collapse), inflation, currency crisis (sudden devaluation of a fixed currency), or a combination thereof (refer to Box 5.4). Since the 1950s, the vast majority of these types of shock have occurred in emerging markets. During the 1980s, for example, most emerging markets faced a debt crisis. During the 1990s, there were currency crises, followed by banking crises and in some cases debt crises, in Argentina, Brazil, Mexico, Russia, Indonesia, Thailand, Malaysia, and the Philippines.

The poorest emerging markets have a very small formal economy and hence their stock market and officially monitored macro environment are at best irrelevant, at worst confusing. Many other emerging markets, including Argentina, Venezuela, Nicaragua, China, Belarus, and Pakistan, have a large formal economy but their macro variables and financial markets are strongly influenced if not fully controlled by their governments. The reason why all of this is relevant is that it is an important characteristic that distinguishes emerging markets from the Triad. It means that stock markets in general are not a good reflection of the real economy of emerging markets. And it emphasizes the fact that emerging markets are riskier, less predictable economic environments, which can very quickly move from growing at record speed to getting into severe crises.

Stock market capitalization is another factor that distinguishes emerging markets—partly because the most developed financial markets are in the Triad, they concentrate most of the global financial transactions. New York, London, and Tokyo continue to dominate global finance. However, as several emerging markets have gradually liberalized their stock markets and "normalized" their economic policies, reducing inflation and debt, they are also developing a financial industry. Brazil, for example, boasts one of the most highly capitalized stock markets in the world thanks to the sophistication of its local financial industry, its economic growth, and the stabilization of its macroeconomic policies. China may eventually wish to become a financial hub, too, and to make its currency a reserve currency like the dollar. For now, however, it has a long way to go because its banking system and state-owned enterprises remain far from transparent.

These factors not only contribute to explaining the volatility of emerging markets, they also explain why it is more difficult to get access to credit and financial instruments and to trade in international markets. All of these factors are well known to firms operating in emerging markets but often come as a surprise to firms used to operating in the Triad. For example, a company producing electrical equipment based in Italy can easily export its equipment to German buyers who use it in their machinery without having to worry about currency and regulations. Trading with the U.S. is slightly more complex because it would mean having to deal in a different currency. Yet, the regulations are clear, and credit for this sort of transaction is easily available. Profits made in Italy can easily be exported, if needed, and there are no restrictions on currency exchanges. However, if the same producer were based in Argentina or Malaysia, it would take a much longer time to complete the transaction—besides legal issues, foreign exchange values would have to be negotiated, as well as ways to repatriate profits. Macroeconomic instability and less open financial markets make it more difficult to invest in emerging markets and even more difficult to export one's profits back home.

Political Instability and Economic Performance

There is another factor that distinguishes emerging markets from developed economies—political stability. Between 1914 and 1945, several Triad countries were affected by insurgency and coups, which eventually unleashed the most terrible and destructive wars in history. Entire generations were wiped out, together with factories, roads, railroads, and agricultural produce. By 1945, Europe was unable to feed itself, the UK had overstretched its economic resources to fight the war, a number of German and Japanese cities were reduced to rubble, and Germany was divided in two. Since 1945, the Triad countries have benefitted from a long period of internal stability and international peace. They have witnessed few conflicts near their shores and have consolidated their democracies, abandoning political violence.

Emerging markets went through the opposite developmental trajectory. They suffered little from the two world wars, but since the 1950s, most emerging markets have gone through a long cycle of political instability, violence, and internal conflicts, which at times have erupted into border wars. With the exception of Costa Rica, all countries in the Latin American region toyed with authoritarianism, either in the personalist caudillo form, à la Fidel Castro, or in the more subtle, bureaucratic form of the Brazilian military juntas. African countries suffered from a similar problem—the independence heroes that liberated them from their colonizers often became despots who ruled through brute force. Guerrilla movements, military coups, and civil wars became a common feature of many emerging markets, ranging from Colombia to India, Nigeria, and Cambodia.

✱ Political instability and internal conflicts affect economic policy principally by making it less predictable and by generating incentives for authoritarian governments to manipulate prices and regulations to benefit specific groups. Political instability also affects macroeconomic variables. A sudden change in leader can bring about a dramatic change in economic policy, thus causing inflation or debt to rise. This makes it yet more difficult to identify emerging markets by looking only at their economic performance—a given market may perform badly because of political violence, yet have the potential to boom in coming years.

Egypt is a densely populated country, with a large urbanized, educated middle class. It has a diversified economy, which, unlike that of other African countries, does not depend only on natural resources. It hosts one of the most important universities of the Arab world. It is endowed with beautiful natural resources and a unique historical heritage, which has the potential to attract millions of tourists. It controls access to the Suez Canal, one of the most important navigation channels in the world. Yet, Egypt's economic growth has been dismal, especially since 2009. Egypt's slow growth is currently exacerbated by its political transformation. Although the demise of the despotic leader Mubarak may lead to a more promising future, in the short run it has caused a dramatic decline in tourism and foreign direct investment. Tourists have chosen other destinations, fearful of street violence and lower security at tourist sites. Foreign investors are worried about future changes, and prefer to wait for the situation to become clearer. Yet, Egypt is, by all measures, an emerging market. It has the potential to become one of the most important markets in Africa. Most managers and investors do not necessarily limit their attention to economic growth, but also look at the potential that markets have. The question, then, is how to calculate potential?

Wealth, Productivity, and Inequality

After GDP and GDP growth, the level of wealth of the population is another common way of identifying emerging markets. Triad countries concentrate most of the world's wealth. Even Triad economies with a small population, such as Denmark, have considerably higher wealth than several emerging markets, precisely because their per capita GDP is higher. Given that GDP is a measure that captures both wealth creation and wealth consumption in any given economy, that means Triad citizens produce and consume on average more wealth per capita—they are more productive workers and can afford to consume more (refer to Box 1.1).

The fact that they produce more does not necessarily mean they work harder. In fact, the contrary can also be true. Most of it can be explained by superior allocation of capital and technology. An example of this is agriculture—a large share of the fields cultivated by small farmers in China, India, and Africa could be vastly more productive if only they were properly irrigated. Many farmers simply cannot afford to irrigate their fields because they lack access to capital or credit. Pumps are too expensive, and in many regions, water is scarce or unavailable. Unless a farmer can borrow the money to install a pump, he or she may continue to produce in a less than optimal way, depending on rainfall. In other cases, electricity is not available or too expensive to power irrigation pumps. As a result, such fields are far less productive than they could potentially be. Their owners produce less and earn less than farmers based in developed economies. These examples illustrate why emerging market workers are less productive in terms of the value per head they generate. It also hints at the business opportunities that these factors permit. In the case of irrigation equipment, if credit institutions paired with pump producers, they could develop specific loans to facilitate farmers' purchases. Pump vendors could also sell their equipment in gradual installments instead of a lump sum or develop cheaper pumps. There are also related opportunities for electricity companies and producers of electrical generators. Infrastructural deficiencies also limit productivity. If, for example, it costs more to carry produce to the nearest port than it does to cultivate it because there are only a few, badly maintained roads, farmers in that village may simply decide to produce less and sell only in local markets. Again, that means on average they will produce and earn less than their developed economy counterparts—and hence consume less.

Another reason why the workers based in developed economies are more productive is that they are more educated. Training and basic education provide skills, which contribute to labor productivity. At a very basic level, a worker who can read signs and count is more productive than a worker who is illiterate; for example, he or she can operate machinery via written instructions. Countries such as Japan and South Korea, which transformed quickly from emerging to rich markets, invested heavily in education, and continue to do so. Many emerging markets, however, continue to suffer from poor educational systems. The market opportunity is twofold. On the one hand, poor performing public schools open the market for affordable private schools. On the other hand, if schooling improves, new pools of skilled workers will be trained (see Box 1.2).

Box 1.2: Modern Growth Theory and the Role of Education

Classical economists such as Smith, Ricardo, and Malthus laid the foundations for the modern theory of economic growth, but it is with Frank Ramsey's article "A Mathematical Theory of Saving" (1928) that the theory of economic growth started attracting more attention from scholars (Barro and Sala-i-Martin, 2004; pp. 1–22). Subsequently, Harrod and Domar developed a model in which the growth of the economy was determined by the ability of the economy to save and the capital-output ratio. Solow and Swan (1956) argued that the capital-output ratio is an endogenous variable, which means that it is determined in the economy by the relative endowments of capital and labor (Ray, 1998; pp. 45–94). This led to two main conclusions: the convergence hypothesis (which states that the lower the level of initial per-capita GDP, the faster the growth rate), and the prediction that, in the absence of continuous technological change, the growth per capita of an economy eventually ceases (Barro and Sala-i-Martin, 2004; pp. 1–22). Since then, research framed by growth theory has focused on the role of technological change, and since the late 1980s, it has also included human capital (Barro and Sala-i-Martin; pp. 1–22). In previous models, only physical capital and labor were included, and both were considered as homogeneous factors. However, as Barro and Sala-i-Martin noted, in real economies there are different kinds of labor, skilled and unskilled, and this affects the productivity of physical capital. Therefore, human capital, defined as skilled labor that can be created or increased through education or training, was included in growth models (Ray, 1998, pp. 95–124). The Solow-Swan model was extended to include savings through physical capital accumulation (traditional model approach) and through human capital accumulation (the workforce becoming more skilled). Given that education is the most important mechanism for generating and accumulating human capital in an economy, modern macroeconomic growth theories support the view that education is an essential element of economic development (Ray, 1998; pp. 95–124).

Going back to the topic of the division of wealth in the world, Triad citizens do not just consume more because they produce more. They are also more heavily indebted. They have more credit instruments available (e.g., credit cards and mortgages) and benefit from lower interest rates. They borrow and consume more than what they produce, which is already higher than what emerging market workers produce because of the aforementioned reasons. As a result, the average Briton or American is far more indebted than the average Mexican or Chinese. Hence, the average Briton or American consumes more not only because he or she earns more, but also because he or she can spend more than what he or she earns. Triad governments also consume more wealth than they generate. They provide more public goods than they can pay for with taxation thanks to their capacity to borrow (and hence the astronomic public debt of Italy, Spain, Ireland, the UK, and the U.S.). The result of this is a concentration of consumption in Triad countries, especially when examined at the individual, per-capita level.

The average German produces and consumes almost three times as much as the average Mexican, four times as much as the average Chinese, eight times as much as the average Indonesian. The implication of the term "emerging" is that all of this is changing. Although Triad countries continue to concentrate wealth, emerging markets' share of the world economy has been growing at a dramatic speed for at least 20 years, whereas Triad markets have been growing very slowly, stalling, or, in some cases, shrinking. Most areas outside the Triad, with the exception of South Korea, Israel, Hong Kong, Taiwan, and Singapore, are characterized by lower average incomes. But in good times, such as the 2000s and, it seems, the 2010s, their wealth has grown faster as total GDP growth has outpaced population growth. This phenomenon can be explained in terms of "catch-up growth"—the tendency of the economies in less wealthy countries to converge with more developed economies by growing faster (see Chapter 2, "Markets and Institutions," and Chapter 3, "A Historical Perspective"). In simple, non-theoretical terms, when you already have roads, cars, and housing, it is more difficult to find new products and services to invest in and to sell. On the other hand, in places where even the most basic infrastructure is lacking and where consumer goods have not yet been diffused, little investment can generate great opportunities.

If electricity is not available, irrigation systems powered by sun, wind, and human muscle could provide a temporary means of increasing land fertility by pumping water through the fields during dry seasons. Some systems based on bicycles and other man-powered mechanisms, such as the "KickStart MoneyMaker Pressure Pump" have been successfully tried in rural Africa. Hundreds of thousands of this man-operated pump have been sold, allowing small farmers to grow multiple crops per year, or to switch to crops with a higher commercial value. In this case, the key is affordability of the equipment, which sells for less than US$50, and the fact that it does not rely on electricity. Additionally, it uses less water than flooding the fields because the farmers can bring water to the specific areas where it is needed. One of the insights of this story is that the product was developed for the needs of emerging-market farmers—can you imagine a U.S. farmer irrigating his fields manually? Another insight is that infrastructural deficiency and lack of training contribute to explaining why small farmers continue operating in ways that do not maximize the productive potential of their land. Such locked-up productivity is precisely the sort of potential that businesses see in emerging markets. Small, incremental, often basic innovations can open up new markets and unleash a growth in output and consumption.

The key problem with using GDP/GNI per head as indicators of wealth is that national wealth is not divided equally among the population. A 1% increase in GDP per capita can have different meanings in different countries. The distribution of national income is generally discussed as "income inequality," precisely because it never is fully equitable. The most commonly used indicator of income inequality is the Gini coefficient, which measures income concentration and measures of the share of national income absorbed by different income groups (for example, the percentage of GDP absorbed by the 10% that earns the least). The point here is that we often compare GDP/GNI per capita across countries, but income inequality varies strongly, thus confusing the meaning of the statistics we read. Inequality tends to be on average higher in emerging markets than in developed economies, though it also varies among different developed countries.

There are several reasons why emerging markets are on average more inequitable. First, they tend to have a smaller number of highly skilled people, such as doctors and lawyers, who demand high salaries because of their scarcity. If they are paid too poorly, they can leave to work in other countries. The poor and the unskilled, on the other hand, may find it more difficult to leave because they lack the funds and have less access to information. This in itself reproduces inequality: those with skills are likely to descend from higher income groups that can afford to support their children for several years during their studies. Because of their skills, they earn much more than the average worker in their country, who is in turn likely to be unable to afford to pay for their children's studies.

Access to education and the quality of education are factors that reproduce and occasionally strengthen inequality. A large number of emerging markets are affected by impoverished public education systems. Studying in poorly staffed schools, most pupils do not acquire the needed skills to become professionals and hence end up in low income jobs. The few who can afford private schooling will get access to better jobs, and hence again reproduce existing inequalities. More educated people tend to protect their investments and savings better; they may, for example, buy foreign currencies to diversify risk. This means that the violent macroeconomic fluctuations that often occur in emerging markets (though now more frequently also in the Triad), such as high inflation or default, affect the poor, the old, and the badly informed most. The income groups that concentrate most of the wealth generated in emerging markets tend to be largely protected from them thanks to their skills and access to information.

There are many more reasons that explain income inequality in emerging markets. Many emerging markets have authoritarian governments and are ruled by small groups of networked people who control access to the most productive parts of their economies. Think about Libya, Tunisia, and Egypt before the Arab Spring overthrew the families that ruled them. The key axes of their economies, ranging from oil in Libya to tourism and banking in Egypt and Tunisia, were controlled by the extended families of the ruling elite. Through monopolies, state concessions, subsidies, and tax exemptions, they generated wealth that benefitted their networks while effectively limiting the opportunities for other locals to develop businesses. In this sort of context, when the economy grows, rulers enrich themselves. When the economy declines, they suffer the least because they invest their riches abroad and make sure their sons study in top-ranked institutions and acquire the skills needed to operate in different economies.

Authoritarian regimes, corruption, and clientelism are co-determinants of income inequality because they limit access to power and high-earning jobs. In many emerging markets, discrimination on the basis of ethnicity, gender, or religion is widespread. In India, for example, low caste citizens are still subject to forms of discrimination despite the existence of laws aimed at tackling this problem. The existence of discrimination and marginalization means that certain parts of the population (often indigenous people and minorities) have inferior access to education and jobs and hence less chances to climb up the income ladder—another factor contributing to income inequality. Its implication for business is that in certain countries we find groups of people who have very different income levels, consumption habits, and access to credit and services than the rest of the population. Integrating these groups is a challenge, and yet a great opportunity for both policy makers and businesses alike to cooperate and, if desired, to pursue an objective that is simultaneously social and economic in nature.

Another reason why income inequality matters for businesses operating in emerging markets is that it strongly affects consumption patterns and their evolution as total GDP grows. In a very inequitable country, it is likely that a change of 3% in GDP per head is absorbed mostly by the top 2–5% of the population. This would mean that despite an improvement in GDP on a per-capita basis, most people continue to earn the same. The top 2–5% that benefit from higher incomes would consume more. However, the goods and services that top earners consumer are different from those consumed by middle classes and by the poor. They are likely to include luxury goods and foreign vacations. By contrast, in a less inequitable country increases in GDP are more likely to result in an increase in consumption across different income groups. That would translate into more leisure activities of the cheaper kind—cinema tickets, bars, cheap restaurants, and more expenses in food and clothing. It is very important for consumer goods producers to keep this mind. Different income inequality across markets means that similar levels of growth in GDP per head can generate different types of business opportunities.

A graphic reminder of this is the exotic habits of Teodorin Nguema, son of the current ruler of Equatorial Guinea, an oil-rich African country. In August 2012, his French villa, worth 150 million Euros, was seized by the French authorities who are charging him with corruption. Despite an oil boom that has made it the third biggest African oil exporter after Nigeria and Angola, Equatorial Guinea remains a very poor country, where the majority of the roughly 700,000 inhabitants lack access to water and electricity. Meanwhile, Teodorin, son of the president and currently minister of agriculture, owns several multimillion (U.S. dollar) properties in the U.S. and Europe and sports cars of the likes of the Bugatti Veyron, worth over one million U.S. dollars. In this case, wealth per capita provides a completely distorted measure of the business opportunities that may have developed in Equatorial Guinea throughout the 2000s when oil prices continued to increase (Silverstein, 2012).

Demography and Wealth

Discussing GDP per head leads us to focus on demography. All Triad countries have very low demographic growth. In some cases, as in Italy and Japan, the population is already shrinking. There is a clear relationship between wealth and the propensity to have children. As countries become richer, their citizens have fewer children. The economic boom of most Triad economies occurred in periods when their populations were still growing. The U.S., for example, boomed between 1880 and 1929, and then again between 1945 and 1970, when its demographic growth was much higher than it is today. Aging populations mean less young workers available in the workforce, which results in higher average wages and pension costs. Emerging markets typically have younger populations, a higher percentage of whom are part of the workforce, and hence can potentially be integrated as producers and consumers in the economy. Economies that used to be considered as emerging but are by now rich, such as South Korea and Ireland, by now have similar demographics to Triad countries, which makes it likely that their economic performance will also converge, gradually slowing down and stabilizing.

Changes in GDP per capita measure how much extra income per person is created every year, at least from a statistical perspective, given that income is not divided equitably. If a given population does not grow, any marginal improvement in total GDP must be created by roughly the same number of workers generating a higher output (for example, through the use of better technology). Equally, keeping population constant, an increase in total GDP means an increase in GDP per capita too. By contrast, in a country where the population is increasing fast (for example, Pakistan), total GDP could increase simply because more people are brought into the workforce. If demographic growth surpasses GDP growth, it means that even if the total size of the economy is expanding, in per-capita terms the country is getting poorer—a slightly larger cake is being shared by a much larger number of people, resulting in a smaller slice per person.

Countries with fast population growth find it difficult to grow sufficiently fast for that growth to be translated into an increase in GDP per head. However, countries such as Japan and Italy, which have an aging population and some of the lowest birth rates in the world, face the opposite problem: a shrinking workforce that has to generate enough wealth to pay for the welfare of an increasing group of older people receiving pensions.

Speaking of demography, it is important to note that what matters for the overall economy is how many people can work and are contributing to GDP as opposed to the number of people who are "dependents"—who consume what others produce. Children and the elderly are dependents. It is likely (and hopeful) and that they are not in the workforce. If they are, they are less productive than a young adult. This means that an economy reaches its ideal demographic balance when most of its population is within the most productive age—between 18 and 35. This phenomenon, called the "demographic dividend," is defined as follows:

> "The demographic dividend is the accelerated economic growth that may result from a decline in a country's mortality and fertility and the subsequent change in the age structure of the population. With fewer births each year, a country's young dependent population grows smaller in relation to the working-age population. With fewer people to support, a country has a window of opportunity for rapid economic growth if the right social and economic policies are developed and investments made" (Gribble and Bremmer, 2012: p.1).

The poorest emerging markets, such as Mali, Somalia, and Ethiopia, have such high birth rates that most of their population is made up of children. They have yet to reach their demographic dividend. China, due to the specific birth control policies it enacted, is currently riding the wave of its demographic dividend, though that will soon end. Richer emerging markets, such as the Eastern European countries, have already gone beyond that point and are approaching Western Europe in terms of the aging of their populations.

Triad countries now have a growing proportion of their citizens in the elderly dependant category, whereas many emerging markets, especially the poorest, are limited by having too many young people who are still not in the workforce. In both cases, it is likely that on average populations will age. The impact is, however, very different. In most emerging markets, the share of the population that is part of the workforce will increase, generating positive economic effects. In developed economies, a shrinking number of people are having to pay for a growing number of older citizens (Lee and Mason, 2006).

Most emerging markets have faster population growth than Triad countries, though this varies a lot. Birth rates are affected by several factors, notably education and income levels, which, among other things, allow for the diffusion of contraceptive methods. Life expectancy at birth, which depends on access to hospitals, is another important determinant. Countries where public health systems reach a high share of the population have higher life expectancy. In countries where health systems are concentrated in just a few areas, or are insufficiently staffed and equipped to provide the required services, many citizens remain outside the health provision systems. As a consequence, their life expectancy at birth is lower. When life expectancy is low, birth rates tend to be higher. In other words, women tend to have fewer children when it becomes more likely that their children survive. Having many children is an ancient way of compensating for the probability that some may die through illness. Both Italy and Japan had much higher birth rates than Britain or France in the previous century. The development of sophisticated and affordable health systems then dramatically increased the survival chances of new born Italian and Japanese babies. Both countries now have among the lowest birth rates in the world.

Education also plays a role. It helps to prevent illness through better practice, contributing to increased life expectancy. Educated women are more likely to enter the workforce, which in turn may lead them to have fewer children. Education also fosters the diffusion of contraceptive methods, which reduces birth rates. This can be seen in countries such as Argentina and Uruguay, which have relatively high educational standards among emerging markets and have similar birth rates to those of developed economies, despite having much lower average incomes. Countries affected by lower education and access to health, such as Ethiopia, tend to have higher natality (and mortality) rates. China is a peculiar example—the Communist Party one-child policy has kept birth rates much lower than those of countries with similar income levels. It thus benefitted in the past from having a lower share of young people as dependants, but it has a population that is aging faster than its income or life expectancy rates would suggest. In other words, China will soon also get to the point where its share of old people surpasses those who are in the workforce, though its average citizens will remain far poorer than the average Italian or Japanese citizen.

Having a younger population is one of the key advantages of emerging markets, though in the short run, it may make it difficult to become richer on a per-capita basis. A younger population means a potentially expanding market, it means a pool of labor that can be trained to work in new industries, and in most cases, it means a yet-to-end, or yet-to-come, demographic dividend. And it is one of the features that characterizes, though to different extents and in different ways, emerging markets (Lee and Mason, 2006). For businesses, it means locations where large numbers of people will enter the workforce in the coming decades. It also means that there is potential for targeting the sale of goods and services aimed at children and teenagers in emerging markets where economic growth is effectively generating higher disposable incomes for citizens. More rollerblades, more music players, music shows, and fashionable clothing. In some markets, it may mean more baby food and specialized items for children. In others, such as Russia and Argentina, which are gradually aging, it means more demand for products for the elderly.

Consumption and First-Time Buyers

Emerging markets are characterized by lower average incomes and hence lower consumption than developed economies. This means that there is more scope for expanding consumption: there are people who have never owned a car, a fridge, or a TV, but who, as soon as their incomes allow it, will purchase one (see Table 1.1).

Table 1.1   Durable Consumer Goods Ownership per 1000 Households

	China	India	Japan
Motorcycles*	21	218	177
Washing Machines	95	93	1092
Refrigerators	94	203	1235
Color TV Sets	135	558	865
Cameras	47	67	1350
Air Conditioners	81	118	2478
Computers	42	46	1157
Video Cameras	4	–	475
Microwave Ovens	48	–	1032
Cell Phones	137	670	2131
Telephones	94	–	–
Automobiles	3	35	1414

Data Source: China Statistical Yearbook 2010, Japan National Survey of Family Income and Expenditure, Household Consumption of Various Goods and Services in India.

*Motorcycles data includes scooters.

First-time consumption is a powerful driver of business opportunities and economic growth. In the Triad, most consumers went through their wave of first consumption several decades ago and have since moved to a process of cyclical substitution of such goods. They all go to the cinema, have tens of pairs of shoes and DIY tools (perhaps hundreds, depending on the household), and an array of electronic gadgets. As they go through their second, third, and fourth purchase of the same type of good (say, a mobile phone), consumers become increasingly more informed, more sophisticated, and more specific about what they want. They can afford to delay consumption because they already own an old version of the good—it is up to the producer to really convince them it is time for a new model. An example of this is this snippet of conversation we heard between two teenagers on the bus from Waterloo Station to Dalston in London, UK: "Should I buy the new iPhone or wait for the new Samsung? I prefer the Samsung, the screen is larger...."

The first purchase of a mobile phone constitutes a life-changing event for a consumer for the simple reason that it allows communication on the move; you are no longer dependent on a fixed landline (assuming you could afford or had access to fixed telephony in the first place). Even the simplest phone performs that great function, and it opens up the possibility of accessing information about prices, of not missing the bus back from work, or knowing that there is a monsoon coming and hence avoiding going out fishing that day. The same applies for a car—the fact that it can transport people and objects faster and more cheaply than animal-pulled vehicles (still used in many places) makes it a great good. It allows people to go to work in places that would otherwise be out of reach or to bring their potatoes to the market. Yet, as consumers get used to the fundamental functions of the goods they purchase, they look for an infinity of other uses, often unrelated to the basic reasons why they own such a good.

Seeing this from a company strategy perspective, unless we offer new reasons for buying, such as new functions, all consumers would happily stick with their first car, phone, and fridge, reducing the scope for increasing revenues and profits. Hence, companies *have to* make their products and services more sophisticated to appeal to consumers and, of course, to distinguish themselves from competitors. And consumers become ever more difficult to convince. However, there are still millions of potential customers who never have had two pairs of shoes, and many more who have never had a fridge or a car. They want these goods for their key functions, which will have a dramatic impact on their lifestyles—and, of course, as symbols of status.

The average emerging market consumer consumes much less than the average developed economy consumer. Statistics about the diffusion of consumer durable goods reveal this very clearly, illustrating the potential for expanding and developing these consumer markets. In places like the U.S., there are almost more cars than people, whereas in many emerging economies, most people have never driven one (see Tables 1.2 and 1.3).

Table 1.2   Car Ownership (Millions)

	U.S.	India	China	Advanced Economies (Except USA)	Rest of the World	World
2005	153	7	21	304	161	646
2010	171	9	51	332	197	760
2020	211	19	134	390	292	1046
2030	253	55	255	442	460	1465

Data Source: Chamon et al. (2008)

Table 1.3   Car Ownership Per 1000 People (2010)

U.S.	Germany	Bangladesh	Kenya	Philippines	China	Bulgaria	Mexico
797	572	3	24	30	58	393	275

Data Source: World Bank Development Indicators, accessed 4/20/2013 at http://data.worldbank.org/indicator/IS.VEH.NVEH.P3

Infrastructure

In the Triad, only the very oldest citizens remember living without electricity. The positive economic impact of electrification occurred long ago. A large share of emerging-market households still have only occasional or no access to electricity. Emerging markets tend to have inferior infrastructure compared to Triad markets, at least for now (see Figure 1.1). A large proportion of roads are unpaved, and often dangerous, particularly outside the capitals and main commercial hubs. With the exception of India and China, most emerging markets lack train connections. A vast number of people still live without access to clean water and sewage systems. And statistics about infrastructure development are often over-optimistic. If you were ever naive enough to try drinking the tap water in Moscow or Salvador do Bahia, you would know that being connected to a fresh water source does not necessarily mean having access to clean fresh water. Access to electricity is also difficult to measure because many areas of the emerging world, including coal-rich and economically booming India, have to endure electricity shortages. Even areas that are officially connected to the electrical grid often need generators to compensate for blackouts. In areas where there is no electricity, an improvement in the grid can generate a quick boom in demand for refrigerators and air conditioning units. It can also help small businesses work for longer hours and allow them to install electric motors, both of which increase productivity.

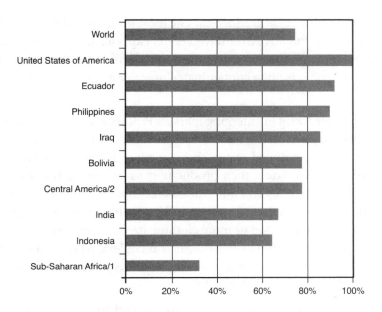

Figure 1.1 Access to electricity (% of population).

Data Source: World Bank Development Indicators (2013)

/1 Central America includes Guatemala, Honduras, El Salvador, Nicaragua, Costa Rica, and Panama.

/2 Sub-Saharan Africa includes Angola, Benin, Botswana, Burkina Faso, Burundi, Cameroon, Cape Verde, Central African Republic, Chad, Comoros, Côte d'Ivoire, Democratic Republic of Congo, Djibouti, Equatorial Guinea, Eritrea, Ethiopia, Gabon, Gambia, Ghana, Guinea, Guinea-Bissau, Kenya, Lesotho, Liberia, Madagascar, Malawi, Mali, Mauritania, Mauritius, Mozambique, Namibia, Niger, Nigeria, Republic of Congo, Rwanda, Senegal, Sierra Leone, and Togo.

Electrification has multiple effects on consumption and productivity. It allows for longer working hours and more flexibility over work times, benefitting employers and workers alike. It also allows for mechanization of simple production processes by applying small motors to existing human power machinery. A pedal loom can very easily and cheaply be converted into a more efficient and faster electric-powered loom. A study of the early Japanese economy by Professor Hunter, from the London School of Economics, demonstrated how the introduction of electric pumps in rice irrigation systems increased rice yields substantially and freed up some of the labor previously used to this purpose that then migrated to urban centers to work in new factories (Hunter, 1989).

The diffusion of sewage systems and fresh water pipes also has important implications. Prahalad has noted that the price of water in the slums of Delhi is much higher than in the richest areas, precisely because there are no clean water pipes. The same situation applies in most countries in Latin America. The most modern and costly neighborhoods of Rio, Sao Paolo, and Buenos Aires have very cheap, clean, drinkable water available from the tap, even though their dwellers may only drink imported Evian or Perrier. In the slums, however, water is often contaminated or water pipes may not even reach housing units.

The majority of people living in emerging markets lack access to clean fresh water. Either they consume unclear, polluted water, or they buy bottled purified water at very high prices. If they consume polluted water, they are more likely to fall ill and contract a myriad of illnesses, which reduce their productivity as workers. If they have to purchase clean water at high prices, they will limit their consumption of other goods and services to make sure they can buy water. Therefore, if they could save on water, they could buy more of other goods, such as food or more clothing items. Sewage systems have a similar effect—they reduce the diffusion of diseases such as cholera, which can be very costly for the health systems of poor countries. Ultimately, a healthy population is more productive and makes both better workers and better consumers.

There are several reasons why emerging markets tend to have worse infrastructure than Triad economies. The primary one is income—average growth since the late 1800s in Triad countries made public resources available to electrify their cities and rural areas and to build sophisticated railroad networks. Another reason is that Triad economies went through an exceptional period of peace and prosperity between 1945 and 2008, which allowed their public sectors to engage in long-term, costly infrastructural investments. Many emerging markets never had the needed public funds to subsidize or entirely fund major infrastructure developments, relying instead on sporadic projects promoted through aid. Other emerging markets have been affected by conflicts and unpredictable political changes, which have reduced the scope for long-term projects. For example, all Latin American countries, with the exception of Costa Rica, have had at least one violent, non-democratic government takeover since 1950. Many of them, such as Argentina, Bolivia, Ecuador, and Guatemala, have been through several such episodes. Others, such as Colombia, have been affected by decades of internal conflict involving armed groups. Many African countries have also suffered from violent struggles, including Nigeria, Algeria, Mali, Sudan, Congo, Rwanda, Burundi, Sierra Leone, Liberia, and most recently, Libya.

Internal conflict often makes it impossible to develop infrastructure in certain areas because roads, pipelines, and railroads are often targeted by insurgent groups. Political instability also interrupts the process of economic policy making, creating incentives to focus on short-term projects, which can be finished quickly and generate visible political return. Lack of continuity contributes to explaining why long-term infrastructure developments were not pursued in many emerging markets. China exemplifies the opposite—having a stable authoritarian government, it has long pursued a policy to improve its infrastructure, engaging in expensive and ambitious projects. Political continuity and the fact that it has a very resourceful public sector explain how it has been able to build an impressive network of roads and railroads in a very short period.

Other factors also contribute to explaining the infrastructure deficiencies of emerging markets. One of them is population density—many emerging markets, such as Kenya, Tanzania, and Afghanistan, have very small populations scattered across a large territory. Building roads, laying water pipes, and extending electric wiring to each of their inhabitants is much more costly than for populations that are concentrated in densely populated areas. Many more kilometers of road and pipes would be needed, and they would be used less intensively.

Another factor to be taken into account is that emerging markets have lower average taxation levels than developed economies. The latter tax their citizens and companies more and are more effective at collecting taxes. Calculating taxation and enforcing tax collection is complex. It requires a skilled bureaucracy and state control over the transactions that take place in the economy, together with functioning legal and judicial systems. Many of the lower-income emerging markets have not yet developed these institutions. Large shares of economic activities occur outside the formal and taxed spheres, even in countries that have sophisticated institutions and complex tax systems, such as Brazil and China.

The easiest taxes to collect are indirect taxes, such as VAT and tax on gasoline. Import duty is also easier because it is collected as goods enter the borders of a country. Typically, emerging markets rely more on these types of taxation than on direct taxation (income and corporate tax). With the exception of countries that are very rich in natural resources, this means that emerging market governments collect only a small share of GDP in the form of taxation and as a result have few funds to finance infrastructure developments.

Historically, emerging markets have struggled to attract investment because of their instability. Most emerging markets, including Cuba, have special economic zones where foreign investors can operate in low-tax or tax-free regimes and benefit from better treatment than local companies. They offer lower corporate tax than Triad countries, which helps convince investors to bring with them capital and technology. Having lower income taxes can also be part of a specific development policy because it helps to attract skilled professionals. But it is a double-edged sword in that it also contributes to the country's low tax revenue receipts. Again, China is an exception. Its authoritarian government is capable of mobilizing vast resources and has a penchant for infrastructure projects that can showcase its initiative. This explains why China, still a very poor country in terms of income per capita, has shiny new high-speed railways and state-of-the-art highways.

Triad economies tend to benefit from a more extensive diffusion of roads, fixed landlines, water pipes, railways, canals, electric grids, and fiber optic cables. A consequence of the 2008–2012 economic downturn is that Triad economies also have fewer and fewer resources to invest in repair or new infrastructure. If this trend continues, the advantage they have experienced for many years vis-à-vis emerging economies in terms of infrastructure will fade out soon. Nevertheless, businesses used to operating in Triad countries where the functioning of roads, the electricity grid, and water systems are taken for granted can often overlook the negative consequences of the very different operating environment of emerging markets. This can lead, first, to an underestimation of the costs needed to work in emerging markets (for example, additional generators to ensure a continuous electricity supply). Second, it can limit businesses to developing new products and services with a Triad mindset, without first scanning the faster growing emerging markets.

Emerging markets have plenty of scope to improve their infrastructure, or to build it up from scratch. The lack of infrastructure presents an attractive opportunity for business. Many emerging markets now have the necessary public funds to finance new pipes, though they may lack the organizational or technological capabilities or the will to do it. Companies that can seize this opportunity can simultaneously benefit from a source of demand and contribute to a positive social goal. In cases where the public sector is unwilling to fund the diffusion of fresh water and sewage systems, companies can engage local communities in community development projects and experiment with price segmentation—there is plenty of scope to reverse the situation described by Prahalad and to change things so that the richest neighborhoods pay higher prices for their water, subsidizing the poorest (Prahalad, 2006).

Transport infrastructure also has a strong effect on local economies: it creates new markets and links existing ones. A canal, for example, can make it economically feasible to transport heavy, bulky, nonperishable goods for long distances. It can hence make operating a mine or cultivating a crop in an area located far from the main export markets profitable. Roads and railways have similar and cumulative effects. The more connected a given location is to others, the more their markets integrate, thus opening up the possibility of selling a given product to a larger number of potential customers. Improved transport infrastructure also increases the number of potential available suppliers for a company in search of inputs. This feature of transport infrastructure is fundamental, and yet often forgotten in the Triad, where such transformations occurred at least a century ago.

One of the consequences of infrastructure deficiencies is that emerging markets are *not*, in most cases, integrated markets. They are the sum of many local markets, many of which are loosely integrated, others of which are almost entirely isolated. The markets around the capitals and biggest cities are generally integrated among themselves and linked to the world economy. Smaller urban centers and rural areas are more isolated. Poor infrastructure means that local prices in each of these markets are distorted by the limited availability of alternatives. A truck takes a minimum of four hours to go from the capital of Costa Rica to its main port on the Caribbean coast, though it is a distance of less than 100 kilometers, despite the fact that there are no road blocks and no insurgencies in the country. Some rural areas of emerging markets such as Nepal and Thailand require days of traveling to reach them. The consequence of being de-linked from markets is that refined local goods may be sold at puny prices because by the time they have reached the closest harbor, the cost of transporting them has surpassed what was paid to the producers. Supplies thus also may have to be bought at very high prices, making it difficult for companies to remain profitable when they have to substitute their parts or machinery. Improvements in transport infrastructure can progressively link such markets, transforming business opportunities for both local and global business.

Linking markets also allows for higher labor force mobility. Poor workers that depend on seasonal jobs (for example, harvesting of sugar cane or coffee beans) often remain idle or with partial employment for several months because they cannot afford to commute to other locations. Better roads can allow villagers to move around more freely, giving them access to different sources of income, and hence also providing available labor where it may be needed.

Sometimes markets are separated by communication deficiencies even more than by physical barriers; people may not hear about opportunities to sell their wares in a nearby village, or that a factory is looking for workers. For this reason, the sort of infrastructure that lowers the cost of transmitting information—ranging from the telegraph, to antennas for mobile telephony and broadband Internet connections—has strong potential to stimulate business development and economic growth. Experiments with mobile telephony show that becoming aware of prices and demand patterns affects the strategies of poor agricultural producers, making them shift to growing the crops that are most in demand, which benefits them as well as their global buyers. It also allows best practice to be shared more widely. It can, for example, put an injured person in a remote area in touch with a nurse or doctor who can provide advice.

The whole concept of the e-economy was based on the idea that lowering the cost and time needed to transmit information would unleash a huge economic potential by integrating markets. It has already occurred in developed economies, leading to the development of giant companies such as Amazon, to a change in consumption habits, and to yet further sophistication of consumers, who can inform themselves more easily than before. However, the strongest potential for this sort of change is in emerging markets, precisely because in such markets workers and employers as well as producers and consumers are more de-linked than in developed economies and have been so for many years. Within Europe, North America, Japan, South Korea, and other developed economies, consumers can easily move from urban centers to cheaper locations for their shopping. Many of the millions who inhabit emerging markets live in badly connected areas or have insufficient income to take their products or their labor to different markets. All of this is changing fast, however, as emerging markets invest in new infrastructure and investors look for opportunities to employ their capital and know how outside of their depressed home markets.

Cities in emerging markets are catching up with the Triad, installing new subways and airports and improving their road networks. To do so, they are contracting architecture studios, engineering firms, construction businesses, and sourcing all of the related materials needed. The train that links Shanghai airport to the city, the first magnetic levitation train to operate in the world, was developed by Siemens, one of the largest German companies. The governments of several large emerging markets, notably Argentina, Brazil, China, and India, are often reluctant to contract foreign firms for publicly funded projects. But Triad companies have the advantage of greater experience in complex engineering and infrastructure projects. A common solution to this problem is creating joint ventures that include both local partners and Triad companies.

Market Institutions

Basic economics teaches us that markets are made by consumers and producers. Consumer demand, producers sell. Consumers will buy more if lower prices are offered, whereas producers will sell more at higher prices—and this logic is why the demand curve is downward sloping and the supply curve is upward sloping. Where demand and supply meet we find the equilibrium point in the market for any given good. What classic economics does not take into account is that markets do not work automatically. They require both buyers and sellers to have access to information. For example, a consumer who knows little about wine is unlikely to pay a premium for a wine of a special year, even though it is highly valued by a connoisseur.

As we explain more thoroughly in Chapter 2, markets also require supporting institutions, especially instruments that facilitate transactions, such as means of payment and contract enforcement. If all transactions have to be carried out in cash because credit cards and other instruments are not available, it becomes difficult and risky to make large purchases such as a house or a car. More importantly, the simpler and more transparent the regulations and law enforcement mechanisms are, the lower the costs of completing a transaction (Williamson, 1998; North, 1990). Emerging markets typically have more complex regulatory frameworks than developed economies. And they have less transparent law enforcement mechanisms. It is more difficult to draw up a contract, and yet harder to ensure it is enforced in case of noncompliance. Complicated legislation makes it easier to find loopholes for local experts. And inefficient courts mean it may be cheaper to search for a settlement than to wait for the case to be dealt with. Porous frontiers and cheap means of changing identity documents also mean that even winning a battle in court does not guarantee recovery of losses—the guilty can escape or change identity.

Tarun Khanna and Krishna Palepu, two Harvard professors who wrote the influential book *Winning in Emerging Markets,* qualified all of these barriers to business as "institutional holes" (Khanna and Palepu, 2010). They point out that all emerging markets have some institutional holes, or lack institutions to support markets in specific areas. To win in emerging markets, it is important to identify such holes, and possibly turn them into an advantage (for example, developing intermediary firms that compensate for lacking institutions). Institutional voids are present, to different extents, even in the Triad. For example, it is easier for a foreigner to register property in Turkey than in Germany. Emerging markets tend to have less developed markets and to be affected by more institutional holes. Transparency International, a think tank based in Germany, ranks countries according to perceived corruption. Its Corruption Perception Index shows some Triad countries, such as Italy, as more corrupt than many emerging markets, such as Chile, Botswana, and Qatar (Transparency International, 2012). But the worst offenders are always emerging markets, and the vast majority of emerging markets rank as more corrupt than the largest Triad economies (the U.S., Japan, Germany, France, Canada, and the UK).

Corruption is one of the more commonly used indicators of institutional voids. Other indicators may include the extent to which property rights are respected, the complexity of taxation, and the regulation of the labor market. A look at the indexes compiled by the World Heritage Foundation, another think tank, illustrates that most Triad economies are freer in terms of trade and financial market regulation and provide better protection for property rights. The "Doing Business" index of the World Bank and the International Finance Corporation, two multilateral organizations, shows a similar picture (World Bank and IFC, 2013). It is a combined measure of the difficulty of doing business in a given country, and includes items such as the number of days required to start a business or to compile income tax forms. The 100 countries that rank the lowest are all emerging markets. In 2011, none of the top ten performers were emerging markets, though two markets that have long emerged, Singapore and Hong Kong, have been ranking among the top every year for over a decade (see Table 1.4).

Table 1.4   Measuring the Business Environment

	Country	**Doing Business Ranking** (World Bank and IFC). Ranking Out of 185 Countries, with 1 Being the Best Rank.	**Corruption Perception Index** (Transparency International). Ranking Out of 174 Countries, with 1 Being the Best Rank.
Largest Triad Economies	USA	4	19
	Japan	24	17
	Germany	20	13
	France	34	22
	UK	7	17
BRICS	Brazil	130	69
	Russia	112	133
	India	132	94
	China	91	80
	South Africa	39	69
N11 and Civets	Bangladesh	129	144
	Colombia	45	94
	Egypt	109	118
	Indonesia	128	118
	Iran	145	133
	South Korea	8	45
	Mexico	48	105
	Nigeria	131	139
	Pakistan	107	139
	Philippines	138	105
	Turkey	71	54
	Vietnam	99	123

Data Source: "Doing Business," World Bank and IFC, accessed on 4/25/2013 at http://www.doingbusiness.org/rankings, and "Corruption Perception Index," Transparency International, accessed on 4/25/2013 at http://cpi.transparency.org/cpi2012/results/.

In sum, operating in emerging markets is different because less efficient institutions are supporting transactions. It entails more risk, more complexity, and longer time to complete a deal. But there is great variety among emerging markets, ranging from economies such as Somalia, which function in an almost total absence of formal supporting institutions, to countries such as Chile, where it may be easier to do business than in Greece or Spain.

Sophistication of the Economy

Emerging markets tend to have less diversified and sophisticated economies than Triad countries. And we use the word "tend" precisely because it is a generalization, which applies to the majority of emerging markets, but not to some of the largest of them, such as China, Brazil, and India. The majority of emerging markets generate most of their wealth from a handful of activities, often depending on natural resources. Nigeria, for example, despite being a densely populated country and having fertile land, continues to rely on oil for a large share of the wealth it generates. In Venezuela, also rich in fertile land and benefitting from a relatively well-educated population, most of the GDP comes from oil. Botswana relies on diamond exports, Malawi on tobacco, and Cote D'Ivoire on cocoa. Triad economies, on the other hand, have more diversified economic structures. Even small Triad economies, such as Finland or Belgium, have specialized manufacturing industries, some engineering companies, and an array of service industries. Triad economies are thus less vulnerable to fluctuations in prices of specific goods.

Triad economies are also different in terms of resource endowments. With the exception of Norway, most Triad economies are poor in resources. Some, such as Italy, France, and Japan, depend heavily on imports for their natural resource inputs. Others, such as the U.S. and Canada, are richer in resources but still not self-sufficient. Most of the world's mineral and energy resources are located in emerging markets. Emerging markets also concentrate the vast majority of fertile land. The world's production of food, energy, and minerals depends strongly on the development of sources located in these markets.

Mineral riches have already generated economic booms in countries such as Qatar and Kazakhstan, transforming them into respectively rich and mid-income economies. Resources have the potential to transform many other economies, ranging from Peru to Indonesia and Mongolia. Economic growth always generates business opportunities. When it benefits only a small share of the population, it generates demand for luxury goods. After the end of communism, for example, Russia became one of the most profitable markets for companies as Ferrari and Louis Vuitton. When economic growth trickles down to the upper-middle classes, it generates demand for consumer durables, such as fridges, TVs, and cars. And when it also benefits the lower-middle and poorer income categories, it boosts demand for mid-priced clothing items, restaurants, bars, and other entertainment services. Resource-fueled economic booms hence open up markets not only for the companies directly involved in resource extraction and production, but also for other businesses, which can tackle the needs and desires of wealthier citizens.

Agro resources are another important area of potential business in emerging markets. In the Triad, most wealth is generated by services, such as banking, engineering, consulting, and manufacturing. Agriculture contributes to a minor share of national wealth and employs a minor fraction of the workforce, even in countries such as the U.S. and France, which have very vocal agro-producing lobbies. By contrast, in several emerging markets, such as Argentina, Brazil, Paraguay, Malawi, and Kenya, agriculture generates an important share of national income and drives exports.

Some emerging markets, such as Brazil, have already developed large-scale, high-tech agro producers and companies supplying seeds and machinery. But most emerging markets, including China, India, and Russia, lack expertise in these fields. Their agro production is often characterized by low technology and low levels of mechanization. As incomes rise in emerging markets, new opportunities will develop for Triad companies producing irrigation equipment, agricultural machinery, seeds, and other inputs.

Triad economies concentrate the production of scientific knowledge, measured as the number of published articles in peer-reviewed journals or the number of patents (though China is catching up very fast in this field too). Triad economies invest more in research and development, and they innovate more. It is important to note that until now, this was because Triad economies were richer—their companies and governments could afford to spend more on innovation. In the post 2008 crisis context, where governments and companies in the Triad are cutting down on R&D, emerging markets may easily become the new loci for innovation. The opportunity here would be for companies that specialize in highly innovative technologies that require initial support from governments, such as green technologies. The United Arab Emirates have, for example, created Masdar, a new city that is being built using advanced environmentally friendly technologies. They have attracted several Triad businesses there, and are providing seed capital to help them kick-start their projects. Even if emerging markets continue, by and large, to be net importers of technology, they will produce an increasing share of the world's innovations.

Their economies will gradually change and become more sophisticated and diverse, following the path of Triad countries. As consumers spend more on entertainment, local music, and cinema productions, these areas will become more sophisticated. The Hong Kong, Indian, and Nigerian cinema industries have, for example, benefitted greatly from the economic boom of China and India. They have exploited their growing revenues, investing in new technology. They increased the average budgets of their movies and have internationalized, launching in neighboring countries and capturing markets from lower quality local producers and Hollywood cinema. An indigenous music industry has emerged in Angola, fuelled by demand from a new urbanized middle class enriched by the oil boom, and exported to other African and Latin American countries.

References

Aggarwal, V. (2003). The Evolution of Debt Crisis: Origins, Management and Policy Lessons. En V. Aggarwal and B. Granville. *Sovereign Debt: Origins, Crises and Restructuring* (pgs. 11–35). London: Royal Institute of International Affairs.

Amieva, J. and Uriza, B. (Enero de 2000). *Crisis Bancarias: Causas, Costos, Duración, Efectos y Opciones de Política*. Santiago: CEPAL.

Barro, R. and Sala-i-Martin, X. (2004). *Economic Growth.* Massachusetts: Massachusetts Institute of Technology.

Blanchard, O. (2006). *Macroeconomía.* Madrid: Pearson Education S.A.

Chamon, M., Mauro, P., and Okawa, Y. (2008). Cars: The Implications of Mass Car Ownership in the Emerging Market Giants. *Economic Policy, Vol. 23 (54)*, 243–296.

Dornbusch, R. and Fischer, S. (1987). *Macroeconomía.* USA: McGraw Hill, Inc.

Durán, R. and Torres, C. (2007). *Hacia un Entendimiento del Fenómeno Inflacionario: El Caso de Costa Rica.* San José: Banco Central de Costa Rica.

Esquivel, G. and Larraín, F. (2000). Determinantes de las Crisis Cambiarias. *El Trimestre Económico, Vol. 67 (266)*, 191–237.

García, S. and Vicéns, J. (2007). Últimas Aportaciones en la Explicación de Las Crisis Cambiarias: El Caso de las Crisis Gemelas. *Spanish Journal of Economics and Finance, Vol. 30 (82) (Cuadernos de Economía)*, 75–99.

Gavin, M. and Hausmann, R. (1998). *The Roots of Banking Crises: The Macroeconomic Context.* Inter-American Development Bank (Working Paper No. 318).

Gribble, J. and J. Bremmer (2012). The Challenge of Attaining the Demographic Dividend. *Population Reference Bureau.* Accessed on 4/20/2013 at http://www.prb.org/pdf12/demographic-dividend.pdf.

Kamisnky, G., Lizondo, S., and Rainhart, C. (1998). Leading Indicators of Currency Crises. *IMF Staff Papers, Palgrave Macmillan, Vol. 45 (1)*, 1–48.

Khanna, T. and Palepu, K. G. (2010). *Winning in Emerging Markets: A Road Map for Strategy and Execution.* Harvard Business School Press.

Lee, R. and Mason, A. (2006). What Is the Demographic Dividend? *Finance and Development, the IMF, Vol. 43, N.3.*

Mankiw, G. (2006). *Macroeconomía.* Barcelona: Antoni Bosch, Editor.

North, D. (1990). *Institutions, Institutional Change and Economic Performance.* Cambridge University Press.

Prahalad, C. K. (2006). *The Fortune at the Bottom of the Pyramid: Eradicating Poverty Through Profits.* New Jersey: Wharton School Publishing, Pearson Education.

Ray, D. (1998). *Economía del Desarrollo.* Barcelona: Antoni Bosch, Editor.

Silverstein, K. (2012). Bipolar Policy on Equatorial Guinea, June 15th, Foreign Policy.

Transparency International (2012) Corruption Perception Index. Accessed on 4/23/2013 at http://www.transparency.org/research/cpi/overview.

Williamson, O.E. (1998) *The Economic Institutions of Capitalism,* Free Press.

World Bank and International Finance Corporation (2013). Doing Business Index, accessed on 4/23/2013 at http://www.doingbusiness.org/rankings.

World Bank Development Indicators (2013). Accessed on 4/23/2013 at http://data.worldbank.org/indicator/.

2

Markets and Institutions

Introduction

This chapter traces the evolutionary journey from hunter gatherer societies through the development of the first markets, institutions, and formal forms of organization, such as government. Our objective is to explain some of the concepts we use throughout the book, such as institutions, and outline the factors that shape markets and business environments. To do so, we draw extensively from economics and economic history. The story takes in the development of credit institutions, the formalization of private property rights, and the pioneering steps of companies working in far-flung regions and breaking new ground in commerce, and then reflects on what these things meant for the further expansion of trade. For readers with a background in economics and history, it will be a reminder of their first years of study, whereas for others it will provide a summarized explanation of the development of market institutions. The next chapter will further develop this topic by looking at how multinational companies have contributed to the integration of the global economy in the past, and how they operated in emerging markets. We believe that these history-based chapters provide an insightful background for the more hands-on chapters that we develop in the second and third parts of the book. Nonetheless, readers anxious to get to the strategic part of this book and learn how to operate in emerging markets can skip to the second part and read the two historical chapters as a complement later.

Understanding the Functioning of Markets: A Look to the Past

The creation of wealth, as opposed to the pure transfer of existing wealth via pillaging or theft, lies at the basis of most human societies. It can be traced back to the shift from hunting to agriculture and the development of the first settlements about 11,000 ago, described elegantly in Jared Diamond's book *The World Until Yesterday* (Diamond,

2012). Hunters and gatherers focused on using resources to fulfill their immediate needs. Settlers employed the resources they had available, land and labor, not only to gather fruit to feed themselves, but also to generate future resources—growing food rather than simply gathering what nature made available in a specific place and time. In other words, they not only consumed "wealth," they experimented with the production of some of the goods they needed. This led to the demand for further goods, such as tools to cultivate the land. Early settlers continuously innovated with agro production technology, discovering new crops, introducing basic irrigation techniques, and experimenting with domestic animals. They also improved their hunting and fishing skills by building new weapons, such as bows, inventing traps and nets, and fine-tuning their understanding of the habits of their prey. As they moved out of caves to form agricultural settlements, their need for shelter from the elements and predators pushed them to develop the first rudimentary shacks.

Demand for a rising number of goods and services made it necessary for early settlers to search for ways to coordinate their efforts. Tasks that required more than one person, such as hunting large animals or building an irrigation trench, were shared. Other tasks were gradually assigned to specific individuals. It is unclear whether this happened by chance, whether some members of these communities actively chose to specialize in specific skills, or whether they were perhaps ordered to do so by their elders or leaders. It is clear, however, that the shift from pure resource exploitation for the purpose of survival to resource management and production, together with the fact of creating settlements, generated demand for increasingly sophisticated goods and services. Naturally, humans began dividing tasks among themselves, generating the division of labor—one of the basic principles of the modern economy (Durkheim and Coser, 1997).

Gradually, settlers became specialized leather workers, animal caretakers, weapon makers, and so on. Dedicating more of their time to a particular set of activities, humans began developing specific knowledge about such activities—how to best sharpen the tip of a spear, which wood makes the most resistant arrow, and which wood is flexible enough for bows. Weapon makers searching for harder and harder materials for the tips of their spears discovered metals and later metalworking techniques. Those specializing in producing shelters experimented with stones, wood, and other materials and building techniques to improve the solidity of their structures and the extent to which they provided protection from the elements.

The gradual accumulation of a body of specialized knowledge allowed settler societies to improve the techniques used in all of their activities by building on past experiences (Mokyr, 1990). By discarding techniques that had proven inferior, skilled workers could save their efforts and focus them instead on extending the search to yet-unproven materials or processes. By training apprentices and teaching skills to their offspring, they ensured that they transmitted their knowledge to others. This generation and diffusion of knowledge are key elements of what in the modern economy we define as "innovation." Through innovation (gradual, cumulative improvements in the way different tasks were performed), early settlers learned to be more productive, though this is a very modern way of defining the process. They learned how to extract an ever-increasing amount of resources or wealth from a given stock of resources—for example, by working out how to catch more fish in an hour by using different kinds of nets or by increasing the yield of a plot of land through better irrigation. By becoming more efficient in their use of time, muscle power, and land, they began generating what Marx calls "surplus"—more wealth than they strictly needed to survive (for example, more food than they could consume before it perished, or periods of idle time between the performance of different tasks). As humans began to produce more than they immediately needed for their survival, they searched for ways to exchange the extra goods they had no need of for other goods and services, leading to the development of the first markets.

The division of labor and the development of specialized skills fostered wealth creation and provided incentives to exchange goods and services (Smith, 2006). This fueled a positive cycle whereby specialization allowed primitive societies to be more productive and simultaneously made it necessary to exchange some goods and services. The extra wealth generated by specialization and trade provided further reasons to trade, and the possibility of generating further extra wealth justified the development of yet more specialized skills. By no longer performing all the tasks needed to survive for themselves and specializing instead on a small set of specific activities, humans became more interdependent and reliant on others for many of their basic necessities. Workers who specialized in producing bows began to demand strings for their weapons, which in turn were made by others specializing in processing animal skin to make other wares. This rise in the frequency and sophistication of the exchanges that occurred within self-standing societal units, such as villages, made it necessary to develop mechanisms to regulate and facilitate transactions, which leads us to the emergence of the first markets (Ferguson, 2011; Landes, 1998).

Markets link buyers and suppliers, allowing the results of improved productivity to be absorbed and exploited across society. The first prerequisite for this to occur is the availability of information. If I do not know whether anyone is willing to buy my product, I may not be able to sell it. Indeed, I may not decide to produce it at all and choose to provide the goods I need myself instead, even though I will likely not be very skilled at doing so. On a more general level, different parties need to exchange information in order to trade—information about the characteristics of the goods and the conditions of the transaction. How many eggs can I get for this fish? Having exchanged information ("This fish was caught two hours ago, so it's very fresh"), the two parties can agree on a set of conditions and complete the transaction. Repeating this exercise can lead to the development of an idea about the approximate value of some goods in terms of other goods. A fisherman, for example, may begin to learn how many eggs or how much corn he may receive in exchange for different types of fish.

Information and information exchange are necessary conditions for the development of markets (Williamson, 1979). Yet, they are not sufficient by themselves—if, for example, exchanging goods in a given location is very dangerous because of thieves, a seller may refrain from transacting even if he or she believes there are available buyers. Transaction cost economists, such as Williamson (1979), explain this by demonstrating that as exchanges, or transactions, become less costly in terms of the risks involved, more incentives to trade emerge and thus more incentives to continue innovating, specializing, and becoming more productive. We can infer that markets developed when early settlers found ways to facilitate commercial exchanges (Acemoglu and Johnson, 2003). What allowed for this decline in transaction costs? What were the mechanisms that facilitated the diffusion of trade beyond each community or region and eventually reached a global level?

Three basic elements allow different parties to carry out exchanges: information exchange, rules, and rule-enforcing mechanisms. These rules are often defined as "institutions." Nobel Prize winner Douglas North (1990), one of the founding fathers of new institutional economics, argued that institutions, or the rules that exist in a given society, regulate human behavior through incentives—positive incentives (rewards) to promote a certain type of behavior, and negative incentives (sanctions) to discourage other behavior. If thieves were not punished in ancient societies, there would have been greater incentives to obtain food and shelter by taking it from others than by generating it through one's own work (Greif, 2006). This, in turn, would have made it illogical to attempt to innovate and become more productive—by this logic, it would have made more sense to find better ways of thieving. Undoubtedly, a few members of any society at any time do specialize in theft and criminal enterprise. The fact that society at large condemns these activities on moral grounds, together with the existence of punitive mechanisms to discourage crime, explains why crime remains the "specialized skill" of only a minority of people.

Specializing in different tasks meant that settlers moved from being equal members of a community performing a broad range of tasks to being "the" members of the community assigned to one or another task, not so far removed from what can we can observe in a beehive (Hayek, 2013; Durkheim and Coser, 1997). It would have become necessary to attempt to coordinate actions in order to avoid duplication and, in some cases, to pull resources together to achieve common goals (Ostrom, 1990). It is likely that the first forms of local government emerged as a response to the need to coordinate an increasingly complex set of tasks and activities, some of which required the joint work of several members of society at once. We do not know exactly when this happened, but we do know that ancient communities developed rules to shape the behavior of their members, rewarding communal efforts and punishing theft and other acts. Rules also regulated transactions—we can imagine that if every time two parties attempted to exchange goods they ended up in a deadly fight, trade would pretty quickly cease and each community member would focus on providing for his or her family nucleus's basic needs, ✳ rather than specializing in particular skills (Greif, 2006). Trade was not only a result of the division of labor, it was instrumental in ensuring the sustainability and continuation of such a division of labor (Cipolla, 1965; Ferguson, 2011; Landes, 1998).

Rules are meaningful only as far as they are known and enforced. This truth feeds back into the reasons why different forms of government and governance emerged (North, 1990). Enforcing rules entails the capacity to deploy force when needed, to monitor behavior and deploy incentives accordingly. In its basic definition, the government has jurisdiction and the exclusive right to the use of force over a certain territory and the subjects that live within it (Williamson, 1998). Jurisdiction, again a modern and sophisticated definition, means that a government designs the rules that will regulate human behavior—that is, the institutions (Rodrik, Subramanian, and Trebbi, 2004). Various civilizations have generated a broad range of government forms and found different justifications for the authority of government, ranging from divine right to communal tradition. But they all developed their own sets of institutions, which helped to structure and cement existing traditions and to coordinate societal life (Acemoglu and Robison, 2012). Even in a very small, self-governed village in a primitive society, it is safe to assume that there were rules, individuals in charge of designing and amending the rules, and ways of ensuring compliance. By developing institutions and mechanisms to enforce them, humans prepared the basic conditions for markets to emerge (Greif, 2006).

Among the most important institutions regulating social and economic life was the definition and protection of property rights (Smith, 2006; Hayek, 2013; North, 1990). Even societies that rely on communal assets—for example, communal land and tools—allow individuals to own and exchange some of their possessions and have found ways to define rights to ownership and usage of assets (Rodrik et al., 2004). Before the development of institutions to protect property rights, the concept of ownership was related to an individual or family group's capacity to defend their possessions. The idea that property should be respected, and that society at large stands by this principle, justifies trade and attempts to generate extra wealth through innovation.

North (1990) emphasizes that institutions are important where they actually regulate behavior, whether formally or informally. They do not have to be written. Customs, or the well-established, understood, and generally respected ways of doing things in a societal context, are institutions—they explicitly or implicitly regulate behavior. Opening the door for an elderly woman is not a law, it is a custom, yet one that tends to be agreed upon and respected in multiple cultures. Embracing and kissing among men is a custom that is accepted and even expected in a number of cultures but frowned upon in others. The institutions regulating markets are sometimes structured and formalized, in others they are customary, but not necessarily less effective for this. Although we may not have records of it, it is likely that institutions regulating exchange developed as markets emerged, albeit in primitive forms (Greif, 2006). For example, historical accounts of the ancient Babylonians illustrate that private property was well established and that well-defined systems existed to regulate trade. Another example of the early emergence and acceptance of market institutions is the fact that all of the monotheistic religions strongly condemn theft, the clearest form of attack against private property. We can find many examples of societies where most assets were communally owned and managed, such as the indigenous communities that populated the area between the South of Brazil and the North of Argentina. Yet, communal organization did not exclude the existence of markets within these communities and across different villages and groups, nor did it forbid individual ownership of specific items. Property rights put borders to what was available and to whom, specified how these goods may have become available, and at what conditions or price.

With the modern nation state, this sort of communal ownership receded, substituted by direct state ownership and management of assets that produced goods and services that were used by its subjects communally—for example, infrastructure, defense, sanitation, education, and health services (Landes, 1998). Communal ownership and state ownership did not preclude property rights, however. They generated a different form of right where the owner was an organization that represented and served, at least in theory, its subjects, rather than an individual. Just as a state-owned factory was not freely available for any use by all and sundry, communal land was regulated for a specific use, and its owner (the commune organization or the state) had the right to buy it, develop it, modify it, and often to sell it. This contrasts strongly with the organization of the hunter-gatherer societies that were developed around the pursuit of freely available resources.

Clarifying the rules of the game created incentives to trade, both within and across the borders of a community. The intensification of transactions led to the development of another pillar of capitalism—the means of exchange. Instead of bartering, exchanges began to be denominated in third goods, which were external to the transaction, generally rare and sought-after materials and objects—these included not only precious metals, but also different types of gems, stones, and even cocoa seeds. The diffusion of primitive forms of currency freed an immense potential for trade, further specialization, and wealth creation (Hayek, 2013). Instead of searching for a party who had the exact good needed, it became possible to sell goods or services to anyone willing to pay for them and then use the earned currency for other purchases. Markets became a central feature of settlements, which often included specific spaces for them, such as a square or covered area. With the development of the institutions that permitted transactions to occur and the establishment of different currencies to carry exchanges beyond bartering, the next key step in the development of markets was de-linking exchanges in the present from income in the present (Ferguson, 2012). As commerce became more sophisticated, the first credit instruments emerged to allow buyers to purchase beyond their current means and defer payments to the future. This eventually generated modern banking institutions and the practice of lending, borrowing, and paying in installments, freeing further potential for exchanges (Cipolla, 1965).

The complexity of exchanges brought about another institution of the modern economy—the company or firm (Coase, 1937). As Chandler elegantly argues, the firm exists because some transactions are just too complex to be carried out without some form of coordination (Chandler, 1990). If it requires multiple workers and a complex organization of tasks to produce a good, some form of top-down organization becomes necessary to avoid conflict and repetition and to establish a work sequence. This justifies the existence of the company—an organization that serves the purpose of internalizing all of the needed activities and transactions to generate a certain good or service. The birth of companies was the last step in a long evolutionary journey that generated modern markets (Landes, 1998; Coase, 1992). Private companies developed the capacity to perform multiple tasks and very complex production sequences, which would have been impossible for individual artisans. Trade fostered the emergence and development of modern corporations (Chandler, 1990).

The concept of the multinational company, in the sense of a company that operates simultaneously in multiple locations, finds its origins in the British and Dutch East India Companies. These were large hierarchical organizations that grew for the purpose of establishing and defending trading posts (Dunning and Lundan, 2008). As trading became more dangerous and logistically difficult, they diversified into other activities, building their own warehouses and armies. It is important to note that these organizations, notwithstanding some despicable actions and consequences, developed in order to expand trade and the benefits that could be extracted from them. It is also noteworthy that they were the first examples of private enterprises managing diverse multinational (in some cases global) operations, in spite of the logistical challenges this entailed (Jones, 2000). The managerial and organizational innovations introduced by the first multinational companies occurred precisely to allow trade to expand by establishing new routes and creating new markets.

What is striking is the fact that we can find evidence of private property and the development of some forms of markets in most of the civilizations we have records of, despite their geographic location, religious preferences, or ethical values—there were markets in Babylon, in the Greek city-states, the Egyptian Empire, the Roman Republic, the Moghul Empire and the Chinese Empire (Acemoglu and Robinson, 2012). The Carthaginians and Phoenicians established trading posts all across the Mediterranean sea. The Mayans and Aztecs traded through the impenetrable forests and high mountains of Latin America. The Arabs were skilled traders, and so were many Jewish tribes. Trade motivated explorers, allowing the meeting and cross-fertilization of different civilizations. The Venetian Republic, one of the longest-standing independent republics of Europe, was ruled by traders. Its arch-enemies, the Ottomans, who ruled vast parts of Asia and the Middle East for centuries, fought for the control of trading routes. The modern banking institutions, as well as the principles of modern accounting and the first universities, were founded in small cities that thrived on commerce: Antwerp, Amsterdam, Lubeck, Florence, Pisa, Bologna, and Venice (Cipolla, 1965). The Atlantic crossings of the Spanish and Portuguese explorers were motivated by trade, and the British Empire's actions against the Spanish crown were partly motivated by the desire to free Atlantic trade from the Spanish monopolies (Landes, 1998). The Austrian-Hungarian Empire flourished because it promoted free trade and communal tariffs across its multinational territory, fostering market integration and specialization. The accumulation of capital and market sophistication that trade fostered in Great Britain and Northern Europe provided the basis for the industrial revolution, which pushed the global economy into its current, fast-paced evolutionary trajectory (Kindleberger, 2011).

This brief skim through some of the key turning points in the development of markets and institutions serves a basic purpose: to illustrate their reasons for existing and their key pillars. The basic foundations of markets, and thus of modern capitalism, are institutions: property rights, rule-enforcement mechanisms, means of exchange and financing (currencies and credit instruments), and the private company. Markets exist because of the capacity to produce surplus wealth and the fact that, by specializing, individuals need to exchange the products of their work in order to provide for all their necessities. They also exist because of the desire to trade and acquire goods and services that are not strictly necessary. Despite philosophical and religious criticisms of consumerism, there is plenty of historical evidence of the production and possession of superfluous goods of the likes of toys, makeup, and decorations in ancient civilizations. Markets developed because men and women not only needed but also wanted to trade. And the same could be said for the institutions that regulate markets, ranging from currencies to the rules of exchange and credit instruments.

Barriers to Trade and the Integration of International Markets

Markets are a dominant feature of a diverse range of human societies, and precisely because they arose autonomously in different unconnected societies, it would be naive to imagine that markets are exactly the same in different social and cultural contexts. They have similarities; they share the basic fundamentals, such as property rights and credit. But they also exhibit subtle differences. To understand this, it is useful to think of a metaphor—the family nucleus. Family continues to be, by far, the most common societal form of organization, to the point that a lot of statistics are compiled using households rather than individuals as the unit of analysis in order to allow for the sharing of resources that occurs in family nuclei. Yet, the meanings, ways of functioning, and legal implications of family change across religious, cultural, historical, and geographical settings. The same goes for markets—the level of formalization of the rules, the roles of intermediaries, the ways of negotiating, the costs of transactions, and the ways institutions are understood and operationalized change dramatically across civilizations and locations.

One of the main drivers of economic growth, wealth generation, and development is the integration of markets—the linking of buyers and suppliers that were previously unconnected. This generates efficiency by pushing for resources to be allocated to their most efficient use. Let's imagine a small mountain village that produces excellent cheese, which, being isolated from the nearest large market, has also had to produce the majority of the other goods it consumes, from bread to leather tools, even though at this altitude it is extremely inefficient to cultivate grain. A road that dramatically reduces the time to reach the closest market would allow this fantastic imaginary cheese to be sold to a much broader range of customers, in turn stimulating demand for it. Leather, tools, corn, and other products would become available at cheaper prices, brought from locations that are more efficient at making them, and more people would dedicate themselves to making cheese. Otherwise known as the concept of "comparative advantage," this explains why and how commerce can generate wealth (see Box 2.1).

Box 2.1: Comparative Advantage

David Ricardo explained the concept of "comparative advantage" in his 1817 book *On the Principles of Political Economy and Taxation*. The basic idea behind the concept is that every individual (and every country) has an advantage in performing some activity, such as producing a particular good or service. As such, there tend to be always gains to be made by trading. Even when a party (say, an individual) is best at doing everything, his or her advantage is likely to be more marked in a particular set of activities. For example, if an Olympic runner is also quite good at performing administrative tasks, such as accounting, she may do her own accounting and indeed work in an accounting company. Yet, there is an opportunity cost in pursuing accounting and running simultaneously. Because she is also working as an accountant, she will have less time to train in the activity in which she excels (i.e., running). If she focuses on running, she can hire an accountant to perform her admin tasks and will achieve a superior outcome overall. The same concept applies to private firms and to countries. Every activity has an opportunity cost, which is the cost of focusing resources on that activity and not others. Given that resources are scarce, opportunity costs are always involved in the economic choices that people, countries, and companies make. For example, should we, the authors of this book, become writers of fiction as well as working as academics? If we do, some of our time and resources will shift from being used for academic research to being used for fiction writing. It is very unlikely that we would become famous fiction writers, yet it is certain that we would focus less on our academic work, and there is a similar opportunity cost for every such choice.

When talking about countries, it is important to remember that they have very different endowments of resources. By trading, they can exploit these differences—for example, an abundance of labor or fertile land—and focus on the activities they can perform best. Nationalist leaders, such as Mussolini and Hitler, did not fully grasp the concept. They pursued economic autarchy, or autonomy from trade. Italy channeled resources toward producing grain, in which it never had a competitive advantage, instead of focusing on apparel, mechanical engineering, and wine production, in which it excelled. German engineers, under the direction of Hitler, managed to produce oil out of coal. Yet, that oil was extremely costly, and their efforts could have been better spent developing new automobiles to be sold on the international market. After World War II, Italy and Germany became open to trade and investment again. They focused on their respective advantages and developed innovative products that the rest of the world was willing to purchase, ranging from luxury clothing and sports cars to sophisticated engineering services and tasty wines, while importing oil, grain, and all of the products for which they were not very competitive.

Source: Mankiw (2007). Chapter 3: Interdependence and the Gains from Trade (pp. 31–38); Kindleberger (2011).

We can find an example of the opposite process in history—in the fall of the Roman Empire. Rome built and maintained a road network that connected the whole of Southern Europe and North Africa, through France, Britain, Greece, Turkey, and parts of Germany. Along Roman roads commerce flourished, creating markets for everything that was available at that time. When the Empire collapsed, its territories were divided into different and ever changing political entities that generally failed to protect and maintain the roads. All of a sudden commerce declined dramatically, forcing reverses in specialization, trade, and wealth generation (Acemoglu and Robinson, 2012). The economic consequences were dire—this period is defined as "the Dark Ages" for a reason. The "Renaissance," the period when economic growth resumed, was driven by the development of new production and trading routes linking Europe with Asia (Cipolla, 1965).

What are the most significant obstacles to market integration? We have discussed markets by showing that their function is linking potential buyers to potential suppliers. To do so, they presume the exchange of information and, in the case of goods markets, the movement of goods. In the case of services, integrating markets may entail the movement of people or capital—a client going to a barbershop or the transfer of credit from a bank to an entrepreneur. Any barriers limiting the movements of goods, people, and capital also limits market integration. The most significant barriers are political and physical, though many other factors can hinder market integration. Let's outline them briefly, starting with political barriers. The borders of political entities, such as states, regions, and empires, can and generally do constitute barriers to trade. One of the easiest ways for states to collect revenues is by taxing wealth-generating activities, especially trade. Both exports and imports can be taxed. This reduces the benefits of trading, and thus also limits the volumes traded across such borders. Political barriers can also limit trade by establishing ad hoc regulations—for example, prohibiting the import of a specific good that is produced by a neighboring country. Markets are now more integrated than they have ever been in history, but there are still political barriers dividing potential consumers from buyers. In any country of the world, whether developed or emerging, there are import taxes on certain goods and probably strict regulations over the import of other goods. Political agreements that reduce these barriers foster trade and thus also the generation of wealth (Smith, 2006; Hayek, 2013; Kindleberger, 2011).

Physical barriers are the oldest form of obstacle to trade. Mountains, rivers, oceans, and forests have stopped the flow of goods and, up until relatively recently, of people, information, and capital. Infrastructure that overcomes physical barriers linking markets has a great impact on wealth generation. The building of the interstate highway system that linked the U.S. states contributed to a dramatic rise in inter-state trade, allowing for the movement of people to areas where jobs were available and the development of previously remote locations. Other notable major infrastructure projects that have linked markets are the Panama and Suez Canals, which opened new, more direct, and safer shipping routes. Overcoming physical barriers entails the use of technology, capital, and political will. Without the use of motorized cranes and pumps, it would have been impossible to dig the Panama Canal. Deploying technology is expensive, which is why capital is also needed, and in very large sums. And last but not least, political will—the building of the two canals, just like the development of the Roman road network thousands of years before, was possible because there was strong political will to get it done. When infrastructure links different countries and political entities, developing it also means finding compromises and agreements about sovereignty—the Euro tunnel, for example, was co-developed by British and French teams, and the organization that manages and operates it is floated on both the London and Paris exchanges.

Although technology has helped us to overcome many literal and metaphorical obstacles, physical barriers continue to play a role. Lack of access can isolate villages and communities from international and even local markets. It can take days of travel from the capital to reach certain remote areas of Senegal or Colombia—the people who inhabit these areas are cut off from the main national market and have access to a much narrower range of goods and services for which they must pay a premium to compensate for transport costs. A large share of the road network in emerging economies is made up of unpaved roads, many of which become muddy quagmires during rainy seasons. Mountains are passed through long sequences of zigzagging perilous routes because tunnels are too expensive to build and maintain. Main highways often lack overpasses or sidewalks. Heavy trailers travel side by side with animals, and children take their lives in their hands daily crossing all this to go to school. Traffic is slow, and infrastructure tends to be old and overloaded—in many of the poorer emerging economies, roads have not been built or maintained for decades, though China's spurt of investment in infrastructure development provides a vivid example that much progress can be achieved in a very short period of time. Rural areas remain by and large disconnected from the capital and the main industrial hubs of emerging economies. Their markets are only lightly integrated into the national market as natural barriers and infrastructure raise the cost of commerce.

Political disagreements, conflict, and lack of capital and technology can explain why, in spite of the impressive progress in many fields, there are still inaccessible areas and unconnected markets and peoples. There are also cultural barriers to trade. Language, one of the most significant manifestations of culture, creates an ancient barrier to market integration. This has often been solved by using a lingua franca, a commonly understood language—Latin, for example, performed this function in Europe for several centuries after the fall of the Roman Empire; Arabic facilitated trade in North Africa and the Middle East, while now English is the language of choice for business and trade.

Taking the long-term perspective, the trend has been for international markets to become more and more integrated, reaching a historical peak in our age. Technological innovations at the beginning of the twentieth century, such as steam-powered boats and railways and the telegraph, have dramatically reduced the cost of transmitting information and shipping goods (Mokyr, 1990; Wolmar, 2009). Refrigeration expanded the advantage of steamboat shipping to perishable goods, fostering the development of modern farming in areas ranging from Argentina to New Zealand, Canada, and the U.S. In economic terms, these innovations have reduced transaction costs, generating incentives to produce and trade more. The diffusion of combustion engines, container shipping, and commercial aviation have created a whole new range of opportunities to link potential buyers and sellers. They have created new markets and integrated fragmented markets. These factors have pushed the productive frontier out further and sustained economic growth throughout the twentieth century.

Through history, political barriers to trade have also tended to decline, though events such as the 1930s depression and the two World Wars have interrupted this trend. Various events in history have promoted the economic linking of previously divided and often hostile territories. After World War II, the existence of a common enemy, the Soviets, together with the scars of two devastating wars, pushed European countries to put the past behind them and gradually eliminate the barriers that hindered trade across their frontiers. The initial efforts to rebuild Western Europe in a coordinated manner planted the seeds for what is today the European Union, which, in spite of the current economic turmoil, has been one of the most successful attempts at international market integration in history. Economic integration in Europe has allowed for a continuous decline in trade barriers, which in turn has fostered specialization and economic growth (Eichengreen, 2008).

The end of communism was the other major political event that significantly influenced international market integration. When the Berlin Wall fell, the virtual walls that separated Eastern Europe and the Soviet Union from the global market also fell. Barriers to investment, trade, and migration declined, bringing about new opportunities for business, entrepreneurs, and skilled workers. With the end of the Cold War, many emerging markets began to open their economies to trade—countries such as China and Vietnam, which were once almost completely isolated, are now major exporters of manufactured goods. These experiences show that hostility and history can be overcome where there is the will to do so.

Regional trade agreements, such as the North American Free Trade Agreement (NAFTA), contribute to reducing barriers to trade within their geographic areas, stimulating cross-border market integration. The extent to which they affect wealth creation depends ultimately on political will. The signing of the World Trade Agreements (WTO) contributed another global-level push to trade. First, it established clearer rules for multilateral trade in goods and services. Second, it created a dispute-settlement mechanism—a sort of institution enforcement system—and provided it with the authority and neutrality needed to be credible. Third, the WTO entailed reducing average tariffs for manufactures, which stimulated commerce in industrial and manufacturing goods. Fourth, it established regulatory frameworks for the exchange of services.

The twenty-first century has been characterized by a number of political factors that have contributed to the decline in trade barriers. Technological change further enhanced this process. The main economic contribution of the Internet was to make the transmission of information faster and cheaper. The diffusion of ever more powerful and more affordable computing tools (PCs, telephones, etc.) and the exponential growth in Internet connections and Internet traffic have changed forever the way information moves across barriers. Not only are these innovations increasing the speed and lowering the cost of transmitting information; they link people across the globe in real time, literally creating new markets and marketplaces, even virtual ones that can make you real money like *Second Life*. Their importance is underlined by the fact that some of the most admired U.S. companies, such as Apple, Google, and Amazon, made their fortunes in this industry. Amazon's very business model is to link buyers and suppliers across frontiers.

Governments and Markets

We have discussed the role of markets and institutions, highlighting that some of the barriers to the integration of markets are political in nature—throughout history, governments have influenced the extent to which the territories they ruled were open to trade, investment, and migration. There has been lively debate about the role of the state since the 1930s. It continues to be the source of much disagreement between supporters of the Democratic and Republican Parties in the United States, among different political groups in Brazil, Colombia, Malaysia, and Turkey, and even within the Communist Party in China. The necessity of the state as an actor that supports development is entwined with the reality of the imperfections of the market: there are many cases where the market may not be the best system to allocate resources (Stiglitz, 1989). Individuals are unlikely to pay directly for things such as street lighting and roads, and construction companies may not be willing to undertake long-term risky projects, such as improving the road network of a country or lighting the streets of town, unless they have some certainties that their investment will generate good returns. Yet, having better roads benefits all users, individual and corporate, and, by reducing transport costs and linking markets, it also has a positive effect on the economy. This is an example where market forces per se cannot generate the best outcome—that is, well-made and well-lit roads. The state can compensate for this sort of market failure; it can provide the private sector with the necessary incentives to build infrastructure, and find indirect ways, such as taxation, to fund it. The same applies for many other examples of public goods, such as sewage systems and public transport networks in urban centers (Mankiw, 2011).

If we look at economies that have developed fast, lifting millions of people out of poverty, ranging from the United States to Japan or South Korea, we find a common factor—the role of the state in shaping institutions and also in coordinating, though not necessarily executing directly, the improvement of infrastructure, education, and health. On the other hand, the regions of the world where the state is all but absent and fails to exercise control over its subjects and territory—for example, Somalia and Haiti—have experienced prolonged periods of decreasing living standards. Even staunch critics of the state tend to accept that it is needed to provide basic prerequisites for economic growth and development, such as the protection of property rights (Smith, 2006; Hayek, 2013). The absence of the state, or its failure to address the needs of its citizens, is one of the reasons why it is challenging to operate in emerging markets. For example, it is costly to distribute goods in the slums of big emerging market cities because they are often controlled by armed criminals, who effectively substitute for the state in their respective turfs (the Brazilian movies *City of God* and *Elite Squad* provide a shocking, if entertaining, illustration of this).

Having a strong state does not guarantee positive outcomes in development. The state can, for example, be dominated by a ruling elite that pursues policies that deter economic growth, such as that of North Korea. For business, the excessive presence of the state can be as much a problem as its absence. The state can easily modify the rules of the game—for example, by demanding new taxes or setting up subsidies—and by doing so generate extra costs for business (Olson, 1982). It can also threaten the property rights of foreign companies and control foreign exchange. However, in these cases, it is not the state per se that affects the business environment; it is the policies that governments implement through the branches of the state. From the 1960s, the state played an important role in the economy of both Taiwan and Myanmar, yet the results were very different. In the former case, the state invested strongly in education and infrastructure; in the latter case, it invested mainly in its military. As a result, the Taiwanese state helped to create a highly competitive electronics industry by providing an environment where foreign companies could thrive and by co-funding research and development activities. In Myanmar, the state attempted to substitute the role of private firms through direct control of large shares of the economy. By 2013, Taiwan ranks similarly to most developed economies in terms of wealth per capita, incidence of poverty, life expectancy, and literacy, whereas Myanmar remains one of the poorest economies in Asia.

Most emerging markets combine state failure in some areas with damaging state intervention in others. For example, between 1999 and 2013, under the rule of the president Hugo Chavez, Venezuela became a much more state-centered economy, with large numbers of private businesses nationalized or prevented from operating. The state intervened in the economy by fixing prices, limiting the repatriation of profits by foreign firms, controlling the exchange rate, and setting up new import taxes. Government spending increased astronomically, fueled by a rise in the price of oil, which finances most state revenues, together with borrowing from abroad. In spite of this expansion of the state, Caracas, the capital of Venezuela, became one of the murder capitals of the world, where the death toll surpassed that of war-ravaged countries such as Iraq and Afghanistan. The Venezuelan government made the business environment challenging through both state absence and excessive intervention. Managing in environments that share these characteristics entails understanding and "managing" the state in some areas of business life, but also compensating for its absence in other realms, such as security in the case of Caracas.

Governments and the Economy

Government policies are important not only because of their direct effect on the business environment, but also because they affect long-term economic growth. During the first period of industrialization, between 1800 and 1914, the state played a relatively minor role in the economy of most countries, partly because it lacked resources, partly because there was a widespread liberal consensus that it should, by and large, stay out of economic affairs (Landes, 1998). As a result, economic development was shaped mainly by multinational corporations, which, as we discuss in the next chapter, managed most of the investment, trade, and economic activities occurring across the globe.

The First World War changed everything—all of a sudden European states had to mobilize resources and people and direct the economy towards the military effort. To do so, they developed the means to collect resources more efficiently (new taxes and tax collection systems) and the technical bureaucracy to "direct" some economic affairs. New schools of economic thought, such as Keynesianism, the Swedish economics school, and, last but not least, scholars of the command economy, diffused the idea that the state should play an active role in the economy, though they provided different recipes for doing so (Kindleberger, 2011). The First World War also sparked economic nationalism, championed by leaders such as Hitler, Mussolini, and Stalin. During the economically turbulent inter-war period (1918–1939), governments erected tariffs and other barriers and abandoned the principle of free trade and nondiscrimination against foreign enterprises (Eichengreen, 2008).

The Second World War continued the trends that began during the inter-war period. To sustain the war effort, the state became a much more central actor in the economy, not only of totalitarian states such as the Soviet Union, but also in democracies such as the United States. It developed the bureaucratic and institutional capacity to channel resources toward specific industries and to coordinate economic and scientific activities. When the war ended, the state did not automatically retreat in most countries. It shifted its priorities from funding the war to funding reconstruction and development (Crafts and Toniolo, 1996).

In the post–World War II decades, most countries in Western Europe, Africa, Asia, and Latin America adopted state-centered economic models. Some of them, such as China and, at a later stage, North Korea, Cuba, and Vietnam, became command economies. Most emerging markets, such as India, Brazil, Mexico, Argentina, Egypt, and Turkey, chose hybrid systems, where the state "directed" the economic activities of the private sector through a series of policies ranging from subsidies to import duties and, in some cases, private ownership. The state promoted industrialization, urbanization, and the diffusion of literacy, and invested strongly in public health systems. In Western Europe, Japan, Taiwan, Singapore, and South Korea, the state succeeded in generating not only accelerated economic growth, but also a significant improvement in living standards for most of the population. However, in most of the economies that we define as emerging markets, state-centered development was far less successful. In spite of the fact that the state managed large shares of the domestic economy with the purpose of promoting development, it failed to address poverty, education, and health and to manage urbanization. Moreover, in most emerging markets, especially in Latin America and Africa, state-centered development depended on external financing. In other words, the governments of most emerging markets borrowed money from foreign banks, governments, and multilateral organizations to sustain these hybrid development models (Thorp, 1998).

During the 1980s, global interest rates increased as the U.S. changed its monetary policy. As a result, for many emerging market governments it became unsustainable to service debts. This generated strong macroeconomic imbalances, as governments attempted to generate resources by printing money, which caused inflation (Reinhart and Rogoff, 2009). Many economists started pointing out that the state was not efficient at allocating resources and that its excessive intervention in the economy was deterring as opposed to promoting development, especially in emerging markets. The economic decline and eventual collapse of the Soviet Union further discredited state-centered economic development. Political leaders such as Reagan and Thatcher, backed by an array of neoclassical economists, also contributed to popularizing liberal economic reforms. Soon the idea of deregulating, privatizing, and opening economies became a new widespread consensus, often defined as "the Washington Consensus," because it was officially supported by the multilateral organizations based in Washington, such as the International Monetary Fund and the World Bank (Williamson, 2000).

By the 1990s, most emerging markets changed their models. First, they reduced their imbalances through economic reforms—not dissimilar to what Southern European countries have been trying to do since 2010 up to the present day. Second, they reduced state intervention in the economy by selling state-owned assets and opening their markets to foreign investment and trade. These changes attracted a growing inflow of capital to emerging markets, and integrated them more into the world economy. In spite of the criticism that these reforms attracted, the economic reforms allowed emerging markets to exploit their competitive advantages and start the long road to catching up with developed economies, which we discussed in the first chapter of the book (Bhagwati, 2007).

Although emerging markets have gradually opened to foreign investment and trade, the state remains an important player. What has changed is the form in which the state coordinates economic activities. Instead of closing the economy and attempting to insulate it from global trends, in most emerging markets the state attempts to attract foreign investment and support the internationalization of local companies. The most evident form of state intervention in the economy is the direct ownership and control of multinational corporations, which we discuss in Chapter 8, "Multinationals Based in Emerging Markets: Features and Strategies." The implications for business are that although it may be easier to operate in emerging markets than it was during the 1970s, it continues to mean having to get to grips with how the state operates and developing links with the technical bureaucracy involved in economic policy making.

References

Acemoglu, D. and Johnson, S. (2003). *Unbundling institutions* (No. w9934). National Bureau of Economic Research.

Acemoglu, D. and Robinson, J. (2012). *Why Nations Fail: The Origins of Power, Prosperity, and Poverty*. Crown Business.

Bhagwati, J. (2007). In Defense of Globalization: With a New Afterword: Oxford University Press, USA.

Chandler, A. D. (1990). *Scale and Scope*. Belknap Press of Harvard University Press.

Cipolla, C. M. (1965). *Guns, Sails and Empires: Technological Innovation and the Early Phases of European Expansion, 1400–1700*. New York: Pantheon Books.

Coase, R. H. (1937). The nature of the firm. *Economica*, 4(16), pp. 386–405.

Coase, R. H. (1992). The institutional structure of production. *The American Economic Review*, 82(4), pp. 713–719.

Crafts, N. and Toniolo, G. (Eds.) (1996). *Economic Growth in Europe Since 1945.* Cambridge University Press.

Diamond, J. (2012). *The World Until Yesterday: What Can We Learn from Traditional Societies?* Viking Adult.

Dunning, J. H. and Lundan, S. M. (2008). *Multinational Enterprises and the Global Economy.* Northampton, Massachusetts: Edward Elgar.

Durkheim, E. and Coser, L. A. (1997). *The Division of Labor in Society.* Free Press.

Eichengreen, B. (2008). *The European Economy Since 1945: Coordinated Capitalism and Beyond.* Princeton University Press.

Ferguson, N. (2011). *Civilization: The West and the Rest.* Penguin Books.

Greif, A. (2006). *Institutions and the Path to the Modern Economy: Lessons from Medieval Trade.* Cambridge University Press.

Hayek, F. A. (2013). *The Constitution of Liberty: The Definitive Edition* (Vol. 17). Routledge.

Jones, G. (2000). *Merchants to Multinationals.* Oxford University Press.

Kindleberger, C. P. (2011). World Economic Primacy: 1500 to 1990. *OUP Catalogue.*

Kirzner, I. M. (1973). *Competition and Entrepreneurship.* University of Chicago Press.

Landes, D. S. (1998). *The Wealth and Poverty of Nations: Why Some Are So Rich and Some So Poor.* Abacus, London.

Mankiw, N. G. (2011). *Principles of Microeconomics.* South-Western Pub.

Mokyr, J. (1990). *The Lever of Riches: Technological Creativity and Economic Progress.* Oxford University Press, USA.

North, D. C. (1990), Institutions, *Institutional Change and Economic Performance.* Cambridge University Press.

Olson, M. (1982). *The Rise and Decline of Nations: Economic Growth, Stagflation, and Social Rigidities.* Yale University Press.

Ostrom, E. (1990). *Governing the Commons: The Evolution of Institutions for Collective Action.* Cambridge University Press.

Reinhart, C. M. and Rogoff, K. (2009). *This Time Is Different: Eight Centuries of Financial Folly.* Princeton University Press.

Rodrik, D., Subramanian, A., and Trebbi, F. (2004). Institutions rule: the primacy of institutions over geography and integration in economic development. *Journal of Economic Growth, 9*(2), pp. 131–165.

Smith, A. (2006). *An Inquiry into the Nature and Causes of the Wealth of Nations.* Echo Library.

Stiglitz, J. E. (1989). Markets, market failures, and development. *The American Economic Review, 79*(2), pp. 197–203.

Thorp, R. (1998). *Progress, Poverty and Exclusion: An Economic History of Latin America in the 20th Century.* Inter-American Development Bank.

Wolmar, C. (2009). *Blood, Iron and Gold: How the Railways Transformed the World.* London: Atlantic.

Williamson, J. (2000). What should the World Bank think about the Washington Consensus? *The World Bank Research Observer, 15*(2), pp. 251–264.

Williamson, O. E. (1979). Transaction-cost economics: The governance of contractual relations. *Journal of Law and Economics, 22*(2), pp. 233–261.

3

A Historical Perspective

Introduction

This chapter provides an overview of the internationalization of multinational companies in late modern history. Multinational organizations were fundamental in transforming the world economy, making it more integrated through their trading and investment activities. Globalization is a term that became fashionable during the 2000s as emerging markets opened their economies to trade and investment. In this chapter, we examine two other periods in history when the world economy was also highly integrated: The period 1850–1914, which we refer to as Global Economy I, and the period 1948–1980, which we refer to as Global Economy II. We look at the context in which multinational companies were operating during these periods and at the way they grew and internationalized in the emerging markets of their time. This chapter can be used as a reference to the origin of multinational companies and their relationships with governments and the state.

Israel Kirzner, the famous economist of entrepreneurship, maintained that market-based decision making was significantly less complex than political choices (Kirzner, 1973). Similarly, because the risks of investing and operating in developing countries are as much political and social as economic, they raise particular points of consideration for international business strategy. There is, as we illustrate in Chapter 4, "The Determinants of Attractiveness and the Four Dimensions," and Chapter 5, "Managing Risk," no index that easily captures these complexities. A look at the history of investing and operating in developing territories is, we believe, an essential part of assessing the suitability of a location and the risk of doing business there. It can help account for the international, home country, and host country factors that have determined the policies of multinationals in the past and their impact on the present.

Through the period of Global Economy I, multinational companies expanded their reach into emerging markets in the search of resources and business opportunities. They built all manner of infrastructure—from railways to harbors to electricity grids—all over the world. They managed armies and had unique capabilities to mobilize capital, skills, and technology. Among them were companies mining copper, bauxite, and coal; oil firms; and trading companies that owned and organized plantations, processing plants, and transport networks. These last commercialized tea, bananas, jute, and numerous other products and sold them to an international market. Some multinationals were engaged in building infrastructure, sometimes trade related; others, predominantly in Mexico City, Sao Paolo, Buenos Aires, and other major cities in Latin America, erected and ran electricity, water, transport, and telephone systems. Interestingly, many multinationals in this period also employed forms of cross-border network organizations and high levels of vertical integration, now perceived as innovatory among the international businesses of the twenty-first century.

During Global Economy II, most emerging economies reacted to the often undiplomatic strategies of former colonial powers and multinational companies by closing their economies and nationalizing private concerns. As a result, between the 1950s and 1980s, the axis of the world economy shifted toward the Triad of the U.S., Western Europe, and Japan. Multinational companies, by and large, kept emerging economies as a marginal part of their activities. We describe a new, distinct and ongoing phase of the Global Economy from the 1980s in Chapter 1, "What Are Emerging Markets?" This contemporary phase has been characterized by the opening of emerging economies to foreign investment and trade, which has resulted in a dramatic acceleration in their economic growth and development. Debates over the causes and implications of the growth potential for Triad businesses in emerging economies normally overlook the earlier history of multinationals. This chapter discusses the fortunes and misfortunes of multinational companies throughout late modern history (Global Economy I and II), anticipating topics that are discussed in more depth in the second part of the book referring to the current conjuncture. As with the previous chapter, this chapter can be read to set the stage for the conceptual part of the book (Part II, "Operating in Emerging Markets: A Step-by-Step Guide"), or it can be read subsequently, as a complement to it.

Global Economy I: 1850–1914

Can the period before 1914 be meaningfully labeled as a global economy? One component of a global economy that we might anticipate is the existence of multinational enterprises operating across borders, linking continents and investing in overseas economies. A large volume of evidence shows that between 1850 and 1914, multinational enterprises became an established feature of the international economic system, and they impacted the politics of countries and international affairs as well as the nature of commerce. The period of Global Economy I was also the era of imperialism, and international businesses could and did benefit from the security that empire could provide for their investments. During this period, countries in Asia, Africa, and the Americas were integrated into the world system, within which Europe exported manufactured goods in return for imported primary products. In undeveloped regions, especially those rich in natural resources, there was thus a need to transfer European capital, management, and technology and a need to build infrastructure and establish trade routes. Multinational companies were pioneers in building the physical and organizational infrastructure needed to integrate emerging markets in the world economy. As such, they prepared the basis for the first period of economic growth of emerging markets, which was driven by the exports of natural resource-based products, in which these economies had a comparative advantage. Natural resources accounted for roughly half of all foreign direct investment from Britain and the U.S. by 1914, and Asia, Africa, and Latin America were still hosts to some 60 percent of foreign direct investment (FDI) assets as late as the 1930s (Fitzgerald, 2014; Corley, 1994; Wilkins, 1970; Fieldhouse, 1965).

By the nineteenth century, the principles if not always the actual practice of open international competitive markets and waged labor had replaced a system of mercantilism and slavery in long-term decline. Mercantilism implied the exploitation of colonies for the benefit of the imperial power, whereas the flow of free trade and investment, so the new economic theories ran, could benefit all participants in the international economy (although not equally). While many of the new multinationals of Global Economy I enjoyed colonial privileges, their success depended to an important degree on their competitive capabilities, rather than on a state-sanctioned monopoly granted principally for the exploitative gain of the imperial power. It also depended on their capability of operating in very difficult environments, often with minimal communication with their headquarters, and managing the complexity of local political, social, ethical, and religious conflicts. In Chapters 1 and 4, we illustrate that emerging markets now concentrate not only the majority of natural resources, as they did in the period Global Economy I, but have also become highly attractive for their internal markets and as hubs for global production. For this reason, multinationals are again focusing on these economies. The world of today is much better linked in terms of communications, which means it is much easier and less costly to manage global operations. Nonetheless, as we illustrate in the second part of the book, emerging markets continue being challenging for business. A look at history can provide some interesting lessons for Triad businesses interested in emerging markets.

World output per head grew by an average of 7.3 percent per decade between 1800 and 1913. This upsurge in global economic growth was mainly the result of the activities of multinational companies, which linked markets through their operations, generating new opportunities to exploit comparative advantages and exchange goods and services.

Per-capita world trade in merchandise expanded yet faster, at 33 percent. To put it another way, the value of trade was some 3 percent of total global production in 1800, but, mostly thanks to accelerating change after 1850, it was equal to 33 percent of global production by 1913. The commerce in primary products (intercontinental in its reach, but revolving around Europe) multiplied three times between 1880 and 1913 alone. This is why we define this period as Global Economy I. It is estimated that 22.5 percent of Britain's imports came from its colonies (1892–96 average), and that 33.2 percent of Britain's exports went back to its colonies in return. The commercial significance of their colonies to most European economies was less important, economically, but imperial ties had a greater effect on colonial economies. So, some 53 percent of the trade conducted by Britain's colonies went to or came from the ruling power, whereas 61 percent of French colonial trade was connected to France. By 1913, Europe took nearly 85 percent of all imported primary products, obtained increasingly from tropical or far-off locations (Maddison, 1993; Lougheed and Kenwood, 1999; Fieldhouse, 1965).

With respect to total FDI assets, one estimate puts the figure to be a third of all overseas investment, or some $14.6 billion. In which case, FDI stock was equal to some 9.0 percent of global GDP in 1914, above the situation in 1960 (4.4 percent) and even 1990 (8.5 percent). The percentage of British FDI located in the dominions and colonies stood at 66 percent, in 1910, in destinations where the capital and expertise of multinational enterprise were needed. If we look at the distribution of world FDI assets in 1914, the U.S. and Canada were the largest recipient host nations, but the majority of these assets (some 60 percent of the total) were to be found in the developing regions of Latin America, Asia, and, to a lesser extent, Africa. India and China were the principal destinations in Asia; in Latin America, it was Brazil, Argentina, and Mexico that were notable. Most likely, one half of world total FDI stock was invested in natural resources (renewable and nonrenewable), and nearly a third in trading and services, more frequently for commercial projects in developing territories; only a minor part, the remaining sixth, supported manufacturing, almost entirely located in Western Europe and North America (Dunning and Lundan, 2008).

Trade was particularly important to developing economies because their home markets were characterized by low total demand and per-capita consumption and low endowments of capital, infrastructure, and technology. Their infrastructural deficiencies meant great opportunities for investment for multinational companies, but also great logistic challenges. Most operations (establishing a plantation, for example) entailed clearing forests and building roads, railways, and housing, and the whole infrastructure needed to produce and export the goods. In most cases, developing economies offered their natural resources for export and needed international investment in transport, machinery, and landed estates. Trade, as a result, became associated with economic growth and modernization, but it brought, in parallel, the threat of colonization. To succeed and to manage risk, international traders relied on business networks, and built trust relationships with clients—a strategy that we discuss in Chapter 5. Personal entrepreneurship, reputation, contacts, and market knowledge fostered and secured deals. Traders thrived by connecting international demand to supply, and they were prepared to deal flexibly and opportunistically in a highly varied range of goods and services, involving the building of railways and manufacturing as well as commodity deals and finance (Fieldhouse, 1965; Jones, 1998; Jones, 2000).

Multinationals and Colonization in Asia

The most famous and infamous of the chartered firms founded under the mercantilist system was Britain's East India Company (EIC), which controlled territory across South and Southeast Asia. It is often called an early example of modern multinational enterprise, though there is much disagreement about this definition (Bowen, 2006). The EIC had a monopoly over trade with India and also controlled British commerce with China. In return for these commercial privileges, the company had administrative responsibilities in conquered territories, necessitating a large bureaucracy, and, furthermore, a statute limiting its sphere of operations.

The EIC was a remarkable organization, which managed a globally stretched trading network in spite of the fact that communication was at best slow and at worst nonexistent between its headquarters and its Eastern hubs. The lesson for modern business is that centralization may not always lead to the best results. The EIC, as did many of the earlier multinational companies, also abused its position, wishing to benefit indefinitely from monopolistic control over trading routes. It used its relationship with the government in London and with local rulers to achieve this. Several independent traders began operating in spite of the monopoly rights of the EIC. In stages, beginning in 1813, and by 1833, in part because of lobbying by independent merchants, the British government ended the EIC's control over both India and the China trade, a share of which consisted in the narcotic opium. Eventually, the EIC's focus on preserving a monopolistic position instead of becoming competitive, together with its excessive meddling in local political affairs and use of violent means, planted the seed of its demise.

One of these dynamic independent merchants who lobbied against the EIC monopoly was Jardine Matheson, which came to control a third of the foreign trade at Canton (modern Guangzhou), the key entry port to the mainland (Blake, 1999; Farooqui, 2005; Darwin, 2009; Bowen, 2006; Bowen, Lincoln, and Rigby, 2006). Western traders brought opium into China from the Indian subcontinent and traded it for tea and other Chinese products. Opium was a highly profitable trade for European merchants, which conveniently ignored the negative effects it was having on the Chinese population and the fact that it had been banned since 1729. In 1839, the Chinese government reacted to the increasing diffusion of opium in society by sending the army to seize the property of Western companies suspected of involvement in the illegal trade, including Jardine Matheson. The traders lost valuable stocks of the narcotic, and thus lobbied London to intervene on their behalf. Britain was quick to declare hostilities and send the Royal Navy to China, starting the First Opium War.

The First Opium War was an early instance of the rights of international traders running counter to the concept of national sovereignty. Western companies, Britain, and its allies ensured that the rights of international traders were preserved. One of the concessions China made, in the Treaty of Nanjing, in 1842, was to hand over Hong Kong in perpetuity, and, two years later, Jardine Matheson transferred its main office to the new colony, where it was protected and enjoyed easy access to mainland China. A supplementary treaty increased the number of entry ports and granted foreigners extraterritorial privileges and the right, in China, to be judged by the laws of their homeland. Similarly, when the British established sovereignty over the free port of Singapore, supplanting the Sultanate of Johor, it reduced the risks of trading firms such as Guthries and Edward Boustead, which were developing their operations and processing plants in the new colony. These firms worked with regional traders, often Chinese, whose commercial contacts were essential and whose willingness to share the commercial risks was a major boost (Jones, 2000; Blake, 1999; Keswick, 1982; Yonekawa, 1990).

Jardine Matheson's branches throughout China, most prominently those in Shanghai and Hong Kong, invested in railways, silk, sugar, harbors, shipping, and banking, and also built China's first cotton mill in 1895. In China, Western traders relied on local partners, investors, buyers, sales agents, and managers for their success. Jardine Matheson and Butterfield & Swire's significant role in importing to and exporting from mainland China rested on indigenous agents. Multinationals evolved a network of "compradors" to supply finance and make deals. In time, many compradors gained enough experience and resources to establish themselves as independent commission agents (Jones, 2000; Blake, 1999; Keswick, 1982; Cochran, 2000). Meanwhile, anti-Western and anti-capitalist feelings began to develop among Chinese high society and intellectuals, largely as a result of the actions of Western traders and Western military powers.

The actions of the EIC in India sparked the First War of Independence (Britain's "Indian Mutiny") in 1857. This ended the EIC as a proxy in India for the government back in London, and the subcontinent was converted into a crown colony in the following year (the EIC wound up as a commercial enterprise in 1874). Defined by the terms of their charter, and formally without competitors, mercantilist firms did not have the adaptability of commercial rivals, which were better suited to the new, open international system. Within colonies, they competed with each other for businesses.

After the "First War of Independence," the Raj became a mixture of direct rule and subordinate princely states, but investors could everywhere rely on a system of law and courts modeled on Britain's. Andrew Yule, a Calcutta-based trading firm, grew into one of its largest business groups in India, and ran four jute mills, a cotton factory, 15 tea companies, four coal enterprises, two flour mills, a railway, and an oil distribution business. Western traders transacted with Indian businessmen to gain entry into their markets, commerce, and investment networks, and learned from their experience. Indian merchants were able to mobilize investment networks. As well as providing capital for India's plantations, mines, commodity trade, transport, and infrastructure, Indian merchants were major partners and investors in Burma (through the Bombay Burmah Trading Corporation) and in Hong Kong (through the Hong Kong Bank, the forerunner to today's HSBC). One of the consequences of the integration of India in the world economy was that the imports of British manufactures temporarily displaced local handmade clothing industry. The event, which put numerous textile workers out of job, also inspired Indian business houses to import machinery and develop what later became one of the world's most competitive clothes manufacturing industries. (Fitzgerald, 2014; Roy, 2006; Jones, 2000; Allen and Donnithorne, 1954; Macaulay, 1934; Pointon, 1964; Webster, 1998; King, King, and King, 1998; Jones, 1996; Jones, 2005; Tomlinson, 1989).

Burma (currently known as Myanmar) became a British colony by stages, beginning with the First Anglo-Burmese War (1823–26), which secured coastal ports and territories, whereas the Second Anglo-Burmese War (1852–53) led to the annexation of what became known as Lower Burma. Inside this newly acquired land were rich teak forests and other valuable resources. Wallace Brothers, in 1863, founded, with a group of Indian merchants, the Bombay Burmah Trading Corporation to exploit the opportunity more fully. When the Burmese government fined the company for unlicensed activities, it led to the Third Anglo-Burmese War (1885) and the annexation of Upper Burma. Britain was reacting to France's occupation of Tonkin (in modern, southern Vietnam), itself brought about by rivalry with China, treaty disputes with local rulers, and the desire of international merchants in Saigon to extend French control over the Mekong delta. Therefore, Britain was looking for a diplomatic cause for war, and, simultaneously, its actions simplified the operational difficulties of interested British firms. They could now move their businesses to Rangoon, while increasingly investing in forestry and rice fields, and importing the labor they needed from nearby India (Fitzgerald, 2014; Allen and Donnithorne, 1954; Pointon, 1964).

British government policy toward the Malay Peninsula followed a similar path of securing coastal bases, stabilizing borders, protecting business interests, and expanding trade. Between 1874 and 1910, the Malay sultanates one by one accepted "residents" or representatives of the British government, which, with the ultimate backing of the Indian army, brought about effective colonization. Intervention helped safeguard the assets of British investors, mostly in tin mining, and to a lesser extent gold. From 1877, they introduced the rubber tree as an export crop. The Federated Malay States, formed under British direction in 1896, streamlined the administration of Selangor, Perak, Negeri Sembilan, and Pahang, and embedded British power in the peninsula's most developed regions. The traders, Guthrie, arrived in the same year, opting to invest in coffee, and, in partnership with a local Chinese businessman, rubber (Jones, 2000). Business dealings between British firms and Chinese entrepreneurs and financiers were common. Yap Ah Loy was, by the 1890s, Malaya's richest individual, through his ownership of mines, plantations, and shops. It was the Chinese who controlled the local banking and insurance industries that financed the Malay sultans whenever they fell, as they frequently did, into debt (Fitzgerald, 2014). These are early examples of private businesses managing in spite of political and social instability, leveraging personal connections and a sophisticated understanding of local politics. They are also early examples of emerging-market businesses operating internationally.

Western firms involved in trade, shipping, and finance and operating in Asia had numerous advantages. Having increased the scale and distances of transcontinental commerce, they controlled access to the rich markets of Europe and North America; they could call on international sources of finance; they had a lead in technologies, including those associated with the steamship, mining, and preventing crop disease; and they often had support and concessions from imperial authorities. Western firms transformed transcontinental commerce, and they had an impact on intra-regional commerce, too, but they formed only part of the Asian international system. Indian, Chinese, and Arab merchants had already pioneered the region's trade routes. Their pivotal role in Asia's economy did not disappear: indeed, economic growth and trade expansion gave them new entrepreneurial opportunities. Although Western firms in Asia might compete against local businesses, they equally needed their cooperation, partnership, commercial expertise, market knowledge, and, as recorded in prominent cases, their finance. Through diaspora and family relationships, cross-border networks cemented trust levels between traders, strengthened the capacity for striking and managing deals, and quickly transferred commercial information (Fitzgerald, 2014). Finding Chinese and Arab businesses working side by side in a place such as the current territory of Indonesia or Malaysia was not surprising during the late 1800s. Many observers, students, and managers are surprised at the diffusion of business links among emerging markets today, such as Chinese firms building roads in Ghana or Malaysian companies extracting oil in Sudan, but as the history of multinationals highlights, this is not a new phenomenon.

In Borneo, Britain's imperial government had preferred to avoid policing actions, so long as native governments did not discriminate against British businesses. In 1841, the Sultan of Brunei appointed the adventurer James Brooke as the Rajah of Sarawak, for his help in quelling a local rebellion, but Brooke ultimately supported a ruling dynasty that lasted 101 years (that is, until the Japanese army arrived in 1942). The Borneo Company Ltd., which was founded in 1856, based in Singapore, was associated with the Brookes, who consequently granted the enterprise special trading privileges. In Sabah, in northeast Borneo, several powers contended for the right to rule, and the Sultan of Brunei needed outside help to deal with rebellions and piracy. At first, in 1865, he granted a lease to the American Trading Company of Borneo, owned by a group of U.S. and Chinese investors, and appointed its leading figure as the Rajah of Ambong and Maudu, and as the Maharajah of North Borneo. American Trading sold the lease to a businessman and Austria's consul in Hong Kong, who wanted at first to sell North Borneo to Germany, and then looked among other European powers for a buyer. Leading partners in Britain's Dent trading company, who had made their fortunes in opium, argued that no investors would come forward until a government guaranteed their security. Britain did this, in 1882, through the anachronistic mechanism of a royal charter, so reminiscent of a mercantilist past, which created the British North Borneo Company. Six years later, both North Borneo and the Brunei Sultanate became British protectorates, although in practice North Borneo continued to be administered by the Company—again, until the watershed year of 1942 in Asia (Fitzgerald, 2014; Longhurst, 1954; Galbraith, 1965).

Britain and The Netherlands were imperial rivals along the Southeast Asian archipelago that forms modern Malaysia and Indonesia. To exploit the commercial possibilities, The Netherlands took the mercantilist and chartered Vereenigde Oost-Indische Compagnie (VOC, or United East India Company) as its model, and founded the Nederlandsche Handel-Maatschappij (NHM) in 1824. NHM's first duty was to revitalize The Netherlands economy, and its control over colonial trade dampened innovation and economic development at home and in the Dutch East Indies (DEI). Over time, the company extended its control beyond directly ruled Java and West Sumatra over the archipelago's local rulers, and, by 1850, some 50 to 60 percent of imports to The Netherlands were colonial products, mostly from the DEI. After 1856, military action and formal colonization became more frequent, and the NHM and its appointed commercial agencies, banks, and shipping lines expanded quickly. Between 1861 and 1870, The Netherlands government loosened and then ended the company's commercial grip on the DEI, and private enterprise took the initiative in growing and exporting commodities, and in developing shipping and infrastructure. Deli-Maatschappij and Tabaksmaatschappij "Arendsburg" developed tobacco estates in East Sumatra; it had had cinchona, copra, and light railway interests, and it pioneered the cultivation of rubber. Borsumij, headquartered in The Hague, owned river and local shipping, traded in gum and rattan, and branched into coalmining, rubber plantations, coffee exports (sold directly to the U.S.), and paraffin (acting for what became Royal Dutch Shell). Investment by The Netherlands (almost all of it in plantations, mines, and commodity processing industries) doubled between 1900 and 1914 (Jonker and Sluyterman, 2000; Sluyterman, 2005).

Alongside Western companies, Chinese merchants continued to operate important multinational companies. Chang Pi-Sheh, who emigrated to the Dutch East Indies in 1856, founded a steamship line between Penang and North Sumatra, and later gained fame as one of the world's richest Chinese. He had a contract from the Dutch navy, and his ships flew the Dutch flag. Guo Chunyang, from Fujian, joined his uncle's firm in Samrang, in the Dutch East Indies, in 1872. By 1914, he had founded trading enterprises in Taiwan, Hong Kong, Xiamen, Zhangzhou, Shanghai, and Tianjin. He owned sugar plantations in China, and refined the commodity in Hong Kong. Politically, he was pragmatic. He was involved with the Taiwan Oolong tea trade, and, when China lost the Sino-Japanese War of 1894–5, and Japanese forces occupied Taiwan, Guo claimed residency of the island and took Japanese nationality. Thanks to this decision, his Taiwanese enterprises received greater legal protection and reduced taxation; anti-Chinese sentiment in the Dutch East Indies was another motive. He had good relations with both the imperial Qing government and its Republican successor after 1911. Khaw Soo Cheang and his family became major figures in the mining, smelting, and exporting of Siamese tin. For this, they established close relations with the government, collecting taxes on its behalf, and accepting appointments as regional governors (Fitzgerald, 2014).

The Americas

Latin America and the multinationals operating there were quite different from Asia. It was colonized much earlier, mainly by Spain and Portugal, which were minor players in Asia, and was (and still is) less densely populated. The wars of independence that liberated the Spanish-speaking part of Latin America from its colonial power during the first decades of the 1800s brought about huge business opportunities. The Spanish extracted their riches through monopolistic control over trade—high taxes had to be paid to the Spanish crown for all that was produced, exported, or imported. The independence movements were partly financed by local businessmen who had interests in expanding their trading links and building an export-oriented economy. When independence came, foreign investors flowed in, and Latin America went through a period of accelerated economic growth. However, political instability affected most countries, as competing local elites struggled for control over the newly independent economies (Abel and Lewis, 1985; Platt, 1972).

In Latin America, multinationals had to deal with governments and economies often destabilized by events and policy failures. Latin American nations were heavily reliant on natural resources for exports and currency, and needed the world market access that the foreign trading firms could provide. An example is Peru, whose government became heavily dependent on revenues generated by the export of guano, which was used as a fertilizer during that time. In 1842, Peru offered the concession to the firm Anthony Gibbs & Sons, recognizing its organizational skills, as well as its ability to commercialize the commodity overseas; in return, the firm won local acceptance by financing the government and its officials. Not everyone in Peru was a beneficiary, and, by 1861, agitation against Gibbs was so strong that the contract could not be renewed. Gibbs adapted to the situation and instead took up the production of nitrate in both Peru and Bolivia, selling the product throughout the Pacific Coast, California, and Europe. As well as its nitrate, copper, mining, and flour interests in Chile and Peru, Gibbs built businesses in freight agency, coastal shipping, sheep and cattle ranching, and mining; it had interests in Australia as well as organized securities and loans in London for overseas projects.

Managing relationships with highly volatile governments and unpredictable political contexts was one of the most important competitive assets of multinational companies operating during Global Economy I, and it continues to be important in many emerging markets even today (Gibbs, 1958; Mathew, 1981; Maude, 1958; Jones, 2000; Jones, 2005; Abel and Lewis, 1985; Platt, 1972). The novel *Nostromo* by Joseph Conrad illustrates the challenges of operating businesses in emerging markets at the time, and also the extent to which capital, trade, and labor was becoming integrated in the world economy. It tells the story of a British investor who purchases a mine in a fictional Latin American country. The investor begins his operations with the support of a skilled workforce brought from Italy and other European countries to build the railway that will service the mine. Having imported capital, skills, and machinery, the prospects of profit seem endless. The challenge becomes carefully playing the local politics: the emergence of competing military leaders, social unrest by the indigenous population that was used as unskilled labor, and frictions between the capital and the mining town. Eventually conflict, rebellion, and shifting loyalties bring the venture to its ruin.

Not surprisingly, U.S. traders were active at an early point in Latin America, and they were large investors in Cuba's sugar estates, railway system, and ports. As an early indication of international business's influence on emerging countries, Alsop & Co. bought a percentage of Bolivia's custom revenues, notably those from silver, and acquired future concession rights when it helped the government with its debt obligations (Wilkins,

1972). William Russell Grace left his native Ireland to work in Peru, where, in 1854, he set up his own business, W.R. Grace & Co., exporting sugar and guano, founding his own merchant steamship line, and, ultimately, establishing cotton spinning, woolen manufacturing, and sugar refining. Grace & Co., having set up offices throughout Latin America, was a major influence on the whole region's development, and Grace himself was a twice-elected mayor of New York. Dozens of U.S. mining and processing companies could be found in Mexico by the 1880s (Clayton, 1958). The country was nearby and, under the rule of Porfirio Díaz, stable and business friendly. There were few labor problems, and firms could negotiate on duties, levies, taxes, and other concession terms.

After 1890, M. Guggenheim's Sons built lead and silver smelters in Mexico and a silver smelter in Bolivia. Mexican Coal and Coke Company, by 1899, established self-government at its Coahuila township, where it owned a machine shop, a hospital, a drugstore, schools, a jail, a post office, and a telegraph office. Founded by the Guggenheim banking family, in 1901, with the support of J.P. Morgan, the Kennecott Mines Corporation bought copper mines in Chile, among them the world's largest underground mine in El Teniente, in the Andes. Through American Smelting and Refining Company (ASARCO), the Guggenheims emerged as Mexico's largest investors (Wilkins, 1972; *International Directory of Company Histories*).

In Costa Rica, Minor Cooper Keith was an entrepreneur adventurer, who began by building railroads and ports, and ended with a personal grip on the economy and politics of a region. To further the transport of coffee to overseas markets, the Costa Rican government commissioned a railroad in 1871. To build it, the company brought foreign workers from Jamaica and Italy. As the line lacked sufficient freight revenues, Keith decided to plant bananas along the route. The railway was never a great success, though Costa Rica became a very competitive banana exporter. Keith next developed banana plantations in Panama and Colombia, and came to dominate the fruit's production in Latin America. Financial difficulties drove Keith into a merger with the Boston Fruit Company, in 1899, to create the United Fruit Company: it controlled a quarter of a million acres in Central America, owned 112 miles of railroad, and ran 11 steamships. In Guatemala, the President, Manuel Estrada Cabrera, in 1902 commissioned Keith to construct and control railroads, ports, and telegraph services on the Atlantic side of the country, in return for land grants and tax exemptions, and the chance to lay out banana plantations. United Fruit—a union of trading, railway, and plantation projects—became so associated with the economies and politics of Central America that it earned the nickname "el pulpo" (or the octopus). As in the fictional story by Conrad, the multinationals that operated the plantations and mines had the technology and resources to develop infrastructure, which local governments lacked. This, in principle, created symbiotic relationships. In practice, however, the prospects of extracting resources from foreign private businesses contributed to inflaming frictions among local groups that attempted to gain political power. Multinational companies, in turn, used their influence and resources to protect their interests, which at times stabilized and at other times destabilized the social and political environment where they operated.

In Latin America, multinational companies built virtually all of the railways, although ownership gradually passed to local interests (Lewis, 1983). A U.S. company was responsible for the Panama Railway Company, founded in 1851 and completed in 1855. Its project could claim to the first large-scale U.S. overseas investment. In the case of Cuba, the fall of sugar prices hurt the local planters who had built the island's railways, and British and U.S. investors bought up much of the network. A shortage of cash and a conflict with Chile halted railway building in Peru, and the British-controlled Peruvian Corporation took over the country's rail system in 1890. British multinationals greatly influenced Argentina. William Bragge won the first railway concession in Argentina, and completed the line from Buenos Aires to Flores, in 1857. However, within three years, through financial difficulties, it passed to the Buenos Aires government (later extended and called the Buenos Aires Western Railway). British capital owned and operated the Central Argentine Railway, established 1870, and the Buenos Aires & Pacific, opened in 1888. By 1914, out of a total of 142 British-owned overseas railways, 75 were located in Latin America (Wilkins, 1972; Wolmar, 2009).

The engineers Pearson & Son, from Britain, forged close links with the government of Porfirio Díaz in Mexico, in power for most of 1876–1911. They drained the Valley of Mexico, reconstructed the Tehuantepec Railroad, and established electricity supply for a number of important cities. The company used its experience in Mexico to run utilities in Chile, and built Santiago's hydro-electric capacity. On the eve of the First World War, British-owned gas, electricity, tramway, bus, and dockyard companies were located in Argentina, Brazil, Chile, Uruguay, and other parts of Latin America (Jones, 2000; *International Directory of Company Histories*). Over time, utility multinationals tended to divest. One problem was the almost inevitable tension between the foreign ownership and management of public utilities, and public pressure for local control and regulation. Political uncertainties and a downward pressure on price in Latin America challenged the profitability and security of investments in utilities. During this period, from the closing decades of the nineteenth century, multinationals formed a primary force behind the endeavor of global electrification. Developing countries hired contracting engineers to construct or run systems of generation or transmission, but, in many major examples, ownership and financing resided overseas. It was German companies that took the lead in electrical engineering projects in Europe and Latin America, and they created a world-wide market for German electrical plant and products. In Latin America, AEG, Deutsche Bank, and eight other German and Swiss banks were the major partners in a subsidiary that financed, built, and operated electricity generating and using enterprises, beginning with power stations, lighting, and tramways for Buenos Aires, and establishing a strong presence throughout Argentina, Uruguay, and Chile. AEG's strategy—like that of Siemens—was gradually to hand over control to local interests, and to recycle capital for the next engineering project (Hausman, Hertner, and Wilkins, 2008).

Canadian multinationals were also substantial players in the region. The Montreal-based Mexican Light and Power Company organized, from 1902, hydroelectricity and tramways in Mexico City. The Canadian-owned Sao Paulo Tramway, Light and Power Company (formed 1898) and the Rio de Janeiro Tramway, Light and Power Company (1904) additionally managed gas and telephone services in these cities. In 1912, the Toronto-based Brazilian Traction, Light and Power Company Limited acquired both businesses. Stockholms Allmana Telefon (SAT) had the technical expertise to run telephone systems in Warsaw and Moscow, and, with its competitor Ericsson, in more distant Mexico. The Société Générale des Chemins de Fer Économiques, owned by a consortium of Belgian banks, possessed tramways worldwide by 1914, and we know that a total of 23 Belgian companies were running tramway systems in Russia (McKay, 1970; Jones, 1996; Hausman, Hertner and Wilkins, 2008; *International Directory of Company Histories*).

International Rivalry and Business in Africa

Africa became the most conspicuous example of late-nineteenth century imperialism, when European powers divided the continent into spheres of interest. Until the Berlin conference of 1884–85, some 80 percent of Africa had remained uncolonized; after that date, the entire continent fell under colonization or occupation. To make good the hoped-for economic gains, Belgium, Germany, and even free-trading Britain resurrected the charter company. They contravened the accepted nostrums of the day, but, clearly, European investors saw the risks of free markets as too uncertain to venture into undeveloped and untried lands without guarantees of support, monopoly, or both from their governments. During the 1884–85 conference, Leopold II of Belgium gained the Congo as his personal fiefdom, in return for a promise (mainly unfulfilled) to open up the whole territory to European investment generally. Initially, Leopold had only debts to show for his seizure of the Congo. It was the sudden demand for rubber in the 1890s that rescued his business venture, economically, but demand for this new export ended with international outrage over the barbarity inflicted on indigenous people. The Belgian government, very reluctantly, assumed control over the Congo from its king in 1908 (Fieldhouse, 1965; Hochschild, 1998).

Another winner from the Berlin conference was George Taubman Goldie. British, French, and German commercial interests had long vied for control of the Niger Delta.

By buying out French traders along the lower part of the river, and attending the conference as a Niger expert, Goldie had facilitated the decision in favor of his National Africa Company. No longer wary of international disputes, the British government was willing to reconsider the advantages of a charter for his company, which it had previously refused. In 1886, the necessary legislation was passed to convert NAC into the Royal Niger Company, with prominent positions in palm oil, palm kernels, groundnuts, tin, hide, and rubber. Yet, with these newly chartered territories still surrounded by French and German protectorates, the British government became more and more concerned at leaving a hotspot of international relations under the supervision of the RNC. In 1900, the company transferred territorial control, for the very large and profitable sum of £865,000, and Nigeria reappeared as a formal part of the British Empire, one year later (Fieldhouse, 1965; Darwin, 2009; Jones, 2000).

The fact that no German company wanted to invest in Cameroon or Togoland was a disappointing setback for Bismarck, and his government had to assume direct rule of these colonies. The principal figure in the founding of Germany's East Africa colony was Karl Peters. He lobbied the Berlin conferences on behalf of his East African Company, but Bismarck, uninterested in some unknown lands of unproven value, was more concerned with stabilizing Anglo-German diplomatic relations. Imperially inclined members of the Reichstag nonetheless brought about the EAC's charter for the territories. Without the sanction of the German government, Peters tried to acquire concessions in the kingdom of Buganda (in modern Uganda), but a larger expedition from the Imperial British East Africa Company, part of the MacKenzie-McKinnon trading conglomerate, drove him out. The 1890 Heligoland-Zanzibar Treaty settled a number of disputes, mostly over African territories, between Germany and Britain, and left the East Africa Company with the uneconomic territories inland from Dar-es-Salaam, and eventually Germany took administrative control of what became German East Africa (later Tanganyika, and today's Tanzania), although the EAC enterprise continued to dominate the colony's mining activities, and took revenues from customs duties, land deals, and banking in the colony. "Hangman" Peters fled when he was convicted of crimes against indigenous people in 1897, although he was welcomed back to Germany in 1914 (Fieldhouse, 1965; Jones, 1986; Jones, 1989; Griffiths, 1977).

Punitive punishment and forced labor were part of Africa's colonial story. The scale of the atrocities and their notoriety especially distinguished the Belgian Congo, yet Portugal's policies attracted international outrage, too, after 1904, when the brutal working conditions on the cocoa-producing islands of Sao Tomé and Principe were exposed. Although settler capital was the main source of investment in Portuguese-controlled Africa, Belgium's Banque d'Outremer is known to have bought land for cultivation in

Sao Tomé. When borrowers defaulted, the Banco Nacional Ultramarine acquired cocoa estates, coffee planters, river navigation companies, and tobacco factories in Portuguese South West Africa (modern Angola). Foreign firms frequently rescued failed enterprises, too: in the Zambezi delta, the Sena Sugar Estates, exporting to Portugal and the Transvaal, became British owned, and French investors took control of the Boror and Madal copra enterprises. The Companhia de Moçambique, which had received a royal charter in 1891, with monopoly and sovereign rights in the area between the Zambezi and Save rivers, exercised the power to use forced labor. Within a short period, it was controlled by France's Banque Impériale Ottomane. The company's gold mine and railway projects did not generate positive revenues, and it relied on land leases and on an African head tax instead. The South African miners Lewis and Marks owned the chartered Niassa Company in northern Mozambique (Fitzgerald, 2014; *International Directory of Company Histories*; Fieldhouse, 1965).

In Southern Africa, it was the adventurer-capitalist Cecil Rhodes who most prominently and personally identified international mining with empire building. By 1887, the De Beers Company dominated the Kimberley diamond fields. Rhodes had been the architect, but he relied on his connections with Lord Nathaniel Rothschild, the head of the London bank, who became the company's largest shareholder. Within a year, Rhodes was drawn by the possibility of gold deposits north of the Limpopo River. Once granted a concession by the chief of the Matabele, he hoped to end local control, and, on behalf of the British Empire, sweep onward into central Africa. In 1889, the chartered British South Africa Company was formed, with the commercial tasks of establishing trade and making treaties with Africans, distributing and managing lands, and organizing a police force. Rhodes referred to his enterprise as "another East India Company." Eventually, BSAC carved out a territory, named Zambezia, and then Rhodesia (covering modern Zambia and Zimbabwe). Conflict with the Boers (the Dutch and Afrikaans word for "farmer," which was applied to the descendants of the Dutch-speaking settlers) was principally economic: the Transvaal produced a quarter of the world's gold supplies, and mining operations were largely financed through British capital. In 1889, the British Colonial Secretary, Joseph Chamberlain, provoked the Boer War, which, by 1902, allowed Britain to take over the Transvaal and the Orange Free State. Nonetheless, the Union of South Africa in 1910 was a remarkable example of rapid reconciliation between enemies, and offered security to those interested in economic pursuits. Two-fifths of world capital invested in mining by 1914 went into the digging of South African gold (Fitzgerald, 2014; Roberts, 1988; Darwin, 2009).

Oil, Diplomacy, and Foreign Investment

Multinationals had a central part in the development of the oil industry across the world, building wells and pipelines. The oil industry requires costly and risky long-term investments and, as a result, oil companies tend to be very large, even today. From 1871 onward, oil multinationals played an important role in founding the first oil-extracting installations in the Caucasus Mountains. Refineries soon turned Baku, recently annexed by Czarist Russia from the Ottoman Empire, into "Black Town." The Nobel Brothers Petroleum Producing Company—founded by the Swedish business family and armaments manufacturers—opened its refinery in the city in 1873, and the Paris Rothschilds completed the railway from Baku to Batum on the Black Sea, creating the world's most important oil ports. Through their subsidiary, the Société Commerciale de Naphte Caspienne et de la Mer Noire (called, by its Cyrillic acronym, Bnito), the Rothschilds built a kerosene distribution network throughout Europe.

At the time, there was only one source of oil under British control, and it was the well-known trading enterprise of Finlay, Fleming & Company, which was behind the formation of Burmah Oil, in 1886. It was the year that brought the final annexation of Burma, ending for traders and investors the difficulties of royal monopoly, bribes, and extortion. The colonial authorities pledged not to allow foreign exploration, as an incentive for Burmah Oil. The Royal Dutch Company, established in 1890, also had a privileged position in the Dutch East Indies. Royal Dutch merged with British-owned Shell Trading, in 1907, and linked its sources of supply with a worldwide tanker and distribution operation. Although a Dutch-controlled company, its joining with Shell allowed it publicly to be a substantially British business. In 1911, Royal Dutch Shell took over the Rothschild operations in Russia, and two concerns—the Shell group and the U.S.'s Standard Oil—had come to dominate the world oil industry (Corley, 1984; Zanden, Jonker, Howarth, and Sluyterman, 2004). Shell remained throughout history one of the top players in the oil industry. Standard Oil by the 1900s had become the world's largest oil company, developing and controlling most of the U.S. oil industry, and managing large investments in China. It was broken up by the U.S. anti-trust legislation in 1911. Its break up generated some of the future leaders in the industry, such as Exxon.

Turning from Burma to Mexico next, we can see S. Pearson and Son, a famous firm of international construction engineers. Weetman Pearson used his influence with Mexican dictator, Porfirio Díaz, to begin drilling for oil in 1902. He thought it would be politic to register his interests as Compañia Mexicana de Petroleo El Aguila (Mexican Eagle) in 1909, but he retained a majority or controlling holding. Big discoveries from 1910 quickly turned Mexico into the world's third largest oil producer and one of the largest UK-based companies. The greatest achievement of Pearson is that it succeeded in managing its business even during the Mexican Revolution. After the First World War, Pearson sold El Aguila, avoiding the consequences of the changing political climate, which by the 1930s resulted in the nationalization of the oil industry. During the inter-war period the political climate changed again in Latin America. The war interrupted the success of the export-oriented economic growth driven by the activities of multinational companies. The nationalist and protectionist ideas that were prevailing in Europe had reached the Americas, too. A new range of leaders, such as Cardenas in Mexico, Peron in Argentina, and Vargas in Brazil, adopted more closed economic models, erecting barriers to trade and investment and nationalizing some foreign businesses. After the 1940s, all of Latin America moved in this direction and foreign businesses had to adapt.

The story in Persia is different again: In 1900, an agent of the Persian government approached the British entrepreneur William Knox D'Arcy to buy an oil concession. Persia was a buffer territory between an expanding Imperial Russia and the British Raj. Despite the very apparent practical and commercial difficulties of the project, D'Arcy, in May 1901, bought rights for 60 years over some 75 percent of the country. Inhospitable terrain, climate, and local tribes hindered exploration. It proved a risky and speculative venture, which ran up huge losses, but D'Arcy had the support of the Royal Navy, anxious to secure a plentiful source of fuel oil. Admiralty connections finally secured the intervention of Finlay, Fleming—Burmah Oil's owners—and, in 1905, once it was assured that the British government viewed Persia as a protectorate, it led a syndicate that took on the task of oil exploration there. When the Shah was deposed in July 1906, the new Majlis (the administrative council) questioned the sweeping terms of the 60-year oil concession. In response, the British government dispatched a token troupe of Indian troops to guard the syndicate's facilities. The first large oil strike occurred in May 1908, and the Anglo-Persian Oil Company was created. The British Admiralty regarded the flow of Persian oil as a strategic asset, but it continued to hesitate over the crucial decision to convert its main battle fleet away from steam coal. The Agadir Crisis in 1911—in which Germany threatened to annex the Mediterranean port as compensation for a French protectorate over Morocco—galvanized Winston Churchill as First Lord of the Admiralty. As APOC continued to struggle from a shortage of working capital, the British Parliament, in 1914, agreed to a 51 percent stake in APOC, and acquired the right to appoint directors (Ferrier, 1982; Zanden, Jonker, Howarth, and Sluyterman, 2004).

Global Economy II: 1948–1980

The period that we have defined as Global Economy I was characterized by the expansion of multinational companies and their often unscrupulous activities in emerging markets—often not only condoned but supported by the governments of their home countries. Nonetheless, the investments of these companies linked the global economy, generating an unprecedented period of economic growth. This changed with the two World Wars. The inter-war period saw two decades of political, international, and economic instability, and, as well as undermining democratic institutions, the Great Depression of the 1930s brought a worldwide collapse in trade, policies of autarchy, unemployment, and poverty. The global economy, so prominent in the era before 1914, unwound, and the Second World War inflicted further dramatic destruction on an international system that was already broken. Former allies, united during the Second World War, history's most destructive conflict, split in the years 1945 to 1948. On one side was the Communist bloc led by the Soviet Union; on the other side were the free market, democratic countries of the North Atlantic—the U.S., Canada, and West European nations—and allies such as Australia and New Zealand. The division was part ideological, part international power-play, and part economic. The trade and investment barrier between East and West established a new system of international political economy, and the Communist bloc was effectively closed to multinational investors from the West. The "iron curtain" across Europe created diplomatic crises—even the threat of war, in 1948, 1956, and 1962—but, elsewhere in the world, their rivalry proved bloody.

Despite the economic calamities of the inter-war period, and the physical destruction of the Second World War, the return to peacetime and the principles of open trade had a remarkable and rapid effect. Commentators gave the post-war decades the title of the "Golden Age," noted for long-term rises in output, demand, trade, and productivity. The Communist bloc, however, excluded itself from the expanding international economy, and, by the end of the 1960s, its economic failings, initially hidden by propaganda, had become all too evident. Multinational enterprises, too, resumed their investments overseas, and U.S. firms led and stimulated advances in technology and management worldwide. U.S. capital and know-how, in the immediate post-war decades, made a vital contribution to world recovery (Fitzgerald, 2014; Gaddis, 1997; Kenwood and Lougheed, 1999).

The vast proportion of U.S. multinational investment, in the 1950s and 1960s, went to Canada and Western Europe, and it was industry that explained a large part of the increase. U.S. manufacturers, replete with capital, had acquired international leadership in management, technology, products, and brands, and, once assured that European recovery was underway and permanent, turned to strategies of market-seeking FDI. After 1958, the lifting of currency controls and other restrictions in Europe lifted operational difficulties and increased the confidence of investors. The "Third World," however, raised quite different issues for multinational companies. Because so many developing economies had experienced colonization, they were unsurprisingly wary of "economic imperialism," or dependency and exploitation by foreign businesses, and they associated progress and national sovereignty with central planning and import controls. Most opted for mixed models, which combined capitalism with a strong state coordinating the economy through trade barriers, subsidies, and direct ownership. This was not only detrimental for most multinational companies, as it made the business environment more complex and unpredictable, it also failed to generate the levels of economic growth and development that the more open economies of Europe and Japan experienced during the same period of 1950–1980.

The value of world exports rose by 7 percent per annum over the period 1950 to 1973, compared to world GDP at 4.9 percent and world GDP per capita at 2.9 percent. Much of the gain went to a small number of rich market economies, which received about 63 percent of world imports, by value, in 1960. These industrialized countries in North America and West Europe accounted, in addition, for 64 percent of world exports. In 1960, the ratio between exports and world GDP reached 8.3 percent; by 1973, the figure was 11.2, and, therefore, finally higher than for 1914 (at 8.7 percent) and for 1929 (at 9.0 percent); by 1980, it was 11.4 percent. This was the period during which the economic power of the Triad consolidated, pushed by investments in infrastructure, education, and the growing integration of the Western European, North American, and Japanese economies (see the Appendix, "From Third World to Emerging Markets: Definitions, Contexts, and Meanings").

The role of multinationals in international business grew, too. Total outward FDI stock grew to 4.0 percent of world GDP in 1967, and to 4.2 percent in 1973; yet, admittedly, these ratios still remained well below those created in the first wave of globalization by 1914. By 1960, U.S. businesses alone owned some 48.3 percent of outward FDI stock, nearly four times the share of its nearest rival, the UK; their 40.0 percent of world FDI stock in 1980 was still nearly two and half times larger in real terms than their 1960 holdings. The top ten investing nations still dominated by 1980, because developing nations were responsible for between 1.1 and 3.1 percent of all outward FDI for the whole of the period from 1948 to 1980. Furthermore, in contrast to the world of 1914, when some 66 percent of world FDI stock was located in developing territories; some 67 percent was, by 1960, in developed nations; and Western Europe, the U.S., and Canada remained, in 1980, the locations for nearly two-thirds of FDI assets (Maddison, 1993; Lougheed and Kenwood, 1999; Dunning and Lundan, 2008). Multinationals not only generated a large share of the world's trade and investment during Global Economy II. They also invested heavily in technology, developing commercial aviation, affordable fridges, cars, television sets, and a range of less visible but equally important engineering and chemical products.

Post-War Manufacturing Multinationals

U.S. FDI was a key motor of the post-war international economy, and, as we have seen, much of the increase came from its manufacturing sector, flowing north to Canada and across the Atlantic to Europe. It was U.S. multinationals that developed the techniques of standardization, mass manufacturing, and the assembly line, diffusing them across the world. They pioneered the development of multidivision, complex organizational and managerial structures, capable of mobilizing large numbers of employees and resources. They were also innovative in the fields of product development, branding, advertising, and distribution, which continue to be critical strategic areas for any consumer good producer.

U.S. multinationals, engaged on market-seeking strategies for their products and brands, gave small priority to emerging economies, with their smaller markets and lower per-capita income. But there were exceptions, with most of them being supports rather than the mainstay of their international strategy. Goodyear Tire established itself throughout Latin America, and Caterpillar had opened a subsidiary in Brazil by 1956. Coca-Cola, which, after the attack on Pearl Harbor, had followed the G.I. abroad, opened some 15–20 bottling plants a year during the 1950s and created a global icon and a tribute to Americana. H.J. Heinz went to Venezuela, while Kellogg built a factory in South Africa, in 1948, and another in Mexico, in 1951. General Foods—whose brands Maxwell House coffee, Birdseye frozen foods, Jell-O, and others had high recognition—was, by the 1960s, a worldwide food giant, with subsidiaries in Latin America alongside those in developed countries. S.C. Johnson—the maker of Johnson's Wax, Glade air freshener, and Pledge spray polish—owned, by 1968, some 20 overseas firms, including subsidiaries in Latin America, Africa, and South East Asia (Fitzgerald, 2014).

Post-war British companies showed an initial preference for investing in the Commonwealth countries of Australia, Canada, and South Africa, through calculations of familiarity, growth opportunities, and low political risk. Both the Australian and South African governments pressured foreign companies to invest, as a means of promoting local industry. Pilkington, the glassmakers, founded a subsidiary in South Africa in 1951, and the same considerations led to its 1954 investment, in partnership with local capital, in India. It was the invention of the float-glass process, which came into production in 1960 and then transformed the industry, that inspired a change in international business policy at Pilkington. Seeking quickly to exploit its technical advantage, it founded eight overseas subsidiaries over the next 20 years, in developed economies mainly, but in Latin America too. The Anglo-Irish Guinness followed its trade, and went where its products had already won brand loyalty: it built, after 1962, four breweries in Nigeria, its largest national market outside Britain, and began to make its distinctive stout beer in Malaysia,

Cameroon, Ghana, and Jamaica. Stout remains very popular today in the West Africa and the Caribbean.

Like other Swedish manufacturers, Ericsson had a competitive advantage in technology and engineering and owned 21 overseas subsidiaries by 1970, mostly in Europe, but also had Brazilian and Mexican subsidiaries. With its leading radial tires, France's Michelin had built factories, by 1970, in Nigeria, Algeria, and Vietnam, and, subsequently, in Brazil. Pechiney took stakes in aluminum fabrication companies in Argentina and Brazil in 1947–48, founded an aluminum plant in Cameroon in 1954, and constructed an alumina factory in Guinea in 1960. The big three of the German chemicals industry reestablished themselves in Latin America, sometimes, ironically, purchasing companies they had lost during the Second World War. Bayer acquired Quimicas Unidas, in Mexico, during 1952, and, thereafter, bought back Allianca Commerciale de Anilinas, in Brazil. Mannesmann AG, by 1955, had established steel and tube mills in Turkey, and, in Brazil, its Companhia Siderurgica Mannesmann evolved into a group of companies, active throughout Latin America, and engaged in high-grade steels, industrial machinery, compressors, excavators, control systems, mining, and trading (Fitzgerald, 2014).

The most prominent case of multinational investment by a German multinational was Volkswagen. The Beetle proved itself to be VW's greatest post-war asset, both at home, and, very notably, in export markets. As a result of pressure from governments, the company built assembly plants in South Africa (1950), Brazil (1953), and Mexico (1954). In Brazil, the post-war presidency of Eurico Gaspar Dutra, from 1946, and that of re-elected former dictator, Getúlio Dornelles Vargas, from 1950, initiated a policy of "developmentalism," which led to the nationalization of oil and mining, including the assets of firms such as Jersey Standard (the future Esso/Exxon) and Shell. However, a friendly approach was adopted toward foreign direct investment. By 1956, Brazil had banned the import of foreign cars and imposed local content rules. VW sold 20 percent of its subsidiary, in the following year, as a means of shoring up the support of the government and indigenous business interests. In a short period of time, it became the first car manufacturer in Brazil, effectively diffusing the mass-produced automobile in what will become the largest market in Latin America. VW continues to be an aggressive player in emerging markets—it is among the top three automotive companies by market share (depending on the year) in Brazil, China, and Mexico.

Capitalism in the Communist Bloc

As we discussed, the coming of communism insulated a large group of economies from international trade and investment. However, by the 1960s, planned economies were failing to provide their citizens with mass-produced goods such as cars and fridges. Their centralized resource allocation and absence of price systems were efficient at fostering the defense industry, much less at guessing what consumers may want. Moreover, they lacked the technological and managerial skills to do so. Gradually, they made a few exceptions to their policy and accepted investments in the industries where they were most backward.

Having brought the mass-manufactured, affordable car to Italy, Fiat expanded and became one of the top European and global automotive producers by the end of the 1960s. Its management had global ambitions and built assembly plants in India, Morocco, Egypt, South Africa, and Latin America. Pragmatic in pursuit of commercial opportunities, Fiat signed a long-lasting technical assistance and licensing agreement with Zavodi Crvena Zastava Automobiles, in Kragujevic, Serbia, which began making variations of the Italian company's cars, moving eventually from an assembly operation to fuller production (its well-known Yugo brand was to appear commercially in 1981, and Fiat subsequently acquired Zastava).

The Soviet Union was ideologically inimical to foreign multinationals, but, when the grey apparatchiks, Leonid Brezhnev and Alexei Kosygin, replaced the very volatile Nikita Khrushchev, they attempted to revive the country's industry with capitalist methods of management. Fiat was able, therefore, in 1966, to sign a deal with the Soviet Union to establish a turnkey factory, the Volga Automobile Plant (AutoVAZ), which gained fame for making the Lada. Its management had to negotiate with the U.S. government in order to gain permission to invest in the USSR without suffering from boycotts or legal issues in the North American market. Its Soviet Union factory became one of the world's largest car manufacturing plants, and to operate it Fiat brought to the USSR engineers, machinery, and technicians from Italy. It contributed to the building of Tolyatti, the town which hosted the factory, named after a famous Italian Communist, and to develop the supply chain necessary to provide inputs to the factory. These are great examples of creative management, which offset ideological and geopolitical barriers in the pursuit of business opportunities. Among the list of Western multinationals in the Soviet Union, by 1980, were Dow Chemical, IBM, ITT, AEG Telefunken, and Pechiney Ugine-Kuhlmann (PUK), but it is well to recall that the total inward FDI in the Soviet Union was worth only some $1 billion (Fitzgerald, 2014; *International Directory of Company Histories*).

Post-Colonial Asia and Africa

Once the Second World War had bankrupted European empires, they began their long retreat from Asia and Africa, withdrawing support for the firms that operated there. The government of liberated Burma, in 1948, took permanent control of the teak forests once exploited by British trading firms. A military government, later, in 1963, embarked on policies of autarchy and the full nationalization of major industries, transferring the assets of foreign multinationals, including those of Burmah Oil. Because of the large demand for its products in the Indian subcontinent, the Schweppes tonic water company, from Britain, decided to invest in newly independent India. The overall trend, however, was disengagement. Heavier taxation on private firms, exchange controls, rupee devaluation, and discouragement of foreign ownership made overseas companies unwilling to sanction new investments in India, from the country's founding in 1947. The Indian coal industry was nationalized, in 1970, and the 1973 Foreign Exchange Regulation Act (FERA) sought to boost the indigenous ownership of business by penalizing all firms that were 40 percent or more foreign controlled. From the date of independence onward, British trading companies had sold up, in some cases, to the Indian government, and, in other cases, to local enterprises, with the Tata Group often appearing in prominent acquisitions.

The Borneo Company, from 1953, announced it was strategically withdrawing from Asia. In Malaysia, multinationals retained their place in rubber and palm oil, thanks to their access to capital and their control of technological knowledge, but the New Economic Policy, introduced in 1971, given its aim of favoring native Malays, was a clear signal to begin divesting. After several years of warfare, an independent Indonesia was formed in 1949. The Netherlands trading firms returned, but Indonesia restricted imports and profit transfers, and gave preference to indigenous merchants. Then, in 1957, Indonesia nationalized all Netherlands companies within its borders—about half of all the European country's overseas assets—and replaced their managers. Some Asia-based traders attempted to transfer their skills in commodities and developing economies to Africa. Wallace Brothers bought plantations and ranches in many African countries, between 1950 and 1954, and Finlay acquired tea estates in Kenya and trading interests in Rhodesia in 1956. On the whole, and over time, most British trading firms evolved into companies investing in a wide range of industries and services in their home economy, while those from The Netherlands tried to become, with mixed success, Europe-wide businesses (Jones, 2000; Jonker and Sluyterman, 2000; Sluyterman, 2005; *International Directory of Company Histories*). This was in line with the general refocusing of multinational companies from emerging economies to the Triad, which responded in part to the increasingly anti-business climate prevailing in emerging markets, in part to the fact that the Triad, being more open to trade and investment, was growing faster and hence providing more business opportunities.

The Arab countries of North Africa, beginning with Libya in 1951, gained their formal independence, and Ghana initiated the process for sub-Saharan Africa in 1957, with the pace greatly quickening across the continent in the 1960s. New nation states were suspicious of enterprises with imperial histories, and often linked multinationals with blocking their economic independence in the era of political sovereignty. Multinationals felt disadvantaged against local or state companies, and increasingly dealt with import, profit, and currency controls on imports and profits and non-convertible currencies. Some trading companies, nonetheless, proved adept at deal-making and commercial opportunism in the changed political climate. From 1946–57, new constitutional arrangements ensured that Nigeria exercised greater autonomy, before formal decolonization in 1960. Under pressure from the Nigerian government, the United Africa Company (UAC), an arm of Unilever, began the assembly of motor cars in 1958, and so protected an import and distribution business it had created. From 1961, Roland "Tiny" Rowland transformed the London and Rhodesia Mining and Land Company (Lonrho) into a sprawling conglomerate with worldwide interests but, above all, deep involvement in Africa. His greatest skill was a talent for forming relationships with Africa's new rulers and political elite: the Malawi government, for example, commissioned the company to take on all its sugar refining needs. Elsewhere in the world, Gray Mackenzie managed the new Dubai port, from 1972, and Ocean Wilsons and Inchcape established a joint venture to offer support services to Brazil's off-shore oil industry (*International Directory of Company Histories*; Jones, 2000).

The British government, in 1949, on behalf of the Anglo-Iranian Oil Corporation (AIOC), which effectively monopolized its oil supplies, offered Iran revised terms for its operating concession. The Iranian government remained, however, highly aggrieved by the royalty returns, by AIOC's failure to give it any say in the management of the business, and by the wages paid to workers. When the Arabian American Oil Company (Armaco)—owned by Standard Oil of California (Socal), Texaco, Jersey Standard (Esso/Exxon), and Socony Vacuum (Mobil)—agreed to a 50-50 profit share with Saudi Arabia, in late 1950, anger intensified.

In 1951, the Majlis (administrative council) voted for nationalization, and Iranians democratically elected Mohammed Mossadegh, who supported the policy, as their Prime Minister. The seven large oil majors from the U.S., Britain, The Netherlands, and France all combined and, with their control over markets in developed countries, refused to buy oil from Iran. The U.S. supported a 50-50 profit split but the British government rejected the proposal. The Shah arrested Mossadegh, with the tacit support of Washington and London.

Having bought assets in Iraq and Kuwait, AIOC changed its name to British Petroleum (BP), but public opinion in Iran was too strong to allow it to resume operations as before, and the other oil majors and the U.S. wanted a revision of the concession. An international consortium composed of BP, Gulf Oil (which ultimately merged with Socal to form Chevron), Shell, Compagnie Française des Pétroles (CFP, and later transformed into Total), and the Aramco partners owned and managed the newly founded National Iranian Oil Company (NIOC). It agreed to the 50-50 profit split that the British had once adamantly rejected, but continued to deny any Iranian government control over its management or scrutiny of the accounts (Bamberg, 1994; Bamberg, 2000; Van Zanden, Jonker, Howarth, and Sluyterman, 2004). The aggressive stances of oil companies and their refusal to allow the Iranian government better concessions stirred popular resentment, which later resulted in the Iranian Revolution. This was an example of short-term strategy and colonialist mentality, based on an overestimation of the extent to which their economic muscle could be used to engineer political outcomes. After 1979, Iran nationalized the oil industry and closed its economy, damaging not only the current but also the future business prospects of Triad-based firms, and with it also the potential for growth and development of the Iranian economy.

Sovereignty Versus Property

There had been few instances of the forced nationalization of foreign enterprises before 1945: combatants had sequestrated enemy property during the First and Second World Wars; the Bolshevik Revolution of 1917 led to the end of private enterprise; after disputes about concession terms, royalties, or profit share, Bolivia, in 1937, and Mexico, in 1938, took control of their oil industries; Argentina expropriated American & Foreign Power, during 1943–45; and, in 1946, the Canadian-owned Mexican Tramways entered public ownership. In the immediate post-war decades, forced divestments were relatively few and, on the whole, ultimately settled by agreement. Under the presidency of Juan Perón, elected in 1946, Argentina paid generously for the remaining British-owned railways. British companies resolved any disputes with India, Pakistan, and Burma after 1947, and later with Malaysia. The Netherlands, similarly, came to terms with nationalizations in Indonesia, from 1957 onward. Petrobras, in Brazil, controlled the country's oil assets, but continued to work with foreign multinationals to effect exploration, production, and export. ITT, Rio Tinto, and Ford felt that operational difficulties and discriminatory policies had effectively forced them out of Fascist Spain by 1954, although terms, however grudgingly accepted, were agreed upon. British-American Tobacco, by agreement with Chiang Kai-Shek's Nationalist government, reentered China, only to be wrong-footed by the victory of Mao Zedong's Communists in 1949. In return for its managerial personnel being released, in 1953, BAT signed over its assets to the new Chinese government, which began to sequestrate all private businesses (Fitzgerald, 2014; Encarnation, 1989; Jones, 1996; Jones, 2005; *International Directory of Company Histories*; Fritsch and Franco, 1991).

Egypt's nationalization of the Suez Canal marked the beginning of a turning point. In response to the levels of nationalist feeling in Egypt, Britain had withdrawn its armed forces from the Suez Zone in 1953, but retained ownership of the Canal itself, still registered in France, and largely British owned, for another 25 years. When President Gamal Abdel Nassar came to power in 1956, he nationalized the Canal and prompted a combined military reaction from Britain, France, and Israel. The U.S., seeking to minimize Soviet influence in the Middle East, forced a withdrawal of the occupying forces. The Suez Crisis had long-lasting implications for international politics, but, among those of multinational enterprise, the Canal remained a foreign-owned asset nationalized without compensation (Piquet, 2004; *International Directory of Company Histories*). One year after becoming independent in 1958, Guinea provided another example of nationalizations not being reversed, in land ownership and wholesale distribution, which were dominated by French interests. But the new state saw itself as too economically vulnerable to appropriate the mining firms and banks. U.S. companies, in 1958, controlled 37 percent of Cuba's sugar crop. The victory of Fidel Castro, during 1959–60 quickly brought about the nationalization of foreign-owned assets. Despite the weight that a nearby superpower could bring on its small neighbor, U.S. investors permanently lost their sugar and fruit estates, hotels, and other leisure businesses (Safarian, 1993; Fitzgerald, 2014; *International Directory of Company Histories*).

In 1962, the General Assembly of the United Nations adopted a resolution on Permanent Sovereignty over Natural Resources, which called for "appropriate" compensation for the nationalization of foreign businesses in accordance with national state and international law. The Soviet Union—with so little outward FDI, and wanting to discourage outside interference in its internal affairs—argued for the inalienable rights of nation states. The United States was uneasy over the vagueness of the word "appropriate," but there had been so few examples of appropriation. Congress passed the Hickenlooper Amendment, in a reaction to the Cuban Revolution, and to the acquisition of ITT in Brazil, demanding the withdrawal of aid if no compensation was forthcoming. Yet the provision was hardly ever used, and the State Department applied it pragmatically, in order to secure room for negotiations with host governments. The pace of nationalizations and host government interference in multinational subsidiaries hastened, and investing countries and companies increasingly accepted the principle of national sovereignty over ownership, while arguing for the principle of proper compensation. Beginning with Iraq's acquisition of mineral rights in 1961, oil-producing countries over the next decade or so took control away from the majors, culminating in Saudi Arabia's nationalization of Aramco in 1976 (Safarian, 1993; *International Directory of Company Histories*).

The Congo imposed state ownership on the Société Générale de Belgique's mining operations in 1966, because the company was a domineering influence on its economy, in addition to being a colonial legacy. Zambia did the same to U.S.- and British-owned copper mines in 1969, and converted the assets owned by the Roan Selection Trust and the Anglo-American Corporation into Zambia Consolidated Copper Mines (ZCCM), as much an instrument of social as economic development.

With the backing of the Communist bloc, capital-importing economies at the United Nations had, in 1972, won a motion declaring that the nationalization of foreign assets was an expression of political sovereignty. The Gonzalez Amendment, passed by the U.S. Congress, declared that it would halt all World Bank and other international loans to offending nations, and legislation in 1974 allowed the imposing of sanctions. The State Department had identified 106 disputes with U.S. multinationals in 39 countries, affecting $3.5 billion out of the $25 billion total American FDI in Asia, Africa, and Latin America, almost all of it in minerals and natural resources. Multinationals, however, showed themselves to be pragmatic, and generally preferred to come to terms. Firms such as Rio Tinto Zinc and Kaiser Aluminum followed strategies of seeking state or local partners as a means of off-setting commercial risks, although leading miners additionally switched as far as possible to investments in developed and politically favorable countries such as Australia and Canada, just as oil firms explored Alaska, Canada, and the North Sea (Safarian, 1993; *International Directory of Company Histories*).

International Political Economy

As we have seen, in our historical survey of the first and second global economies, the ways in which countries have conducted their economic relationships with each other, and that the nature and role of multinational enterprises have varied considerably over time and place. One of the advantages from looking at issues chronologically is to identify the key factors determining economic relationships between states—the international political economy—and how they have changed. From ancient times, military conquest determined the relationship between peoples, and frequently involved economic exploitation of the losing power, including forced labor. Nonetheless, more endurable empires offered security, stability, systems of law and administration, and the deepening trade routes. The combined drives of trade expansion and military conquest, led by European merchants and adventurers, brought about global transformation from the fifteenth century onward. In South America, the conquerors came looking for precious metals, and the flow of natural resources across the Atlantic boosted the economies of Spain and Portugal; in Asia, incorporated businesses, acting under charters from their governments, and with their own militia forces, began by establishing coastal trading forts, and, as in the case of the East India Company, ended up as rulers of India. Mercantilism and slavery epitomized, by the eighteenth century, the prevailing international political economy. The trend was toward the economically successful European nations trading and exploiting undeveloped territories, but, in the case of India, military power brought the subjugation of regions arguably more or equally as advanced as Europe (Bayly, 2004; Darwin, 2009; Fitzgerald, 2014; Stopford, Strange, and Henley, 1991).

What differentiated the international system that emerged in the nineteenth century was the existence and expansion of these multinational enterprises, which, in principle, could transform the workings of the global economy because of their intrinsic competitive advantages. With few new company charters being issued, and with the fortunes of charter companies on the wane, independent multinational enterprises, after 1820, and more emphatically after 1840, brought about the unprecedented boom in exports and imports. They had competitive capabilities in management, technology, finance, international logistics, or market access. They invested in mines and plantations, roads, ports and transport, water, and utilities. They laid the basis for the integration of the world economy and a period of accelerated economic growth. Many emerging markets continue to rely, even today, on the infrastructure built by multinationals during Global Economy I. FDI flowed mainly from Europe, and went to mostly politically independent Latin America and to an Asia that was increasingly colonized. Africa, later divided between the European powers, received small amounts of FDI in global terms, but the investment would have significant impact on the economies and peoples of the continent. The trading and investment imperative in many instances became intermixed with colonization, and, from 1870 onward, the cause of imperialism gathered impetus (Bayly, 2004; Fieldhouse, 1965; Darwin, 2009).

Although historians have traditionally located the period 1870–1914 as the high point of colonial imperialism, the British, French, and The Netherlands empires reached their greatest geographical extent during the inter-war decades, although freedom movements and resistance grew to significant strength in many ruled territories. The retreat began as late as the 1950s and 1960s—although the Portuguese tried to hold on to their African colonies for another decade—yet the legacy of colonialism continued to have implications for multinational investors in recently created nation states. The U.S. emerged out of the Second World War as the world's lender of capital, and its firms possessed unmatched managerial and technological capabilities. It hastened the end of European empires and promoted the integration of emerging markets in the world economy.

In post-colonial countries there was, not surprisingly, residual resentment over the hold of foreign multinationals on the oil, mineral mining, or plantation commodities that were the mainstay of their economies and exports. In Latin America, social unrest, democratic pressure, and the pursuit of industrialization and national economic development similarly brought a challenge to the control of overseas multinationals on national economies and their vital resources. Multinationals continued, in many places, to cope with the problems of poor infrastructure, but had to learn how to cope with governments opposed to the implications of multinational investment and, potentially, ideologically opposed to free enterprise and open markets. Political and economic instabilities within host countries similarly raised the levels of risk and uncertainty. In Chapters 4 and 5, we discuss at length the topic of business risk and strategies to manage it in emerging markets. Our conceptual tools draw from management theories and from historical evidence.

Concluding Remarks

The aim of this chapter was to illustrate that private businesses have been operating in emerging markets for centuries, that it has never been easy to do so, and that failure to understand and respect the local political, social, ethnic, religious, and cultural context damages business interests in the long term. The nationalist, protectionist, and often anti-foreign business policies that developing economies adopted during Global Economy II were a reaction to the events of Global Economy I. They were a reaction to the abuses of colonialism, and to the fact that the first period of economic integration benefitted only a small share of the local population, such as the political elites linked to multinational companies. They were also a reaction to the perceived, and in many cases real, interference of foreign business with local politics. The consequences were negative for business and also for the economies of emerging markets, many of which lagged behind the Triad during Global Economy II because of their insulation from international trade and investment and their unstable business climates. Since the 1980s, emerging markets have opened their doors to foreign investment and trade again. We have shown in Chapter 1 that by opening they have and are growing fast, and now account for a key share of the global economy. Once again, emerging markets are becoming a fundamental part of the picture for multinational companies. It is to be hoped that contemporary firms based in developed economies will adopt more sustainable strategies (for example, by making products and services accessible to the poor), as we discuss in Chapter 7, "Targeting Emerging Market Clients II: Strategies for the Base of the Pyramid." Multinational companies continue to be at the forefront of technological and organizational innovation. If they invest more resources in studying and managing the environment risks of operating in emerging economies, they will be able to benefit greatly from the economic growth of these markets, while simultaneously contributing to their development.

References

Abel, C. and Lewis, C. M. (1985). *Latin America, Economic Imperialism and the State*. London: Athlone.

Acemoglu, D. and Johnson, S. (2003). *Unbundling institutions* (No. w9934). National Bureau of Economic Research.

Allen, G. C. and Donnithorne, A.G. (1954). *Western Enterprise in Far Eastern Economic Development*. London: George Allen.

Amsden, A. H. (2001). *The Rise of "The Rest"—Challenges to the West from Late-Industrializing Economies*. Oxford University Press.

Bamberg, J. H. (1994). *The History of the British Petroleum Company, Vol. 2: The Anglo-Iranian Years, 1928–1954*. Cambridge University Press.

Bamberg, J. H. (2000). *History of British Petroleum, Vol. 3: British Petroleum and Global Oil, 1954–1975: The Challenge of Nationalism*. Cambridge University Press.

Bayly, C. (2004). *The Birth of the Modern World 1780–1914: Global Connections and Comparisons*. Oxford: Blackwell.

Blake, R. (1999). *Jardine Matheson—Traders of the Far East*. London: Weidenfield & Nicholson.

Bowen, H. V. (2006). *The Business of Empire: The East India Company and Imperial Britain, 1756–1833*. Cambridge University Press.

Bowen, H. V., Lincoln, M., and Rigby, N. (2002). *The Worlds of the East India Company*.

Bucheli, M. (2005). *Bananas and Business: The United Fruit Company in Colombia: 1899–2000*. New York: New York University Press. Suffolk, England: Boydell.

Bucheli, M. (2004). Enforcing Business Contracts in South America: the United Fruit Company and the Colombian Banana Planters in the Twentieth-Century, *Business History Review*, Vol. 78.

Bucheli, M. (2008). Multinational Corporations, Totalitarian Regimes, and Economic Nationalism: United Fruit Company in Central America, 1899–1975, *Business History*, Vol. 50.

Chang, H. J. (2003). *Kicking Away the Ladder: Development Strategy in Historical Perspective*. London: Anthem Press.

Chapman, P. (2007). *Jungle Capitalists*. Canongate.

Clayton, L. A. (1985). *Grace: W.R. Grace & Co., the Formative Years, 1850–1930*. Illinois: Jameson.

Cochran, S. (2000). *Encountering Chinese Networks: Western, Japanese, and Chinese Corporations in China, 1880–1937*. University of California Press.

Corley, T. A. B. (1994). Britain's Overseas Investments in 1914 Revisited, *Business History,* Vol. 36.

Corley, T. A. B. (1984). *A History of the Burmah Oil Company, 1886–1924.* London: Heinemann.

Corley, T. A. B. (1984). *A History of the Burmah Oil Company, 1924–1966.* London: Heinemann.

Darwin, J. (2009). *The Empire Project: The Rise and Fall of the British World System, 1830–1970.* Cambridge University Press.

Dosal, P. (1993). *Doing Business with the Dictators: A Political History of United Fruit in Guatemala, 1899–1944.* Wilmington: Scholarly Resources.

Dunning, J. H. and Lundan, S. M. (2008). *Multinational Enterprises and the Global Economy.* Northampton, Massachusetts: Edward Elgar.

Encarnation, D. J. (1989). *Dislodging Multinationals: India's Strategy in Competitive Perspective.* Ithaca: Cornell University Press.

Farooqui, A. (2005). *Smuggling as Subversion: Colonialism, Indian Merchants, and the Politics of Opium, 1790–1843.* Lexington Books.

Ferrier, R. W. (1982). *The History of the British Petroleum Company: Vol. 1, The Developing Years, 1901–1932.* Cambridge University Press.

Fieldhouse, D. K. (1965). *The Colonial Empires: A Comparative Survey from the Eighteenth Century.* London: MacMillan.

Fitzgerald, R. (2014). *Rise of the Global Economy: Multinational Enterprise and the Making of the Modern World.* Cambridge University Press.

Fritsch, W. and Franco, G. (1991). *Foreign Direct Investment in Brazil: Its Impact on Industrial Restructuring.* Paris: OECD.

Gaddis, J. L. (1997). *We Now Know: Rethinking the Cold War.* Oxford University Press.

Galbraith, J. S. (1965). The Chartering of the British North Borneo Company, *Journal of British Studies*, Vol. 4. Gerschenkron, A. (1962). *Economic Backwardness in Historical Perspective.* Massachusetts: Harvard University Press.

Greenhill, R. and Miller, R. (1998). British Trading Companies in South America after 1914 (G. Jones, Ed.), *The Multinational Traders.* London: Routledge.

Griffiths, P. J. (1977). *A History of the Inchcape Group.* London.

Hausman, W. J., Hertner, P., and Wilkins, M. (2008). *Global Electrification: Multinational Enterprise and International Finance in the History of Light and Power, 1878–2007.* Cambridge University Press.

Hochschild, A. (1998). *King Leopold's Ghost: A Story of Greed, Terror, and Heroism in Colonial Africa.* Mariner Books.

Hunt, W. G. G. (1951). *Heirs of a Great Adventure: Balfour Williamson, 1851–1901.* London.

Hunt, W. G. G. (1960). *Heirs of a Great Adventure: Balfour Williamson, 1901–1951.* London.

International Directory of Company Histories (1988–2010). London: St James Press.

Johnson, C. (1982). *The MITI and the Japanese Economic Miracle.* Stanford University Press.

Jones, C. (1958). *Antony Gibbs & Sons, Ltd: A Record of 150 Years of Merchant Banking, 1808–1958.* London, Antony Gibbs.

Jones, G. (1996). *The Evolution of International Business: An Introduction.* London: Routledge.

Jones, G. (2000). *Merchants to Multinationals.* Oxford University Press.

Jones, G. (2005). *Multinationals and Global Capitalism.* Oxford University Press.

Jones, G., ed., (1998). *The Multinational Traders.* London: Routledge.

Jones, G. (1981). *The State and the Emergence of the British Oil Industry.* London: MacMillan.

Jones, S. (1989). *Trade and Shipping: Lord Inchcape 1852–1952.* Manchester University Press.

Jones, S. (1986). *Two Centuries of Overseas Trading: The Origins and Growth of the Inchcape Group.* London: Macmillan.

Jonker, J. and Sluyterman, K. E. (2000). *At Home on the World Markets: Dutch International Trading Companies from the 16th Century Until the Present.* Montreal: McGill-Queens University Press.

Kenwood, G. and Lougheed, A. (1999). *Growth of the International Economy, 1820–2000.* London: Routledge.

Keswick, M. (1982). *The Thistle and the Jade.* London.

King, F. H. H., King, C. E., and King, D. J. S. (1988). *The History of the Hongkong and Shanghai Banking Corporation: Volume 1, The Hongkong Bank in Late Imperial China 1864–1902: On an Even Keel.* Cambridge University Press.

Kirzner, I. M. (1973). *Competition and Entrepreneurship.* University of Chicago Press.

Lewis, C. M. (1983). *British Railways in Argentina, 1870–1914.* London: Athlone.

Lewis, C. M. (2002). From Developmentalism to Neoliberalism, 1946–2001 (P. Heenan and M. Lamatagne, Eds.). *The South American Handbook.* London.

Longhurst, H. (1954). *The Borneo Story. The History of the First 100 Years of Trading in the Far East.* London: Newman Neame.

Macaulay, R. H. (1934). *History of Bombay Burmah Trading Corporation 1864–1910.* London.

MacCameron, R. (1983). *Bananas, Labor & Politics in Honduras, 1954–1963.* New York: Syracuse University Press.

Maddison, A. (1995). *Monitoring the World Economy, 1820–1992.* Paris, OECD.

McCann, T. (1988). *An American Company: The Tragedy of United Fruit.* New York: Random House.

McKay, J. P. (1970). *Pioneers for Profit: Foreign Entrepreneurship and Russian Industrialization, 1885–1913.* Chicago University Press.

Morgan, G., Whitley, R., and Moen, E., Eds. (2005). *Changing Capitalisms? Internationalization, Institutional Change, and Systems of Economic Organization.* Oxford University Press.

North, D.C. (1990). *Institutions, Institutional Change and Economic Performance.* Cambridge University Press.

Piquet, C. (2004). The Suez Company's Concession in Egypt, 1854–1956: Modern Infrastructure and Local Economic Development, *Enterprise and Society,* Vol. 5.

Platt, D. C. M. (1972). *Latin America and British Trade, 1806–1914.* London.

Pointon, A. C. (1964). *Bombay Burmah Trading Corporation 1863–1963.* Southampton: The Millbrook Press.

Roberts, B. (1988). *Cecil Rhodes, Flawed Colossus.* New York: Norton.

Roy, T. (2006). *The Economic History of India, 1857–1947.* Oxford University Press.

Safarian, A. E. (1993). *Multinational Enterprise and Public Policy.* Aldershot: Edward Elgar.

Sampson, A. (1972). *The Sovereign State: The Secret History of ITT.* London: Hodder and Stoughton.

Schlesinger, S., and Kinzer, S. (1982). *Bitter Fruit: The Untold Story of the American Coup in Guatemala.* Harvard University Press.

Schoenberg, R. J. (1985). *Geneen.* New York: Norton.

Sluyterman, K. E. (2005). *Dutch Enterprise in the Twentieth Century: Business Strategies in a Small Economy.* London: Routledge.

Stanley, D. K. (1994). *For the Record: The United Fruit Company's Sixty-six Years in Guatemala.* Guatemala City: Editorial Antigua.

Stopford, J. M., Strange, S., and Henley, J.S., Eds. (1991). *Rival States, Rival Firms: Competition for World Market Shares.* Cambridge University Press.

Sutherland, D. (2003). *China's Large Enterprises and the Challenge of Late Industrialization.* London: Routledge Curzon.

Thomas, H. (1971). *Cuba: The Pursuit of Freedom*. New York: Harper & Row.

Tomlinson, B.R. (1989). British Business in India, 1860–1970 (R.P.T. Davenport-Hines and G. Jones, Eds.). *British Business in Asia Since 1860*. Cambridge University Press.

United Nations (2004). *World Investment Report*.

Wade, R. (1990). *Governing the Market*. Princeton University Press.

Webster, A. (1998). *Gentlemen Capitalists: British Imperialism in South East Asia 1770–1890*. London: Tauris Academic Studies.

Whitley, R. (1992). *Business Systems in East Asia: Firms, Markets and Societies*. London: Sage.

Williams, E. (1992). *The Penguin History of Latin America*. London: Penguin.

Wilkins, M. (1970). *The Emergence of Multinational Enterprise: American Business Abroad from the Colonial Era to 1914*. Harvard University Press.

Wilkins, M. (1974). *The Maturing of Multinational Enterprise: American Business Abroad from 1914 to 1970*. Harvard University Press.

Wolmar, C. (2009). *Blood, Iron and Gold: How the Railways Transformed the World*. London: Atlantic.

Yonekawa, S. (1990). *General Trading Companies: A Comparative and Historical Perspective*. Tokyo: United Nations University Press.

Yule & Co., Andrew (1964). *Andrew Yule & Co.* London.

Zanden, J.L. van, Jonker, J., Howarth, S., Sluyterman, K. (2004). *A History of Royal Dutch Shell*. Oxford University Press (four volumes).

PART II

Operating in Emerging Markets: A Step-by-Step Guide

I*n the previous chapters, we have introduced the concept of emerging markets, outlining their characteristics and explaining how they differ from developed economies. Acknowledging that "emerging markets" is an encompassing description, which includes a broad variety of economies, we looked at factors that tend to be common across them, such as having a population that is, on average, younger than that of Japan or the U.S.*

In Chapter 1, "What Are Emerging Markets?," we provided a brief description of the different groups of emerging markets that researchers and market analysts have identified, ranging from "Third World" to the BRICS and Frontier Markets. A detailed reference list with definitions of these is provided in the Appendix. Chapter 2, "Markets and Institutions," undertook a historical review of emerging markets through two distinct phases of the global economy: 1850–1914 and 1948–1980. Chapter 3, "A Historical Perspective," examined the role of markets and institutions. To quote the title of Part I, we have "opened the black box of emerging markets," attempting to grasp the most important features of the subject. Now that we have a better idea of what emerging markets are, we shall discuss how business functions in these contexts.

In this part of the book, we present our conceptual model (Figure II.1)—a step-by-step analytical approach to business in emerging markets, which we developed working closely with practitioners and scholars in the field. Its aim is to equip managers and entrepreneurs with an easily applicable tool to develop their emerging-markets strategies. It also provides business students with a practical understanding of how management theories can be combined and applied to operate in emerging markets. The model is composed of the following steps:

- Identifying the Determinants of Attractiveness for each market

- Examining the other features of these markets using the Four Macro Dimensions tool

- Examining business risk

- Developing a strategy to target different segments of emerging markets clients

Chapter 4, "The Determinants of Attractiveness and the Four Dimensions," discusses the Determinants of Attractiveness and the Macro Dimensions. Risk and strategy are discussed in Chapter 5, "Managing Risk," and the Conclusion. Finally, developing strategies to tackle emerging-market clients is split across two chapters: Chapter 6, "Targeting Emerging Market Clients I: The Rich and the Middle Classes," looks at targeting elite and middle-class clients, and Chapter 7, "Targeting Emerging Market Clients II: Strategies for the Base of the Pyramid," tackles strategies for targeting the mass market or clients at the bottom of the pyramid.

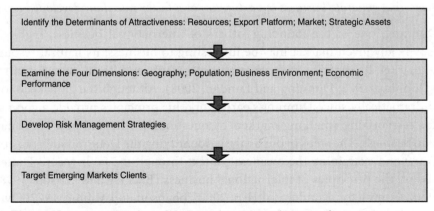

Figure II.1 Conceptual model: a step-by-step evaluation of emerging markets.

4

The Determinants of Attractiveness and Four Dimensions

Introduction

In Part I, we outlined the elements that distinguish emerging markets from developed economies, ranging from incomes to economic sophistication, demography, and infrastructure. We made clear that there is no precise or scientifically proven way to define which country is or is not an emerging market. Emerging markets are the majority of countries in the world; they are effectively all countries bar the few economies and geographic regions that have thus far concentrated most of the wealth production and consumption (North America, Europe, Japan, Australia, and New Zealand) and a few that have joined the ranks of developed economies during the last decades (South Korea, Singapore, Hong Kong, Taiwan, and Israel). What matters most for us is that emerging markets are changing in ways that generate business opportunities at a faster rate than developed economies.

John Dunning, one of the founding fathers of international business, highlights key reasons why any given market may be interesting to business: its natural resources, its internal market, its capacity to serve as an export hub, and its endowment of strategic assets (Dunning, 1988; Dunning and Lundan, 2008). Although the global economy has evolved dramatically since Dunning's early work, his principles provide a good starting point for categorizing emerging markets by questioning why and how they may be of interest to business. The steps of our analysis, identifying the Determinants of Attractiveness (DoA) and examining the business context through the Four Macro Dimensions, are based on the principles of international business (Buckley and Casson, 1998; Dunning, 1998; Contractor, Kundu, and Hsu, 2002; Johanson and Vahlne, 1977; Oviatt and McDougall, 1994; Rugman and Verbeke, 2004). In the following sections, we outline the four main reasons that make emerging markets attractive to business and explain how to identify these drivers of attractiveness.

Natural Resources

As we anticipated in the first chapter, the abundant natural resources found in many emerging markets have long been attractive to business. A brief walk through history thus serves well as a starting point to discuss this specific issue: the first private firms to have operations in multiple markets, such as the British and Dutch East India Companies, internationalized to emerging markets rather than expanding their operations in Europe (Chaudhuri, 2006). In terms of natural resource availability, it made sense to establish their businesses in Asia because they specialized in trading tea, spices, and other goods that were not available in Europe but abundant there. The challenges were also abundant; they were investing and trading in parts of the world that were relatively unknown, where they were obliged to draw maps of the territories where they operated, create the infrastructure needed to transport the goods they traded, make deals with local political constituencies, and negotiate little-known tropical diseases. Despite this, they expanded by hiring linguists and creating armies to defend their businesses (they were also responsible for several less noble affairs, such as fostering local wars, though this is not, at this point, relevant for our discussion). The reasons for embarking on such a risky business were all related to natural resources. They are not far different, for example, from Shell's reasons for operating in the highly unstable Niger Delta.

The trade in tea, pepper, and silk used to be a key driver of the world economy. Businesses engaged in this trade attracted investment and stimulated the formation of financial instruments to provide credit and insurance. Searching for spices and other sources of precious exotic products led to the missions that explored and mapped the world, the establishment of new trading routes, and, notably, the development of the first approximations to multinational enterprises such as the British and Dutch East India Companies (Sen, 1998; Robins, 2006). Modern capitalism does not revolve around trading *these* goods anymore. It does, however, continue to rely on resources that are scattered around the world. Our modern economy is very resource intensive: metals, woods, and minerals are needed to build houses and factories, cell phones, and computers. Sources of energy, especially oil and gas, are needed to power these factories as well as the trains and trucks that transport inputs and finished goods around the world.

Just as adventurous traders traveled around dangerous, sometimes war-ravaged areas to find new sources of pepper and silk during the 1300s to the 1600s, today specialized companies venture into inaccessible and conflict-prone areas searching for untapped sources of natural resources. Finding and extracting resources is necessary for our societies to continue to function in the way we have grown used to, and even more so for emerging economies to converge and become wealthier. It is not a coincidence that China's rapid growth has also generated a surge in demand for iron, oil, gas, wood, and other materials.

That fact that commodity prices have increased by almost 150 percent since the year 2000 illustrate the extent of this phenomenon (Dobbs, 2011).

Developed economies are become gradually more efficient in their use of resources. Yet, they continue to rely on oil and gas for heating and energy and on metals, minerals, wood, and plastics for their manufacturing (see Figure 4.1 and Table 4.1).

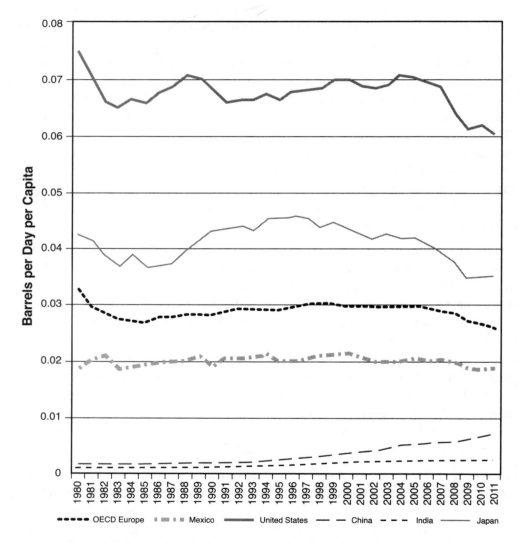

Figure 4.1 Per-capita petroleum consumption (barrels per day per person).

Source: U.S. Energy Information Administration

Table 4.1 Petroleum and Gas Consumption

	Petroleum Consumption				Gas Consumption			
	Total		Per Capita		Total		Per Capita	
	Thousand Barrels per Day		Barrels per Day Per Person		Billion Cubic Feet		Thousand Cubic Feet per Person	
	1980	*2011*	*1980*	*2011*	*1980*	*2011*	*1980*	*2011*
World	63,120	87,421	0.0158	0.0127	52,943	11,2607*	13.26	16.52*
USA	17,056	18,835	0.0749	0.0604	19,877	24,365	87.32	78.11
OECD Europe	14,640	14,284	0.0323	0.0260	9,300	19,878*	20.54	36.39*
Japan	4,960	4,464	0.0425	0.0349	903	3,976	77.33	311.07
Mexico	1,270	2,133	0.0188	0.0188	799	2,089	11.82	18.37
China	1,765	9,790	0.0018	0.0073	505	4,624	0.51	3.43
India	643	3,292	0.0009	0.0027	51	2,158	0.07	1.79

Data Source: U.S. Energy Information Administration

In some cases, technological advances lead companies to switch from using abundant resources to more efficient, scarcer, or more difficult to produce inputs. Audi, a parent of the Volkswagen corporation, makes intensive use of aluminum, a more expensive and energy-intensive input than steel for its vehicles, as it permits weight saving. Toyota's hybrid propulsion system uses batteries and components that contain rare minerals, mostly sourced from China and Latin America. Most of these inputs are too costly to recycle (plastics, wood, metals) or are not recyclable (oil and gas). As a result, it is likely that the world will use an ever-growing quantity of resources. As it happens, the vast shares of these resources are located in emerging markets. Searching for them and extracting them is a multibillion, high-tech business that involves thousands of specialized companies.

Resource extraction—especially that of minerals, gas and oil—is capital and technology intensive. It requires high-tech equipment, which is costly and sophisticated. Most of the sophisticated technology used in the oil, gas, and mining industries is produced by companies based in developed economies, though both China and Brazil have local companies capable of performing high-tech extraction operations. There are, and there will continue to be, great opportunities in emerging markets for businesses that specialize in resource extraction—for example, companies developing the exploration technology needed to find new gas and oil fields.

Emerging markets are not just rich in nonrenewable resources, such as oil, gas, and minerals. Many are also rich in fertile land. In some cases, as with the tea and spices imported by the British East India Company, they are of interest to businesses because their climatic conditions are suited to producing crops that cannot grow in the temperate climates of Europe, North America, and Japan, which for now remain the largest consumers. Coffee and cocoa are prime examples of crops that could not grow in North America, Europe, and Japan, although these countries account for most of the global consumption (see Figure 4.2).

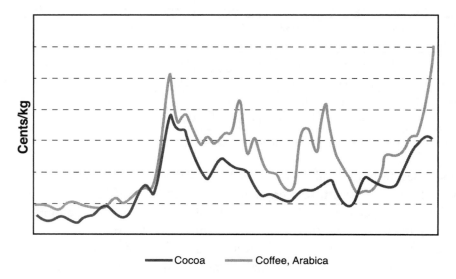

Figure 4.2 Annual nominal prices of selected commodities (cents per kilogram).

Data Source: Global Economic Monitor, World Bank

In order to make chocolate and sell coffee in China, as in the U.S., you need a supplier of coffee or cocoa beans, which means doing business in an emerging market or buying from a trader who does. The interest for businesses here is not just in locations where export crops have been grown for centuries, such as Colombia or Costa Rica for coffee. Searching for new locations where high-value-added crops can be grown is also of interest, as is looking for opportunities to cooperate with local farmers to increase the quality of their crops and their yield. There are thus opportunities for buyers of coffee and cocoa as well as for producers of agribusiness equipment and services.

Other emerging markets are key global producers of grains, meat, vegetable oils, rice, and fish—products that are farmed in the Triad, but that require either intensive and costly labor or large extensions of fertile land. Brazil, for example, has already become the world leader in soy and meat production, whereas Thailand and Vietnam lead global rice production. Developed economies continue to produce agricultural commodities only because they heavily subsidize their farmers and protect them by means of import duties and other measures. Rice, grain, maize, sugar, and meat produced in emerging markets are dramatically cheaper than anything produced in Europe, the U.S., or Japan, if we allow for the subsidies that farmers receive. In some cases, such as beef production, emerging markets are competitive exporters in spite of such subsidies.

In Europe, there is already a strong pressure to reduce subsidies on agricultural commodities because, thus far, they have been granted disproportionally in favor of old members of the European Union (France, Italy, Germany, the UK, Spain, etc.). Eastern European countries, notably Poland, have poorer farmers and a less productive but also less costly agriculture. Yet, they have received only a minor share of the agricultural funds allocated by the Union. Pressures from Eastern European countries to get access to agricultural subsidies are likely to cause a fall in the overall level of protection granted to agriculture, which will entail a shift of the production of cheap, generic agricultural goods toward the Eastern European members of the Union and also more imports from outside of the Union.

At the global level, demand for food has been steadily increasing since the 1990s, as have the prices of all commodities. Energy prices have increased before in history—for example, in 1973, as a result of the formation of the Organization of the Petroleum Exporting Countries (OPEC). Food prices, on the other hand, declined steadily for 50 years after the Second World War as a result of many factors, such as the restoration of agricultural production in Western and Eastern Europe, the widespread mechanization of agriculture, and the introduction of new technology, notably high-yield seeds and irrigation systems. Food prices, however, began to rise in the late 1990s and have continued to do so, reversing the previous trend (see Figure 4.3).

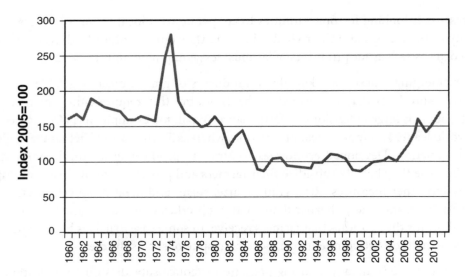

Figure 4.3 Annual real prices of food commodities.

Data Source: Global Economic Monitor, World Bank

The reason for this is twofold: first, global population growth, and, second, the economic success of many emerging markets. As Brazil, India, and China become wealthier, millions of their inhabitants are experiencing an increase in their incomes. They are consuming more meat and fish—in fact, more food in general. As a result, demand for food has boomed beyond what population growth would have suggested. When demand for a set of goods increases faster than its historical trend, it outstrips supply, generating a rise in prices—exactly what we have seen happen in the case of food prices.

When prices increase, it becomes profitable to cultivate more land, develop new fields, and in some cases switch to more valuable crops and invest in new technologies and methods of production. All in all, food production has become an expanding and more attractive business than it used to be. And it is a business that is driven by expanding demand from emerging markets and new sources of supply based in emerging markets. Europe and Japan's agro production is insufficient to serve domestic markets and is heavily subsidized. Economic stagnation may lead to these regions lowering their subsidies, which would open the market for several products, such as sugar and rice. Products which emerging markets can produce more efficiently.

There are many areas where the climatic conditions would allow for the cultivation of goods that have traditionally been grown mainly in Europe and the U.S., such as oranges, lemons, grapes, olives, and the production of related processed goods—juices, wines, and olive oil. This in itself is a great opportunity for agribusinesses. Countries such as Argentina and Chile are experimenting with the production of citrus fruit and olives, developing new competencies as they have already done in wine. North African countries also have a great potential for becoming global producers of grapes, citrus fruit, and vegetables and benefit from much lower labor costs than European countries. Lebanon, Armenia, Syria, and even areas of Iran and Afghanistan were historically important producers of wine, and could return to being so. The U.S., Canada, Australia, and New Zealand remain competitive producers of grains and meat, but they may find it increasingly difficult to compete with Brazilian and African farmers who are adopting similar techniques and machinery.

Emerging markets are already very important in the global production of food and have the potential to expand their role. Chinese agriculture, for example, is characteristically old fashioned, unproductive, small scale, and low tech. Chinese farmers are poorer on average than urban dwellers. They are affected by strong state regulations that limit their capacity to borrow, invest, and move across regions, and large food buyers depress the prices at which farmers can sell. China has modernized its industry and services but not its agriculture. It has only limited the extent to which poor farmers can migrate to cities in order to contain the formation of slums and excessive urban poverty. It has succeeded in avoiding the slums that characterize most emerging market cities but it has failed to ensure greater productivity in farming. As a result, China's imports of food continue to rise. If the Chinese government, worried about food security, decided to modernize its agricultural industry, China could also become a much larger and modern player in food production. A graphic example of the extent to which emerging markets are rich in opportunities in the agricultural sector is Vietnam, a country that in about 20 years became one of the largest coffee producers in the world, thanks to targeted policies and aggressive business strategies.

To summarize this section, most of the world's resources are located in emerging markets. They are rich in energy sources, metals, and also fertile land. Historically this has been the primary and most basic of reasons that makes emerging markets attractive to business. There are opportunities for the exploration of new sources of resources in existing locations, for searches in new, yet unexplored locations, and for more efficient production using new technology and methods in existing locations.

Export Platforms

Emerging markets are not just attractive for their mineral riches, as they once were to the Spanish conquistadores. They are also attractive platforms for producing and exporting a broad range of products and services. The personal computers we used to type this manuscript were assembled in emerging markets. Their hard disks, RAM memory, DVD readers, and other components were designed and produced by companies based in Taiwan, which have production units in Shenzhen, China. The software companies that developed the programs we have used for our analyses have large offices in India, Brazil, Costa Rica, Uruguay, and the Czech Republic.

Since the 1990s, the global structure of manufacturing has changed. Up to the 1990s, most manufacturing was concentrated in the U.S., Japan, Germany, Canada, Italy, South Korea, France, and a few other economies. Since then, a few notable geopolitical events have taken place that have contributed to changing the spatial organization of industrial production (Amsden, 2003). First was the collapse of the Soviet bloc, which brought into the global market several economies that had thus far been isolated. The end of communism in Eastern Europe and the ex–Soviet Republics meant not only the opening of markets but also the privatization of several businesses, especially utilities and telecommunication. This helped ex-communist countries modernize their economies while creating attractive investment opportunities for business.

Second, since the 1990s most economies in the world lowered their tariff barriers on manufacturing, opening their markets to imported finished goods and intermediary inputs. Several countries, including China, signed multilateral trade agreements such as the WTO (see Figure 4.4 and Box 4.1).

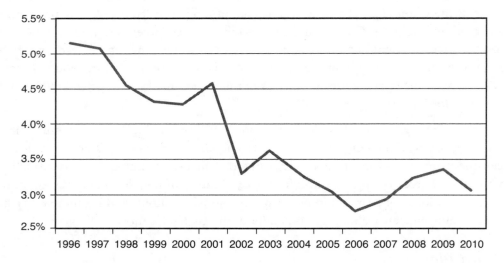

Figure 4.4 World's tariff rate applied—weighted mean, manufactured products (%).

Data Source: World Development Indicators & Global Development Finance, World Bank

Box 4.1: Trade Barriers Definitions

Tariffs: Customs duties on merchandise imports, otherwise defined as import taxes. Levied either on an ad valorem basis (percentage of the value of the good imported) or on a specific basis (e.g., $7 per 100 kg). Tariffs give price advantage to similar locally produced goods and raise revenues for the government. The vast majority of countries in the world have import taxes of different types. Only a few countries, however, tax exports because this can have negative effects on local companies and on overall economic performance. Argentina is a notable case of a country that often taxes its agricultural exporters.

Non-Tariffs Barriers

Incentives: Different means (monetary or otherwise) used by governments to stimulate or discourage external trade (e.g., import licenses, fixed prices, and government procurement only from local firms).

Subsidies: Benefits conferred on a firm either to encourage international trade (exports or imports) or domestic production of a given product or service.

Health and safety regulations: Measures established by government authorities to ensure that export and import products do not harm human, animal, or plant health and food safety (e.g., sanitary and phytosanitary conditions). Although their function is not to limit trade, per se, they are often used for this purpose.

Environmental regulations: Measures established to ensure that products or services do not pose environmental threats (e.g., the regulation or prohibition of import or export products related to polluting substances). Again, these measures are not intended to be trade limiting but are often used for this purpose.

Source: WTO Glossary

Many others signed bilateral free-trade agreements—for example, the agreements of Chile and Colombia with the U.S. Others entered into regional trade agreements, such as Mexico with Canada and the U.S., and Eastern European countries joining the European Union. These agreements were designed to facilitate international trade. They pushed countries to lower their tariff barriers and protectionist measures while improving protection over intellectual property rights. The result of this was a dramatic increase in trade in manufactured goods from 1990 (see Figure 4.5). Agriculture was liberalized to a much lesser extent, partly because agro lobbies from developed economies pushed for continuous protection from products grown in cheaper emerging-market locations.

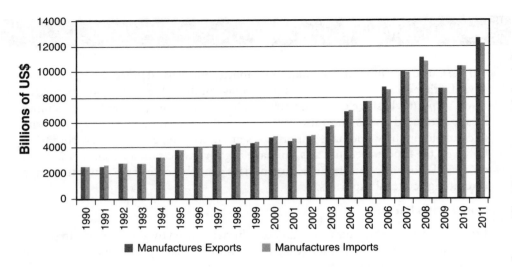

Figure 4.5 World manufactures trade (billions of US$).

Data Source: World Development Indicators & Global Development Finance, World Bank

Third, barriers to investments also declined as emerging markets sought to attract capital and technology from the Triad. Before the 1990s, most investment went from Triad economies to other Triad economies (see Figures 4.6 and 4.7).

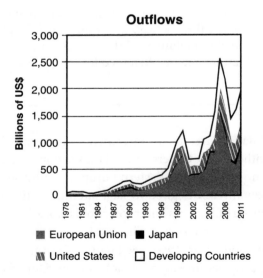

Figure 4.6 Foreign direct investment in current US$: outflows.

Data Source: World Development Indicators & Global Development Finance, World Bank

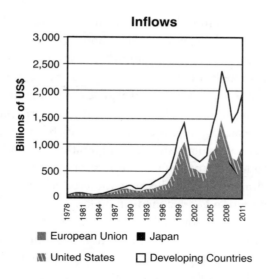

Figure 4.7 Foreign direct investment in current US$: inflows.

Data Source: World Development Indicators & Global Development Finance, World Bank

The Triad had the largest markets, they were also the most stable, and they were often growing faster than emerging markets. Several of them (for example, the U.S. and Japan) also had a large population. Besides being attractive markets, the Triad economies were also more integrated economically and geopolitically: they were military allies, had lower barriers to trade, were signatories of several trade agreements, and had much lesser, if any, controls on foreign investment. By contrast, most emerging markets had strong regulations over foreign investment. As they gradually relaxed these regulations, making it easier to invest, operate, and repatriate profits, foreign investors rushed in. Most new flows of investment between the 1990s and 2012 have been toward emerging markets. New factories and new technology have allowed them to become more productive. Hence, their incomes have increased, attracting yet more new investment. Finally, technological advances, especially the diffusion of Internet- and intranet-based communication systems, now allow for faster transactions, more efficient logistics, and the coordination of longer and more complex supply chains. New technology also reduces the costs of communicating and concluding transactions.

Transaction costs are the costs needed to establish a commercial exchange—for example, legal costs, costs of exchanging information, costs related to taxes, costs for transporting the products traded, and the costs of complying with regulations. The higher the transaction costs, the more expensive it is to trade. The lower the transaction costs, the more individuals and companies are willing to trade, and hence the greater the potential gains from specialization. A simple example of this is the use of the Web as a source of information for buyers. Gathering information about prices and product characteristics previously required physical visits to a broad range of shops. It was time consuming and provided information limited to the number of shops visited and the spatial area covered. Gathering information by phone could also be costly and limited to the directories that one had at hand. Now a potential buyer can gather information about the product she intends to buy (for example, a new chair), the availability of different models, how they are ranked by other consumers, and the comparative prices of different shops without moving from in front of the computer. The cost of accessing and transmitting information has declined dramatically. If she buys the product online, that also means the cost of making the transaction has declined—it no longer requires a journey to the shop, which costs both time and petrol or public transport fares. As a result, one can buy more products, and more importantly buy them in a more informed way. And as consumers become more informed, companies also have more tools to make their goods visible and have a greater incentive to compete on both quality and prices.

At the inter-firm business level, this is even more important. A German-based producer of machinery (let's say a company making machines to cut glass) can now search for component suppliers not only in its neighboring areas but across the globe. The purchasing department of the firm can use industrial forums and contact other companies that use similar components to get an initial idea about the existing suppliers. It can then contact the firms directly and get a range of quotes in a very short timespan. Specifications and even 3D designs can be sent over the Internet. In other words, finding a supplier or a client has become significantly easier, faster, and cheaper for both individuals and companies. It has also become easier to invest and to trade across barriers thanks to the geopolitical changes outlined in the previous parts of this section.

The fall in trade and investment barriers and technological change have opened up new possibilities for businesses based in developed economies. American manufacturers have led the way in experimenting with new manufacturing business models. They have broken down their production and supply chain. They have generated modular product architectures—products that can be assembled by putting together a few self-contained modules, as opposed to products made by a large number of components, which have to be constructed altogether. They began to outsource different components of complex consumer goods—the chairs and transmission systems of cars, the microprocessors and hard disks of personal computers, the screens of televisions. Designing new products, which could more easily be produced in different locations, led them to the next step—offshoring.

Taking advantage of the lower trade barriers, from the 1990s American manufacturers began offshoring the production of a growing share of their goods, either by buying factories located abroad or using plants owned by other firms. Intel, the world's leading microchip manufacturer, has factories in the U.S., its home base, but it has also offshored production to fully owned subsidiaries in locations where costs are lower, including China, Ireland, Israel, Costa Rica, and Vietnam. Nokia, one of the world's largest mobile phone producer, is based in Finland. It has factories in both Finland and China, and it also outsources the production of some components to companies based in Taiwan and China (see Table 4.2).

Table 4.2   Intel and Nokia Manufacturing Locations

Intel		Nokia
Fabrication Plant Sites	*Assembly/Test Sites*	*Production Facilities*
USA	USA	China
Israel	Costa Rica	Brazil
Ireland	China	China
China	Malaysia	Hungary
	Vietnam	South Korea
		India
		Mexico
		Vietnam

Data Source: Intel, Nokia

European and Japanese producers also affected by high labor costs, as well as costs such as social security and costs incurred because of regulation in their home countries, followed this trend by relocating their factories and outsourcing many of their inputs to other companies. It was more profitable to produce in emerging markets—and it still is.

The fundamental reason for this is that emerging markets remain poorer. A factory worker in Thailand earns less than in the U.S. (and has a lower cost of living); hence, it is cheaper to produce the same good in Thailand than in the U.S. The vast majority of emerging markets have lower labor costs than the U.S., Japan, and South Korea, which are home to the world's leading electronics and software producers. Yet, it is economically feasible to produce electronic manufactures, such as smartphones and video game consoles, only in a few emerging markets. If the cost of labor explained the whole picture, it would make sense to produce *any* good in *any* emerging market. In some fields of manufacturing that are not very high tech and are labor intensive, such as clothing manufacture, this holds true; countries with lower costs of labor are more competitive. However, only a few emerging markets have a large pool of labor with the necessary skills to work in factories producing electrical items. China, Thailand, and Vietnam are among them. Geography also plays a role. Transporting bulky and not very valuable goods for long distances is expensive and takes time. This explains why North African countries, such as Tunisia, which have higher costs of labor than China or Vietnam, are in fact important export hubs for companies producing clothes that target the European market.

There are other reasons why only *some* emerging markets make excellent platforms for global production. Having a well-functioning export-supporting infrastructure helps: if it takes too long to take goods from the factory to the port, or if ports take too long to load containers, the cost advantages gained by having cheaper workers may be lost. This is especially true for the export of manufactures that require imported inputs—for example, a video game console assembled in China, incorporating a microchip produced in Israel, a memory card made in Thailand, and the rest of the components made in Japan. The infrastructure in most emerging markets is poor, and this hinders them from becoming globally competitive export platforms. Some, however, such as China, have already passed many Triad economies in terms of their export supporting infrastructure. Others, such as Brazil and Colombia, are investing large sums to catch up.

Emerging markets often have investment incentives to attract multinational companies in specific areas; these vary across countries and sectors. They include free land, free or discounted utilities, ad hoc infrastructural improvements, and discounted or zero cor- porate tax, among others. Markets outside the Triad also tend to have less stringent labor and environmental regulations, which mean lower costs of complying with local rules. When a company is choosing a location for a manufacturing plant, a key step is to fig- ure out trade rules. Countries that have high barriers to trade in the form of import or export taxes are not only costlier but also more complex to manage as export bases. Most countries in the world have some form of import taxation. Several emerging markets rely on import taxes as their main source of government revenue and are hence unwilling to lower it. Some other emerging markets, such as Argentina, also tax their exports to col- lect government revenue.

Whether a country is engaged in bilateral or multilateral free-trade agreements is another important factor in choosing the right location for export-oriented production. Mexico, for example, is fully integrated with the U.S. market, being part of the North American Free Trade Agreement (NAFTA). All of the businesses, local and foreign, that export to the U.S. are already integrated into the infrastructure and regulatory systems. Mexico's southern neighbor, Guatemala, has much lower labor costs, but has a much less func- tional infrastructure and is not part of NAFTA, which makes it more complex in terms of the regulations you have to navigate to export from there.

Lower labor costs, easier regulation, lower taxes, and in some cases incentives and subsidies mean that the costs of producing a good can be considerably lower in an emerging market than in developed economies, unless there are limitations to the import of inputs. Most complex goods incorporate components produced in different parts of the world. Countries that have import duties generally fail to become export hubs because they make it more costly and complicated to access the needed inputs. China, for example, is very competitive as a hub for the manufacturing of consumer electronics, a sector on which there have very low trade barriers. However, it is still more costly to make cars in China than in Europe because it entails paying import taxes on key imported components. As a result, there are relatively few emerging markets that are competitive export platforms, and this varies across products. Thailand, for example, is a competitive export platform for cars, whereas Vietnam is a competitive export platform for microchips and apparel (see Table 4.3).

Table 4.3   Exports of Transport Equipment, Automotive Products, Textiles, and Apparel (Millions of US$)

Thailand			
	2000	2005	2011
Machinery and transport equipment	29,997	49,192	85,848
Automotive products	2,417	7,983	18,279
Textiles	1,958	2,764	4,072
Clothing	3,759	4,085	4,561
Vietnam			
	2000	2005	2011
Machinery and transport equipment	1,256	3,130	18,690
Automotive products	8	161	640
Textiles	298	725	3,772
Clothing	1,821	4,681	13,154

Data Source: World Trade Organization, Statistics Database

The main point here is that, although Triad markets are not growing, they remain large markets. Despite the current economic climate, Triad economies remain very rich as well as costly bases for producing manufactured goods. By contrast, emerging markets are growing, and some are also competitive locations to manufacture a range of products, depending on the good and the market they target. Thailand and Vietnam, for example, are fast-growing markets and they are also competitive export hubs. China is one of the largest markets in the world, and it is growing fast, and it remains a competitive base for manufacturing goods aimed at other markets. Its growth means that labor is becoming more expensive, gradually eroding its advantage vis-à-vis other emerging economies.

Other emerging markets, such as Brazil and India, are fast growing as consumer markets but they are not convenient export hubs for manufacturing. Why? First, they have a complex, and hence costly, regulatory framework. Second, only a small share of the population has the skills needed to work in manufacturing. Third, they have high corporate and income taxes, though they do also have zones where they give concessions on them. Fourth, they have high import taxes that make it costly and inefficient to produce there. Fifth, they have high levels of unionization that make it difficult to lower salaries as more people get trained and enter the workforce. Lastly, their infrastructure does not suit the needs of export-oriented manufacturing: their ports have long lead times, their road networks get clogged with traffic, and their electricity supply is less reliable than in other locations.

Emerging markets are also competitive locations for the production of services. India, the Philippines, and Colombia are, for example, key hubs for call centers and information technology support. Companies locate offices in these economies that provide remote assistance to clients and also more complex services, such as software programming and technical advisory services. Another example is medical services. Costa Rica, Thailand, and India are net exporters of medical services. They provide high-tech facilities for foreign patients. Having cheaper nurses and doctors, and often cheaper taxation regimes, allows them to operate at lower costs than private clinics based in the Triad. Again, only a few emerging markets have the necessary pool of trained medical staff to compete in this field. Yet, their business has been growing exponentially in the last ten years, as the aging population of the Triad seeks alternatives to the long queues of public sector health systems and increasingly costly private hospitals. In the service sector, emerging markets also have an immense potential for becoming attractive locations to which to outsource and offshore operations.

Summarizing this section, the fall in average trade barriers together with technological and managerial innovations have allowed firms to outsource and offshore parts of their activities to more cost-effective locations. As a result, a large and growing share of the world's manufacturing and services now originate from emerging markets. However, only a few emerging markets are competitive locations for export-oriented production. For the export of services, skilled, low-cost multilingual workers, such as doctors and software developers, that can work in English are needed. In manufacturing, good infrastructure, skilled, low-cost factory workers and low trade barriers are the key.

Markets

The attractiveness of emerging markets as markets is a fairly recent phenomenon. Though China has attracted foreign investment since the 1980s, a large share of it has been to establish export platforms that produce manufactured goods consumed in the Triad. Other smaller economies have become attractive now mainly because of the crisis that has affected both the U.S. and Europe, the two largest economies of the Triad.

The reason why Triad businesses historically focused on the Triad is that these were the largest markets. The investments, resource extraction, and relocation of manufacturing and services to emerging markets fueled economic growth in the Triad economies. The share of the world's wealth concentrated in the Triad economies has been declining now for a couple of decades. Hence, not only is the Triad not growing, its share of the global economy is shrinking (see Figure 4.8). The opposite is true of emerging markets. More and more of the world's wealth is being created and consumed in emerging markets. In other words, emerging markets are becoming attractive to business not only as sources of cheap labor and resources, but also for their consumers.

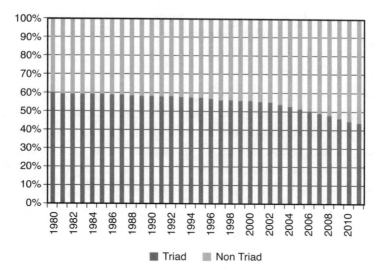

Figure 4.8 World GDP.

Data Source: World Development Indicators & Global Development Finance, World Bank

In 2010, for the first time in history, the U.S. has been overtaken as the largest market for cars. This top spot has been taken by China. China not only produces, but also consumes, more cars than the U.S. The U.S. continues to be the largest market in terms of value, as the average car sold in the U.S. is more expensive than the average car sold in China. But this too may soon change as Chinese average incomes continue to rise and many more millions of Chinese households eagerly save to pursue the motor car dream.

There are two dimensions to the development of emerging markets as consumer markets: their size and the dynamism of their growth. Some emerging markets, such as China, India, and Brazil, have large populations. They are naturally large markets, whose total economy has thus far been limited in size only by the fact that their average citizens were very poor in comparison to an American, European, or Japanese consumer. As incomes rise, these markets will overtake most Triad economies. China has already become the second largest economy in the world, overtaking Germany and Japan, the two industrial powerhouses of Europe and Asia. Among the top ten economies in the world we now find not only China, but also Brazil, Russia, and India. Other economies, such as Turkey, are catching up fast, whereas France, the UK, and Italy are struggling to remain in the top league as both their economies and populations are failing to grow.

India, Indonesia, the Philippines, Vietnam, Mexico, Colombia, Pakistan, and Nigeria are other emerging markets with big populations that have the potential to become very large economies. Even if they remain much poorer in terms of income per capita, their total populations are so large that, assuming they continue to grow even modestly, the total size of their markets will soon match that of the large developed economies, save for the U.S. and perhaps Japan.

The second dimension that matters for the development of local markets is the speed at which they are changing. Business opportunities emerge where incomes increase. The faster they increase, the more consumers diversify their demand. Even in very poor economies, such as Bangladesh, a small rise in incomes would mean dramatic changes in consumption. In this sense, markets that are growing fast are rich in opportunities, even when they do not have as large a population as that of China or Brazil.

It is also important to note that large populations do not necessarily make up integrated or homogenous markets: India, China, Mexico, Brazil, and other large emerging markets have very different regional economies, characterized by diverging incomes, customs, ethnicities, and access to infrastructure. When they grow, they generate a set of individual regional-level opportunities that may be similar in terms of economic value to the opportunities found at the national level in less populous economies such as Kazakhstan.

One of the reasons why emerging markets are becoming large, fast-growing consumer markets is the development of local middle classes. Some scholars estimate that there are already about 2 billion middle-class consumers in emerging markets, and the figure is growing fast (OECD, 2012). As poor people become less poor, they begin investing in shelter, clothing items, televisions, and white goods. They consume more cosmetics, shampoo, and health and beauty products in general. Wherever incomes rise, especially among the poorest 20 to 30 percent of the population, they generate boosts in consumption.

Another way of seeing this is that as poor people rise into the lower middle class, they change the way they live, and, not only do they consume more, but they develop new patterns of consumption. This opens a great window of opportunity for businesses to shape these demand patterns by providing goods and services that are fully targeted to the spending power and needs of the new consumers. These may converge with those of developed economy consumers, or they may be entirely different.

One of the challenges of targeting these new middle classes is that they are not a homogenous group; they range from the family that has just managed to climb above the poverty line to the single professional that just falls short of being among the top 10-percent richest citizens in their country. The former is likely to consume more food and beauty products, and perhaps purchase a few items of kitchenware and shelter-related goods. The latter is likely to emulate the consumption trends seen in the Triad—earning a similar salary as he would in the Triad and spending it on entertainment, new electronic gadgets, fashion goods, property, and perhaps a new car. Hence, we need to take a more nuanced view than simply arguing that emerging markets are attractive because they are producing *a* new middle class. If anything, they are producing different types of new middle *classes*, which alter consumption patterns and which business can profitably target.

It is very difficult to qualify exactly what a middle class is because of relative prices and because the term has different connotations in different countries. An American citizen living on US$2 per day can afford to purchase less than a Malaysian living on the same salary, simply because average prices are higher. Though several scholars try to fix a minimum earning level to qualify as middle class rather than poor, this sort of generalization never gives an accurate picture. It can either underestimate or overestimate the dimension and dynamism of a given consumer market. A better way to look at this is to consider income groups within each consumer market as this picks up people's capacity to spend vis-à-vis other consumers in their same economy.

Summarizing this section, emerging markets are becoming important consumer markets because of their large and young populations and also because their average incomes are growing. They will remain much poorer on a per-capita basis for decades to come. But they will displace Triad economies in terms of total market size. Emerging market success in exporting resources, manufactured products, and services explains why their average incomes have been rising, generating business opportunities for producers of consumer-oriented goods and services.

Strategic Assets

This section explains why emerging markets have thus far lagged behind as locations with attractive strategic assets. It also discusses why this is changing, showing how emerging markets are also developing strategic assets that will make them more attractive to business.

Dunning (1988; 1998) proposes that companies may be interested in investing in a market in order to exploit its strategic assets. Strategic assets are difficult to picture or identify because they are intangible and their value can be subjective. They include knowledge, reputation, and entrepreneurial culture. Strategic assets are so specialized they tend to be concentrated in only a few locations in the world. A clear example can be seen in Italy, which hosts a disproportionate number of car design studios, which, notably, are thriving despite the decline of Italy's car manufacturing business. A history of car racing, together with the Italian flare for design and fashion, contribute to explaining this concentration of activity. The result is that several companies that are not interested in producing or selling in Italy, including Chinese and Indian companies, may invest in Italy to tap into this strategic resource by hiring Italian designers and learning to design better looking cars. The software industry provides another example: having an office in Silicon Valley confers high reputation, even if it may not be as efficient as locating it in Manila or Medellin.

Given that Triad economies have had a long history of investment in research, development, design, and high technology, they still concentrate a high share of the globally attractive strategic assets. They have also had more sophisticated consumers and producers for several decades. Hence, in terms of reputation, it is Triad economies that benefit. A car made in Germany or Japan, for example, benefits from the German and Japanese reputation for engineering and reliability. The opposite applies for a car made in India or China. However, even in this field things are slowly changing.

Emerging markets are developing different strategic assets. Costa Rica, for example, has been experimenting with eco-tourism and sustainable policies for more than 20 years. It is now reaping the benefits from the reputation it has cultivated in this respect, attracting Spanish and biology students as well as tourists in search of the unspoiled natural environments of the rainforests and cloud forests, nature reserves, and yoga retreats. Brazil has been at the forefront of policies to subsidize biofuels since the 1970s, though initially it did so to become less dependent on imported oil, as opposed to environmental concern. As local technology improved and oil prices increased, Brazilian producers of biofuel became not only competitive with gasoline, but also the most eco-sustainable in the world. At present, Brazil is the only country that produces biofuel at market rates without using subsidies and while generating a low carbon footprint. Companies and researchers working on biofuels now use Brazil as a benchmark. Other Latin American countries, such as Venezuela and Mexico, are famous for their soap opera industry—their "tele-novelas" are exported everywhere and they are attracting new investments from Triad producers. India exports its Bollywood movies to several neighboring countries as well as the Indian diaspora around the world, catering to and creating a consumer taste that differs from the Triad-derived Hollywood blockbusters. As emerging markets grow and become more sophisticated economies, they will also develop strategic assets, derived from their historical heritage, their natural resources, and their human skills.

Classifying the Determinants of Attractiveness: Necessary, Highly Desirable, Desirable, and Not Necessary Features

Emerging markets can be attractive to business for their resources, markets, as export hubs, or for their strategic assets. There are specific traits that distinguish economies from each other—one example being their most important exports in terms of value. Economies that export mainly products based on natural resources, such as wood, oil, or minerals, are likely to be rich in resources. Economies that also export manufactured goods are likely to be industrial export hubs. And economies that have a broad range of exports are likely to provide attractive business opportunities in different fields.

Most emerging markets combine several elements. Brazil, for example, is a competitive location for the production of soy and meat, and it is also a large and growing consumer market. Kazakhstan is a prime location for oil extraction and a small but booming consumer market. The fact that emerging markets tend to be attractive for several reasons simultaneously makes it difficult to develop a precise taxonomy, so how can we scan for opportunities in these markets and distinguish them from each other?

Thinking about the Determinants of Attractiveness (resources, export platform, market, and strategic assets) in relation to our business is a good starting point. In order to do so, we need to focus on different aspects of emerging markets and identify whether they are more or less important for a given type of business. We classify these as *necessary, highly desirable, desirable,* and *not necessary* features of the economy (see Figure 4.9 and Table 4.4).

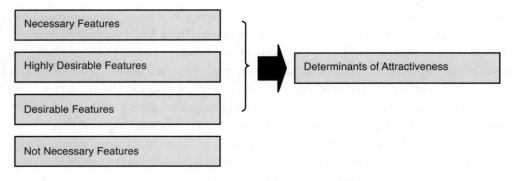

Figure 4.9 The Determinants of Attractiveness.

The preliminary step for this analysis is identifying *necessary* features. In other words, what are the minimum necessary requirements for a given market to be attractive in one of the aforementioned areas (for example, as a platform for service exports)? Drawing on the discussion so far in this chapter, the *necessary* features that shape attractiveness could be the following:

- Resources (land, minerals, oil, gas, forest, tourist sites)
- Skilled labor
- Consumers with growing purchasing power (both private and corporate)
- Strategic assets

Having identified whether a given market has the necessary features to be attractive as a platform for service exports in this instance, we need to look at the other factors that may affect costs. Among these are *highly desirable* factors. For example, to be attractive as a resource exporter, it is *necessary* to have resources, but it is also *highly desirable* to have a regulatory framework that allows investment from foreign companies. To be attractive as a consumer market, it is *necessary* to have a population whose average incomes are growing. It is also *highly desirable* to have a large population, because the larger it is, the larger the potential market. *Highly desirable* features are more numerous and therefore more complex than *necessary* features.

There are other features of economies that may not be *highly desirable,* yet may also influence the attractiveness of a market. We call these *desirable* features. To be an attractive location for the export of information technology (IT) services, it is *necessary* to have a low-cost skilled workforce and it is *highly desirable* to have the needed institutions to support the trade in services (for example, protection of intellectual property rights). Having a good physical infrastructure, such as good roads and airports, is *desirable*, but is not *necessary* or even *highly desirable*. The provision of IT services requires electricity and Internet connections, but companies can, and often do, provide these themselves. India, for example, has long been the leading global exporter of information technology services, and continues to be a very competitive location to offshore services despite recurrent blackouts and gridlocked roads. Because services do not require the flow of physical goods required by manufacturing, the badly congested road system has a relatively minor effect on this kind of business. Furthermore, all companies have private generators to ensure the continuity and stability of the electricity supply. There is also a trend to build campuses to minimize travel for their employees and provision of other services, such as nursery and collective transport, to compensate for infrastructural deficiencies.

Finally, there are features that may be important for a specific type of attractiveness. The availability of fertile land is a *necessary* factor to be attractive as a resource-producing location. It is not *necessary* for any of the other Determinants of Attractiveness. We suggest you try the following exercise.

Use Table 4.4 to think about different markets and rank them according to the features that are *necessary, highly desirable, desirable,* and *not necessary* to be attractive in a certain field. By doing so, you will get a picture of the sort of combined opportunities that businesses may find in emerging markets. For example, an open economy with a small but highly skilled workforce, such as Uruguay, can be an excellent export platform, especially for sophisticated services. A market with a workforce that is on average less skilled than Uruguay but much more numerous and dramatically less costly, such as Vietnam, can be an excellent export platform for labor-intensive manufactures. A country such as Nigeria, with a large but relatively unskilled population, growing average incomes, abundant resources, and a decrepit infrastructure, can be attractive as a resource-exporting location and as a market, though less so for the export of manufactures.

We provide a few examples in this chapter and others throughout the book. We do not rank each market ourselves because emerging markets are changing so fast that our ranking may be outdated before the book is published. Our interest is to provide you with the tools to generate your own rankings and evaluations, which you can update when needed.

Table 4.4 Necessary, Highly Desirable, and Desirable Features

	Resource exploitation	Export-oriented manufacturing	Export-oriented services	Consumer market	Strategic asset
Availability of resources	Necessary	Not needed	Not needed	Not needed	Not needed
High average incomes	Not needed	Not needed	Not needed	Desirable	Not needed
Large population	Not needed	Desirable	Desirable	Highly desirable	Not needed
Young population	Not needed	Desirable	Desirable	Desirable	Not needed
Growing average incomes	Not needed	Not needed	Not needed	Necessary	Not needed
Low inequality	Not needed	Not needed	Not needed	Highly desirable	Not needed
High access to shelter, sanitation, health	Desirable	Desirable	Desirable	Not needed	Not needed
Skilled, low cost labor	Desirable	Necessary	Necessary	Desirable	Highly desirable
Physical infrastructure (roads, electricity, water, ports)	Highly desirable	Necessary	Desirable	Highly desirable	Desirable
Openness to trade	Desirable	Necessary	Desirable	Desirable	Not needed
Openness to foreign investment	Highly desirable	Highly desirable	Highly desirable	Highly desirable	Highly desirable
Supporting institutional framework (e.g., property rights)	Desirable	Desirable	Highly desirable	Desirable	Necessary
Openness to investment	Desirable	Desirable	Desirable	Desirable	Desirable
Macro-economic stability	Desirable	Desirable	Desirable	Desirable	Desirable
Political stability	Desirable	Desirable	Desirable	Desirable	Desirable

Once you have worked through the checklist of the factors that are *necessary, highly desirable, desirable,* and *not necessary,* you can use this table to categorize different markets according to their Determinants of Attractiveness (see Figure 4.10). We suggest a simple method that we have tested and that benefits from its simplicity: ranking the attractiveness of a range of markets for their resources, as export platforms, for their markets, or for their strategic assets on a 1–7 Likert Scale. The Likert Scale is a useful means to reflect subjective judgments about certain issues—in this case, your evaluation of a given market. If you want to do this in a more rigorous way, you can also assign numerical values to the *necessary, highly desirable,* and so on evaluations you provided in Table 4.4, and then add them up and compare them across markets. The market evaluations that add up to higher scores for a specific Determinant of Attractiveness (e.g., as markets) will have a higher Likert Scale value in the tables.

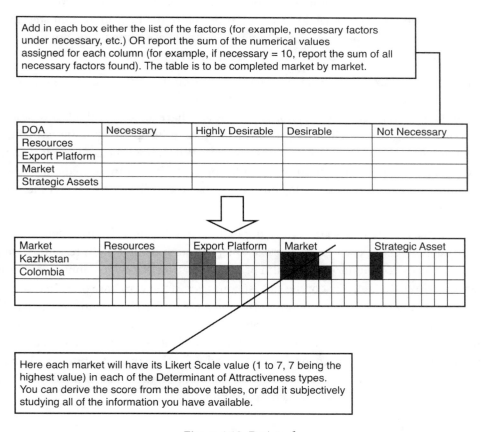

Figure 4.10 DoA tool.

Four Macro Dimensions That Shape Emerging Markets

One of the most common reasons that businesses based in developed economies fail in emerging markets is a lack of understanding of the local context. We believe that the first step for doing business in an emerging market should be identifying the elements that can make a market attractive for certain activities—the Determinants of Attractiveness—and we have provided a simple methodology to do so. We also believe that to understand emerging markets—or any market for that matter—it is essential to build a broader and more multifaceted picture as well as to think about the characteristics that define how the market you are examining differs from other markets in order to ensure opportunities are not missed or challenges underestimated. All of these aspects then need to be brought together to see whether or how they interact with each other, and this is the function of the Four Dimensions tool. An analysis of the Four Macro Dimensions that summarize the features of an economy is therefore the next important step in our model to prepare for business in emerging markets. These dimensions are geography, population, business environment, and economic performance.

To give an example, once we have clarified that an economy (say, Uganda) is oil rich, we know it has the *necessary* feature to be a resource exporter. If we follow the steps outlined in the previous sections, we should by now also have an idea of the *highly desirable* and *desirable* features, ranging from its infrastructure to its openness to investment and trade. But what about other aspects of this market? What about the context? Is its population young or aging? Is it a populous country or not? Though these elements may not be *necessary* for a resource-extracting business per se, they will give us a better idea of the market we will be operating in.

The first three dimensions—geography, population, and business environment—are relatively independent of each other. For example, although being rich in resources would seem to logically contribute to the wealth of the population of a given country, it does not necessarily do so. In fact, most of the richest countries in the world are poor in resources, whereas several resource-rich economies (for instance, Sudan) have impoverished populations. The first three dimensions contribute to shaping national-level economic performance, which feeds back into the characteristics of the population: if an economy is performing well, its average incomes will grow, hence the costs of labor may increase together with the purchasing power of consumers (see Figure 4.11). The following sections provide a brief discussion of each dimension.

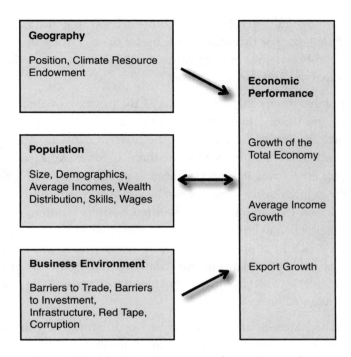

Figure 4.11 The Four Dimensions of emerging markets.

Geography: Land, Location, and Resources

The main way in which countries are defined is by their territory—their place on the map of the world, and the stretch of land they exercise sovereignty upon, at least in theory. This is why we have geography as the first dimension. Geography is also the only dimension that changes very slowly, if at all. Whereas business environments can change rapidly, countries tend not to move! They can be invaded or divided, so geography is not immutable. However, in those cases, the changes are in frontiers and the names of countries, as opposed to the physical characteristics of the territory we are examining. The latter is unlikely to change as fast as characteristics related to population or business environment. A greater problem for analysis of this dimension is related to the unit of analysis: the concepts of borders and national government have only a relative application in some emerging markets. Central governments may not have control over large parts of what is defined as a sovereign country. Where on the map we find a country with clear-cut borders, in reality we may find several regions or areas that are ruled independently from the central government, by groups that exercise effective control by making laws and enforcing them. Nonetheless, most of the available information on emerging markets is collected by multilateral organizations, such as the World Bank, using "countries" as units of analysis. For this reason, it is useful to start using the state as a unit of analysis and only subsequently moving on to smaller units of analysis, ranging from regions to municipalities and barrios.

The first aspect of geography that we consider is the position of emerging economies: are they close to Triad economies? Are they located near strategic navigation routes? Though these factors do not directly affect the Determinants of Attractiveness, they shape the way in which companies can operate there. If, for example, a country is rich in resources but these are located in inaccessible areas and there are no pipelines, ports, or other ways to export them easily, it may be not be viable or worth the expense of extracting them. Libya, an oil-rich country, has benefitted from its location, relatively close to Italy, in that it was possible to build a pipeline to export oil and gas rather than shipping it. Chile, a country rich in copper, benefits from its long coast on the Pacific Ocean, which provides natural export platforms for Asian markets. Proximity to key navigation routes is also an important asset because it provides the opportunity of establishing hubs for refueling and maintenance.

Other aspects related to geography that can be worth considering are natural beauty and historical heritage—does the market have locations that may be developed for tourism? And though it may not seem important to companies interested in oil and other resources, the existence of tourist sites may affect the operations of other types of businesses that rely directly or indirectly on tourism—tourists interested in beautiful natural landscapes are unlikely to appreciate the sight of imposing oil and gas extraction rigs. On the other hand, in areas that have a low potential for attracting tourists, extractive industries can provide an important engine for economic growth and development.

Tourism is a largely underdeveloped industry in emerging markets. Spotting unexploited sites can generate interesting business opportunities. Populous emerging markets such as China, India, and Brazil have a huge potential for developing domestic tourism. Thus far, their tourist industry has been geared toward catering for foreign tourists, mainly from the U.S., Europe, and Japan. Now they have a growing middle class of domestic consumers who will gradually spend more on tourism. In China, the majority of tourists are already domestic, thanks to the enormous size of its population, the existence of different climates and historical sites, and also to the fact that travelling across the country is still novel for most Chinese because it was previously limited by government regulation and low average incomes. In India and Brazil, this could soon be the case as well.

Besides China, India, and Brazil, other populous emerging markets, such as Russia, Indonesia, Vietnam, Turkey, and Mexico, have an array of unique historical and natural locations that can be exploited for tourism. Some of them, such as Brazil, have been very successful at marketing their tourist sites. Others, such as Vietnam, are relatively new to the game. Developing tourist locations, providing services, and catering to the different needs of local and foreign tourists is in itself a challenge for local governments and companies operating in these areas. Emerging markets that are near other, fast-growing emerging markets can also target the latter to attract tourists. Jordan, for example, attracts tourists from the richer United Arab Emirates and Saudi Arabia.

A further element worth investigating is climate. It is of relevance in different ways to a variety of businesses: resource extraction, tourism, to businesses interested in export platforms, and even for identifying new markets for products for pensioners. Is the climate prohibitive to the point that it may require machinery and technologies be specially adapted? Or is it pleasant enough that overseas pensioners may decide to retire there? A country with a pleasant climate is likely to be a preferred destination for expatriates, a positive factor if we intend to use the market as an export platform or to develop knowledge-intensive activities, such as research laboratories and design studios. Locations with extreme climates, such as the Mongolian desert, generate stress for both machinery and personnel and require compensation in the form of higher salaries or investment in special equipment. Technological innovation is making adaptation to climate increasingly possible. However, such adaptations always entail extra costs. And for these reasons it is important to examine climatic and geophysical conditions when developing a strategy to operate in a certain location, even in cases where climate may seem to be a secondary factor for our specific business.

Perhaps the most obvious aspect of the analysis of the Geography dimension is scanning for resources. Mapping the resource endowment of different countries is tricky; most are rich in more than one resource, and information may be jealously guarded or not recorded at all. For emerging markets, it is yet more complicated. In some emerging markets, such as Uganda, the government has little control over regions that may be rich in resources. In such areas, armed groups battle for control of territory among themselves and against the official army or police. In countries such as Libya, this is a relatively recent and hopefully temporary situation. In others, armed violence has been affecting parts of the territory for many years. The borders of the Democratic Republic of Congo (DRC), which are very rich in minerals, have been affected by the presence of multiple armed insurgents for many years, in spite of the presence of a large United Nations peace-keeping mission.

The result of long periods of armed violence is that in several emerging markets there are vast areas of land that have never been fully explored for resources. In addition, government records and reports are often outdated and unreliable, either because of the dangers of accessing these locations or because of poor resourcing and lack of personnel and resources. We can, at best, estimate which regions of emerging markets are rich in resources and which resources these might comprise, unless there are already well-established businesses operating, in which case, of course, the most profitable opportunities may already have been exploited.

Angola was for many decades one of the poorest countries in Africa, affected by a violent civil war that prevented local and foreign companies from investing and operating there. As the country emerged from its decade-long war, foreign investment flowed in and several new oil and gas fields were discovered in less than a decade. Now it is clear that Angola does not just have abundant oil, it is one of the most important oil producers in Africa, and it is also rich in gas. In other instances, political factors or serendipity may have led to under-exploration of resources. Mongolia, for example, has just become one of the most important locations for mineral extraction. The discovery of mineral resources is new, and was not predicted to be a key driver for the economy for many years after the fall of communism.

In summary, when you're evaluating the structural characteristics of a given market, its geographic position, climate, and resource endowment are factors to consider.

Population

Examining the Population dimension involves not only researching how many people live in your target market or country, but also identifying present consumption patterns, how consumption may change in the future, and the type and level of skills of the local workforce. As discussed in the first chapter, this depends on average incomes and the way wealth is distributed. The richer the population, the more it will consume. And the more inequitable the distribution of wealth, the more consumption is skewed toward certain types of goods and services, in particular luxury items. The Population dimension is explored in greater detail from a consumer perspective in Chapter 6, "Targeting Emerging Market Clients I: The Rich and the Middle Classes," and Chapter 7, "Targeting Emerging Market Clients II: Strategies for the Base of the Pyramid," which deal with targeting consumers in emerging markets.

Considering demographics is also an important part of this dimension: aging populations and predominantly young populations will generate different patterns of demand. Furthermore, a young population can supply the workforce for labor-intensive operations for many years, whereas, in economies with an aging population, the share of people at their most productive age is bound to decline. This is an important long-term consideration for businesses interested in emerging markets as export platforms.

The level of education and skills is another important factor, especially if we're planning to establish export-oriented manufacturing or offshore service provision operations. It can be difficult to work out whether our desired investment location has the skills we need for our operations. Some countries, such as Pakistan, have a simultaneously large pool of unskilled workers and very skilled workers in specific market niches. Pakistan is a world-leading exporter of surgical instruments. Instruments made by Pakistani companies and by German companies with operations in Pakistan are used by hospitals in Europe, the U.S., and Japan. This example neatly illustrates the value of having both a generic overview of the average skills in a given economy and a sector-by-sector understanding of specialized skills. We can investigate these factors by looking at indicators such as the percentage of the population that can read and write (literacy levels), enrollment in secondary education, and secondary school graduation rates (often a better indication than enrollment because dropout rates in many developing countries are high).

As illustrated, we also need to examine whether there are fields in which the emerging market has a particularly skilled workforce. To do this, we can look at whether it already has clusters of local producers in a specific field, such as the surgical manufacturers of Pakistan, and whether such companies export or operate only in the domestic market. Exporters tend to be subjected to more stringent quality controls, which entail having a skilled workforce. We can also look at the presence of technical schools that prepare skilled workers and verify whether any of our competitors already operate there. Even if there is no history of previous activity in our specific sector, having related industries indicates that the workforce can be successfully trained in a related field. When Intel invested in Costa Rica in 1996, for example, the country had no history of electronic manufacturing. However, it had some of the highest educational attainments of Latin America, and several local software and engineering firms. Intel took this as a "right" set of conditions, invested, and cooperated with the government to ensure that technical schools provided workers with the right set of skills to work on its premises. Many other firms followed the example of Intel, and Costa Rica has become the top producer and exporter of information and communication technology goods and services in Latin America (on a per-capita basis). If Costa Rica had very low educational standards, it would have been more expensive and challenging to develop the needed skills for the electronic manufacturing industry.

When examining the Population dimension, we should also look at gender. You may be surprised to learn that different economies have a very different share of men and women. In several Asian countries, including China, India, and Pakistan, which alone account for about a third of the world's population, the share of male births in relation to female births has been increasing for decades. This results from culture-related preferences for male children who will carry on the family name and inherit businesses as opposed to female children, who may entail expense in the form of a dowry. Despite legal prohibitions, a large number of families attempt to avoid female births by means of abortion, infanticide, and other practices. The result of this is that there are, and there will be, more men than women in these populations. This means that, in these economies, demographic growth will likely slow down as many single men fail to find a partner and form a family. This is important because demographic growth is an important factor shaping both consumption demand and labor supply.

Women in emerging markets tend, much more markedly than in developed economies, to do different types of jobs and have different consumption patterns to men. When women earn extra income, they are more likely to spend it on food, save more than men do, invest in improvements to their shelter, and eventually consume beauty products and clothing (Deolalikar and Rose, 1998; Floro and Seguino, 2002). Consumption-oriented businesses need to pay careful attention to these trends. Gender also affects the availability of skills, and thus the attractiveness of a location for export-oriented manufacturing or service provision. Men and women tend to train in different fields. Men are more likely to train for mechanical and industrial jobs, whereas women are more likely to train as nurses and teachers. Depending on the business, demographic trends can benefit or threaten certain investments.

The average health of a given population is also an important factor. If the majority of people lack access to clean water and sanitation, for example, workers are likely to regularly fall ill with diseases such as malaria and dysentery, which reduces their productivity dramatically. Businesses can engage in socially responsive projects that boost productivity—for example, improving the infrastructure their workers use or building better housing. Such situations can thus be both a cost and an opportunity, as we discuss in Chapter 7.

Religion may not at first sight seem relevant to business opportunities and development, but, as you shall see, it does in fact influence some important variables. Religion impacts on demography. In places where religion plays an important role in structuring behavior—for example, where church, mosque, or temple attendance is higher than average—natality rates tend to be higher. The teachings of the most widespread religions, such as Christianity and Islam, are supportive of having many children—this tends to contribute to the trend of large families, alongside alternative explanations related to education, poverty, and gender. Religion also influences consumption habits. Religion explains, for example, why beef consumption is limited in India while pork and alcohol consumption are limited in the Middle East. This kind of knowledge can help avoid trying to introduce inappropriate products into certain markets. Religious practices do not just affect consumption, they also influence policy making, and hence rules and laws. Some countries, such as Saudi Arabia, prohibit the sale and consumption of alcohol altogether. Others may limit alcohol sales to specific venues and tax it highly to discourage consumption.

Religion is often intertwined with culture and customs; it shapes the way people behave, what they eat, what they wear, and at times also how they think. It is our responsibility to identify factors that can potentially generate threats as well as those that can generate opportunities. Firms can best manage their relationships with local communities by showing sensitivity to local beliefs and norms. The general behavior of a company and its employees and how it issues public statements needs to be thought through to avoid inadvertently offending believers or touching on cultural sensitivities. Behavior perceived to do so can backfire in the form of demonstrations and violent attacks on property or a boycott of that company's product. There are opportunities in understanding the religious and cultural context, too; fashion is one field where religion and culture have a strong influence. If you walk around the streets of Kuala Lumpur, the capital of Malaysia, a Muslim country, you will see plenty of women dressed in traditional clothing—elegant, brightly colored silk gowns that cover the whole body, with a head scarf that leaves the face uncovered. These are very different from the abaya, the traditional dark decorated dress that women wear in Saudi Arabia. In both cases, in what may seem to be simple traditional clothing to Western eyes, there are subtly different fashions that distinguish products to appeal to different tastes and identify fashion trends.

Religion affects the basic style and characteristics of the clothes used by both Saudi and Malay women, yet local taste and customs differ. Thus far these products have been the realm of local businesses. As average incomes rise in countries with a large Muslim population—countries such as Malaysia and Indonesia—more women will be willing to spend more on more fashionable clothing items. This kind of trend can generate appealing business opportunities for design houses and clothing manufacturers that have the necessary knowledge to target these markets. Thus far, Triad-based businesses have largely ignored the fast-growing markets for traditional clothing, failing to apply their advanced know-how of design and production techniques to products that differ from what they have been specializing in for many years.

Finally, we can also consider the impact of ethnicity within this dimension—a factor related to both religion and culture. Many emerging markets are made up of different ethnic groups, who may have different cultures, languages, religious beliefs, and customs. Some countries, such as India, Pakistan, and Afghanistan, are characterized by particularly fragmented populations and frequent clashes among these different groups. Understanding the dynamics of different ethnic groups within a market, how they relate to each other, and how they may affect consumption can be winning factors in these markets. Returning to our previous example, Malaysia is inhabited by Malays, Chinese Malaysians, and Indian Malaysians. The three ethnic groups operate in very different businesses. Malays, the largest ethnic group, dominate state-owned enterprises, such as the oil company Petronas, as well as political and administrative jobs. Chinese Malaysians, roughly one quarter of the population, are the wealthiest group, owning a large share of the private enterprises of Malaysia, and operating in trade, manufacturing, and tourism. Indian Malaysians tend to work in professional services (for example, as lawyers, doctors, and nurses). These groups specialize in different trades, and tend to eat and dress differently—targeting the Malaysian market does not mean targeting an integrated market, it means targeting a market made up of three groups of consumers who may share some customs, while insisting on keeping others distinct.

Business Environment

In the first chapter, we highlighted several features distinguishing emerging markets from developed economies. Many of those, such as the poorer quality of market-supporting institutions, generate barriers to business. The Business Environment dimension was conceptualized to contain all of these factors. This includes obvious physical barriers to business, such as infrastructural deficiencies, and also more subtle but not less important obstacles, such as regulatory and institutional barriers. Infrastructure as an element of the Business Environment dimension becomes linked to the Geography dimension—for example, a country with particularly difficult terrain but modern transport infrastructure (say, a rail network) may, in the final calculation, result in lower operating costs than a country with relatively easy terrain but with decrepit roads.

Intangible factors are no less important. They include regulations that limit, forbid, or simply make it more expensive to invest in a given market, disinvest from it, or move profits to other locations—namely, barriers to investment, macroeconomic instability, and trade barriers. Investing in Venezuela, for example, is complex and costly because the country has specific rules that limit the repatriation of profits and the conversion of local currency into foreign currencies. Violent macroeconomic fluctuations such as sudden changes in the value of a currency make it more difficult to plan costs, such as the cost of importing a given component. High inflation also generates extra costs in terms of accounting and uncertainty in planning.

If your business is targeted toward exporting and requires imported inputs, barriers to trade become especially important. Selling European food items in China, Colombia,

Brazil, and many other emerging markets involves paying high import taxes, which make the products unaffordable for most consumers by the time they reach the market. Given their final selling price, products that target mass consumption in Europe become luxuries for the top earners in emerging markets. A jar of spreadable chocolate produced in Europe, for example, costs almost six times less in London, one of the most expensive cities in the world, than in many emerging market capitals. This difference in price is the result of two factors: First, import tax. Second, given that average incomes are much lower, selling the product for mass consumption while making a profit would be difficult in many emerging markets, especially when import taxes are factored in. A better strategy is to sell a lower volume of the product and target it to upper-middle class consumers. If it becomes a luxury, its high price ceases to be a problem, and it can offset high import costs. For such strategy to work, however, companies need to make sure they improve the packaging and target distribution to high-end retail only, ensuring that the product acquires a "luxury" image.

The complexity of regulation and the efficiency of the bureaucracy in charge of implementing it, or the "red tape," is another element that can greatly increase the costs of doing business in emerging markets. Paying taxes in Brazil is an almost impossible task for foreigners, and a difficult one even for locals. It involves juggling several levels of state and federal taxation and getting to grips with all of the possible exemptions and subsidies. Several emerging economies have regulatory frameworks that are extremely complicated and difficult to comply with, and the best way to deal with these is to hire established local experts that can help us navigate through the labyrinth of rules and regulations.

The more complex the regulations, the greater the incentive to find loopholes. Unsurprisingly, the most corrupt countries in the world also tend to have very complex regulation. Corruption can be thought of as an operational cost because companies operating in corrupt environments may find they have to make under-the-table payments simply to have rights recognized or legal procedures implemented. At its worst, corruption affects the functioning of the institutions that make commerce possible. Where it is impossible to have contracts enforced without bribing the police and the judiciary, transaction costs are very high. In such environments we often find that formal rules are applied inconsistently, at times randomly, or even ignored. Conversely, we find that business transactions are actually regulated by informal, unwritten rules. To do business in these environments means understanding both the formal and the unwritten rules. Such complications may make it altogether unprofitable to do business in corrupt environments, despite the appearance of lucrative opportunities.

Economic Performance

Economic performance is determined by a combination of other factors, ranging from the skills, demography, and wealth of the population, to the resource endowment and the business environment. It can be measured in different ways, and we are interested in all of them. We have already discussed the key measures of economic performance, such as GDP and GNI and the way in which they are calculated, in Chapter 1, "What Are Emerging Markets?" There are, though, other elements of economic performance to which we should also pay attention. One of these is the level of foreign investment in a country of interest and how it changes over the years. Markets that receive high flows of investment are typically already performing well or are the loci of new resource exploration or discovery (see Box 4.2). They are also generally relatively open, or else investment would flow to other destinations.

Box 4.2: Investment, Economic Growth, and Development

There are two main types of investment: portfolio and foreign direct investment (FDI). Portfolio investment is capital invested in stock markets, which typically flows rapidly in and out of countries. FDI is investment in productive facilities—an office, a factory, a mine. It is riskier because it entails a longer-term perspective. In case things go wrong (for example, if a war breaks out and a recently opened factory has to be closed), a company may incur very high losses. "Exit" strategies are not quick and tend to be very costly. For example, it may be difficult to sell the land and equipment in a difficult economic climate. FDI is an important driver of economic growth for emerging and developed economies alike. First, it injects capital into an economy, which is particularly beneficial for capital-scarce economies such as the many emerging markets. Second, it increases production capacity, thereby contributing to future increases in wealth generation. Third, it brings with it technology and managerial skills. Generally when a company invests in a different country, it improves facilities or establishes new ones, installs new machinery, and updates managerial practices. For this reason, FDI can have positive effects on development, generally characterized as "spill-overs" of technology and knowledge. Economic historians and development economists have shown that FDI is a very important motor of economic development, especially if there are mechanisms in place that facilitate technological learning by local actors, such as linkages between foreign multinational corporations and local firms. For further reading on the topic, please see:

Chang, H. J. (1994). *The Political Economy of Industrial Policy*. New York: St. Martin's Press, p. 88.

Lall, S. (1990). *Building Industrial Competitiveness in Developing Countries*. Paris, France: Development Centre of the Organisation for Economic Co-operation and Development; Washington, DC: OECD Publications and Information Centre.

Lall, S. (2001). *Competitiveness, Technology and Skills*. Edward Elgar Publishing Inc.

Narula, R., and Dunning, J. H. (2000). Industrial Development, Globalization and Multinational Enterprises: New Realities for Developing Countries. *Oxford Development Studies, 28*(2), pp. 141–167.

Humphrey, J., and Schmitz, H. (1996). The Triple C Approach to Local Industrial Policy. *World Development, 24*(12), pp. 1859–1877.

Exports are a good indicator of competitiveness—if, for example, a country's exports of coffee decline, this means that it has become unprofitable to produce coffee in that specific location. This could result from any number of factors or a combination of factors: it could be that the price of coffee in the world market has gone down to a point that makes it impossible to offset production costs. It could also be that our location has been growing fast and hence labor costs have increased so much that it is unfeasible to produce coffee at the current prices. It could be that a plague has temporarily affected coffee plantations, reducing output. Finally, there could be political reasons, such as the government imposing a tax on coffee exporters. The Argentinean government, for example, has been taxing exporters since 2001. As a result, in spite of rising meat prices in the world market, Argentinean production of meat has been steadily declining.

Imports are an indicator of growing internal consumption. When imports increase, it means that extra wealth is being created in the internal market and spent on imported products. Trade (imports and exports) also provides an idea of the economic structure, employment, and competitiveness of markets. Looking at China's international trade, we can see how its imports of commodities—especially oil, metals, minerals, and food—have increased dramatically. Its exports of manufactures have also increased, but at a slower pace. We can thus deduce that a share of the extra inputs has been used for internal consumption—higher incomes have generated demand for extra food, and large construction projects have consumed cement, iron, and other materials. This means that the Chinese internal market has been growing and becoming more sophisticated, and that the government has been pushing for an accelerated infrastructural development. We can predict that China will have much higher wages in the future, but also a much better export-support infrastructure.

The level of household savings is another macroeconomic indicator that can provide useful information. In countries such as China, where household savings are high, it is possible that domestic consumption will increase dramatically in future years. In countries such as Brazil, where the consumption share of the domestic economy is already very high, this is unlikely to happen. The Brazilian government has, however, much scope to improve infrastructure by channeling public and private investments to it.

Given the integration of the global economy, it is important to keep the economic performance of a given market in relation to other markets in a given year in perspective. It is also useful to draw comparisons within specific regions and across markets that share key features.

Although there are many features of economic performance that we can consider, one of the most important ones is the wealth of the population, and with its capacity to consume—or in technical terms, its "purchasing power" (see Box 4.3). When the total wealth generated in a given market increases, there are opportunities. If this occurs in a diffused way, involving the majority of the population, these opportunities may be larger than if this wealth accrues to only a small part or specific group within the population. The opportunities may also be more sustainable. If wealth generation occurs only at the top, opportunities may be more narrow and volatile, subject perhaps to changes in the ruling class. Structural changes in the economy and especially increases in average wealth per capita generate opportunities. Stability and maintaining the status quo, which policy makers are attempting desperately to achieve in the Triad, do not. Examining economic performance is particularly useful because it begins to give us an idea of when, where, and how these changes occur.

Box 4.3: Purchasing Power and Disposable Income

Both the UN and the OECD accept the definition of disposable income of the Canberra Group: "Total income less current transfers paid." For an individual the disposable income represents the amount of income left, available for spending and saving, after taxes and other contributions (e.g., cash transfers to charities or social insurance contributions) have been paid. The purchasing power of an individual represents the quantity of goods (or services) that their personal income allows them to buy.

Data Source: OECD Glossary of Statistical Terms, Canberra Group: Handbook on Household Income Statistics, United Nations Statistics Division

---

Operationalizing the Four Dimensions Analysis

Once we have analyzed the context by looking at these four key dimensions, we can put the information together into a comparative table to see whether it is bringing up any

---

aspects that the DoA analysis failed to capture. For example, say we found a specific country to be the perfect source for new investment to extract gas. We may have also noticed that it is a growing market, though its total size is still small because the population is, on average, very poor, and thus its purchasing power is low. Perhaps we missed the fact that its population is very young and growing fast—an indication that the total market and the labor force is going to grow. We may also have overlooked the fact that our location has a favorable business environment, with low inflation, little in the way of red tape, and very investor-friendly regulation. All or any of these factors may impact on the way we choose to do business or how different potential locations compare in the final summing up. This kind of analysis can throw up surprises as well—for example, analysis of a location that is well-known only for resource-extracting businesses may reveal that the area is also distinctly attractive as a market for other products and services.

The next step of our analysis is to build an archive of the emerging markets we are interested in. We can then compare our markets by their Determinants of Attractiveness, and also by their Four Dimensions. A basic cross-country comparison builds a more complete picture of any market we wish to assess (see Figure 4.12).

Country	Geography	Population	Business Env.	Ec. Performance
Uganda	Fertile Land Copper, Cobalt, Oil, Gold Borders with Congo (DRC), South Sudan, Rwanda, Kenya, Tanzania.	36 million 50≤14 years old Av. income 1300 US $ per head (PPP) 65% Literacy Majority employed in agriculture Ethnic Divisions 6.5% HIV Infected	Economic Reforms Stabilized Economy Low Inflation Open to Investment and Trade	Growing at 5-6% Average Most Exports are Agro Commodities (For Example, Coffee) New Investment in Oil Extraction

Determinants of Attractiveness:
  1) Oil and Gas Extraction
  2) Agro Production: Coffee, Fruit, and Vegetables

Figure 4.12 From the Four Dimensions to the DoA.

Besides building a cross-country comparative table, we suggest generating a specific card for each emerging market, where you can plot the information you gather as you progress through your investigation of business opportunities. You can begin by developing a basic version of your country card by specifying the *necessary, highly desirable, desirable,* and *not needed* factors for each Determinant of Attractiveness and for each of the Four Dimensions (see Figure 4.13). You can then assign values to the elements of your analysis—for example, under "Corruption," one of the items that should appear in the Economic Performance dimension, a good indicator is the Transparency International Global Corruption Index value. Again, our intention is to illustrate a method for categorizing emerging markets and their opportunities, not to impose on you our own judgment. Therefore, we leave it to the reader to decide which indicator to use for each cell of the matrix, and indeed whether to use numeric values or not.

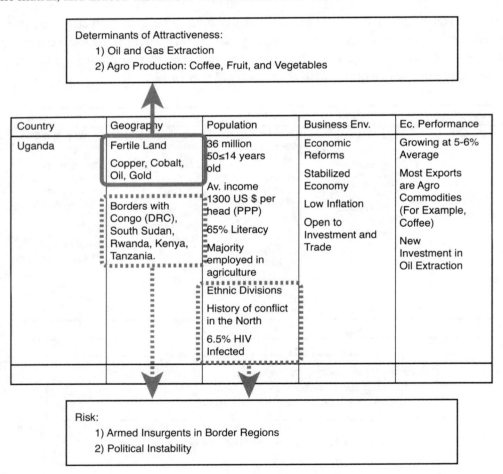

Figure 4.13 Four Dimensions, DoA, and risk.

References

Amsden, A.H. (2003). *The Rise of "The Rest": Challenges to the West from Late-Industrializing Economies.* Oxford University Press, USA.

Buckley, P.J. and Casson, M.C. (1998). Analyzing Foreign Market Entry Strategies: Extending the Internalization Approach. *Journal of International Business Studies,* pp. 539–561.

Chaudhuri, K. N. (2006). *The Trading World of Asia and the English East India Company: 1660–1760.* Cambridge University Press.

Contractor, F.J., Kundu, S.K., and Hsu, C.C. (2002). A Three-Stage Theory of International Expansion: The link Between Multinationality and Performance in the Service Sector. *Journal of International Business Studies,* 34(1), pp. 5–18.

Deolalikar, A. and Rose, E. (1998). Gender and Savings in Rural India. *Journal of Population Economics,* 11(4), pp. 453–470.

Dobbs, R. (2011). Resource Revolution: Meeting the World's Energy, Materials, Food and Water Needs. McKinsey Global Institute.

Dunning, J. (1998). Location and the Multinational Enterprise: A Neglected Factor? *Journal of International Business Studies,* 29(1): pp. 45–66.

Dunning, J. (1988). The Eclectic Paradigm of International Production: A Restatement and Some Possible Extensions. *Journal of International Business Studies,* 19(1), pp. 1–31.

Dunning, J. H., and Lundan, S. M. (2008). *Multinational Enterprises and the Global Economy.* Edward Elgar Publishing.

Floro, M. S. and Seguino, S. (2002). Gender Effects on Aggregate Saving. *Gender and Development Working Paper Series,* (23).

Johanson, J. and Vahlne, J. E. (1977). The Internationalization Process of the Firm—A Model of Knowledge Development and Increasing Foreign Market Commitments. *Journal of International Business Studies,* pp. 23–32.

Krugman, P. and Obstfeld, M. (2001). *Economía Internacional.* Madrid: Pearson Education.

OMC (2008). Los Acuerdos Multilaterales Sobre el Comercio en la OMC.

Oviatt, B. M. and McDougall, P. P. (1994). Toward a Theory of International New Ventures. *Journal of International Business Studies,* pp. 45–64.

Robins, N. (2006). *The Corporation That Changed the World: How the East India Company Shaped the Modern Multinational.* Pluto Press.

Rugman, A. M. and Verbeke, A. (2004). A Perspective on Regional and Global Strategies of Multinational Enterprises. *Journal of International Business Studies,* 35(1), pp. 3–18.

Sen, S. (1998). *Empire of Free Trade: The East India Company and the Making of the Colonial Marketplace.* University of Pennsylvania Press.

United Nations (2012). Statistics Division Glossary. Retrieved from http://unstats.un.org/unsd/default.htm.

World Trade Organization (2013). Statistics Database: Time Series on International Trade [Data file]. Retrieved from http://stat.wto.org/Home/WSDBHome.aspx?Language=E.

5

Managing Risk

Introduction

The previous chapter presented the first two steps in assessing emerging markets as potential business locations, starting with identifying the Determinants of Attractiveness, or the reasons for investing in a given emerging market, and then introducing the Four Dimensions to help us define the context in which investors may operate. We have considered risk in passing, and we turn now to look at the concept and implications of "risk" in greater detail. Emerging markets are, on average, less transparent, more economically volatile, less certain in their rules and institutions, and more prone to conflict than developed economies. They have tended to be the theatres of almost all recent armed conflicts, whether in the form of official inter-state wars, as when Russia invaded Georgia in 2008, or, this being the more common case, confrontation between armed groups within nation states, such as the ongoing violence in the northern and eastern part of the Democratic Republic of Congo.

A long-established rule in business is that the more risky the opportunity, the higher the potential rewards. For multinationals, mainly from developed economies, and historically with their assets in developed economies, the stakes are rising because the rewards of operating in their home economies are declining at record speed. Learning how to manage the complex risks of emerging markets is becoming a sought-after skill—a skill that distinguishes the businesses from developed economies that will continue to expand in the global market from those that will merely defend their positions in their home markets. It is important for any manager interested in emerging markets to understand that there is no easy way of knowing or predicting risk. The most accurate analysis can only be done by the stakeholders themselves. This is why we do not propose yet another index with slightly different values, but suggest a way of examining operational realities through a set of analytical tools.

Chapter 8, "Multinationals Based in Emerging Markets: Features and Strategies," goes on to consider the subject of risk from another perspective—that of companies from emerging markets internationalizing their operations and the advantage their experience of operating in risky conditions gives them, which they can exploit internationally. This chapter concentrates on companies moving into emerging markets from less risky locations. It discusses the different components of risk. In the first section, we consider commonly used categories of risk, what these capture or fail to capture, the reliability of data on risk and risk reporting, and ways to interpret the information that is available. The following sections look at *expected* and *unexpected* risk and provide a guide for assessing risk and for developing risk management strategies for emerging markets.

Defining Risk

In economics and business, the idea of risk is commonly associated with the finance and insurance industry—insurance risk, risk premium, investment risks, and so on (Fitch Ratings, 2013b). Much of the discussion and analysis on risk focuses on investment in the stock market of a given country or the purchase of assets. There are very few books or reports weighing the risks of doing business in emerging markets. By "doing business," we mean the actuality of operating in an emerging economy as opposed to buying emerging-market stocks or bonds in New York or some other financial center. The scarcity of research on this topic does not mean that individuals and companies shun emerging markets. On the contrary, there is a growing flow of capital going toward emerging markets, with new companies being established and facing new or unexpected tests. It is with these companies in mind—the firms that venture into unfamiliar markets and must learn to manage the risks involved—that we have developed the risk assessment methodology presented in this chapter.

Most of the existing literature and practical manuals on risk make a clear division between country risk and political risk (Alesina and Tabellini, 1989; ICRG, 2013). **Country risk** is the sum of risks related to the macroeconomic performance of a country, generally compiled by rating agencies such as Moody's and Standard & Poor's (Fitch Ratings, 2013a). Country risk indexes are designed for financial market investors (see Box 5.1). Their evaluations do not just give information to potential buyers of national treasury bonds; they also have a direct effect on the market's perception of such bonds. The events that have been occurring in Triad economies since 2008, such as the Euro crisis, illustrate the effect when one of the large rating agencies downgrades a country or company; its value in international markets immediately declines. Country risk is a measure of the financial solidity of a given country: it can include an assessment of its national income growth (actual and forecasted), the extent to which it is indebted, and the likelihood that it can and will honor its payments to creditors (Fitch Ratings, 2013b). Within the category of debt, country risk indices examine public debt (that is, the debt owed by a country to its own citizens in the form of treasury bonds) and external debt, or the debt owed to foreign banks and creditors (Standard & Poor's, 2010).

Box 5.1: Country Risk

Country risk measures the risk of investing in a country. Given the characteristics of imperfect information in the real economy, particularly given the asymmetries that characterize the financial market, lenders are always subject to the possibility that borrowers will be unable or unwilling to fulfill all of their obligations (Eaton, Gersovitz, and Stiglitz, 1986). This risk of default, when strictly and directly related to a state that is financed by debt, external or internal, is known as **country risk** (Mankiw, 2006, p. 510). There are many reasons why country risk may be high in a given economy, ranging from economic imbalances (such as high fiscal deficit) to political instability (which affects economic variables). The interest rates of borrowers differ precisely as a form of compensation for different levels of perceived risk (Kiguel and Lopetegui, 1997).

Risk-rating agencies are agents responsible for monitoring the capital market—they determine the risk grades or scores of countries, which form an important basis for the decision-making of investors (Restrepo et al., 2007). The three major rating agencies in the world are Standard & Poor's, Moody's Investors Service, and Fitch Ratings. Each agency applies its own methodology in measuring the risk. Typically, ratings are expressed as letter grades that range, for example, from "AAA" to "D" to communicate the agency's opinion of the relative level of credit risk.

Country risk focuses mainly on measures related to economic performance, or macroeconomic dimensions. If a country is forecasted to grow, it is more likely to honor its debts (see Table 5.1). Country risk gives us an indication of how an economy is perceived in international financial markets. As the fall of Lehman Brothers and the 2008 crisis graphically reminded us, rating agencies are far from "all knowing." They have their own perceptions and assumptions, their business is paid by the very clients they assess, and there is no external independent regulatory authority overseeing their evaluations and rankings. Therefore, countries such as Spain and Italy, which had very low country risk for many years, face the risk of default as credit agency reports unsettle financial markets in 2012–2013. Several emerging markets that have never received the coveted triple-A status, such as Brazil, have not veered near a debt default or a banking crisis for more than a decade. We would thus suggest that the reader use country risk only as an initial and very descriptive measure.

Table 5.1   Country Risk Ratings

Rating Scale			Meaning
Standard & Poor's	**Fitch Ratings**	**Moody's**	
AAA	AAA	AAA	Highest quality and minimal risk
AA	AA	Aa	Very high quality and very low risk
A	A	A	High quality and low risk
BBB	BBB	Baa	Good quality and moderate risk
BBB-	BB	Ba	Speculative and substantial risk
BB+	B	B	High risk
B	CCC	Caa	Very high risk
CCC	CC	Ca	
CC			
C	C		Exceptionally high levels of risk
D	D	C	Default

Data Sources: Fitch Ratings (2013a), Moody's (2009), Standard and Poor's (2010)

There are additional reasons why country risk reports could have a limited use for companies operating or wishing to operate in emerging markets. If we assess the value of their information, we find that most country risk indexes deal mostly with large, financially sophisticated markets, and information on smaller markets is at best limited and at worst inaccurate. From an operational viewpoint, country risk reports do not provide sufficient information to understand the practical implications of risk—how likely it is, say, that a truck will be hijacked once it has left the factory. This sort of consideration has little to do with the tidiness of macroeconomic indicators, yet it can represent very real risk for a business. The first lesson we can draw from this is that there is a broad range of very real risks not captured by the most commonly used instruments of risk measurement (essentially, country risk) that have been developed by, and are targeted to, the finance industry. The second lesson is that macroeconomic risk can, but does not always, converge with broader business risk.

Other risks, those not related to investing in the stock market, are captured by the concept of **political risk** (Eurasia Group and PricewaterhouseCoopers, 2006). The categorization of political risk can be confusing because some of these risks are not, strictly speaking, political (see Box 5.2). Our assessment of risk here is more in line with analysis carried out by organizations specialized in political risk than the output of organizations that provide country risk reports.

Box 5.2: Political Risk

The International Country Risk Guide has established a political risk rating, measuring political risk in ways that are comparable across countries. It determines the political risk looking at a number of dimensions, such as Socioeconomic Conditions, Investment Profile, Internal Conflicts, External Conflicts, Corruption, Military Situation, Religious Tensions, Law and Order, Ethnic Tensions, Democratic Accountability, and, finally, Bureaucracy Quality (ICRG, 2013). The *Financial Times* (2013) defines political risk as follows: "The risk of operating or investing in a country where political changes may have an adverse impact on earnings or returns. This concerns not only politically unstable countries, but also places where normal democratic procedures may bring about a change of government and thus a possible negative change in policy, for example, on tax, regulatory constraints and tariffs, etc."

According to Culp (2012), a journalist writing for *Forbes:* "Political risks are taking new and different forms. In advanced economies, governments are dealing not only with real and perceived income inequalities but with high levels of sovereign debt, as illustrated by the Eurozone discussions. Other types of political risk—including state actions to promote state-owned companies; actions to tap into the cash flow of companies operating within national borders; and the building of trade barriers—are ongoing and have the potential to pose significant problems to many companies." According to a report by PricewaterhouseCoopers and Eurasia Group (2006, p. 5), political risk can be defined as follows: "Any political change that alters the expected outcome and value of a given economic action by changing the probability of achieving business objectives."

Most attempts to explain and measure risk have been carried out by private firms rather than by think tanks, multilateral organizations, or universities. Firms such as the ICRG Group, Exclusive Analysis, and Oxford Analytica analyze and evaluate different types of risk beyond the country risk ratings compiled by Standard & Poor's, Moody's, or Fitch. They monitor a broad range of indicators as well as provide insurance companies, investors, and other businesses with reports of the situation on the ground in different markets. These companies tend to assign numbers to different elements of their risk scales in order to facilitate cross-country or cross-regional comparisons. Some of their numbers are derived mathematically from factual indicators, such as measures of inflation and GDP growth. Others are assigned in a more subjective and interpretative way, as a means to summarize the company's understanding of a specific issue—for example, a new election that is likely to stir social upheaval. Given that each company uses a different method, the results of their calculations generally differ. This point emphasizes the fact that risk assessment is not a science—it is based on a combination of estimations and qualitative evaluations summed up with some arbitrary elements and then illustrated through numerical indexes.

A good way to define risk for our purposes is to think of it as *factors that increase the likelihood of failing to complete one or more of the transactions or operations that a company may have in an emerging market, or of incurring unforeseen costs*. There are numerous ways in which a business may incur extra costs or fail to complete a transaction. We will focus more specifically on the factors that occur more distinctively in emerging markets.

Expected and Unexpected Risk

In order to assess risk, we need to break it down into different elements. The first step is distinguishing risks that occur with some degree of frequency, and can thus be expected, from those that are more difficult to predict. **Expected risk** is the sum of risks associated with operating in a given market that tend to occur on a more or less regular basis and therefore can be reasonably predicted. **Unexpected risk** is the risk associated with abrupt unpredictable changes that have negative business effects. For example, when a country has been affected by high levels of violent crime for a long period, we can consider armed assaults as undesirable yet "expected" threats to our operations. Honduras has consistently had an extremely high number of murders per capita, despite not actually being at war for several decades. In Honduras, armed violence has unfortunately become a chronic problem, and as a result an expected risk. Expected risks can be a feature of any or all of the four dimensions: heavy rains (geography), ethnic divisions (population), corruption (business environment) and a high reliance on foreign aid (economic performance).

Assessing expected risk is, of course, easier than predicting unexpected risk. It entails evaluating the aspects of a given market that may limit our capacity to complete intended transactions. A good place to start is to collect as much information as possible on the practices of other businesses operating in the same industry, whether local, based in developed economies, or based in other emerging markets. The next step is to research the history of the country, aggregating available data from multilateral organizations (UN, Inter-American Development Bank, IMF, World Bank) as well as NGOS, think tanks, and local government agencies. This research should include elements related to all of the Four Dimensions—from information about the geography and climate of our intended market, to the composition of its population, its business environment and economic performance. Be aware that government sources in emerging markets are often under-informed. In other cases, especially in countries ruled by authoritarian regimes, government statistics will likely paint a picture that is much rosier than reality in order to attract foreign investment or simply to polish the rulers' image. We thus need to look beyond official statistics to piece together a more accurate assessment.

To build up a comprehensive picture, we need to draw on a wide range of sources and different types of data; both quantitative and qualitative information are useful, but in different ways. We need to enquire into the reliability of our sources and weigh information accordingly, and to follow leads to and from less formal sources. Reports from global NGOs can provide very detailed information on a range of issues—Amnesty International, for example, is a good source for information about human rights abuses, whereas the World Heritage Forum may be able to provide more information about the business environment. Newspapers and magazines can supply useful reports about a specific market, region, or city. Scanning web blogs and forums can also be a good way to acquire information, though it requires an understanding the local language or the use of a translator. Civil society, ranging from journalists to activists or simple observers, can corroborate or contest the official perspective of the government, giving us a very useful insight into what is happening on the ground in different locations. During the Arab Spring uprisings, for example, news about clashes in Libya and Syria were posted by citizens in spite of official censorship and denial.

We are aiming to develop a dynamic idea of trends rather than a static one-moment-in-time picture of our country(s) of interest. We need to look at how companies operating in these markets have dealt with problems in the past and how these problems have shaped their outlook and operational abilities. Between the 1970s and mid 1990s, the Brazilian economy suffered continuously from a high inflation rate. Supermarkets adapted by announcing price changes with a microphone. Banks would fill ATMs with banknotes on payday because their customers would try to withdraw their entire pay immediately and spend it before its value was lost. Businesses had to manage the expected risk generated by high inflation. What else does this tell us? It tells us that Brazilian businesses that are old enough to have lived through that period are highly flexible and capable of operating in environments characterized by high price uncertainty. When they enter emerging markets affected by high inflation, they may have an advantage over firms based in developed economies, which have become used to very low rates of inflation.

Unexpected risk is generated by sudden, unpredictable changes (see Box 5.3). The riots that erupted in London in 2011 were, for example, unexpected. They affected a city that is normally characterized by low levels of violence and crime and where protests are generally peaceful. A day after the riots, one of us took a cab to the airport in London. The Nigerian taxi driver, commenting on the riots, said, "Everybody is scared, but this is nothing. You should see the riots in Nigeria. There, police shoot people, and some of them shoot back. They happen all the time. Here, people are scared because they are not used to it." His comments neatly represent our arguments: first, that emerging markets are on average far more risky than those in the Triad, and, second, that risks that are not expected cause far more damage and fear than risks that are expected. The businesses that were affected by the London riots did not expect such an event and therefore were not prepared for it. During our research, we found that retail businesses operating in cities that are frequently affected by uprisings and riots, ranging from Lagos to Buenos Aires, have specific risk management strategies in place—from strong bars protecting shop windows and entrances to word-of-mouth mechanisms to learn about the movements of rioters and so on. Despite being "poorer" in terms of their available resources and their sales turnover, they have learned from experience how to manage the expected risks that mass mobilizations can cause. Their most important risk management tool is the readiness to close shop whenever the first signs of riots appear.

Box 5.3: Black Swans

In the book *Fooled by Randomness: The Hidden Role of Chance in Life and in the Markets* (2004), Nassim N. Taleb, a Lebanese-American essayist and scholar, explains "Black Swans" as unpredictable events that occur in an apparently random way. He argues that we are unprepared to manage these events and, hence, when they occur, we suffer disproportionately from the consequences. His work became particularly famous because he anticipated the financial crisis. Back Swans can have dire consequences also outside of the financial realm. In March 2011, Japan suffered an earthquake of magnitude 9.0 Mw, which triggered a tsunami that hit the coast with waves of up to 40 meters. This disaster caused terrible environmental damage and the unfortunate loss of many human lives. It also damaged the country's economy and its industry base. Given that Japan is a global manufacturing hub, the event also affected many other countries and locations. The disruption to Japanese electronics makers led to shortages of key electronics components for many industries, such as car manufacturing and electrical equipment affecting, among others, Jaguar Land Rover's plant in Castle Bromwich in Birmingham, UK and Sony and its plants all around the world (Escaith, Teh, Keck, and Nee, 2011; *Supply Chain Risk Management,* 2011, Wright, 2011). Another example of natural disasters affecting the global supply chain were the floods in Thailand in November 2011, which affected the computer industry. At the time, Thailand produced more than 40 percent of the hard disk drives that came in PCs, servers, and other computing gear. The severe damage to manufacturing facilities and infrastructure following the monsoons had consequences for companies such as Hewlett-Packard and Dell (Menn, 2011).

The crisis of 2008–2009 was an unexpected risk, causing shock waves far beyond the finance businesses originally involved. Car manufacturers suffered because of the economic downturn in the U.S. and Europe and a collapse in the demand for vehicles. The fall in property prices and building hurt the producers and lenders of construction machinery. The reason why we are all very familiar with the 2008–2009 crisis is that it affected Europe and the largest component of the global economy, the U.S. The crisis started in the financial hubs of New York and London, taken as symbols of market dynamism by emerging economy policy makers, and shook the U.S. and Europe from a long lethargic period during which it seemed that dramatic economic fluctuations were a problem of the past.

Had this "Black Swan" event occurred in Bolivia or Tanzania, newspapers would have moved more quickly on to other topics (Taleb, 2007). In fact, even if it had affected a large number of emerging markets, as the Latin American 1980s debt crisis or the 1997 Asian crisis did, the media impact would not have been so dramatic. Whereas the Triad has lived through a long period of economic stability, most emerging markets never did. In March 2012, during a meeting at the University of Rio de Janeiro, a Brazilian software entrepreneur remarked, "I am worried—we have been growing, and with no inflation for far too long. Soon something is going to happen." His comment to me was not based on an in-depth macroeconomic analysis. It was gut feeling. After living through 40 years of dramatic economic instability, he did not believe that the Brazilian economic and institutional context could manage a long period of economic growth. This, in itself, could lead to a self-fulfilling prophecy: if large numbers of executives have similar perceptions, they may stop investing, take assets out of Brazil, or adopt short-term strategies to take advantage of temporary growth spurts. Sudden economic fluctuations, often fuelled by political events, occur much more frequently in emerging markets than in the Triad. Indeed, it could be said that it is rather uncommon for emerging markets to go through a couple of decades of stable economic growth unaffected by macroeconomic instability, debt crises, or other events that generate business risks (see Box 5.4).

Box 5.4: Different Types of Crises and Inflation

Debt Crisis

Debt crises originate when, in order to face the accumulation of public budget deficits, governments borrow more. Accumulating extra internal or external debt (or both simultaneously) leads to a point where it becomes impossible to cover the payment of interest or the return of capital. The consequences of high levels of debt range from the difficulty in obtaining new financing in the future, to high interest rates and default declarations by the state, which can have dire consequences on the stability of other macroeconomic indicators, such as the exchange rate, and on the overall economy (Konrad, 1983).

Banking Crisis

Banks and financial intermediaries play an important role, channeling deposits, which are usually given in the short or medium term, to agents that require loans, at different terms (Gavin and Hausmann, 1998). An important pillar of the banking system is that it is based on confidence. The market (or, if you prefer, citizens and companies) trust that banks will honor their debts. For this reason, economic actors leave their assets in banks, which not only protect them from theft, but also provide them with the opportunity to earn interest. Banks, however, hold in deposit only a percentage of the value of what they loan. Generally, this percentage, defined as the minimum reserve requirement, is established by law. The remaining value will be loaned out, which helps to finance the economy. As far as there is confidence in the banking system and in any given bank, depositors tend to withdraw only a minor amount of what they deposited, and not all at the same time. Banks lend to each other and across their subsidiaries too, to compensate for the fact that withdrawals may be higher in a particular geographic area or period of time. When confidence in a bank falls, the bank's customers are likely to rush to the bank to withdraw all of their deposited value to ensure that they obtain it before it is too late—a behavior called a "bank run," which can attack one bank (as with Northern Rock in the UK in 2007, or spread to the whole banking system). Even if all the debtors of the bank honor their debts, the bank is unlikely to be able to redeem the money loaned out in a short period of time. As such, even a bank that has lent in a very conservative way, to borrowers who will certainly repay, would be in distress if all of its savers withdrew their money simultaneously.

Banking crises are characterized by the inability of banks to provide funds that depositors require, either because some external factor has exacerbated expectations of risk and large numbers of depositors go to the financial institution to withdraw money (a bank run) or due to internal problems of management accounting (Amieva and Urriza, 2000). Banking crises can be transmitted to the real sector of the economy, leading to recessions, through reduced consumption and investment (either by generating negative expectations or lack of access to credit) or through fiscal policy, because central governments may intervene to bail out banks, limiting the possible public investment in other sectors of society, and even exacerbating fiscal deficits (Amieva and Urriza, 2000). Globalization and technological advances have led to a high degree of integration in financial markets, which has encouraged the development of different financial products, but also to the fragility of the system exemplified by the failure of individual institutions facilitating financial contagion.

Inflation

Inflation is defined as the increase in average prices in an economy through a particular period of time. The indicator used to measure inflation is the change in the consumer price index (CPI), which indicates changes in the average prices of a basket of goods and services relative to the price of the same basket in a base period (Mankiw, 2006; pp. 145–193). Inflation tends to be considered mainly as a monetary phenomenon, related to mismatch between supply and demand of money (Duràn and Torres, 2007).

Unexpected risk is characterized by its suddenness; it can dramatically change or overturn the commercial environment. Unexpected risk can also occur within all of the four dimensions. There can be unexpected natural disasters (geography), sudden outbreaks of ethnic violence (population), abrupt regime changes that threaten property rights (business environment), and violent macroeconomic fluctuations (economic performance). Unexpected risk is more difficult to assess precisely because it is sudden and infrequent. Country risk indices and political risk analyses are meant, precisely, to make unexpected risk more predictable. In terms of macroeconomics, it should, at least in theory, be possible to predict moments of crisis. It is hard to imagine a debt crisis occurring in a country that has low levels of internal and external debt and no deficits. And yet, in spite of the sophisticated market-monitoring mechanisms we have and the multiple private, public, and multilateral organizations that study indicators, very few analysts predicted the U.S. subprime crisis or the troubles of the Euro. In the case of emerging markets, macroeconomic data is less accurate and often manipulated by official sources for political reasons. It is therefore much more difficult to rely on it to predict macroeconomic crises than in the case of developed economies. For example, several analysts argue that property prices in China have become overinflated, predicting that such a real estate bubble must eventually burst as it did in the U.S. Others rebuff this, pointing to strengths, from manufacturing to innovation, in the Chinese economy that boost growth and hence property prices. Given the unreliability of statistics on property prices and real estate transactions, especially for commercial property, it is very hard to come to a conclusion either way. No matter how accurate and sophisticated are our instruments to predict future economic trends, there will always be elements of risk that manifest themselves unexpectedly, affecting business in both emerging and developed economies.

In some cases, it may be possible to foresee a sudden increase in risk. For example, if we are operating in a hurricane-prone area, we should take into consideration that at some point a hurricane may strike, even though it may never have happened before and might not happen at all. It is generally difficult to assess whether and when a country ruled by an authoritarian regime may descend into internal conflict. We can predict that a situation within an authoritarian or divided country will bring upheaval, but we can't know what exactly will trigger popular revolt or regime collapse. More importantly, it is hard to predict when this will happen. For example, Libya appeared to be a very stable country up to a few months before the 2011 uprisings began. It was the richest country in Africa and had achieved very high standards of living. Like the oil-rich countries in the Middle East, it was ruled by a nonelected authoritarian regime that limited civil rights and political participation but provided generous welfare and state jobs to its citizens. On certain issues, such as women rights, the Libyan regime was more liberal than most North African and Middle Eastern countries. Colonel Qaddafi was a charismatic, if somewhat ridiculous, figure and an able strategist who managed a switch from being an enemy of the West and supporter of terrorism to being an ally in the fight against Al-Qaeda. Yet, Libya quickly descended from civil uprising to civil war, a conflict that drew in foreign armed intervention, generating large losses for the businesses operating there and physical risk for the thousands of foreign workers that operated the oil and gas industries.

A look at historical data and information can help us better understand the market that we operate in, or intend to operate in, but it does not provide us with a crystal ball. Keeping updated with political, economic, and social developments on the ground is the simplest yet most important strategy in anticipating likely sudden changes and being able to make contingency plans in time. A fundamental difference between expected and unexpected risk is the way in which they can be managed. Managing expected risk means understanding how can we run our business safely and profitably in any market. Managing unexpected risk entails having contingency plans—what happens if the current government is violently ousted? Have we clearly sided with the government to a point that we are certain to be damaged by political change? Are the potential future political leaders outspokenly opposed to our business for any reason? If a hurricane strikes, can we protect our facilities and evacuate staff in an efficient manner? The best we can do is to look at comparable events in history and at the how situations are managed in similar locations, perhaps neighboring countries, to pull together an instrumental assessment of the region and of common trends that may be likely to repeat themselves.

Location Risk and Targeted Risk

A good way to examine risk in emerging markets is to start from the broader picture—country-level basic information, for example—and gradually build a more specific analysis. We can do this by distinguishing between **location risk**, or the risks related to operating and probably living in a given location, from **targeted risk**, or the risk related to the specific business we are managing. Location risk is more generic, and it affects most if not all types of businesses in a country. Location risk gives us a general idea of the sort of market we are discussing. Targeted risk, on the other hand, changes across industries and businesses. It is more difficult to assess because it requires an in-depth understanding of both the business we run and the market.

Mineral and energy extraction industries often operate in marginal, difficult-to-access areas, and they frequently pay royalties to the central government in return for mineral and concession rights. They face risks related to environmental damage and often deal with the risks of protest from local communities. The more we know about the type of business, the more we can specify the risks. There are, for example, many opportunities for diamond extraction in Africa. However, there are also targeted risks—diamond-rich areas tend to be affected by guerrilla groups and low-intensity conflicts. Managing a small chain of coffee shops in the main cities of diamond-rich countries involves different levels of risk than actually operating a mine. Unless armed conflict reaches the cities, which may happen, our main concern may be managing our relationship with the local authorities and marketing our services. If, on the other hand, we extract diamonds, there's a good chance of being constantly in the midst of a violent environment, because the very presence of diamonds may fuel conflicts among rival armed groups.

We can derive location risk from the Four Dimensions analysis. The Four Dimensions we identified do not just determine why a given market may be appealing to business. They capture the sources of potential and actual threats to our business. The more detailed and updated our Four Dimensions analysis, the more we will have a first insight into the location risks we may face. For example, let's say that, under the Geography dimension, we focused on the concern that a particular market is often affected by hurricanes and heavy rains. Under the Business Environment dimension, we might note that its infrastructure is outdated and that businesses require off-road capabilities to access the resource-rich areas. In this case, a clear risk is that natural disasters may interrupt the already fragile road network, interrupting the trading routes we intend to use. If our business depends strongly on reliable supply chains, we may have to think about alternative transport systems or ways to manage potential infrastructure breakdowns. Some light and highly valuable supplies can be transported using small airplanes or helicopters. In other cases, it may be more efficient to invest in military-style portable metal bridges that can substitute for collapsed or submersed bridges and roads. Just waiting for disaster to strike may entail heavy losses. The very function of the Four Dimensions analysis is to help us look at the attractiveness of markets while considering the bigger picture of their characteristics. We will look carefully at the Four Dimensions and develop the specific items of business risk. In the next section, we look at location risk, in both its expected and unexpected manifestations, discussing how to examine it using the Four Dimensions analytical tool.

Location Risk

In the Geography dimension, we consider first and foremost factors related to location. These include climate and conflict areas. First, when looking at climate, we need to take into account the characteristics that pose expected risks to business (for example, high temperatures in the desert areas of Mali). Second, we need to consider the likelihood of not-so-frequent (and thus verging toward being unexpected) climatic events such as hurricanes, tsunamis, floods, and landslides.

The damage caused by the earthquake and tsunami that hit Japan in 2012 is a reminder that even rich, sophisticated economies may suffer heavily from unexpected risk. This also remind us that relying on fragile and stretched supply chains is risky. Japanese manufacturers are known to be extremely efficient in their supply chain organization. They developed the nowadays omnipresent "lean production"—manufacturing that reduces waste and storage costs via quality control and tight delivery times for suppliers. As with other industrial producers based in developed economies, Japanese companies have also offshored their manufacturing to the most efficient locations both within and outside Japan. As such, their production is run through a complex supply chain that combines multiple assembly sites with focal production centers that produce components serving several locations simultaneously. Efficient coordination between in-company production centers and suppliers ensures smooth organization of the chain. Their ability to coordinate complex supply chains continues to benefit Japanese manufacturers in terms of the quality of their final products. However, this form of organization does not take into account the possibility that natural or man-made disasters can interrupt the supply chain by severely damaging some of the key hubs for the production of certain parts. As research by Coronado shows, before 2012 certain components needed to manufacture hybrid vehicles were manufactured only in a few factories across the globe (Coronado, 2012). This contributed positively to economies of scale in an industry affected by excess capacity (see Box 5.5).

Box 5.5: Economies of Scale

Economies of scale are the economic advantages that can be achieved by increasing the scale of production of a given good. For example, let's imagine that we want to produce socks. It may be necessary to acquire "sock making" machinery and rent a space to run our activity. Independently of how many socks we make, we will have to pay for the machinery and space. The more socks we make, the better, because we exploit the maximum capacity of the machinery and space (economies of scale), up to the point where, to make one extra sock, we would need to buy another machine and rent extra space. Beyond that point, it will no longer be worthwhile to expand production. The same example could be made for workers. If instead of using machinery, we produce handmade socks, we will rent a space and sit there with our family sewing socks. To make more, we can hire a few friends and fill the room (which costs the same whether empty or full). That is, up to the point where the room becomes overcrowded and it becomes uncomfortable to work (Sullivan and Sheffrin, 2003, p. 157; Clark, 1988).

The tsunami, however, damaged some of the facilities that supplied the whole global production network of Toyota, among others, which used the specific component. As a result, several assembly factories in different parts of the world had to halt production because they lacked certain key components. This increased the disruption of the tsunami far beyond the factories that were physically damaged by it. Since 2012, transport equipment producers and their suppliers have rethought their supply chains, ensuring that they have contingency plans should it become inevitable to have to halt production at one or more of their key production centers. Notably, a less efficient organization of production—one which, for example, relied on a larger number of in-house and external production hubs—would have been better equipped to overcome this kind of unexpected risk (refer to Box 5.3).

The difficulty of managing unexpected risks is precisely that they do not occur on a regular basis and are therefore difficult to predict. However, companies can take certain measures to reduce the potentially disruptive effects of natural disasters and other unexpected risks. Historic statistics on temperature, hurricanes, earthquakes, tsunamis, floods, and other natural disasters can help us define both the normal and abnormal location risks linked to geography. Choosing locations that are far from the source of risk—for example, far from the sea if it is prone to tsunamis and far from the epicenters of earthquake-affected areas—is a possible strategy. Ensuring that evacuation practices are routinely rehearsed can contribute positively to the safety of employees. High-tech buildings designed to cope with the eventuality of natural disasters are expensive but can better protect both installed machinery and the workforce. In old hotels, retirement homes, and hospitals, several key functions were located in basements, below the sea level. These included kitchens, heating systems, and emergency power systems. This organization maximized space, but in case of flood several functions were put at risk simultaneously. Older buildings are also more dangerous in case of earthquakes—instead of bending, they either resist force or act as a brake, causing heavy fragments to fall. Technology now allows us to simulate how buildings respond to different types of stress, facilitating the development of risk-containing measures. New materials such as composites can help in constructing facilities equipped for these eventualities. In sum, a company that decides to operate in an area potentially affected by natural disasters should adopt strategies to minimize damage and disruption should these occur. It should also have contingency plans in place in case the risk overwhelms even state-of-the-art facilities.

Within the Population dimension, we consider all the social and political features that may generate location risk. These include the level of violent crime, whether there are tensions among different ethnic or political groups, whether there are insurgencies or guerrilla movements, and whether people can quickly mobilize and dissent. To detect these elements of risk, we can use different methods. For example, to measure the level of violent crime, we can look at indicators of the number of murders per population per year. The level of mobilization can be extrapolated from newspapers and news reports: how often are there strikes, road blockages, or other forms of protest? In case they are frequent, how often do they cause damage to businesses and what kind of damage? Historical trends can give us a picture of the continuity of risk. If, in a given country, there is a high level of mobilization now, but the causes are rooted in very recent history, then it may be an unexpected event. The problem may also pass relatively quickly. If, on the other hand, violent clashes between different political groups have been common for many years, we should consider them an expected feature of our location.

The Business Environment dimension evaluates a broad range of risks. Expected risks may include high levels of corruption, red tape, or barriers to investment and trade. Unexpected risks are unpredictable changes in the expected risks—for example, a surge in import duties on essential components. If we are already operating in a particular market, we should have arrangements for dealing with the existing policies and know how to work within the regulatory framework. Consequently, the risk is that the policies and regulations change. If, for example, a company is producing cars in a heavily protected market, it will probably use locally sourced components. A sudden opening of the market to imports of components may require the reorganization of that supply chain. It may not be possible to switch from local to global suppliers until all contractual obligations are complied with, whereas a newcomer may be able to build cars more efficiently using imported components.

Changes in the economic policy of a country do not generally occur overnight and in unpredictable ways. Even in the least sophisticated economies, there are lobbies protecting their entrenched interests. Any change to the status quo will raise concern from the groups that will suffer as a result and enthusiasm from those that will benefit. Even in countries ruled by authoritarian regimes, such as Cuba, proposed change to economic policies causes debate, which allows businesses to detect and assess the possibility of change and take measures to adapt. The abrupt fall of the Soviet Union was largely unpredicted in the West. Yet, after the Berlin Wall crumbled and the whole Eastern Bloc went through a fast-paced political transformation, many companies detected the likelihood that such markets would open and prepared strategies for the eventuality. The market liberalization and democratization of Eastern Europe also caused economic damage to firms that had long-term agreements with communist regimes, especially those that failed to predict that change would occur in the run-up to the events of the late 1980s.

There are many other ways in which the business environment can become risky—the most important one is expropriation (see Box 5.6).

Box 5.6: Nationalization and Expropriation

The term **nationalization** refers to the process through which the state acquires an industry or a production sector from private owners, local or foreign, even in cases where they are unwilling to sell their assets (Toro Echeverri, 2012). An example of nationalization in Chile was the repurchase by the state of all activities in the copper industry (which were in the hands of two American companies: Anaconda Company and the Kennecott Copper Corporation) during the administration of Allende in 1971 (Fermandois, 2001). In Mexico, in September 1982, there was a process of nationalization when President Jose Lopez Portillo decreed the reacquisition of private banking, which was held by both foreign and domestic capital (Hernandez, 1986; Del Angel and Martinelli, 2009).

Expropriation occurs when the state acquires control of privately owned assets without providing compensation to their rightful owners. Expropriation is less common than nationalization, and tends to occur particularly during or after conflicts.

Some notable recent nationalizations include Argentina and Bolivia. Argentina renationalized the energy company Yacimientos Petroleros Fiscales (YPF) in 2012. The company was previously owned by the state between 1922 and 1993.

In Bolivia, the government nationalized the country's main hydroelectric plant in 2010 and the power grid operator Transportadora de Electricidad (TDE) in 2012.

Since the liberalization of trade and investment during the late 1980s, expropriations tend to happen infrequently. Yet, they can, and still do, happen. Expropriations in their current modern form can be traced back to the seizures of enemy property during the First World War and the nationalization of U.S. property during the Mexican Revolution, when the rise of popular and nationalist movements challenged the ruling oligarchies and the role of foreign oil multinationals. Most expropriations occurred after the Second World War in emerging economies, as governments attempted to throw off the remnants of imperialism, adopting models of state planning, or to strengthen the position of emergent nation states or ruling groups. Expropriations were more frequent in oil, gas, mining, energy, steel, railroads, and telecommunications industries, where state intervention could be targeted at supporting development, or in industries that were considered strategic from a defense perspective. They have not ceased to occur. Throughout the 2000s, Zimbabwe has been the theatre of widespread expropriations of agribusinesses owned by white farmers and foreigners. Between 2009 and 2013, Argentina, Bolivia, and Venezuela have nationalized different assets in their respective economies.

One indicator of the risk of expropriation is the rhetoric of government—how anti-foreign and nationalistic is it? The more a government builds up a nationalist discourse with its constituency, the more it is likely to engage in showcase expropriations or nationalizations, independent of any economic consideration. In all of the cases just mentioned, ranging from Zimbabwe to Argentina, the discourse of the ruling elites anticipated the policies they eventually implemented. Other potential risks are changes in the regulations related to foreign investors—for example, placing limitations on the repatriation of profits or increases in corporate tax. These are more difficult to predict. Understanding the politics of a given emerging market and especially its ruling coalitions help refine our understanding of how to judge the sorts of risks that arise within the Business Environment dimension.

The Economic Performance dimension covers risks related to the value of the currency, inflation, or banking crises. An economic downturn can generate associated risks because it can contribute, especially in emerging economies, to political and social instability. Most of the risks that stem from the Economic Performance dimension are captured by country risk indicators. Some businesses, however, have their own specific risks related to economic performance. For example, there may be businesses that benefit greatly from a high-inflation environment and would suffer if the economic performance were to improve and the economy in which they operate were to stabilize.

Once we have identified different risks related to a market, we can sum them up in a location risk table (see Table 5.2), dividing them into "expected" and "unexpected." This provides an informative map for a manager considering the possibility of operating in a new market. In cases where the firm is already present in that market, it can usefully summarize the risk factors that are already known, providing a basis for narrowing down the targeted risk analysis and preparing risk management strategies.

Table 5.2   Location Risk

Location Risks	Expected	Unexpected
Geography	High humidity Extreme temperatures Low rainfall Heavy rains, droughts, monsoons Frost	Hurricanes, floods Extreme draught Earthquakes Tsunamis Volcanic eruptions
Population	High unemployment and poverty Level of unionization Political mobilization Friction among ethnic groups Friction among religious groups Violent crime Internal armed conflict (includes guerrilla movements, terrorist groups, and other insurgencies) Refugees from previous conflicts High influence of the military in politics and society	Union strikes becoming violent (e.g., kidnappings of managers, destruction to property) Dramatic increase in violent crime Escalation of violence in the confrontations opposing different political, religious, or ethnic groups Diffusion of the internal conflict to previously unaffected areas Military takeover of the government
Business Environment	Corruption Red tape Trade and investment barriers Complex regulatory framework Government control over certain sectors Inefficient infrastructure	Increase in red tape Surge in trade or investment barriers New limits on profit repatriation or business ownership
Economic Performance	Slow GDP per-capita growth High level of public debt Inflation Trade deficit Reliance on foreign aid High role of remittances in the economy Volatile exchange rates	Inflation peaks Debt defaults Banking crises Sudden import barriers Sudden reductions in foreign aid inflow Sudden reductions in foreign remittances Sudden devaluations of the currency

Targeted Risk

Once we have examined the risks related to operating in a given market, captured by the location risk concept, we move on to narrowing down our assessment and evaluating targeted risk. We defined targeted risk as the sum of the risks that can potentially threaten a specific business. To evaluate targeted risk, we need an idea of the type of activities we intend to carry out, the inputs we may need, and the area of operation. We can start by going back to the location risk table, where each of the Four Dimensions has generated specific risk items, and check whether and how these items apply to our case. For example, under Geography, we may have heavy rains and threat of hurricanes; under Business Environment, we may have a decaying road network. Do these risks pose a threat to the specific area of the country where we intend to operate, and how do they affect different businesses? To address these questions, it is necessary to identify the following:

- The specific area or region of the country where we intend to operate

- The activities that are key to our business

- The inputs that are strategic for our operations

Business Features: Identifying Where, What, and How

Having built a "big picture" map of location risks and plotted them on a table, our next step is asking the "Where, What, and How" questions (see Figure 5.1), which help us detect business features (exact location, key activities, and key inputs). We need to establish a relationship between the specific risks that affect a given area, the activities we carry out, and the inputs we need. The objective of the exercise is to link generic risks associated with a market (summarized by location risk) to a more in-depth look at our specific business and the way it functions. For example, if most of our employees have a mobile phone, the disconnection or malfunctioning of fixed telephone landlines will not be considered an important risk for our activities and inputs. Getting a good signal from telecommunication towers and having access to sources of electricity to charge batteries are, in this case, more important to ensure that operations are linked to the external world.

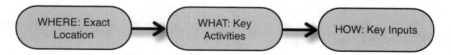

Figure 5.1 The where, what, how sequence.

Although most managers are very familiar with the activities and inputs of the companies they work for, this exercise can remind them of factors they take for granted and help them develop a more structured and accurate risk evaluation. The Where, What, and How questions need to be addressed referring specifically to one subsidiary or production unit at a time. The same company may run very different operations in a market, each having its own specific key activities and inputs. A soft drink and juice producer, such as PepsiCo, may have a juice production plant and a fizzy drink bottling plant. Drinkable water is a key input for both operations. Yet, the factory that specializes in juice production uses large quantities of fruit—a perishable product that needs to be delivered very frequently and stored in cold temperatures. The fizzy drink bottling plant does not handle any perishables, but it is likely to need large quantities of bottles, unless it produces its own. Empty plastic or glass bottles are surprisingly expensive to transport because most of the space they occupy on trucks is filled with air. A bottling plant is therefore likely to rely on bottle producers located in its proximity. Hence, the key input is not just bottles in this case, but bottles that can be delivered at a reasonable price and in timely fashion, which means bottles produced nearby. To have a clear idea of the risks the company faces, it is important to identify risk for each production unit rather than focusing on a broader corporate level. Finally, location may also differ—the fruit plant may for convenience be located near plantations, whereas the bottling plant may be located near industrial areas where producers of bottles and other inputs are based. The plantation area may suffer from hurricanes but be relatively free from mass mobilizations. The industrial area may be farther from the humid tropics and hence more shielded from hurricanes, but it may suffer from frequent violent protests, which block roads and thus potentially access to inputs. This encapsulates why we need to think of the Where, What, and How in a very specific way, linking them to location and targeted risks (see Figure 5.2).

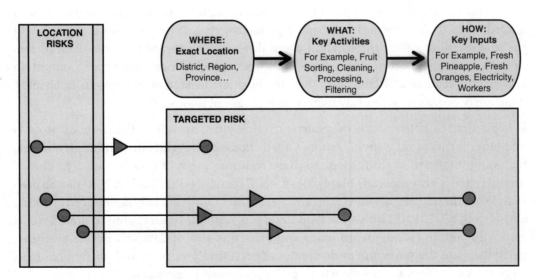

Figure 5.2 Moving from location to targeted risk.

From Location to Targeted Risk

We can start our evaluation by examining the exact location of our activities within an emerging market—are they in an area particularly affected by natural disasters or conflicts? If they are in a city, are they in a safe zone or in an impoverished neighborhood affected by gang crime? Our analysis of the Geography dimension has to become much more specific at this stage, because risks vary considerably across space and economic activity. Country-level indicators are rarely good indicators, especially as risks are spread unevenly across regions in the majority of emerging markets. Images of war-torn Afghanistan conceal, for example, the fact that in Kabul the murder rate is far lower than in Ciudad Juarez, in Northern Mexico. And yet there are several areas in Mexico that are safer than Chicago. For this reason, it is vital to obtain information about different types of risk at disaggregated and subnational levels, not just at the national level.

In most emerging markets, statistics are available for administrative units lower than the national level, such as regions, provinces, and cities. They are typically compiled in ways that reflect the political and administrative organization of a country. They may not be accurate or sophisticated, but they are a starting point for narrowing down our risk evaluation. In some cases, departments and regions may be abstract entities that fail to capture the real political, economic, and social structures of the country. In other cases, they may reveal stark differences between different areas of a market. Not only official government statistics but also the data collected by multilateral organizations, such as the World Bank and often NGOs and civil society organizations, is generally organized according to these criteria (by district, region, city, etc.). If the location is a city, it will become useful to gather information about different areas within the city. Risk factors can affect cities in non-uniform ways—a business perched near the top of a mountain will be at greater risk of landslides than the business located at the bottom of a valley, which may be much more likely to be at risk in case of floods.

It is possible to obtain maps of recurrent traffic jams, as well as the route of protests and other forms of mass mobilization. GPS technology currently links multiple sources, including information from users, to draw real-time maps of such events. The risk of armed crime is also generally highly localized. Depending on the country, it may be possible to obtain statistics about violent attacks, murders, and officially denounced criminal acts (UNODC, 2011). This would help draw geographical borders around areas associated with certain risk items. In many countries this sort of data will not be available, partly because the government does not collect it and process it and partly because a large share of crimes are not reported, and hence cannot be accounted for. However, civil society organizations, such as NGOs, and aid donors, such as the European Union, may attempt to monitor crime as well as natural disasters such as landslides, floods, and other events that can threaten business. Failing that, religious institutions (churches, mosques, synagogues, temples, etc.) may be able to provide information. Magazines, newspapers, and journalists are also good potential sources—they may have access to information that a government refused to make official. By the same logic, newspapers archives can also reveal interesting information about past incidents, where they occurred, and what caused them.

Once we have found information sources about the "where" of our business, we need to assess whether any of the risks we have identified apply to our location. Let's assume that we identified "poor infrastructure" and "heavy rains" as expected risks at the national level under the Business Environment and Geography dimensions. How does our specific location fare on this? Is it in a remote region connected by precarious infrastructure? Is it particularly affected by heavy rains? Or is it in fact in a relatively dry and well connected part of the country? Businesses based in remote locations, such as extractive industries, are more likely to be affected by this sort of risk than businesses that tend to operate in cities, such as retail and services, and in industrial parks, such as export-oriented manufacturing. Urban centers are not safer than rural areas, they just face different types of risks. Cities do not produce most of what they consume, including basics such as water and food. If roads and transport infrastructure are damaged, supply of food, water, energy, and other goods to cities may suffer. Cities are also more often affected by social movements, protests, and other forms of mobilization than rural areas—they concentrate high numbers of people, and, in the case of capital cities, also government, political party, and union HQs and military bases. This makes them ideal locations for organizing rallies and diffusing ideas. When civil wars erupt, however, they do often affect rural areas as well as cities. In Africa, for example, conflicts have tended to be concentrated around resource-rich areas because these allow whoever controls the territory to extract rents.

How do we identify the risks that affect our business? We began this book by pointing out that operating in emerging markets can be, and often is, risky, in the sense that many factors at play can generate extra, unplanned-for costs, or even impede us from completing our transactions. Once we have built a map of the risk factors that affect a country (location risk) and identified which ones apply to a given location, we can focus on the core activities of that business, or "what" exactly it consists of. Which are the activities that generate value for the business, its customers, and the society in which we operate? What is critical to the performance of these activities?

If our business is a coal mine, our first crucial activity will be coal extraction. If, as large mining companies such as Vale and Rio Tinto do, we also take care of transporting the coal, our activities may include moving the extracted mineral from the mine to its assigned port and loading it onto boats. Any factors that may interrupt these activities will cause damage to our business, and hence should be considered as risk. Whether this would amount to expected or unexpected risk depends on the frequency with which it occurs. Some risks, such as a strike among the railroad workers, may affect one or more of a coal mine's key activities—in this case, coal transportation. Other risks, such as the unexpected escalation of a dormant conflict, may affect all of the key activities. There may conversely be risks that affect the area where a business operates but do not touch its key activities. Coal and iron mining often relies on dedicated rail lines. As far as these can withstand extreme weather, the temporary closure of roads due to heavy rains will not affect the mine operator.

After we have identified the crucial activities that characterize a business, and the factors that may affect such activities, the next step is to focus on key inputs. Any factor that may threaten access to key inputs also threatens the business at large. By this reasoning, any factor that puts our labor at risk should be considered a risk. There are several reasons why risks to the workforce are extremely important. Ensuring that employees are safe while conducting their duties is generally considered to be a basic legal and ethical obligation for any business. It also has important economic implications. Accidents and threats to safety, whether or not they actually cause any harm to employees, will have negative effects on the morale of other workers and discourage potential applicants from finding employment. The more skilled the labor, the more risky—skilled labor is not just more expensive, it is also difficult to train, and may be hard to find in certain locations. A company that has a positive reputation regarding the safety of its employees and the environment where it operates is likely to attract high-quality job applicants and retain its skilled labor.

Energy companies often operate in areas affected by armed violence. Hiring the highly specialized workers needed in oil and gas rigs is extremely expensive. Risk demands a premium. Accidents increase such premiums, making it more expensive and difficult to run operations in the area affected. On the 16th of January 2013, the gas field of Ain Amenas, located in the south of Algeria, near the border with Libya, was attacked by armed insurgents claiming to be part of Al-Qaeda, allegedly in retaliation for France's intervention in Mali. Several foreign workers were kidnapped. The accident will have several implications—first, it will cause an immediate increase in the measures needed to protect the Ain Amenas facilities. The private companies involved had to cooperate with Algerian and French troops to attempt rescuing the captured workers. Second, all other oil and gas plants in Algeria and neighboring Libya will require extra security measures to avoid a reoccurrence of this event. Third, the skilled workers stationed at Ain Amenas—and most likely other facilities scattered around Algeria and Libya—will request to be relocated or demand a pay rise to compensate for risk.

Operating near a conflict zone, even if the latter has recently decreased in intensity, entails being in the proximity of armed groups. This is always a risk to our personnel, and hence to our operations. Armed groups may accidentally hurt our workers in the midst of a sudden gunfight. Or they may intentionally use force to obtain a source of income—for example, by kidnapping an engineer or threatening to do so. Deciding to operate in such environments entails expecting the risk of violent threats by armed groups as well as having contingency plans for the eventuality of a dramatic conflict escalation, such as a plan for the evacuation of staff.

All types of businesses rely on their workforce. Factors that threaten employees' safety are cross-sectoral risks—they affect different types of business. For example, operating in an area strongly affected by gang crime entails the risk of violent attacks, theft, kidnapping, rape, ransom, and collateral damage of gunfights among third parties. This applies to a business operating a fast food chain as well as a business running a postal delivery service or a company specialized in laying optical fiber cables. Protecting workers inside corporate facilities via cameras and armed security guards is insufficient to ensure their safety. If they suffer from frequent threats on their journey to work, they may find employment in other locations, even though technically they are safe while at work. Therefore, it is of strategic importance to have an in-depth understanding of the territory—the geography of risk, how employees go to work, the available transport services, and the infrastructure. If several employees commute from a particular area to a business facility, it may, for example, be a good idea to organize a safe, privately run transport service. If the extra cost can improve the safety of workers, it will be a good investment.

Protecting employees from potential hazards is helpful for recruitment and motivation. It also contributes positively to the image of the company in the location where it operates and vis-à-vis its clients, suppliers, and shareholders. One of the most valuable resources of a company is its brand and the associated reputation. These are built through time, by operating in ways that are consistent with a business's mission and also respect the legal and societal context of their location. They are also built through good service, quality, and economic performance. And they are easier to destroy than to create—a single accident can dent the reputation of a company for decades. For an unknown firm, it may take several years to develop a well-known brand. Local governments tend to welcome business operations as long as they generate employment and exports and attract investment. If, however, a business is found to fail in protecting its workers, local governments will be pressured to intervene and possibly impose sanctions. Politicians may even compete to ensure their popularity by bashing the business. Unions are likely to use accidents to pressure for better conditions and higher pay, and with the diffusion of more information, consumers are also becoming more involved in monitoring the activities of large corporations. Responses can include boycotting a certain product and raising awareness campaigns about malpractices—even if these occur in far-flung locations, the impact can affect sales worldwide. Given that failure to protect the workforce can also have effects on clients, they raise the concerns of shareholders and investors. In sum, it is fundamental for business to ensure that its human input is and remains safe.

Another key input for different types of industries, ranging from white goods manufacturing to call centers, is energy in the form of electricity. Interruptions in electricity supply, more than common in the majority of emerging markets, are an important and yet expected risk for many businesses. It is possible to install independent diesel-operated generators. However, certain businesses (say, aluminum smelting) are energy intensive. For them, it would be extremely costly to rely on small generators—and in some cases, it may be technically impossible. Solutions to manage this type of risk may include being connected to multiple sources of electricity, running their own gas or hydroelectric power-generating plants, and striking special deals with energy providers to attempt to ensure continuous supply. In all cases, dealing with potential interruptions in energy supply entails extra costs. Even a small corner shop or a fast food chain will need its own independent generator to be able to function after dark in spite of electricity shortages—it is hard to imagine how a business may avoid closing when not only computers, but also automatic gates, cameras, and lights stop working. Again, if it is well known that electricity supply is unreliable in a market, then it is an expected risk, and one that businesses should be prepared for (see Box 5.7).

Box 5.7: BHP Billiton Energy Problems in Mozambique

BHP Billiton is one of the world's largest producers of major commodities, including aluminum, copper, and other metals. It is based in over 100 locations throughout the world and in 2012 had revenues of US$72.2 billion and underlying EBIT of US$27.2 billion. The company is the result of the fusion of Billiton PLC, a mining company founded in 1860 in The Netherlands and Broken Hill Proprietary Company (BHP), an Australian company created in 1895. Mozal, an aluminum smelter joint venture project, was established in 1998 with BHP Billiton as the major owner. It is responsible for about 30 percent of the country's official aluminum exports. Mozal relies on Motraco, a Mozambican energy company, for the electrical power supply of its large facilities. Motraco, in turn, imports electricity from the South African company Eskom. In 2008 and 2009, Eskom was unable to meet demand, causing blackouts in South Africa and affecting energy exports to Mozambique. This lowered Mozambique's production and exports of aluminum and had strong negative consequences for BHP's smelting plant.

Sources: All Africa (2013), Peakoil News (2008), Webb (2009), Donelly (2012)

Access to water and shelter can be another risk factor. Water is a key input for several businesses, in particular agribusinesses, and also some industrial processes, including specific parts of mining. The development of the mining complex of Oyu Tolgoi, a copper and gold extractive project in South Mongolia, illustrates this very clearly. Since the exploration company Ivanhoe discovered copper and gold in the area, it took Rio Tinto and its partners almost ten years to develop and make the mine at Oyu Tolgoi operational, mainly because of problems related to its location: Oyu Tolgoi is in the Gobi Desert where water is very scarce, infrastructure (especially electrical lines and water pipes) is nonexistent, and temperatures reach extremely low levels (below –40 Celsius). Developing the project entailed building the necessary infrastructure to house the workers and make the machinery operational—for example, bringing electrical lines from China, and water from the closest aquifer, which is located about 50 km away. Depending on far-away sources of key inputs such as water and electricity generates risks—long pipes and cables are more likely to suffer from leakages and damage, and there are no viable alternatives in the vicinity. It is likely that the companies running the mine will provide large water tanks and powerful generators to prepare for such eventualities, all of which entails extra costs. The forecasted potential of Oyu Tolgoi justifies the scale of the investment and the extra measures needed to compensate for the infrastructural challenges of operating in the desert. Should the mine prove to have much less accessible resources than forecasted, or should the government nationalize the project once it is operational, investors would suffer heavy losses.

Developing a list of key activities and inputs is also useful when thinking about the relative importance of the organizational units and processes that a business manages. If the core business is to extract silver in a location frequently affected by armed violence, it may be a good strategy to delegate some processes, such as accounting, human resource management, and secretarial functions, to safer locations. Focusing only on the operations that have to be carried out in a hazardous environment leads to a better use of the investments aimed at protecting facilities and personnel. Thinking of key inputs also helps in identifying potential critical areas of the business that may suffer in case of even minor disruptions. Let's go back to the previous example of two sister plants in the same country, one focusing on fruit juice production, and the other on bottling fizzy drinks. Both require electricity in their processing lines. Yet, if electricity supply should be interrupted, the implications are different. The bottling plant can halt production without damaging empty bottles, one of its key inputs. The juice factory has a very limited time span during which it can halt production without letting fruit perish, unless it has its own generators to power refrigerated storage houses. In countries where electricity supply is unreliable, both plants are likely to have emergency generators, but the juice-producing plant would require generators that are powerful enough for both its processing line and its refrigerated facilities.

Assessing and Managing Risk

As we discussed in the previous sections of this chapter, there are many ways of assessing risk, generally compiled by specialized private firms, which develop their proprietary indexes. We have suggested a method for identifying the elements of risk going from the general, country level, to the specific risks that threaten our specific activities and key inputs (see Figure 5.3).

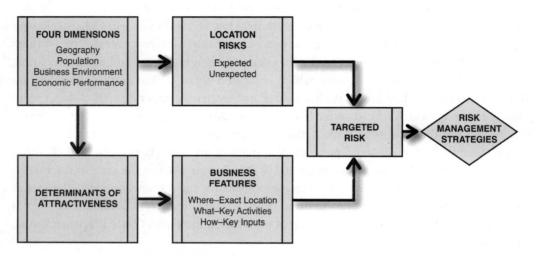

Figure 5.3 From the Determinants of Attractiveness to risk management.

An effective strategy to improve risk evaluation is looking at historical precedents. Searching for archive and historical information can provide a clearer picture of the risks that may seem unexpected but have in fact manifested themselves repeatedly, and the sort of damages they caused to business and society in the past. Historical analysis should focus on three axes: context, own business experience (where that applies), and competitors.

The first step is to look at the context, the country and region, and identify instances when risk has manifested itself—for example, if hurricanes have occurred or if guerrilla groups have attacked an apparel-producing factory. Some industries, such as oil and gas, are more likely to suffer from expropriations and government pressures than others, even within the same location. What are the specific issues related to any industry? If there are local industry associations, we should get in touch with them and learn about the trade. Records of accidents, union mobilization, pollution, and government interference with business can give us an idea of the risks that the sector encountered in the past. The frequency, nature, and effects of these events should improve our assessment of what can be expected. It can also give us an idea of how different elements of risk have affected similar operations in previous occasions.

Our extensive fieldwork has revealed that managers operating in emerging markets often focus on the present and future but have a very vague grasp of history, even of the history of the very firm they work for. They tend to be aware of risks that are manifesting themselves in the present, and to make plans for the future—generally involving optimistic expectations about growth and expansion, and little considerations of risk factors. Large multinationals, such as Ford and Shell, have a long history of operating in difficult environments and in emerging markets. Their past experiences can be very helpful when mapping business risks. A company's history in a given location is like a patient's medical record. It can, for example, explain how the company is perceived by societal actors and why. It can reveal links with specific political parties, confrontations with unions, and other aspects that may, even if events happened several decades in the past, continue to affect the company's image. If the firm is a newcomer in that specific market, we should look for operations in markets that share some characteristics. If, for example, the business is apparel, the first step would be to examine in which of the many locations specialized in apparel manufacturing a company is present. The second step would be to compare such locations and identify common trends as well as differences—for example, costs of labor, levels of unionization, macroeconomic stability, armed criminality, and so forth. Focusing on the few locations that share the most traits, we can identify historical precedents of risk management. Note that corporate units do not always share information, *especially* in case of failure. Finding out whether and how a subsidiary has been affected by risk can be a good starting point for developing new risk management strategies.

Perhaps the most important aspect of studying a company's operations in a specific location is getting to understand how it managed risks. It is likely that certain risks, especially those related to geography, such as landslides and hurricanes, are recurrent. If a meat-processing company has been operating in an area affected by heavy rains, monsoons, and occasional floods for several decades, it probably suffered from these factors on some occasions. It is also likely that it has evaluated the risk and adopted risk management strategies. If the business was sold, or if it left the country for a period, such strategies may have been forgotten and archived. Understanding them is important because it sheds light both on the successes and failures of the firm. If company facilities were flooded and had to close down at some point in the past, it is important to understand whether the risk of floods was suitably taken into account (and hence considered "expected"). If it was unexpected, there may have been no contingency plans, and the damage was partly caused by the surprise factor. If, however, management was aware of the flood risk, why were there no measures to limit and perhaps avoid damage altogether?

Most of the risk elements we have identified and discussed in the previous sections of this chapter are shared across several markets. Hurricanes and floods occur in the Americas as well as in the Indian subcontinent. Political violence affects a large number of emerging markets across the globe. Several economies continue to experience economic mismanagement, which results in high inflation and currency instability. Many others are affected by arbitrary trade rules and threats to private property. It should be easy to find a set of economies that share some salient characteristics. Our risk management strategies need to be developed by taking into account the activities of the firms operating in such economies and their past successes and failures.

First, before designing risk management measures, we advise running brainstorming sessions, studying past events, and defining alternative scenarios. In the flood case, for example, we could start by evaluating the extent of potential damage to the property and workforce as well as the indirect damage of having to interrupt production. Second, we should ask whether the company had taken all of the possible measures to limit damage. Third, we should contemplate alternative scenarios and propose different risk management strategies. Although we can take advantage of cutting-edge technology, and thus implement strategies that were not available in the past, analyzing how a business operates under extreme stress can reveal organizational glitches that persevere through time. Technology is important, but ultimately it is good management that ensures risk is tackled efficiently—even the most advanced technology can become useless if it is not accurately deployed and linked to the practices and contingency plans of a business facility. For example, a factory endowed with a very advanced early warning system can alert its management before government officials do. However, warnings that are too early are liable to be ignored, and evacuations can then be delayed or carried out in a chaotic manner.

In terms of in-house corporate experiences, we should be interested in current and past experiences in the same market, past experiences in similar markets, and past experiences with each of the specific elements of targeted risk we have identified. Having looked at the record of investing and operating in a certain market, and previous experiences in similar markets, it is also important to focus on how a business has dealt with expected and unexpected risks in the past. A firm that has never operated in North Africa, which is about to open a supermarket chain in Egypt, should examine its past experiences in countries that share similar elements of targeted risk. If the firm operates in Bangkok, Thailand, for example, it may be well prepared to operate in urban areas affected by mass mobilization and political violence. If, on the other hand, the firm only operates in cities that have never suffered from this type of risk, it may find it more difficult to adjust in efficient ways—either by overreacting to the threat or by ignoring it and hoping it does not manifest itself.

Another way of examining industry risk is looking at competitors, trying to verify whether they are suffering damages or losses because of specific events and factors. As Porter (2008) points out, looking at competitors is always instructive. For example, does the mining industry have a history of confrontation with local indigenous communities in our area? Even if we set up a different type of mine, and mine a different mineral, this sort of precedent provides an indication that local communities may resist our new operations. If a business never operated in a market, studying how competitors and similar businesses function can provide useful information. Even when a business is already operating in a market, looking at competitors can help identifying risks, as well as benchmark risk management practices. Let's consider banana production in Angola. Who are the players and what risks do they face? Are they local companies or multinational firms? Were they affected by conflict? Did they suffer from natural disasters? What can we learn from this?

Examining and discussing risk in a historical perspective, and benchmarking risk management strategies both against competitors and in relation to in-house past experiences, constitutes the last step of the methodology we propose (see Figure 5.4). It helps to operationalize risk by verifying the sort of damage it has caused in the past, and identifying flaws in risk management strategies that may have failed to tackle it. New measures to manage different aspects of risk should be developed by building on previous experiences and possibly introducing innovative elements to gain some advantage against competitors. Enduring expected risks is a key strategic advantage, especially in emerging markets. The companies that are best prepared for the recurrent risks that affect these markets not will only survive better, they will be better equipped to exploit the business opportunities they generate to sustain their global growth. Risk should be considered as a barrier between companies and the largely untapped natural resources and fast-growing markets of developing regions. Firms that originate from emerging markets are naturally better suited to overcoming this barrier, because their home base shares some of the characteristics of today's most promising locations for business. Firms based in North America, Europe, and Japan need to acquire new capabilities, learn, and adapt. Even firms such as United Fruit that have been operating in emerging markets for decades must adjust their strategies to the continuously evolving political and societal structure of these economies.

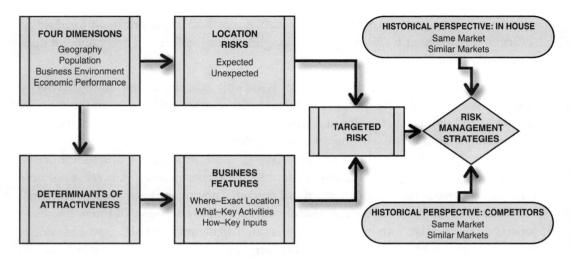

Figure 5.4 Developing risk management strategies.

In conclusion, evaluating the risks of operating in emerging markets is tricky, and depends on subjective judgment, not on objective criteria only. The first step we proposed in this chapter is to use the Four Dimensions to identify the specific characteristics of a market that may entail expected and unexpected risks. The sum of these will allow us to build a table of expected and unexpected location risks. Next, we should focus on the business features, addressing the "where, what, and how" of our business. We should identify the specific geographic areas within the country where we operate (or will operate), our key activities, and our key inputs. At this stage, we should link our location risk table with the business feature table. The elements of location risk that apply to key activities, inputs, and geographic area will generate the expected and unexpected components of targeted risk—in other words, the risks that apply to our case as opposed to the generic location risks that characterize a market. Although this will by no means be an exact measure of risk, it will provide us with a first map of the factors that could damage our business. Next, we should scan for possible risk management strategies related to each type of risk by looking at the practices of competitors as well as in-house current and past experiences. Risk management strategies should be developed by combining past experiences, benchmarking with competitors, and attempting innovative approaches.

References

All Africa (2013). Mozambique: Mozal Aluminium to Be Used in Mozambican Industry. Retrieved from: http://allafrica.com/stories/201302160027.html.

Ayala, J.C., Iturralde, T., and Rodríguez, A. (2000). Construcción de índices simplificados de riesgo país: El caso de Europa. *Investigaciones europeas de dirección y economía de la empresa, Vol. 6, Núm. 1*, pp. 53–70.

Azuela, A. (2011). Cultura jurídica y propiedad urbana en Venezuela. Caracas y las expropiaciones de la era del chavismo entre 2000 y 2009. *Politeia, Vol. 34, Núm. 46*, pp. 47–81.

Clark, J. (1988). Economies of scale and scope at depositary financial institutions: A Review of the literature. *Economic Review*, September/October, pp. 16–33.

Del Ángel, G. and Martinelli, C. (2009). La estatización de 1982 de la banca en México: Un ensayo en economía política.

Díaz, S., Gallego, A., and Pallicero, N. (2008). *Riesgo País en Mercados Emergentes*.

Donelly, L. (2012). Eskom 'must put SA's needs first'. Mail & Guardian. Retrieved from http://mg.co.za/article/2012-01-13-eskom-must-put-sas-needs-first.

Eaton, J., Gersovitz, M., and Stiglitz, J. (1986). The Pure Theory of Country Risk. National Bureau of Economic Research. Working paper No. 1894.

Escaith, H., Teh, R., Keck, A., and Nee, C. (2011). Japan's earthquake and tsunami: International trade and global supply chain impacts. *VOX*. Retrieved from http://www.voxeu.org/article/japans-earthquake-and-tsunami-global-supply-chain-impacts.

Eurasia Group and PricewaterhouseCoopers (2006). Integrating political risk into enterprise risk management. Retrieved from http://www.pwc.com/gx/en/political-risk-consulting-services/pdf/praermfinal.pdf.

FAO (2011). Capacity, Excess Capacity and Overcapacity. Retrieved from http://www.fao.org/docrep/005/y8169e/y8169e0h.htm.

Ferrari, F. and Rofilni, R. (2006). Investing in a Dangerous World: A New Political Risk Index.

Fermandois, J. (2001). La larga marcha a la nacionalización: El cobre en Chile, 1945–1971. *Jahrbuch für Geschichte Lateinamerikas, 38*, pp. 287–312.

Fitch Ratings (2013a). Definitions of Ratings and Other Forms of Opinion. Retrieved from www.fitchratings.com.

Fitch Ratings (2013b). Complete Sovereign Rating History. Retrieved from www.fitchratings.com.

Hernández, R. (1986). La política y los empresarios después de la nacionalización bancaria. *Foro Internacional, Vol. 27, Núm. 2*, pp. 247–265.

Heymann, D. and Sanguinetti, P. (2000) Pseudo equilibrios de expectativas: algunos ejemplos macroeconómicos. *Económica, Vol. 46, Núm. 1*, pp. 23–36.

ICRG (2013). International Country Risk Guide Methodology. Retrieved from http://www.prsgroup.com/ICRG_methodology.aspx.

International Monetary Fund (2012). World Economic Outlook. [Data File]. Retrieved from www.imf.org.

Kennedy, C. (1988). Political Risk Management: A Portfolio Planning Model. *Business Horizons*, 31, 21.

Kiguel, M. and Lopetegui, G. (1997). *Entendiendo el riesgo país.*

Mankiw, G. (2006). *Macroeconomía.* Barcelona: Antoni Bosch, Editor.

Menn, J. (2011). Thai floods may force decline in PC market. *Financial Times.* Retrieved from http://www.ft.com/intl/cms/s/2/cece0090-0bf2-11e1-9310-00144feab-dc0.html#axzz2QzPdRvq9.

Moody's Ratings (2009). Rating Symbols and Definitions. Retrieved from www.moodys.com.

Peakoil News (2008). Mozambique: Mozal Suffers From South African Energy Crisis. Retrieved from http://peakoil.com/alternative-energy/mozambique-mozal-suffers-from-south-african-energy-crisis.

Restrepo, F., Mantilla, G., and Holguín, D. (2007). Calificaciones de riesgo en el mercado de capitales colombiano. Universidad de Medellín.

Standard & Poor's Ratings (2010). Guide to credit rating essentials. Retrieved from http://www.standardandpoors.com/home/es/la.

Sullivan, A. and Sheffrin, S. (2003). *Economics: Principles in Action.* Upper Saddle River, New Jersey: Pearson Prentice Hall.

Supply Chain Risk Management (2011). Five Months On: The Japanese Tsunami's Impact on Global Supply Chains. Supply Chain Risk Management Blog. Retrieved from http://supplychain-risk.com/five-months-on-the-japanese-tsunamis-impact-on-global-supply-chains.

Taleb, N. (2004). *Fooled by Randomness: The Hidden Role of Chance in Life and in the Markets.* New York: Random House.

Taleb, N. (2007). *The Black Swan: The Impact of the Highly Improbable.* New York: Random House.

Thomas, W. and Thomas, D. (1928). *The Child in America: Behavior Problems and Programs.* New York: Alfred A. Knopf.

Toro Echeverri, F. (2012). Nacionalización de empresas en Latinoamérica. *Revista de Negocios Internacionales, Vol. 5, Núm. 1*, pp. 62–66.

UNODC (2011). Global Study on Homicide. United Nations Office on Drugs and Crime.

Webb, M. (2009). BHP confirms Mozal aluminium smelter job cuts. *Mining Weekly.* Retrieved from http://www.miningweekly.com/article/bhp-confirms-mozal-aluminium-smelter-job-cuts-2009-02-23.

What's next Venezuela (2013). Timeline of Expropriations. What's next Venezuela. Retrieved from https://www.whatsnextvenezuela.com/media-kit/timeline-of-expropriations/.

Wilpers, B. (2009). *¿Cómo ha contribuido la influencia de los Estados Unidos en el desarrollo de Chile?* Germany: Auflage.

World Bank Group (2013). World Development Indicators [Data File]. Retrieved from http://databank.worldbank.org/data/databases.aspx.

Wright, R. (2011). Supply chain: Tsunami, floods and storms move logistics up the agenda. *Financial Times.* Retrieved from http://www.ft.com/intl/cms/s/0/754e8758-407a-11e1-9bce-00144feab49a.html#axzz2QzPdRvq9.

6

Targeting Emerging Market Clients I: The Rich and the Middle Classes

Introduction

This chapter turns to an examination of the emerging markets as consumer markets. *People living in emerging markets grow a rising share of the food that an expanding global population consume, work in the assembly lines that produce everything from fridges to iPhones, extract the minerals and energy necessary to sustain global economic growth, develop new high-tech services, and, increasingly, contribute to the global consumption of all of these products and services. Understanding the way these populations live and the production and consumption patterns that characterize emerging markets has become an important new challenge for business. For many managers and entrepreneurs, this will entail getting to grips with realities that differ greatly from their current routines and know-how as well as digging into an unknown that is often less structured and neat than the market forecasts presented in boardrooms.*

Developing strategies that target emerging market clients is a priority for any business that wishes to sell their products or services in emerging markets. A good grasp of the dynamics of emerging markets is needed in order to embed these features in the strategic targeting of products and services. In the next two chapters, we discuss the differences between developed and emerging economies in terms of their markets and clients, showing how companies can exploit such differences to generate new business opportunities. We look at how markets have developed historically to highlight the basic foundations that link emerging markets with developed economies. We examine the specificities of tackling emerging-market customers from a strategic perspective. We draw from the international business and marketing disciplines and from our extensive fieldwork to develop strategic insights for students and practitioners interested in capturing different types of clients in emerging markets (Czinkota and Ronkainen, 2007; Ghemawat,

2001; Hamel and Prahalad, 1993; Kaplan and Norton, 2000; Kim and Mauborgne, 2004; Mintzberg, 2003; Porter, 2008). To achieve this, we propose market segmentation based on income groups, providing some tips about how to develop strategies to win each group of clients and, in some cases, to create markets where they do not exist yet. In this chapter, we discuss targeting the global rich, targeting the upper-middle class, and mass-market targeting the so-called "new middle classes." Consideration of the mass market continues in Chapter 7, "Targeting Emerging Market Clients II: Strategies for the Base of the Pyramid," where we look at targeting the poor (that is, those at the base of the pyramid). The main objective of these chapters is to provide the final step of our conceptual model—after having identified the Determinants of Attractiveness and examined risk, we can now focus on developing strategies suited to successfully targeting the segment of emerging-market clients of most interest to our business.

Targeting the Rich: Globalization and Luxury

With the fall of political barriers to trade and the coming of the "Internet age," we are witnessing an era of increasing international economic integration, often described as "globalization." The iPhone has become as much a global feature as Coca-Cola, desired and available in most markets in the world. Whereas Soviet leaders used to travel in clumsy looking Soviet-built limousines, Chinese government officials prefer the elegance and fine quality of the German-built Audi A8. Globalization has generated a side industry of books examining its political, economic, legal, and philosophical features. It has also stimulated an anti-globalization movement, which helped several artists and writers—Naomi Klein, Manu Chau, and Rage Against the Machine, among them—to boost their sales, riding on the global popularity of their anti-globalization message during the 1990s to 2000s.

Nowadays, a work lunch in Medellin, Colombia, may feature sushi, and your next visit to Ulan Bator, Mongolia, may end up in an Irish pub. Companies that produce luxury goods with a quintessential European flavor, such as Hermes bags, Prada shoes, and Ferrari cars, have more customers in China than in Italy or France. The popularity of their products crosses cultural, linguistic, and political barriers. It can be argued that consumer taste has also converged to a certain extent, creating further demand for the clothes, accessories, cars, and perfumes that American, European, and Japanese companies have been producing for decades. What has really converged are the consumption habits of the world's super rich. The new upper classes from emerging markets have become even more avid consumers of luxury goods than their U.S., Japanese, and European counterparts. They send their offspring to study in the best American universities, drive Mercedes and Bentleys, wear Armani, own football clubs, and mingle with royals and TV celebrities. The super rich differ, however, from other income groups in emerging markets—they often have residency in developed economies, invest globally, and consume globally.

The world market for goods aimed at the rich has become more integrated and standardized. This is not so much to do with falling trade barriers making it cheaper to purchase Louis Vuitton bags, Cavalli dresses, or Crystal champagne. It is because the purchasing power of the wealthiest consumers based in emerging markets has increased strongly, thus making a range of goods and services that were previously off limits affordable for them. Rich emerging market consumers are well informed, travel frequently, and follow the latest fashions and trends. Their taste tends, for now, to converge with the criteria established by the firms that created the luxury industry, such as the fashion designers of New York, Paris, and Milan. They are influenced by Hollywood movies and the style of Western celebrities, ranging from actors to businesspeople and artists. Purchasing the best available Western products is a way of enjoying the recently acquired wealth, a way of living the consumerist dream and displaying their status within their society. Luxury goods producers have benefitted from this by multiplying the offerings of "aspirational goods"—products that consumers buy for the status they attach to them rather than their utility (see Box 6.1). What are the lessons for business here? How do we target the super rich of emerging markets? Is it so different from targeting the super rich anywhere else?

Box 6.1: Aspirational Goods

Aspirational goods are goods that people associate with high purchasing power or social and economic status. Consumers are willing to pay more for a product with an aspirational image, even if it has the same characteristics as others in the same category. Brand and exclusive design often contribute to conferring the aspirational character to the good (Yeoman and McMahon-Beattie, 2005).

Sources: Jan-Benedict, Steenkamp, Batra, and Alden (2003); Bearden and Etzel (1982); Hart, Hoe, and Hogg (2004); Yeoman and McMahon-Beattie (2005); Doyle (1990).

Keep Your Positioning High: Do Not Popularize Exclusive Brands

The rich of emerging markets are growing in number, they are wealthy—even more so than U.S. and European luxury goods consumers—and they are not concerned about small decreases in price (see Figure 6.1). On the contrary, attempts to popularize a brand by making it more accessible may have the effect of alienating consumers that look for exclusivity. There are opportunities to develop new goods that from the inception are exclusive and targeted at the new rich—a special, limited-edition mineral water bottle or a custom-made mobile phone holder. Phillip Starck, one of the most famous designers and artists in the world, provides us with a good example of this. He exploited his reputation as a designer to provide services for the super rich, designing ad hoc yachts and interiors for the wealthy that wanted something truly "exclusive." The best universities in the world (think Harvard, Oxford, Cambridge, Yale, MIT, NYU, and Columbia) compete to capture wealthy emerging-market clients. They have signed cooperation agreements with institutions based in emerging markets and have opened campuses in new locations, such as Brazil, China, and Dubai. The risk of this strategy is that as a degree with the coveted brand of a prestigious university becomes more affordable and accessible through local campuses, it may also become less desirable by the top earners, who would send their offspring to study abroad partly to ensure that they achieve an exclusive foreign degree.

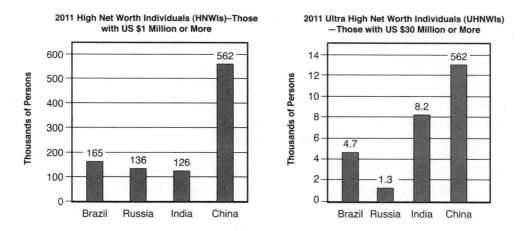

Figure 6.1 Number of millionaires in selected emerging markets.

Data Source: World Ultra Wealth Report 2011 and World Wealth Report 2012

A basic marketing principle that applies equally to developed and emerging markets is the importance of distinguishing products according to the segment of clients they target: if Ferrari started making cheap compact cars, it would certainly sell more cars in terms of volume, but it would also erode the value of its brand for its traditional customers, many of whom would be appalled at seeing their beloved prancing horse on cheap "popular" cars.

Creating and maintaining different offerings for different income groups is fundamental for companies that sell their products and services not only to the super rich, but also to upper-middle classes. In the case of a top ranking university, it is important that the super rich continue to perceive that full-length, higher-priced degrees are more prestigious and add more value than off-campus, distance learning or shorter degrees from the same institution. The trade-off here is value against volume—a firm selling products and services that positions itself as high value can increase volume only to the point where this begins eroding its brand value. Many companies produce limited numbers of their goods precisely to accentuate their exclusivity. By doing so, they limit their potential revenues but enhance the brand value, thus ensuring that their future products will maintain the same appeal, and providing an incentive for current clients to engage in repeat purchases. The strategy involves at times accepting lower sales in the short run to ensure the long-run sustainability of the business, which is, in the case of luxury products, very much linked to how potential clients perceive the brand. All luxury goods producers position themselves high in the market. Ensuring that this positioning is clear and does not dilute over time will help in capturing the wealthy emerging-market consumers.

Build Value on a Product's Origin

The rich of emerging markets want to own goods produced in prestigious locations associated with style. They do not want luxury goods made at home. To maintain their appeal, companies targeting this group of consumers do well to emphasize their links to their home base and to build up or encourage side businesses related to it—visits to the headquarters with exclusive tours, for example. Buyers of Ferrari like to visit Maranello, to learn about the history of the village, to breathe the air, and to try the food and, obviously, the cars. They want to be part of the Ferrari dream, not just to own an expensive toy. Buyers of Bentley and Aston Martin want to tap in to the essence of British class, not just speed. Offering emerging-market clients a taste of the tradition and culture that surrounds most Triad luxury goods can strengthen brand equity while generating extra sources of income. Given that these new consumers may know very little about the particularity of these locations, using location as a strength and competitive advantage also means educating consumers—explaining why making the leather bag in that area of France is important leads to a greater appreciation of the uniqueness of what they have purchased. Château Lafite Rothschild, a wine producer owned by the Rothschild family, has successfully established itself as the most recognized wine brand in China, a market where wine consumption is still relatively new. Its popularity has ensured a rapid increase in sales and the average price per bottle sold. Visiting the Château Lafite Rothschild winery has become a "must" for wealthy Chinese tourists visiting France.

Create Brand Awareness

Although they tend to be informed and aware of fashion and luxury trends, wealthy consumers in emerging markets may not know about *all* of the niche brands that exist. The desirability of luxury goods is related not only to what the consumer knows but also to the fact that others know the brand, too, and may envy the newly acquired product. Creating brand awareness in target markets is important, even when a good may be unaffordable for the vast majority of consumers in that market. Being associated with the consumption habits of people who are famous locally, both local celebrities and popular foreigners, helps to build the image of exclusivity needed to justify the purchase of a luxury. Opening classy stores in exclusive areas of big cities is an expensive strategy, but it can pay off if it helps to build brand image. Bottega Veneta, an upmarket clothes and apparel producer based in Italy, followed precisely this strategy—although it is a relatively small player in Europe, it pursued an aggressive expansionary strategy in China, developing a strong brand awareness there, which in turn contributed positively to sales (see Table 6.1).

Table 6.1   Luxury Goods Stores

	Europe	China
Bottega Veneta	44	38
Louis Vuitton	108	43
Tiffany Co.	34	22
Prada	84	24

Data Source: Companies' websites

Innovate with an Eye to Tradition

In order to ensure they encourage repeat purchases by their consumers, producers of luxury goods need to innovate constantly. The challenge of this is that they simultaneously have to stick to tradition. A Louis Vuitton bag that does not look like Louis Vuitton loses an important element of its desirability. The strategic hint therefore is to introduce elements of novelty while building on the elements of class and tradition associated with origin that contribute toward the product's exclusivity. Louis Vuitton, part of the French luxury goods group LVMH, is a good example of a company that uses continuous innovation and creativity to build on tradition.

Link Exclusive Consumers

The desire of exclusivity drives the consumption of luxury and other high-priced products and services. Producers can emphasize this by generating events and occasions, real and virtual, that make their consumers feel not only individually special, but part of an exclusive group. Using these initiatives, a company can reinforce how owning a certain product is related to particular desired lifestyle and to a set of exclusive preferences (for example, an appreciation of aesthetics), and this can create invisible bonds among consumers.

Plan for the Future

This is the golden age of luxury producers. The number of wealthy consumers has increased, yet their preferences have converged, which contributes to explaining the strong performance of firms specialized in luxury goods. However, the current situation may not last for long. It is not enough to be making healthy profits with an established business model; competitive firms need to look at the future and think about new products, services, and ways of selling them to affluent emerging-market consumers.

The taste of the emerging-market upper classes may change through time, in line with the decline in Western geopolitical and economic influence. Currently, the rich tend to demand a very similar range of cars, yachts, clothes, and vacations, regardless of where they are from. This is the result of several factors. First, up to a few decades ago, the vast majority of rich consumers were based in the U.S., Europe, and Japan. Naturally, they have influenced the fashion industry with their taste. The rich from emerging markets are still a relatively new phenomenon. Perhaps in time, they will not only be consumers but also alter the luxury industry to their taste. An example of this trend is the success of the Porsche Cayenne, the first SUV vehicle launched by the brand. In spite of its break with tradition, the Cayenne was very successful and has provided Porsche with a healthy stream of sales revenues. One of the factors accounting for its success is that it attracted emerging-market consumers who desired a premium vehicle that was not only fast and sporty, but also spacious, with off-road capabilities (and could be made bulletproof, if necessary). Thanks to the Cayenne's popularity in emerging markets, particularly China, the 2008–2012 slump in demand for expensive cars in France, Italy, Spain, and Portugal has not affected Porsche at all. On the contrary, Porsche's sales expanded between 2008 and 2012, sustained by the rising appeal of the Cayenne and the continuing success of the more traditional 911 model.

The economic dominance of Europe, the U.S., and Japan means that the majority of luxury goods producers are based in these countries, especially in Europe and the U.S.

Emerging markets are, however, developing their own luxury brands, especially in food and drinks—think luxury Mau Tai or high-end Tequila. These products are, for now, often used as gifts to foreigners, or consumed on specific occasions by the emerging-market rich. They are, more often, the favorites of the emerging-market upper classes, which, as we illustrate in this section, are less globalized than the rich. It may take some time before these products become as truly global as champagne or caviar. It will likely occur for competitive producers who gradually build their brands, engage in aggressive international marketing, and leverage the appeal of novelty. Whether it happens, and how fast, depends also on the capacity of these companies to emulate Triad luxury producers in developing a prestigious brand image and ensuring consistent high quality.

Targeting the Upper-Middle Classes: Urban and Aspiring to Become Super Rich

A look at the changing tour destinations of the big music stars—from electronic music gurus such as Armin Van Buren, to pop stars such as Lady Gaga and older rock groups such as AC/DC—illustrates the extent to which consumption has become globalized: they attract huge crowds all around the world, and in some cases their appeal is even greater in emerging markets. The Rock in Rio music festival, which takes place in Brazil, has become one of the largest and most prestigious events for rock musicians. Psy trance and techno DJs often play more gigs in China, Mexico, and Brazil than in Europe and the U.S. The fans that pay hundreds of dollars to go to these events are not just the wealthy from emerging markets or else they would not fill huge stadiums. The super rich maintain exclusivity because they also then attend premiere events and obtain special VIP seats for much higher prices, or they may organize their own niche exclusive events. The increasing appeal of the live music industry in new markets is due to the increased affluence of upper-middle income classes. These consumers are far more numerous than the super rich, and yet they have a much higher purchasing power than the average citizen in their respective economies. They live mainly in capitals and large cities. Their taste is urban and inspired by the super rich. Many of the goods that the super rich can afford, such as personal jets and yachts, are beyond their means. Other products, such as luxury bags, vacations in prestigious resorts, and designer clothing are not only available to them but also highly desired because they represent an upward movement in terms of disposable wealth and the status this confers in society.

A key difference between the wealthiest emerging market consumers and upper-middle class consumers is that the latter are less global. They may travel and invest, but they tend to maintain stronger local links. Many of them are not fluent in foreign languages and remain attached to their country of origin for their key business and personal relations. Whereas the super rich may go to places such as Eaton for their high school education, the upper-middle classes tend to study locally. They populate the expensive and exclusive private schools that are mushrooming in the large cities of emerging markets. Some of them will study abroad, but this will most likely be for graduate education as opposed to pursuing their main degree abroad. Many of them will study in the top business institutions of their respective countries, which are growing in number, size, and reputation. Although the number of Chinese, Brazilians, and Mexicans pursuing an MBA in the U.S. is growing, it is a drop in the ocean when compared to the growth in Chinese, Brazilians, and Mexicans studying for an MBA in their top home business schools. For these students, being in home-based institutions has several advantages. To begin with, it tends to be more affordable than studying abroad. It also involves less challenge in terms of cultural and linguistic adaptation. A factor that is becoming increasingly important is that studying in home-based institutions allows students to stay connected to the family business, while also creating or strengthening links to other local businesses. Given that emerging-market economies have been outperforming developed economies for almost two decades, maintaining links to the local economy has become an important factor for upper-middle class prospective students. If 30 years ago studying in the U.S. or UK was appealing in part because it generated opportunities to stay in these countries and work there, now the opposite is occurring: studying in developed economies may be less appealing because it entails being disconnected from the fast-growing economic reality of emerging markets, especially for students that are already involved in business. Conversely, studying in home-based institutions may be a little bit less prestigious but may be compensated for by the opportunities it creates in the local context. Studying in a limited group of prestigious, and yet local, not global, educational establishments strengthens networking at a local or, at most, regional level. This observation helps us to define this group of consumers—aspiring to be elite, feeling exclusive, increasingly well educated, linked to local business and politics, wealthier than most, yet not quite part of the top-tier elite of their country and not as globally connected.

These traits also affect their consumer tastes and consumption habits. They imitate the super rich, acquiring goods and trends observed in London and New York. But, partly because they are less exposed to global trends than the super wealthy, they make their own interpretations of such trends, influencing them and transforming them. In the following sections, we discuss the strategies for targeting upper-middle class emerging-market consumers.

Numerous, Growing in Number, Affluent

This group of consumers is much more numerous than the super wealthy, and it accounts for approximately US$7 trillion of consumption per year (McKinsey, 2010). The fact that they are numerous and concentrated in large urban centers facilitates the cross-fertilization of global and local fashions and trends. Although less wealthy than the rich, upper-middle class emerging-market consumers generate a far higher demand for luxury goods and services in terms of value simply because they are far more numerous. Not only is this group of consumers larger, it is expanding very rapidly as emerging-market middle-class professionals climb the corporate ladder and acquire higher positions and consequently higher incomes. This group also includes millions of local entrepreneurs that lead local companies, which, in spite of being unknown internationally, have been growing steadily for the last 20 years: Chinese manufacturing companies making textiles, apparel, valves, and mechanical parts; Colombian fast food or pub chains; Indian soft drink producers; Vietnamese software houses, and many other types of business. We interviewed hundreds of entrepreneurs from a variety of emerging markets and industries and found that very often they are much less international and globalized than textbooks generally account for—many entrepreneurs, even those involved in exporting, are not able to communicate in English and rely on interpreters and middle men. Often, they only sell locally. The businesses they run have been successful in the past 20 years, benefitting from the growth of the economies they are based in. They have also been a key motor of such growth—in spite of the difficulties that affect business in emerging markets, from bad roads to conflicts, these entrepreneurs have generated jobs, exports, invested in new ventures, and successfully captured an ever-rising share of the world's manufacturing output. We have come across many instances of entrepreneurs who live modestly themselves but fund luxuries for their families. In sum, this group of consumers is much more embedded in local society than the super rich. It wants its offspring to become more global, to live a better life, and to acquire status. For this reason, targeting this group is less straightforward than it may at first seem.

Between the Rich and the Middle Class: Getting the Price Right

The purchasing power of this income group is lower than that of the super rich. Despite this, targeting luxury goods at this group does not entail making it too affordable. These consumers want exclusivity just as much as the super rich, notwithstanding their lower purchasing power. If they perceive a good to be too affordable or insufficiently exclusive, they may shun it. Hence, getting the price right is the trickiest part of targeting this group. It is important that premium products demand a premium price, yet also fall within their buying power. In other words, positioning the product accurately is particularly important for these consumers. It means accurately gauging the position of a product to fit in between the global luxury and the local premium offerings.

Interviewing the managers of luxury good producers operating in China, Russia, Indonesia, and Brazil, we found that a very common mistake is the assumption that the purchasing power of the upper-middle classes in these economies is much lower than that of their Japanese or U.S. equivalent income groups. Although in pure economic terms their earnings may be lower, these consumers benefit from lower living costs (for example, lower average rents). They also have a higher propensity to spend than U.S., European, and Japanese consumers, which can be explained by looking at several factors: first, on average, they have become rich more recently. Second, in most cases, their economies have been performing well and so have their businesses or the companies they work for. This makes them optimistic about spending their newly acquired wealth, while the opposite is true in developed economies—in other words, their positive expectations about future earnings push them to have a higher propensity to consume. Third, precisely because of the novelty of wealth, they may be more likely to engage in consumption that performs a social function—buying goods and services that show their wealth and power in their respective societies. The upshot of this is that products should not be priced too low, or else a given product may cease to be perceived as premium by this group of consumers.

Educating New Consumers

This group of consumers has acquired wealth more recently than the super rich and is less exposed to global trends. As a result, their understanding of the trends and fashions that emerge in New York or London may vary and be filtered by local interpretations. Creating brand awareness for them requires more effort than for the super rich—it is not enough to be visible at the global level; it becomes important to be very visible locally as well as globally. For the super rich meeting world-famous footballers, rockers, and even politicians, it is possible. For the upper-middle classes from emerging markets, the global elite is too distant and out of reach. Its role in influencing their consumption is precisely that—a distant, desirable, yet probably unreachable model, which inspires but is insufficient in shaping taste by itself. These models need to be "localized" in ways that make them closer to the reality of the targeted consumers. This can be done by pursuing links with local VIPs, business leaders, and artists who are closer to their territory and symbolize a more attainable dream of success. Substituting Western models with local beauties in adverts for fashion clothing is, for example, a highly advisable and simple strategy. Visibility needs to be greater and more anchored in the local society and economy in order to generate the sort of brand image that can foster sustained sales of premium products to this group.

Experimenting, Moving Beyond Tradition, and Understanding Local Trends

The upper-middle classes of emerging markets are less traditional than the super rich—they are generally more willing to experiment and embrace the new. This generates interesting opportunities for businesses willing to experiment—for example, introducing products that move away from their established corporate traditions. Another implication of the fact that this group of consumers is less global is that their perception of what is luxurious and exclusive is influenced by local trends, which can be, and indeed are, created and manipulated by successful companies. It is possible to target these consumers by creating a new brand and position it as premium through intensive advertising in a given market. It is also possible to elevate a less prestigious brand to a more prestigious status aimed at these consumers using a market-by-market approach. As far as the brand is perceived to be premium in the target market, it is irrelevant that in Frankfurt the same brand is considered rather lower middle class. This involves understanding exactly what makes a brand premium in a specific emerging market and what actions can help in building such reputation. Raising a brand's profile in emerging markets entails exploiting local factors and combining them with global strengths to generate brand awareness and stimulate consumers' desire. The strategies to target this type of consumer can blend the old and the new and mix in local elements. As long as the pricing and image remain prestigious in the target market a company will be able to maintain its premium positioning.

Capturing these consumers is vital for a broad range of companies that have the capabilities to produce premium goods and services. Their demand generates the high profit margins that characterize premium niches but with high and fast-growing volumes. Given that these consumers' taste is more locally oriented but still very much global in comparison to the majority of emerging market consumers, established companies can easily exploit their accumulated know-how in brand building and brand management. They can also use their own corporate history to achieve this—after all, companies such as Armani, Hugo Boss, and Lacoste built their brands mainly during the 1960s to 1980s, riding on the economic growth of the European and U.S. economies. They may be able to replicate and adapt the basic strategies through which they successfully captured consumers in the developed economies.

Disconnected Markets, Growth Potential: Mass Markets in Emerging Economies

This section moves from a consideration of highly profitable but limited niches of the market to examining how to approach the large, and often untapped, mass markets of emerging economies, which include the majority of the world's population. These markets hold an immense potential and yet are difficult to target. They are often very fragmented, disconnected from the global market, and strongly affected by culture and tradition. The institutional voids, infrastructural deficiencies, and local idiosyncrasies that we discussed in the first part of the book become particularly important for the companies that intend to capture a share of the lower-income emerging-market consumers. Our discussion starts with a brief reflection upon the extent to which the world has become globalized, and for whom.

For those who travel in a similar style to a high-profile politician, IMF officer, or senior executive, it is easy to agree with the idea that the world is becoming more globalized. This kind of travel probably entails staying in a five-star hotel, which can be pretty impersonal and unvarying despite their location, eating in restaurants that cater to a globalized taste, chatting in English, and then moving on to the next country, hotel, or meeting. If we were to travel like this, we may meet some of the global elite, some super-rich businessmen, a president, or a minister. We would certainly meet the upper-middle classes—the entrepreneurs that lead most of the firms that have an important presence in these markets, but that may not yet be global, the senior managers that work at local subsidiaries of multinational corporations, economists, scientists, and a broad range of policy makers. However, we will meet them in "our" setting—a globalized and increasingly standardized setting. In fact, whenever they can, emerging-market upper classes prefer to meet foreigners in settings that are very globalized, partly to make their hosts feel at ease, and partly to emphasize their status as aspiring global elites. This strengthens the impression of convergence and the idea that the world is "flat."

If we were to stroll a little way off from our hotel and grab a local snack from a cart, we would find that the world is not as globalized as many academics and policy makers would have us believe after all. The further we walk from the "business districts," the more apparent this is. Stylish bars playing electronic music and sushi chains are now omnipresent in the big cities of emerging markets. But they cater to a small share of the population, together with a few tourists and expats. Even in large cities, such as Lagos and Jakarta, most of the Western-style bars and restaurants are concentrated in relatively small districts. What about the millions of citizens that do not go to these establishments? Should we assume they do not eat out or drink? Who are they, where do they go, and what do they consume?

Any business interested in emerging markets will do well to recognize that only a minor share of the population of these economies lives and consumes according to trends that are more or less converging to Western standards. Those who do are the wealthier consumers discussed in the previous section. The rest is made up of a growing lower-middle class and a very large number of people who live in poverty. Both these groups are much more disconnected from the global market than the super rich and the upper-middle class and are therefore less visible to the occasional business visitor. Making these consumers visible, understanding them, and targeting them is an important strategic objective for any firm operating in emerging markets that does not focus only on luxury.

The integration of markets across spatial and cultural boundaries has popularized the idea of "globalization"—a world without borders, where consumer tastes converge, distance and cultural differences cease to matter, and people everywhere are linked together by trade relationships. Since the 1990s, barriers to trade and investment have declined dramatically while technology has simultaneously reduced communication costs. This has resulted in a strong increase in the flows of information, capital, and people moving across national borders. Trade in manufacturing goods and foreign direct flows have grown exponentially, benefitting mainly emerging markets—the locations where capital was scarcer, labor costs were lower, and in general where there were more unexploited business opportunities. China's accession to the World Trade Organization in 2001 brought into the international market one of the largest and most populous countries in the world, albeit a very poor one at the time. Japanese, American, and European companies competed fiercely to capture a share of these new markets—in other words, to capture consumers that had previously been inaccessible because of trade and investment barriers. Chinese entrepreneurs were quick to exploit the trend—they established millions of companies manufacturing products for international consumers. They focused on production efficiency, exploiting low labor costs, at times less-than-stringent labor and environmental regulations, and economies of scale. They internationalized, selling to global buyers such as Walmart and Gap and to intermediaries who handled the export of their goods. In ten years, Chinese manufacturers became dominant in several fields: electronic consumer goods, jeans, bras, and shoes, among others (see Table 6.2). Their products are common from London to Dhaka and Kuala Lumpur. Certainly this is a visible sign of market globalization and one that highlights the rising importance of emerging markets.

It may seem odd to argue that there are hundreds of millions of consumers who are delinked from the global economy. What about connectedness, the role of social networks, and cell-phone connections? The number of mobile phone subscriptions and Internet connections has increased steadily in emerging markets from the 2000s, closing the gap in connectedness with developed economies (see Figure 6.2). In 2000, almost 60 percent of the world's Internet users were based in either North America or Europe. Only 1 percent was based in Africa and 5 percent in Latin America. By 2012, the number of users based in North America and Europe had decreased to 32 percent of the total, while

Africa's share rose from 1 percent to 7 percent and Latin America's from 5 percent to 11 percent.

Table 6.2   Footwear Production by Country

Footwear Production 2012		
Country	**Pairs (Millions)**	**World Share**
China	12,887	60.50%
India	2,209	10.40%
Brazil	819	3.80%
Vietnam	804	3.80%
Indonesia	700	3.30%
Pakistan	298	1.40%
Bangladesh	276	1.30%
Mexico	253	1.20%
Thailand	244	1.20%
Italy	207	1.00%

Data Source: 2012 World Footwear Yearbook

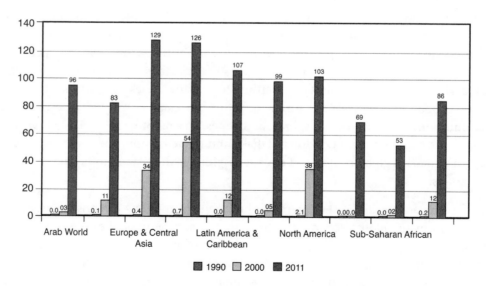

Figure 6.2   Cell phone subscriptions (per 100 people).

Data Source: World Ultra Wealth Report 2011 and World Wealth Report 2012

The impact of "connectedness" is, however, more limited than it may appear at first sight. Using the Internet for business (for example, to advertise or to search for buyers) does integrate markets: it transmits information that overcomes physical barriers. But it does not perform this function in a globally homogenous way. The World Wide Web is supposed to be identical in every location. The reality is that it is not—it is different depending on where it is accessed. Ironically, the very tool that is supposed to overcome geographical and cultural barriers actually mirrors them. The reasons for this are two-fold. The first is political: as with trade barriers, countries have a sovereign right to regulate the Internet. They do so when monitoring websites for illegal activities (for example, terrorism or prostitution). And they do so for political purposes, censoring websites that threaten the establishment. The Chinese government, for example, invests huge sums to monitor and occasionally stamp out dissent on online forums and websites.

The second reason why the Web differs according to where it is accessed is language. Unless a Chinese seller advertises his or her wares in English, or by preference in Japanese, it is unlikely that a Japanese consumer will buy them. The very search for keywords is a function of language and semantic meanings—it is sometimes called a "semantic search." The implication is that consumer groups that are able to communicate only in their own language have access only to the websites published in that language, as permitted by the government that rules that territory. Up to now, English has dominated the World Wide Web in terms of the number of websites and the number of visitors accessing these websites (see Figure 6.3). The movement toward Internet connectedness began and was developed first by entrepreneurs and firms based in the United States. The U.S. also concentrates a high share of Internet traffic simply because of its economic size—it is still the largest economy in the world. Finally, English is the de facto language of choice for international transactions and international communication—many websites are in English simply to increase the chances of being read and understood, even in situations where both the website's owners and intended viewers are not native English speakers. The second key language of the Web is naturally Chinese—in this case, the driving factors are the number of Chinese speakers in the world and the growing importance of the Chinese economy. In spite of the role of English and Chinese, the Web is still fragmented in terms of language, available content, and the way in which search engines show such content to us. Whereas the percentage of websites in English and in languages used mainly in developed economies, such as German, Italian, and Japanese, has slightly declined, the percentage of websites in languages spoken in emerging markets, such as Chinese, Spanish, French, Portuguese, and Polish, has increased (see Figure 6.3).

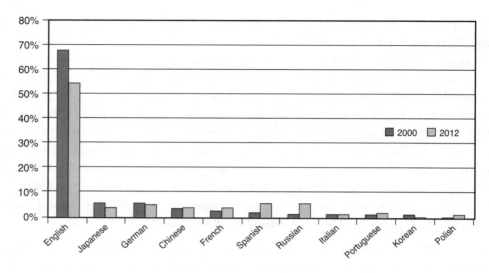

Figure 6.3 Web pages by language.

Data Source: World Bank

English has certainly facilitated the diffusion of the Web and its use as an instrument to link buyers and suppliers. However, as in the Middle Ages, dominance of a lingua franca remains the privilege of native speakers and educated foreigners—there are millions of people worldwide who are unable to communicate in English, many of whom live in emerging markets. In many economies, such as India and Guatemala, there are large shares of the population who are not capable of trading in the official language of their own country—Spanish and Hindi, respectively. Ethnic minorities or marginalized groups can be poorly educated, which hinders their communication skills in the official language and often even more so with English. This isolates them from both the national and global markets, locking them into poorly remunerated jobs. This is an example of the role that language continues to play in integrating and dividing markets, even markets that are virtually integrated on the Web. Failure to communicate means failure to exchange information, a key prerequisite for trade. And misunderstandings increase transaction costs and thus limit trade.

Culture and consumer tastes also affect what is available in a specific language and location on the Web. The preference for sports is a classic example of how consumer demand drives Internet content. Information about Hollywood movies and American elections tend to reach all corners of the globe—the images of Kenyans celebrating the victory of Obama because of his ancestry illustrated the effects of connectedness. Yet, information about American football is not very widespread outside of the U.S. Even the Super Bowl, one of the most popular sporting events in the U.S., is scarcely known in most emerging markets. In the vast majority of cases, this is not because American football is censored. It is simply that emerging-market consumers are not interested in the sport. On the other hand, they may closely follow the English and Spanish football premier leagues, baseball, cricket, or Formula 1.

Another key limiting factor of the global impact of the Internet and Internet devices is the fact that a large number of people continue to lack access to them. There are physical and economic barriers to the diffusion of the Internet. In terms of fixed access, many locations in the developing world have never been linked to a landline. As such, they cannot be linked to the Internet via telephone cables (for example, through modems). A large number of locations are also not reached by the cables used for broadband connections, which limits the possibility of fast access to the Web. In other words, the Web we are used to accessing for work and entertainment reasons, the Web of instant streaming and YouTube, is still very much a Web targeted to, and mainly used by, consumers based in developed economies and the upper classes of emerging markets. The vast majority of emerging market consumers do not have access to the Web. For those that do, access is slow and unreliable, making applications that need constant and speedy connections unusable.

As of 2013, access is still not as pervasive as we may think. Millions of people continue to live without access to information available online, separated from virtual markets and from the opportunities they generate. This is changing rapidly—the advent of portable Internet devices and the decline in their price mean that Internet access will reach more and more people. Indeed, access via mobile phones is already allowing millions of emerging-market consumers who never had a landline or Internet connection to be linked, if sporadically and with limited content, to the Web.

The spread of cheap mobile phone handsets is fostering a new trend that has huge implications for business—the growing connectedness of millions of lower-middle class and poor emerging-market consumers. Although they may be connected, they are very unlikely to have the high-tech, high-speed, reliable connections you can find in Manhattan. The business potential here is not in the potential capacity to download and upload heavy content speedily, but rather in the sheer number of people who are becoming connected and hence forming new markets. The diffusion of mobile phone banking in Africa is a perfect illustration of this phenomenon—technology has brought down communication barriers and has linked potential consumers and providers, creating a market for an innovative service even before the latter became common in the developed world. Technology companies that focus on the type of products and innovations that can be targeted to these consumers will benefit greatly from economies of scale. They will also cater to markets that are still relatively untapped. Conversely, firms that continue innovating with the rich-world consumer in mind may find it harder to grow. The attempt to shift large amounts of Internet content to remote servers or cloud computing, for example, provides interesting potential for cost savings for large companies based in any economy. It can also be appealing for consumers who have almost continuous, fast, and reliable access to the Internet. It becomes irrelevant for any consumer who has less than optimal access and who risks being cut off from their data every time there is an interruption in connectivity.

Per-capita incomes and purchasing power are also important factors to consider. Different economies are characterized by different levels of wealth and wealth distribution. Even if the international car market were integrated, buying a US$40,000 BMW would require more than a decade's worth of salaries for a Chinese or Ghanaian skilled worker (for example, one working in a car assembly factory). Assuming there were no trade barriers, the same car would cost the equivalent or less than a year's salary for a Japanese or German worker carrying out the same task. Most products developed for the average rich-country consumer are simply too expensive for most emerging-market consumers. Because of their lower purchasing power, these consumers are cut off from the market for a broad range of goods and services. Yet their consumption is increasing, and it is highly diversified. However, with their focus on developed markets, Western companies are often not aware of this.

Finally, trade barriers and regulations often contribute to further isolating emerging-market consumers by making products and services more expensive and thus even less affordable to them. To buy a German-built BMW in China or Vietnam, it is necessary to pay an import tax, which makes it almost twice as expensive than it would be if the international car market were truly integrated. The same BMW model would not be affordable to a German worker if it were sold at the final price that it is sold in China; it would be a product for the upper classes. This illustrates that even if purchasing power were exactly the same across the world, trade barriers can still make certain products unaffordable for most consumers. Emerging markets tend to have higher barriers to trade than developed economies as a measure to protect their manufacturing industries and to raise tax revenues. An unintended result is that imported products, including intermediary goods, such as mechanical parts and other inputs for corporate clients, become much more expensive than their average prices in developed markets. Diverging taxation on imported products contributes to explaining why consumption patterns change so dramatically across emerging markets, even when average incomes do not differ much.

Technological change and falling political barriers to trade have undoubtedly brought new markets into the international economy, which has led some observers to claim the world had become "flat," converging toward a presumably Western- and American-dominated cultural standard. Yet language, culture, and persisting political and physical barriers continue to divide markets. Today we can observe continuing diversity, occasional friction between different cultures, and ultimately different customs and different ways of doing things. So although we do find McDonald's in almost every corner of the world, the menus, recipes, and even the layout of the restaurants and the type of clients they target, change. In India, instead of a Big Mac, you can get a Maharajah Mac. *Sex and the City, Desperate Housewives,* and other shows may have been visibly popular in a large number of markets, especially Triad ones, and yet Bollywood blockbusters dominate in Asia, outstripping these series in popularity, but remain largely unknown in the West. To consider food again for a moment, think how popular sushi has become in Western societies, especially among health-conscious consumers who tend to be from higher-income groups. Yet there are thousands of delicacies from different cultures that continue to remain obscure to the majority of consumers, even in the most affluent economies. Culture also divides markets in terms of taste—the use of a main meal prevails in Northern Europe and the North America, whereas in India, Japan, and China, a typical meal out tends to involve several small dishes. In Italy, a set of small dishes "antipasti" precedes a strictly denominated "first course," which can be pasta, soup, or rice, followed by a "second course" of meat or fish.

The differences in markets become particularly obvious when we consider emerging markets and their consumers. If we apply American or European definitions of middle class, the vast majority of emerging-market inhabitants qualify as poor. Yet consumers who earn around US$10,000 per year would not qualify as poor in most emerging markets. They work in different jobs and have different consumption habits than the poor, live in different areas, and tend to have better educational attainments. They perceive themselves to be different from the poor and strive to distance themselves from them. They may not consume what is affordable to a German worker, but their consumption is far higher in terms of value than those of the poorest income groups in their countries, and it is rising fast. Next, we turn to identifying the features of these consumers and discuss how we can target them.

The New Middle Classes

As emerging economies grow, a rising share of their population moves out of poverty into the middle class, reaching the point where consumption increases. In other words, the trend is for this group of consumers to grow fast and become more affluent. According to Bain & Company, between 2010 and 2020 about 1.3 billion people will join the ranks of the new middle classes (Bain & Company, 2011). Their purchasing power is lower than that of the upper-middle classes, but their numbers are far higher—this provides important potential for achieving high economies of scale in industries where fixed costs are high, such as white goods and transport equipment. The emerging-market middle classes are changing their economies and societies in ways that mirror the formation of an increasingly wealthy middle class in the U.S. between the 1900s and 1960s, and in Europe and Japan between the 1950s and the 1970s. They are leading a dramatic change in consumption patterns. They are simultaneously producers and consumers, generating the economic fabric that transformed poor economies into developed, sophisticated ones in the past. They are educated, typically to secondary school level, and tend to have specialized skills. Education and skills distinguish them from the poor, providing them with access to jobs that are not only better remunerated but also often have better conditions in terms of stability, pension, and health benefits. They are an extremely important group of consumers precisely because of their differences with both the wealthier upper-middle class and the poor. They are vastly more numerous than the upper-middle classes—some estimates forecast they will number around 4 billion people by 2020 (Kharas, 2010). And, unlike the poor, they do not spend the majority of their incomes on food and shelter. They have disposable income to spend on other items of consumption. Historical evidence illustrates that consumption increases at the same pace as income until all basic needs, especially food and shelter, are satisfied; it then increases at a faster pace than income as consumers begin spending on not-necessary-yet-useful items (a fridge, a ventilator, etc.). After reaching a peak, consumption grows more slowly—once a consumer has already purchased his or her first car, microwave oven, fridge, and several sets of clothing items, he or she may begin saving to buy a house. Replacement consumption is slower than first purchase consumption (Farrel et al., 2006; Ravallion, 2010). As a result, the new middle classes yield the highest potential for unexploited consumption. This consumption will materialize if the economies where the new middle classes live continue "emerging," providing opportunities for large numbers of poor people to improve their earnings (and thus their lifestyles) and gradually become "middle class."

In the U.S., Europe, and Japan, the rise in demand for fridges, new kitchens, electrodomestic appliances, and cars by the middle class that emerged more than 50 years ago fuelled not only economic growth but also economic diversification and development. The growth of manufacturing and services catering to the middle class, in turn, provided more skilled jobs, which sustained growth and development, reducing the share of the population that qualified as poor and improving nationwide standards of living. For business, the process has a very important implication—many of the market leaders that emerged during the consumer boom sustained by Western and Japanese middle classes are the world market leaders of today, such as Ford, Toyota, VW, Sony, Bosh, Electrolux, and General Electric. Understanding the structural change that is occurring in emerging markets and targeting their new middle classes could provide firms such as these with much needed dynamism to compensate for the slower growth in their domestic markets. There are also opportunities for new firms with more flexible structures and business models that make them better suited to capturing these consumers. Local firms may be in a better position to understand the market, but global players have more expertise and technology. What is certain is that this will be one of the market segments that will define new market leaders, allowing them to carve out a position in the global market. In some fields, it has already happened; in the white goods industry, the Chinese firm Haier has benefitted from its strong position in the domestic market to develop a phenomenal range of products for emerging-market clients and subsequently internationalized to developed economies. Its astonishingly quick rise from local to global player illustrates the potential benefits of successfully targeting the new middle classes (see Chapter 8, "Multinationals Based in Emerging Markets: Features and Strategies," for more details).

Their earnings are lower than those of a poor American or Japanese person, ranging between US$1,500–2,000 per year per capita to over US$20,000, depending on the country in question and the definition used. There is ongoing debate about how to measure this new emerging-market middle class. Some sources, such as the OECD, prefer to define it by means of a universal measure of the average income band, establishing minimum and maximum thresholds. Other sources prefer to use a relative measure—that is, defining the new middle class by segmenting the income groups within each country and creating this category from the group that is clearly above the median income level of the poor. What matters for us here is that it is highly advisable to avoid using rich-world definitions of middle class: in Italy and Portugal, someone earning $12,000 a year is considered poor, yet in most emerging markets, such income is far above average. We prefer the relative measures because they provide an indication of where these consumers stand in comparison to other groups within their society. Another way of identifying the new middle classes is to identify what qualifies as "the poor." Many sources use the US$2-a-day threshold to distinguish those they classify as in poverty from the middle class—anyone earning more than that would thus qualify as non-poor or part of the new middle class. However, what you can buy with $2 again varies from country to country and depends on the relative prices in each one. This factor is normally taken into account in purchasing power parity indicators. Our recommendation is to consider the part of the population whose earnings are among the lowest 20 percent, or the lowest income quintile, as poor. This way, we can have an idea of how many people and what percentage of the whole population has the lowest incomes, independent of the average incomes of a country and its costs of living. The group between the lowest 20 percent and the highest 20 percent is the new middle class—a large and diverse group indeed. Using this measure, the top 20 percent of the population can be considered the upper-middle class, and within that, the top 5 percent would be the super rich (World Bank, 2011; Kanbur and Sumner, 2012).

As the economies of the poorest emerging markets move from agriculture to industry, they demand not only workers with basic skills, but also workers capable of operating complex machinery, reading instructions, using computers, and performing other skills. Industrialization also fosters urbanization, by attracting millions of workers from the countryside to cities. Urbanization then creates extra demand for a broad array of services, ranging from hairdressing to electrical and plumbing services, accountants, lawyers, and private transport. It creates opportunities for entrepreneurial workers to set up their own small stores or to find employment in more specialized positions (for example, as shop managers). New industries also generate opportunities for skilled workers. Call centers, for example, employ hundreds of thousands of lower-middle class people based in emerging markets. A large number of new middle-class consumers are also employed by the state in positions such as low-level managers, teachers, and administrators. The new middle classes take great pride in the educational attainments, which distinguish them from the poor. They invest in the education of their offspring, trusting that this will provide them with new opportunities to progress. They live in areas that are not upmarket but that benefit from good access to electricity, sanitation, and transport. Although they mostly live in rented accommodation, a growing number will purchase their own homes. Given that their relative expenditure on rent is much lower than those of the upper-middle classes, they can afford to spend money on nonessential consumption items such as mobile phones and haircuts. For these reasons, they are a very appealing group of consumers. How can companies target them effectively?

Incomes and Purchasing Power: Getting the Targeting Right

We have emphasized throughout this section that the lower-middle class in emerging markets is very different from the middle class in developed economies in terms of purchasing power. For this reason, we dub it the "new middle class." Most of these consumers have incomes that correspond to those of the average poor of developed economies. They can't afford the products and services that have been developed for American or Japanese middle-class consumers. Yet they are spending a rising share of their rising incomes on consumption goods and want these products and services to have new functions, variety, and, where possible, to be of good quality. There is a distinct gap in the market between what these consumers want and what most companies offer. If we consider clothing, for example, we can see that it is easy to find cheap clothing, generally unbranded, aimed at lower-income groups. These products tend to be lacking in both quality and design. Meanwhile, products aimed at the upper classes are often too expensive for the new middle classes—a pair of branded jeans may cost a third of the monthly salary of an individual in this new middle class! These consumers would, however, spend rather more than the poor on the same clothing item, assuming that it conforms to their expectations.

What is often missing is a range of good-quality, decently designed products, which position themselves in between famous global brands and cheap unbranded goods. Turning to look at entertainment services, we find a similar picture—expensive, Westernized restaurants or cheap, local establishments catering to the poor. The reason for this gap in emerging markets is that these markets have always operated in the absence of a middle class; they have long been characterized by a stark division between the rich and the poor. Part of the story of their recent economic success is precisely the emergence of a middle class. The market has yet to adapt to this new income group by supplying products and services that suit their purchasing power and their consumption aspirations. In order to get the targeting right, it becomes essential for businesses to study the income groups of each market where they operate or intend to operate, assessing the purchasing power of the new middle class and monitoring its consumption patterns. It is also useful to examine the penetration of different consumption items, ranging from cars to fridges and air conditioning units to spot niches with high growth potential. Given their growing but limited purchasing power, these consumers are naturally price sensitive. Even for products that are within their means (for example, beer), they will respond to changes in price. Therefore, getting the price right must be an essential part of any business strategy aiming at capturing the new middle-class consumers.

Functionality

The new middle classes are much more frugal than wealthier income groups. They are, generally speaking, more interested in functionality. Given that the majority of products and services continue to be developed in the rich economies, for rich-world consumers, providing "functionality" entails either adapting existing products or developing new ones to meet the needs of emerging markets. Adaptation is necessary to ensure that quality for low-priced products is raised to achieve the minimum level of durability that these consumers will find acceptable. In some cases, it may be possible to reduce investment in marketing and design and put it into improving the quality of inputs and processes—for example, producing shoes with a more stringent process of assembly and better leather but with a less innovative design. In other cases, it may be necessary to develop ad hoc products and services. Most importantly, companies must rethink their value proposition and examine whether it is suited to targeting this group of consumers or whether it needs to be modified.

In many cases, this segment will be made up of first-time consumers or very occasional buyers of consumer durables, such as cars and kitchen appliances. They may be unaware or uninterested in trends partly because they are less informed and partly because they are more pragmatic. But they are very careful about obtaining functional value for money. If they spend the equivalent of several months of their salary to buy a particular product, they want it to work well and to last. A good example is white goods—a washing machine costing $300 may be as much as a month's salary for an emerging-market middle-class consumer, whereas for a poor, rich-world consumer, it is likely to be less than one-third. The latter may consider it a cheap purchase, chosen for lack of will to spend more or out of strict necessity, in the event of the preceding washing machine breaking down. Buying a product at the cheaper end of the scale comes with the concern that it may break. For the emerging-market middle-class consumer, this is an important investment. It is not "cheap." If it breaks, the income used to replace it will be seen in terms of the opportunity cost of what else could have been purchased with that money. This reasoning explains how targeting the new emerging-market middle class with inferior products can backfire. If they associate the brand with low quality, their future purchases will go toward other products or brands.

Clothing is another set of products that illustrate this preference for functionality well; the new middle classes often have office jobs that require frequent use of formal attire. Fashionable but not very high quality clothes, such as those generally offered by European high street retailers, are not a good bet for them: they may be too fashionable for their intended use and their quality not perceived to be good enough for the price. More conservative looking but more durable clothing would be better suited to these consumers.

Value Differences and Understand the "Local"

New middle-class consumers are not poor, but they are much less globalized than the previous income groups discussed in this chapter. To begin with, they are less likely to speak English or travel abroad and so are less informed about global trends. They may think of foreign products as, at best, a curiosity, and certainly not very related to their lives. They do not aspire to the lifestyles of the global elite; their role models are local and they are much more influenced by tradition, customs, and religion. Targeting them not only entails getting the price right and ensuring that products are functional, it also entails understanding their consumer preferences: what they eat, where they like to go out, what they like to wear. As we anticipated in the previous sections, in the majority of emerging markets, the new middle classes are rather conservative in their habits—they shun the latest fashions not just in terms of clothing but also in behavior and habits. To target them, marketing has to be highly localized, in line with local sensitivities and interests, referring to local customs, and making use of local celebrities and events. Supporting local traditions is an essential element of a strategy aimed at localizing brands and making products appealing to the new middle classes. Globalized advertising is not effective toward this group and may even backfire, suggesting, as it could be perceived, an attempt to impose an alien cultural model.

The products and services that cater to the lower-middle class and poorer income groups of developed economies are therefore often unsuitable for the new middle classes. They live differently: in some cases, they may have spacious houses that can easily host large white goods and furniture. In many cases, they will have maids taking care of most domestic affairs, including cooking and cleaning. Being in a position to afford domestic help depends greatly on the relative cost of labor in the location where they are based, and this changes not only across economies but also within economies. It is, for example, much cheaper to have a maid in the North of Brazil than in Sao Paulo. Whether a household has domestic help or not will define consumption patterns for items such as kitchen utensils and cleaning tools. It also defines what is eaten in the household: why buy a readymade meal when you are paying someone to cook for you everyday? If a business wishes to sell food products in these markets, what consumers eat, how, where, and what food is consumed on special occasions, and accompanied by which types of drinks is all essential information. It gives a first insight into whether we can target them at all with our product, and if so, how to do it. Attempting to sell sweet breakfast cookies to consumers who are used to having a large, heavy, salty breakfast will likely not meet with much success. The same cookies could, however, sell well if marketed as snacks or for other occasions. Local companies have a competitive advantage—they know the market well and can more easily develop better targeted products. In order to compete with local firms, global companies need to gather as much information as possible about the nature of demand and about what their competitors do. They can then exploit their superior expertise in managing stretched supply chains and marketing products to offer higher-quality, better-image goods that cater to local taste.

Brand Building

Building brand awareness with these consumers is much harder than with the wealthier income groups, precisely because they are less exposed to global trends and advertising. The fact that they may be first-time consumers can be a double-edged sword: because they will not have previous experiences of buying these sorts of products, most brands will not yet be associated with either a positive or negative reputation, so well-established brands have less scope to exploit their value. It also means that there is space for any business to build a positive reputation, a great long-term investment given that this is a fast-growing consumer group, which could provide a large number of future repeat consumers. The way to position a brand successfully with these consumers is related to accurate targeting in terms of price and the minimum quality standard necessary to ensure reliability and functionality. Not being able to eat in a five-star restaurant should not have to entail accepting bad service or dirty tables. Though more frugal than wealthier consumers, the new middle classes value the brands that distinguish what they purchase from what they think the poor purchase. After all, all of the consumption that is not strictly necessary (food and shelter) is in some way related to self-satisfaction. These consumers will be less willing to accept the poor quality and poor service that poorer consumers often have to accept. They are willing to spend extra to obtain something different than the offerings at the lower end. They may not yet aspire to purchasing luxury or premium products, but they want an improvement in their consumption, which can be provided through durability, quality, and through effective presentation of the product or service (for example, by better packaging and labeling). It is a good strategy, then, to segment the market to target the new middle classes with basic products that have elements of an aspirational good, as producers of fast-moving consumer goods (for example, shampoo) have done in the Triad since the 1950s by developing a broad range of brands and price ranges. If these strategies are successful, they will become loyal consumers and will upgrade to more elaborate or expensive products and services from the same companies when their incomes rise.

References

Adkins, S. (2011). Ambient Insight Comprehensive Report: The Worldwide Market for Mobile Learning Products and Services: 2010–2015 Forecast and Analysis. Retrieved from http://www.ambientinsight.com/Resources/Documents/Ambient-Insight-2010-2015-Worldwide-Mobile-Learning-Market-Forecast-Executive-Overview.pdf.

APICCAPS (2012). *World Footwear 2012 Yearbook*. APICCAPS.

Bain & Company (2012). *Luxury Goods Worldwide Market Study*. Bain & Company, Inc.

Bain & Company (2011). The great eight trillion dollar growth trends 2020. Bain & Company, Inc.

Bearden, W. and Etzel, M. (1982). Reference group influence on product and brand purchase decisions. *Journal of Consumer Research*, 9 (2), pp. 183–194.

BID (2009). *Poder a través de inversiones*. Retrieved from http://idbdocs.iadb.org/wsdocs/getdocument.aspx?docnum=1904581.

Capgemini and RBC Wealth Management (2012). *World Wealth Report.* Capgemini and RBC Wealth Management

ClickZ (2000). *Web Pages by Language.* Retrieved from http://www.clickz.com/clickz/news/1697080/web-pages-language.

Czinkota, M. R. and Ronkainen, I. A. (2007). *International Marketing.* South-Western Pub.

Doyle, P. (1990). Building Successful Brands: The Strategic Options. *Journal of Consumer Marketing, 7*(2), pp. 5–20.

Ghemawat, P. (2001). Distance still matters. *Harvard Business Review, 79*(8), pp. 137–147.

Global Banking and Finance Review (2012). African telecom investment opportunities attract global interest. *Global Banking and Finance Review.* Retrieved from http://www.globalbankingandfinance.com/Global-Markets/African-telecom-investment-opportunities-attract-global-interest.html.

Farrell, D., Gersch, U. A., and Stephenson, E. (2006). The value of China's emerging middle class. *McKinsey Quarterly, 2*(I), p. 60.

Ferrari (2012). *Ferrari Challenge.* Retrieved from http://www.ferrari.com/english/scuderia/corse_clienti/Pages/ferrari_challenge.aspx.

Kaplan, R. S. and Norton, D. P. (2000). *Having trouble with your strategy?: Then map it.* Harvard Business School Publishing Corporation.

Kharas, H. (2010). *The emerging middle class in developing countries.* Paris: OECD Development Centre.

Kim, C. and Mauborgne, R. (2004). *Blue ocean strategy: How to create uncontested market space and make the competition irrelevant.* Harvard Business School Press.

Hamel, G. and Prahalad, C. K. (1993). Strategy as stretch and leverage. *Harvard Business Review, 71*(2), p. 75.

Harley Davidson (2012). *Harley Owners Group.* Retrieved from http://www.harley-davidson.com/en_US/Content/Pages/HOG/membership-benefits.html.

Hart, S., Hoe, L. and Hogg, G.M. (2004). Faking it: Counterfeiting and consumer contradictions. *European Advances in Consumer Behaviour,* 6, pp. 60–67.

Internet World Stats (2012). *World Internet Usage* [Data File]. Retrieved from http://www.internetworldstats.com/stats.htm.

McKinsey (2010). Capturing the world's emerging middle class. *McKinsey Quarterly.* Dallas, Texas.

Mintzberg, H. (Ed.) (2003). *The Strategy Process: Concepts, Contexts, Cases: Global.* Pearson Education.

Porter, M. E. (2008). *Competitive Advantage: Creating and Sustaining Superior Performance*. Free Press.

Ravallion, M. (2010). The developing world's bulging (but vulnerable) middle class. *World Development, 38*(4), pp. 445–454.

Steenkamp, J., Batra, R. and Alden, D. (2003). How perceived brand globalness creates brand value. *Journal of International Business Studies, 34* (1), pp. 53–65.

The Economist (2010). First break all of the rules. Available at http://www.economist.com/node/15879359. Accessed on 3/15//2013.

W3Techs (2013). *Usage of content languages for websites* [Data File]. Retrieved from http://w3techs.com/technologies/overview/content_language/all.

Wealth X (2011). *World Ultra Wealth Report*. Wealth X.

World Bank Group (2013). World Development Indicators [Data File]. Retrieved from http://databank.worldbank.org/data/databases.aspx.

Yeoman, I. and McMahon-Beattie, U. (2005). Luxury markets and premium pricing. *Journal of Revenue and Pricing Management, 4*(4), pp. 319–328.

7

Targeting Emerging Market Clients II: Strategies for the Base of the Pyramid

Introduction

I n the previous chapter, we discussed how to target the rich and the middle classes of emerging markets. The question we pose here is whether the poor of emerging markets really represent viable markets for profitable business opportunities. The answer to that is a resounding yes: they can and they do for quite a number of savvy organizations. This chapter discusses the poor as a group of consumers that continue to be, by and large, disconnected from mainstream markets. It illustrates some of the reasons why the poor continue to remain poor but it also demonstrates and provides examples of the kind of market this disconnected group can represent and how it can be tapped. Within this chapter, we also promote the idea that private business can make a social contribution, making a positive difference to the living standards of the poor while simultaneously pursuing profit-making objectives, and that this can provide a positive feedback loop for the business. For this we draw from the arguments of Prahalad (2006) as well as London and Hart (2010), providing some principles for managers and students interested in developing inclusive business models to target consumers at the Base of the Pyramid (BoP).

Making the Poor Visible

The most astonishing thing about the poor is their invisibility—this group has been ignored by business for a long time. Poverty is often discussed by governments, multilateral organizations such as the World Bank and United Nations, and NGOs but the vast majority of the policy makers and business leaders who shape the world economy have little or no idea of where and how the poor live. Global-level discussions about reducing poverty have been common for over 50 years. The prevailing approach has been to consider the poor as rather passive—as victims that must be helped. It is with this perspective that most policies tackling poverty have been developed, generating handouts, subsidies, and other instruments that "target" the poor without necessarily involving them or considering them in more active and respectful ways. In recent decades, the language has changed to that of inclusion and participation, but the new rhetoric has often been a whitewash with little change in how interventions are actually operationalized (Williams, 2012).

The ideological basis for these kinds of interventions is that market mechanisms have failed to provide for the poor. The thinking goes more or less along these lines: if the market is efficient at allocating resources, how is it that we have billions of people with poor access to clean water, sanitation, shelter, energy, health services, and education? If the market fails, other organizational actors, primarily the state, but also civil society organizations such as NGOs, should step in and attempt to meet the needs of the poor. We have seen first-hand the effects of poverty in emerging economies—in the slums of Rio, the impoverished countryside of Equatorial Guinea, and many other locations inhabited mainly by "the poor"—and ethically we certainly agree that something should be done about poverty. However, we also know that in the more than 50 years that non-market mechanisms have been in place to attempt to solve poverty, they have not really worked.

Big donors, such as the U.S., the EU, and Japan, have funded poverty-reduction schemes in most countries around the world since the 1960s. Multilateral organizations, such as the World Bank, have invested in all sorts of projects targeting poverty. And many emerging markets, ranging from large economies such as Brazil, highly populated countries such as India, and smaller countries such as Nepal or Nicaragua, have had government policies to tackle poverty for many years. Some of the largest emerging economies, such as Egypt and Indonesia, have invested billions and billions of government money in policies such as fuel subsidies, which are designed to help the poor from above. After decades and impressive sums spent in "helping the poor" by governments, multilateral organizations, and NGOs, poverty remains pervasive. The top-down approach of helping the poor through charity and handouts has also failed to deliver. But why are we discussing this in a book whose objective is to discuss how best to do business in emerging markets? Because poverty is not just a problem, it is an opportunity for business to find a new driver of growth—one that can simultaneously improve the livelihoods of the less fortunate.

C. K. Prahalad, T. London, and S. Hart, three famous business scholars, have been particularly influential in suggesting that business can, and should, take a more active role in developing products and services that improve the living standards of the four to five billion poor people in the world in sustainable ways, which pay off their initial investments and ideally also generate healthy profits (Prahalad, 2010; London et al., 2010).

They developed the "Base of the Pyramid" (BoP) paradigm. Their main contribution was to raise the issue and as a result make the poor more visible, not only as victims, but as potential protagonists in their own forward progress. The poor are generally invisible to business because their purchasing power is extremely low—some measures define the poor as those who earn a maximum of US$2 per day. Given such extreme poverty, can the poor really be viable consumers? The answer is yes—and the following sections discuss how.

Numbers

Perhaps, unsurprisingly, in monetary terms the poor consume very little per head, but, alas, they are the largest part of the world's population, numbering between four and five billion. Collectively, they thus account for a much higher total expenditure on consumption than the global rich, consumption that leading businesses are struggling to tap. In spite of their low earnings, the poor have to consume to survive. Even where there are state-support mechanisms such as the Public Distribution System (PDS), the Indian food security system that distributes subsidized food and non-food items to those below the official poverty line and certain marginalized tribal groups, the poor still purchase most of what they consume. The sum of purchases at the BoP account for an impressive business volume. In other words, the starting point for understanding and developing suitable business strategies to target those at the BoP is that there *is* a demand for a range of products and services, and that it is significant.

Potential

The fact that the BoP has been ignored by businesses for such a long time means that there are plentiful opportunities for business. Where large modern businesses have never ventured, the needs of the poor have been catered for by smaller, less sophisticated outfits. There is a vast gap in the market between the demand from the poor (what they need and what they can pay) and supply (what is available, through which sales channels, and in which areas) and the prices that are charged. The businesses that can target this gap will benefit greatly from the volume that BoP consumers can generate. This potential is amplified by the fact that during the last 20 years the share of people classified as living at the BoP has been gradually but consistently declining. In other words, the poor are becoming less poor and are finally able to get access to a range of goods and services they could not previously acquire.

Do What You Know Best and Help the Poor

In targeting the BoP, businesses can contribute to social development in ways that are more sustainable than philanthropy, because they generate revenue flows. Businesses are good at creating goods and services for customers and at providing them at a profit. They are good at innovating, introducing new products, finding new ways of delivering them, and exploiting and using new technologies. In fact, they lead the world's innovation, spending far more than governments in R&D. With the exception of the BoP, where there is uncatered-for demand, business is more effective at meeting demand than governments. Business is better at identifying potential demand and better at developing sustainable ways to meet it, precisely because, unlike governments, its objective is not to deliver the goods or products demanded per se, but to do so in a way that allows costs to be covered and some profit to be made. Failure to achieve this generally results in bankruptcy, closure, and managers losing their jobs.

Business is capable of designing and running extremely articulated and globalized supply chains, way beyond the reach of most governmental organizations, with the exception perhaps of the U.S. military today or the Roman army centuries ago. Private business has also been responsible for developing most of the infrastructure that links the global market, ranging from roads to fiber optic cables to telecom antennas. Many businesses also have far more resources than governments—even rich-world governments—to dedicate to a particular task. In other words, business frequently has the resources, expertise, know-how, and skills that governments, multilateral organizations, and NGOs lack. By focusing these on consumers that have long been marginalized and ignored, business has the potential to fill the gap between demand from the BoP and the available supply (London and Hart, 2010). This goes beyond the idea of corporate social responsibility. Instead of emulating what NGOs and charities do, a business can target the BoP by doing what it knows best. A company that develops infrastructure could design infrastructural projects to link isolated communities to the main port of a country. A company specialized in health products could develop low-cost remedies for the diseases that disproportionately affect the BoP, such as malaria. This has been the missing factor in poverty-reduction policies for the last 50 years—a business contribution that is not aimed at donating funds, but at incorporating the poor as potential customers and at understanding their specific needs (Prahalad, 2010). By becoming a more active element in the improvement of the BoP living conditions, a business can acquire more credibility in these communities, planting the seeds of future consumer loyalty in income groups that are fast moving from poverty into the new middle classes. Such strategies can also improve a business's image among rich-world consumers who are more often confronted with negative stories of business exploitation of the poor, of polluting rivers, and of dealing with oppressive regimes.

Find New Growth Drivers

American, Japanese, and European companies struggle to make profits in their home markets, which are by now saturated and growing only slowly. Their traditional customers have been subjected to decades of intensive marketing, which has made them more and more difficult to target. They have also become more informed and sophisticated (in other words, more demanding), and competition is high. The economic climate of post-2008 has also negatively affected consumer expectations, reducing spending in many different fields. The BoP is a very large group of consumers that could potentially generate the high volumes needed to spur growth and sustain profits in spite of the crisis. Additionally, this group is not well targeted by existing providers of goods and services, which creates a space not only for marketing but also for developing suitable supplies. In sum, the BoP could be an important growth driver for business.

The BoP and Exclusion from Markets

Base of the Pyramid scholars have appealed to businesses to stop ignoring the billion poorest consumers that populate mainly emerging markets on the basis that ignoring them not only makes no sense from a business perspective, it also effectively preserves poverty. As companies focus on richer consumers, their investment in R&D and their innovations in services and logistics fail to benefit those at the BoP. This section addresses the question, if there are such great business opportunities, why are BoP consumers more often than not overlooked?

The first reason is straightforward—they are poor. Precisely because their purchasing power is very low in monetary terms, the value of anything they could potentially acquire is also low, making them appear unattractive as consumers. The fact that this group represents large numbers and can generate cumulative volume seemed to have escaped mainstream business thinking until the mid-2000s. Another important reason explaining why this group of consumers has usually remained below the radar is that they are the poor of countries that have been on the periphery of the world economy for centuries. Triad-based companies that do target poorer consumers tend to target this group in the Triad only. The poor in Triad markets have a much higher purchasing power than the poor in emerging markets, even though they share a position at the bottom of their respective pyramids, not to mention different consumption patterns and preferences. The majority of firms that target the poor have for many decades failed to consider the BoP consumers as a viable market opportunity. The shifting axes of the world economy toward emerging economies is changing this and raising business interest in the BoP in emerging markets.

The exclusion of consumers at the BoP from business models targeted at these markets can also be partly laid at the door of the paternalistic attitude taken by governments and civil society alike. Even the United Nations failed to include any acknowledgement of how business could contribute to poverty reduction in its Millennium Development Goals (Prahalad, 2010). Thanks to the work of Prahalad and Hart, this was subsequently changed, and the United Nations Development Program explicitly endorsed the BoP paradigm. The point here is that most businesses follow a line of thinking, prevalent among governments and other non-private sector organizations, that sees the poor as subjects who must be helped from above by entities in charge of providing free goods and services, such as governments and NGOs. Such an intellectual bias that leads to a view of the poor as passive explains but does not justify why business has contributed so little to improving lives at the BoP. Governments and multilateral organizations can be considered equally responsible for having mainly only incorporated business into their project strategies in order to raise funds rather than adopting a more market-based approach and tapping into business expertise.

The neglect of this segment of the population is compounded by their virtual invisibility even to the local elite. Multinational corporations operating in emerging markets bring with them the business models and mentality of their home bases—often rich economies. Their CEOs tend to be from the Triad and are mainly male, but a high share of their personnel is often local. Multinational corporations operating in emerging markets do not just employ local secretaries and assembly line workers. The purchasing managers, sales managers, supply chain managers, and very often also the highest managerial positions, such as country directors, are often locals. Would it not be reasonable to assume that these personnel must be aware of the way of life of the poor and have the necessary information to help business develop suitable solutions for the BoP? The reality is that this is not necessarily the case. The managers who work for the likes of United Fruit, BP, and Siemens in emerging markets are local people, but they come from the richest 20 percent of the population, the section of society that can afford to study in the best local or foreign schools, who have been exposed to global trends, and whose consumption patterns are converging with those of North America, Europe, and Japan.

Their ambition is to distance themselves from the poor, and their understanding of the BoP is generally very limited. They do not take the same public transport or go to the same schools as people at the BoP; they do not eat in the same establishments, they prefer different forms of entertainment, and live in different parts of town. Many of the upper-middle class managers we interviewed had never visited the poor areas of the cities where they lived and worked, in spite of being locals. This combination of poor knowledge and the desire to avoid thinking about an uncomfortable reality go a long way to explaining why the managerial elite of emerging markets have often failed to help multinationals target the BoP. Triad managers may have the intention of learning more about the BoP, but they often lack an in-depth understanding of the societal and cultural subtleties of the BoP in different countries. As a result, most companies, managers, and business scholars continue to be ignorant about consumer demand from this quarter: what the poor consume, and in what ways and how much they are willing to pay for goods and services. Without better knowledge of the BoP, we can't target it. There is a clear role here for NGOs, governments, and multilateral organizations to help businesses gather this type of information and to assist in developing products that the market has thus far failed to deliver to the poor at prices they can afford and in places they can access.

In spite of the colorful protests of anti-globalization movements, the truth is that most of the world's poor are delinked from the global market and even from their national markets. Suboptimal access to infrastructure often separates them from markets: many live in rural areas that are badly connected to the main ports, airports, and hubs that link their national economy to the world market. Governments and private businesses that develop infrastructure to link export production areas and wealthy consumers often neglect to connect the BoP as well. Poor local infrastructure further isolates the BoP population in rural areas from the mainstream market and from the eyes of business. In rural areas, access to electricity is often either entirely lacking or very unreliable. Access to clean water, sanitation, and health clinics are also luxuries. There may be schools, though the quality of the education tends to be very low because teachers are reluctant to live in such remote areas even when paid a premium.

The urban poor is much more visible, and yet also often disconnected from mainstream markets. They also live in areas with poor access to drinking water and sanitation, which, in the crammed conditions of urban slums, often contributes to dismal living standards. In many emerging markets, especially in Latin America and Africa, the urban poor live in very dangerous areas where the state is all but absent and may be substituted by heavily armed criminal gangs, which also contributes to isolation from markets. In the slums of Medellin and Rio, potential customers, scared by the risk of violent theft and kidnappings, avoid venturing into these areas. As a result, the volume of business for local businesses is low, unless entrepreneurs take their products out of the slum areas in person or rely on reaching an arrangement with an intermediary that can do so. Both of these solutions entail extra cost. Although they form part of large cities, slums are often badly connected to the rest of town because these areas have been urbanized without any form of planning. Access is often in the form of narrow muddy roads and steps that prohibit access to cars and trucks. Motorcycles and walking are the main means of transport for the residents of slums. BoP consumers, both urban and rural, have to spend a much higher share of their income on transport than any other income group. They live far from opportunities, and the cost of commuting can often eat away most of what they can earn. This prevents many BoP citizens from pursuing jobs in richer areas.

Access to markets can provide opportunities to generate wealth and stimulate development. Conversely, being isolated from the market increases the cost of most inputs, ranging from fuel to heat shelters in cold climates to textiles to produce clothing items. And we are not talking about places where major physical barriers such as mountains or deserts separate consumers from the rest of the population here; as Prahalad observes in his book, the cost of fresh water in the slums of Delhi is almost always much higher than in rich areas of the city, even though the rich can afford to buy bottled mineral water. It is a stark case of the distortion of demand and supply caused by the exclusion from the market of those at the BoP, which is common across many products and services within highly concentrated urban areas.

Isolation, thus defined, reduces the potential market for local products and distorts prices, allowing intermediaries who link otherwise insular markets to speculate. If, for example, a criminal gang controls the distribution of drinkable water in a slum, it can set monopolistic prices. Or if a rural village is served only by one small shop providing all the main inputs for agricultural production, the latter will be able to exploit the absence of competition in the area and charge a premium for its goods. The same negative effect occurs for buyers: a large share of the rural BoP population rely on agriculture; however, because of their remoteness they tend to have to rely on one dominant buyer for their products. The buyer, perhaps a company operating trucks or an intermediary, can exploit its monopsonistic position to extract prices that are lower than the average market price from BoP producers. If BoP producers don't sell their products to these buyers, they may not be able to sell them at all. For these producers, failure to sell can represent the difference between being able to buy food, cooking fuel, medicines, and other basic and essential items, and going hungry or being unable to treat a chronic condition (see Box 7.1).

Box 7.1: Definitions

Monopoly

A situation where one economic actor (a company or an individual) has exclusive control of the trade (or supply) of one good or service. Having monopolistic control over the market generally allows sellers to charge high prices and thus achieve high profits, exploiting a buyer's lack of alternatives.

Oligopoly

A situation of limited competition whereby a small number of players share the market. Oligopolistic players can achieve high profits by agreeing to limit the extent to which they compete on prices.

Monopsony

A situation where there is only one buyer purchasing all of the goods and services in a given market. This can lead to exploitative practices vis-à-vis sellers, who may lack alternative mechanisms to trade their goods and services. This is, for example, the case of intermediaries who exploit their ownership of means of transport to purchase all of the agricultural produce from villages that are isolated from main trading routes (see Chapter 2 for more information on the role of intermediaries, trade, and market insulation at the base of the pyramid).

Source: Oxford Dictionary

Their products are primarily agricultural, so it is risky to wait for another buyer to show up because the products can perish from lack of suitable storage (Gold et al., 2013). A large share of agro production is damaged every year in emerging markets precisely because of insufficient investment in protected storage and training in storage techniques. Again, it is the poorest producers who fail to obtain the market value for what they produce. The reason is often their inferior access to markets, which is easily exploited by whoever is ready to plug the gap and act as an intermediary.

Distance or lack of access to the market limits the potential for specialization: if there are few outlets to sell one's trades, it is more rational to become multi-skilled than to specialize. At the extreme, market isolation can lead to subsistence economies, whereby all activities and resources are employed to generate necessities locally, leading not only to a suboptimal BoP resource allocation, but also preventing people from obtaining goods and services that are not available locally, which may include services such as health and education. Physical and infrastructural barriers isolate the poor from markets and marginalize them in the economy, and this can be enhanced by social barriers, such as ethnic tensions and racism against poor minorities. Crime and state failure to tackle it constitute another factor that contrives to separate the BoP from the market. Institutional failure, partly caused by their invisibility to political and judiciary elites, and partly caused by lack of resources, also negatively affects the BoP.

Lack of recognition and protection of the property rights of those at the BoP is the most manifest example of institutional failure. It contributes to the isolation of BoP citizens from mainstream markets, which in turn exacerbates poverty. Together with the existence of customs and rule-enforcing mechanisms, property rights are one of the foundations of functioning markets (see the discussion in Chapter 2, "Markets and Institutions"). They justify engagement in transactions and the development of businesses. Most housing used by people at the BoP is constructed without permission. States tolerate this but do not recognize the rights of property or even of tenancy of millions of poor people in this situation. Despite living in these homes and often improving them over long periods of time, the poor are often the subject of abuses by companies and governments that can evict them as they please, exploiting their lack of formalized property rights. The majority of people at the BoP have very limited or zero functional literacy, which facilitates abuse and the effective exclusion from state protection of rights, property rights among them. It is common to observe that other institutions, such as the judiciary and the police, may also be captured by special interests or crime in cases where they are underpaid and underfunded. Such insecure property rights exclude the poor from credit markets. Without formal collateral, most banks will not lend to them, even though they are the group of consumers that most need seed money to start any activity. This paradox in the market explains the existence of money lenders who target the people in the poorest income groups and charge astronomical interest and the assertion earlier that this sort of institutional failure exacerbates poverty.

The sight of slums being cleared for new urban developments is a familiar one, and one that governments and donors alike applaud as a sign of positive progress. The inhabitants of the slums that are demolished, however, are seldom compensated or provided with alternative housing. When this occurs, it is often in areas that are furthest from the city, and so their cost of commuting is increased. The driving mantra of most policies to tackle slums has been to make them invisible—to destroy the slums and move the poor, rather than to think about how to incorporate the poor and understand their needs and their demands. Even without this to contend with, the absence of the state and the lack of property rights create an environment ripe for abuse by local criminals, who can impose high rents in spite of bad conditions, and back this up through force.

One of the main arguments of the BoP paradigm is that integrating this group into existing markets would provide huge business opportunities while improving their access to goods and services. In some cases, the BoP is delinked from the market not because of physical access but because of a lack of products that suit the BoP needs and purchasing power. This is precisely where business can employ its superior technical and managerial expertise to innovate in ways that create markets for the BoP rather than just connecting BoP consumers. The next section details how this can be achieved.

How Can Business Target the BoP Effectively?

This section outlines a set of principles for businesses that aim to target the base of the pyramid in emerging markets. It is based on our conversations with companies already involved in BoP business, and on the tenets of the BoP literature.

Getting Your Hands Dirty: Understanding Your Customers and Suppliers and Finding Opportunities at the BoP

Between four and five billion people live at the BoP (London and Hart, 2010). We believe that exactly defining the income above which a consumer ceases to be at the BoP is a pointless exercise: does it really matter if the annual average income of a single mother is US$3,000 or $3,200? It is far more important to understand who the people living at the BoP are and to develop strategies that can deliver business growth while also contributing, even if only marginally, to improving the living standards of those at the BoP. We begin here by exploring some of the characteristics of people living at the BoP.

Some factors that define this group and differentiate it from the new middle classes and richer classes discussed in the previous chapter are low per-capita incomes, being among the lowest earners in their respective economies, and accounting for a low share of national GDP. Populations in this group also share the experience of being excluded and marginalized not only from markets but also from many other aspects of society. Despite these aspects of shared experience, their situations differ greatly between the rural and urban, within countries and across countries. Access to shelter and sanitation vary greatly, as do access to electricity, the availability of clean water, the quality of schooling, and the level of risk related to criminal activities. Customs and culture, of course, also affect consumer preferences, so even in cases where most other variables are equal, BoP consumers may well consume different products and services (Rangan et al., 2011). The first basic step of a strategy targeting the BoP is to gather information about what consumers need, what is currently available, and at what prices. To achieve this, it is necessary to move from theoretical market research to more practical, embedded research that involves observing the living conditions and way of life at the BoP. We consider this to be a very useful exercise on both an ethical and a business level—exposing young managers and market researchers to the challenges that the poor have to face in their everyday lives can help them identify with the consumer, and the whole exercise can provide important strategic information about this little-known market.

Understanding the target consumer also means understanding the cultural, ethnic, and religious elements that affect their receptiveness to marketing messages and their consumption patterns. Advertising a product aimed at the BoP by showing a typical consumer who looks, dresses, and talks like an upper-middle class customer may easily backfire—if the BoP consumer feels that the model consumer portrayed is too alien, the ad may put them off rather than appeal to them. Marketing should not just emphasize cheapness; it can build on the functionality of the product and exploit links with the context—with the food, music, and habits of the consumers targeted. In many economies, bicycles are the most common means of transportation for people in this group of consumers—featuring them in advertising or developing products and services for the bike rider are apt ways to successfully target the BoP. To achieve the latter would mean having to rethink the business model of most Western and Japanese bike producers who have for decades focused on marginal innovations aimed at improving performance and design regardless of rising costs. For a BoP consumer, a new system that allows one to carry heavier loads safely on a bike would be a distinctly more relevant innovation than a cutting-edge gear-changing system that allows the rider to save a fraction of a second when moving from first to second gear. Getting to know how our potential customers live, what they do for a living, and how they spend their time can help us assess what products and services have the potential to be successful in this market and what consumer needs or desires are currently unsatisfied. The next step is to work out why demand is unmet: is it a case of inferior access to markets? Or of products being too expensive or unsuitable for their intended use by consumers at the BoP? With this information, we can develop our BoP strategy.

Getting the Price Right: Value for the BoP

In many cases, customers at the BoP are excluded from the market for goods and services because of their purchasing power. Earning US$1–3 per day, their individual spending power is very low and it tends to be spent immediately on food and shelter. However, as BoP scholars have illustrated, this does not mean that people living at the BoP do not consume, nor does it mean that they pay lower prices for what they purchase. In most cases, they pay prices that are far too high for the quality they receive, which creates business opportunities. Exploiting these opportunities entails understanding not only what consumers *are able* to spend but understanding *what they are willing to spend* on certain products (Rangan et al., 2011). If our objective is to create a new market, to convince people to buy goods that they are currently not consuming, getting the price right is paramount (Schrader et al., 2012). Clearly, it is not only about demand. We have to position our products in such a way that they are attractive for those at the BoP but that allow the venture to be profitable once certain economies of scale are reached. At the BoP, very little movement in the final price can have a disastrous effect. In 2005, Danone, a French multinational corporation specializing in dairy products, in particular, yogurt, successfully introduced a product aimed at the BoP in South Africa. In 2007, it increased its price marginally in order to compensate for rising costs of production. Sales suffered a sudden decline, negatively affecting its ability to recover the investment undertaken to develop and distribute the product.

Linking Demand and Supply: Bringing Physically Distant Markets Closer Through Infrastructure

In many cases, BoP consumers are simply cut off from the market—they live in areas that are difficult to access, which increases distribution costs, making products and services either unavailable to them or too expensive. If the BoP has been ignored because it is delinked from the market, in order to target it we need to find ways to reach these customers or allow BoP producers to bring their wares to the market more effectively. This can be achieved by collaborative operations between business, the state, and civil society organizations. Small infrastructural developments (for example, a bridge or an overpass for pedestrians) can have a strong effect in terms of reducing the cost of commuting and generating opportunities for those at the BoP (Gold et al., 2013). These types of initiative have the potential to expand markets at the BoP in cases where the combination of natural barriers and infrastructural deficiencies seriously increase costs. They can also contribute positively to local economic development, a factor that in turn helps to build a positive perception with both local communities and global customers.

Linking Demand and Supply: Cutting Intermediaries

As already stated, customers at the BoP often pay higher than market prices because they are disconnected from mainstream markets. Their demand is catered for by intermediaries—people and companies who operate in slums and rural areas and who take advantage of the low availability of supplies to extract high prices. These intermediaries perform a useful function—they link demand and supply where the official, formalized market does not work (London and Hart, 2010). However, by charging premium prices for low-quality products and services, they also contribute to maintaining people in poverty—the premium they extract from the poor is a share of their disposable income that they cannot save, invest, or spend on other items (Prahalad, 2010). Basic farming tools, such as spades and shovels, are a good example of this in rural areas—the rural poor tend to pay much higher prices for these sorts of tools than the rich and middle classes because they live far from large shops that offer them at market prices. Paradoxically, the people who most need simple farming tools and who can least afford to pay for them end up paying the most. The same goes for credit—where banks do not operate, money lenders do, charging astronomic interest rates and using violent means to ensure compliance.

These intermediaries are able to operate in this way because the market fails to provide products and services (e.g., tools and credit) that the poor want, where they can purchase them, and at prices they can afford. There is scope then for companies to find creative ways to do away with intermediaries. Opening local branches of shops or distributing products directly to small retailers is one way to reach into the areas where these groups live to break apart the monopoly of intermediaries that result in high prices. If there are several corner shops in a slum and they all sell similar products purchased from a wholesaler, why not target the shops directly and provide incentives for the best performers? Why not provide a franchise business model suited for a BoP context, substituting corner shops with brand stores, such as micro supermarkets affiliated with a main retail brand?

Linking Demand and Supply: Empowering the BoP

Where it is impossible to shorten physical distance by improving infrastructure, companies could invest in different distribution techniques that can reach potential BoP customers. It is, of course, the consumers at the BoP themselves who have the best information about what, where, and how this group consumes. In cases where volume does not justify establishing direct retail systems, large companies can generate entrepreneurial opportunities for individuals interested in operating as sales agents. Direct door-to-door sales may seem an anachronistic method in the age of the Internet, but this sales technique has proved to be very successful at the BoP. First, this kind of business model empowers people at the BoP to become entrepreneurs and acquire new potential sources of income. Second, it takes advantage of and exploits their knowledge of localities to improve distribution efficiency and do away with the need for intermediary shops. Third, they exploit local understanding to refine the marketing message and finalize sales. Several leading multinational companies, such as Danone, Unilever, and Procter and Gamble, have adopted creative new mechanisms to break into BoP markets (Gold et al., 2013). Relying on networks of local entrepreneurial distributors has been shown to be a very effective way of compensating for dysfunctional or absent infrastructure and the often suboptimal reach of conventional retail systems (see Box 7.2).

Box 7.2: HUL and Shakti Women

Hindustan Unilever Limited (HUL), Unilever's Indian subsidiary, is the largest fast-moving consumer goods firm in India. To expand its sales to the BoP, HUL understood that having low prices was not enough. Conventional marketing methods would not work as the rural poor have no access to the Internet, television, and often are not able to read. More importantly, HUL found that there were no mechanisms in place to distribute the products to the widespread rural villages where a large share

---

of the Indian BoP customers lived. In 2000, HUL set up Project Shakti, a pilot project training a network of women to be authorized distributors in the state of Andhra Pradesh. It worked with self-help groups, local NGOs, and microcredit institutions to identify groups of women that could benefit from the program and then invested in providing training on sales, marketing, and book keeping to the women interested in participating. Each of these Shakti Women then received an initial stock of goods at a discounted price purchased using credit provided by specialized institutions, and each became an entrepreneur, earning extra income by distributing HUL products. The project was so successful that it has not only been replicated across India, but it is currently being replicated in Latin America and Africa as well. In India, in only four years, the number of Shakti Women climbed from zero to 13,000, reaching 50,000 villages, or an estimated 70 million customers. The program achieved the dual aims of providing large numbers of women with an additional income source while allowing HUL to reach a large number of new consumers.

Source: Hindustan Unilever, accessed 4/25/2013 at www.hul.co.in/careers-redesign/insidehul/oursucces-sandchallenges/shaktiprogrammeindia.aspx. World Bank and IFC: Promoting Women's Economic Empowerment, accessed 4/23/2013 at http://www.unilever.com/images/es_PromotingWomensEconomicEmpowerment_TheLearningJourneyofHindustanUnilever_tcm13-220813.pdf.

Linking Demand and Supply: Exploiting Institutional Voids

Institutions tend not to work very well in the areas and social contexts of the BoP—property rights are not clear, contracts are not always in written form, the rule of law not always enforced, and policing may be performed by the same criminals it is supposed to deter (Khanna and Palepu, 2010). These institutional voids delink markets and make them dysfunctional. They also provide opportunities for intermediaries. Slums may appear to the onlooker to be made up of provisional self-managed shelters, but in reality they are often managed by unscrupulous criminals who charge surprisingly high rents and exercise de facto property rights over land that they do not own and that has been "urbanized," if not in the most orderly fashion, by others who were responsible for building the shelters, roads, and the little infrastructure that exists within them.

People build their houses with materials they find locally, again often sold at a premium by intermediaries who have access to a truck to move them around, and property in the slums is rented, bought, and sold. The absence of the state means no taxes are collected. But the absence of large companies means that inferior construction materials and unsafe techniques are often used because no others are available. Private business could profitably join forces with local community organizations or NGOs to open stores providing not only materials commonly used by the poor to build basic shelters, such as corrugated iron, but also information on safer and more efficient techniques for building with these materials. This kind of venture would start with a phase to gather in-depth information about materials and the location targeted. Local community leaders would then need to be trained to run the shops as self-managed franchises, and to provide training sessions for future workers. These simple steps would lower the cost of building or improving a house. Helping the poor certify and register their property is another potentially attractive business opportunity—such an enterprise would easily generate a high volume of business because of the sheer number of poor people who have unregistered property, and it would, as a result, improve their access to credit by providing them with collateral. Another result would be to provide the state with better information about who lives where. A better grasp of the demographics of potential consumers can help firms improve their targeting and distribution for the BoP. Cemex, a Mexican multinational enterprise that ranks among the largest cement producers in the world, has pioneered the introduction of initiatives aimed at the BoP, such as providing building materials and technical advice on credit, establishing a network of micro-entrepreneurs who build and sell their own concrete bricks, and coordinating neighborhood efforts to joint-finance access roads.

There are already several examples of innovation at the BoP that have successfully overcome institutional voids. The most remarkable of all is the diffusion of cell phones. The failure of the state in the vast majority of emerging markets to develop landline infrastructure resulted in very poor fixed telephony penetration rates, even in countries with relatively high average incomes, such as Argentina. Now there are more cell phone users in emerging markets than in developed economies, and all of this has occurred in the space of roughly ten years. How did this come about? Advances in technology allowed the cost of a basic handset to reduce dramatically. It also became apparent that infrastructure (i.e., the antennas), which was originally built to target wealthier consumers, was already in place for use in targeting the BoP. Even with cheap handsets and antennas already in place, however, the poor were not in a position to pay a subscription to a network. Besides being too expensive, this often entailed having a bank account or a credit card. In order to skip the institutional void of inefficient state telecom systems, private firms had to innovate with the way in which they sold their services—they began to offer very cheap pay-as-you-go services that could be charged with small amounts of credit. This opened the market for a very large number of consumers who had never had a telephone before. It benefitted these consumers by allowing them to communicate not only with friends and relatives but also with potential customers for their products, thus enabling them to gain information about market prices for their products, for example. It is important to note that technological innovation per se would have been insufficient to create this BoP market; what made it thrive was the innovative thinking in terms of finding feasible ways in which BoP consumers could effectively consume tele-com services, which in turn spurred further innovation. Cell phones need to be charged now and then, and because many BoP cell phone users do not have access to electricity, rural entrepreneurs began catering to this need by setting up kiosks to charge customer's phones or to swap the battery. This innovative service allows consumers to maximize the utility of having a phone in spite of the decades-long institutional failure in the provision of electricity. Cell phone diffusion has allowed another widespread institutional failure to be overcome: the unsophisticated and inadequate banking sector of most emerging mar-kets. Another managerial innovation, telecom banking, has provided a booming number of consumers with their first access to banking services—a means to save and transfer small sums of money to other people. Why has this worked? First, because conventional banking does not; if it did, there would have been no need for telecom banking. Telecom banking has better reach, requires fewer bureaucratic processes and less paperwork, and makes it easier to transfer small sums. Second, technology has brought down the costs of mobile telephony and communication. Third, the whole business model was developed with the BoP customer in mind, allowing for very small, repeated cash transfers, which moves us on to the next section (see Box 7.3).

Box 7.3: Africa's Telecom Sector Opportunities: The Case of M-PESA

The telecommunications sector has great growth potential, particularly in Africa. According to the report *Ambient Insight's 2010-2015 Worldwide Market Forecast for Mobile Learning Products and Services*, growth in African mobile learning products for the five years from 2010 to 2015 will be approximately 50 percent, much stron-ger than in any other region of the world. The Vodafone subsidiary, Safaricom, has developed M-PESA, a cellphone-based money transfer and micro-financing service, in Kenya. M-PESA was launched in the Kenyan mobile money services market in March 2007 and five years later had about 15 million customers. It allows its users to execute a variety of financial transactions using their cell phones, such as depositing and withdrawing money, transferring money to other users and non-users, paying different bills, sending remittances, and recharging pay-as-you-go cell phone sub-scriptions. The success has been such that M-PESA has begun to be implemented in Uganda, Tanzania, Rwanda, and Afghanistan, and it is considered an example to be emulated across the developing world. Notably, mobile phone banking has spread faster in emerging economies where consumers often lack a formal bank account and hence the means to transfer money.

Sources: Mas and Morawczynski (2009), Global Banking and Finance Review (2012), Adkins (2011), Jack and Suri (2010), Safaricom (2012).

Small, Repeated Cash Transactions

Most global firms expanded their businesses by growing during the period of mass consumption in the Triad. Their business model evolved over time and focused on selling, often through credit card purchases, in large retail spaces that concentrated all offerings under one roof, reducing the need to shop around. These innovations allowed consumers to stop carrying large amounts of cash and to maximize their time, which has become ever more pressed. They also responded to the growing participation of women in the workforce: with less time to shop, how much more convenient to buy everything in the same place. Increased car ownership made it possible to drive to cheaper retail stores located outside of city centers. To attract consumers, retailers pushed producers to make large, though nonperishable and highly discounted bulk items available—large detergent bottles, large corn flakes cartons, and so on. They generated an array of new brands and flavors and resorted to aggressive marketing. This whole model of market development does not work for the BoP (Subrahmanyan and Gomez-Arias, 2008).

Consumers at the BoP in the vast majority of cases do not own a credit card and do not have bank accounts. They do not drive a car, and they live in areas that are not close to large shopping malls. They earn little and are often paid in cash. They would, and do, pay a premium to be able to buy smaller quantities, such as one cigarette, a small loaf of bread, or just enough milk for breakfast because they lack sufficient credit or purchasing power and fridges to store perishable items. This may not seem at all attractive as a business environment, but it generates an impressive volume of repeated, very small, cash transactions, mainly benefitting local stores and intermediaries who act as distributors. To target this gap in the market, it is necessary to go beyond understanding what BoP consumers want and consider how they pay for the items they consume (Rangan et al., 2011). From there, we can design items that will be sold in very small quantities, using alternative, low-cost packaging to allow for affordability. As many leading global multinationals have found, instead of opening a large detergent carton and selling spoonfuls to clients, the corner shop could be selling small sachets of the same product packaged by the producer, provided that there is the incentive to do so. Throughout emerging markets, you can see long strings of sachets of different brands of shampoo for sale in the small kiosks or shops that cater to this group of consumers, and often to backpackers who travel through these areas, too! Reducing the size and cost of packaging can make products accessible for customers at the BoP, especially for fast-moving consumer goods, such as soaps, detergents, and beauty products, and food items, such as bread, beans, sugar, and salt.

Brand Loyalty

BoP consumers may not know much about brands if they are first-time consumers. They are, however, not impervious to marketing (Schrader et al., 2012). Each purchase is a relatively large share of their income, which is spent on one product and not another. It is therefore essential that the product works. If it does not, they will immediately switch to another brand. And, more importantly, spread the word to their friends, neighbors, and relatives in order to save them from the same negative experience. On the other hand, a product that seems to be working well (for example, a particularly effective soap) will quickly build its reputation through the same word-of-mouth network. Assuming that a company gets the pricing, packaging, and distribution right, ensuring that the product performs its basic functions is the next feature in effective targeting of the BoP.

Frugal Innovation: Identifying What Features Add Value and Generate New, Cost-Efficient Products

The problem with targeting the BoP is that the majority of products and services that leading global companies have thus far developed have not been developed for this group of consumer. Adapting them can make them more suitable, but not necessarily ideal. Developing products for the BoP entails rethinking the product in terms of the function it performs, focusing on the critical functions and doing away with superfluous functions, and exploring solutions to the environmental shortcomings it may have to withstand. For example, it is not enough to price a washing machine for the BoP cheaply, perhaps by means of cheaper materials and less prestigious branding (Radjou and Prabhu, 2013). It must be a washing machine that can be used with less than crystal-clear water, which is often supplied at very variable pressures. If, furthermore, we are planning to sell in water-poor areas, it also has to be efficient in its water consumption. In terms of size and use of space, design decisions will depend whether we are targeting the urban or rural poor. In the former case, the machine will need to be rather compact. Finally, what about electricity? The machine will need to be able to withstand power cuts without breaking too often and perhaps have alternative means of functioning, such as a manual motion system that can be used when there is no electricity. Fancy design, colors, and brands are significantly less critical factors. The result of this exercise is not simply a cheap washing machine; instead, it is a machine that combines elements of a cheap washing machine (price, materials, brand) with other elements (compactness and ability to withstand power cuts). The ideal product is not a cheap version of an existing washing machine; it is a new washing machine developed for the BoP. Frugal innovation, rethinking, and reengineering products to cater to the needs of the BoP have the potential to create new markets and provide interesting opportunities for the firms that are bold enough to implement this.

Frugal innovation means developing a value proposition that is superior to existing offers. General Electric, one of the most established American multinational enterprises, has been a leader in the incorporation of "frugal innovation" into its philosophy, investing in R&D labs in several countries across the developing world in order to harvest the best minds and ideas. Focusing on the need for a smaller and cheaper device to perform electrocardiograms (ECGs) in India, its Bangalore research department developed a breakthrough ECG device that was simultaneously smaller, lighter, and much cheaper to produce than any other ECG device on the market. Its researchers stripped from the device all nonessential functions and components, from large screens to the mechanical components needed to produce a large printout of the ECG. They eliminated all of the optional functions and components that they found to be seldom used. The result was a much simplified device, as capable of performing its core function, an ECG scan, as any other device, but cheaper and more portable and hence much more suited to the market at which it was targeted. It created a market for new, no-frills ECG devices. Increasing the diffusion of ECG devices has helped to reduce the price a patient pays on average for an ECG, making them available to a larger number of people. Frugal innovation allowed GE to pursue sales growth, which also advanced a social objective (*The Economist,* 2010).

Procter and Gamble (P&G) achieved this in Brazil by launching a new line of female pads for BoP customers. It did not compromise on the key functionality and performance of the product, such as providing good protection and comfort. If it had skimped on these, it would have compromised its overall brand name, affecting the sales of higher priced products too. P&G was savvy with its choice of image, too, recognizing that a product that was perceived to be somewhat fashionable would be more successful in targeting young women. How did P&G reduce the costs of producing this product? The company saved on packaging, developing a new package that used less ink. It also saved by removing marginal innovations, such as extra-length wings, which provide premium performance on its more expensive product lines (Kanter and Bird, 2008).

Save Resources, Save Costs

Consumers at the BoP often experience poor access to fresh water, sanitation, building materials, and electricity. It would be beneficial for companies and BoP customers alike to think of products and services that economize on resources, diverging from the wasteful mass-consumption model that prevails in the Triad. New materials and new technologies are opening the frontier for environmentally friendly frugal innovation. The fall in the price of solar panels, for example, is providing the means to generate cheap electricity in areas that are disconnected from the grid and where fuel is expensive. This will allow for a broader diffusion of electrically powered devices, such as mobile phone chargers.

Depending on the availability of batteries or other means of storing or harnessing power, such as solar power, LED lamps may become sufficiently cheap to displace kerosene lamps, and by doing so eliminate a key risk factor causing both fires and lung diseases.

Flexibility of Use: Embracing Customer Needs

Companies do not always fully grasp how consumers at the BoP use their products. Haier, a Chinese company that specialized in white goods production, discovered that in a certain area of China, its consumers were using washing machines to wash vegetables as well, which resulted in a higher than usual rate of damage under warranty. The firm used this to its advantage: it gathered consumers' opinions and improved its washing machines in ways that made them more suitable for the multiple uses they were put to (Khanna, Palepu, and Andrews, 2011). BoP consumers may well act differently from the patterns established by other types of consumers or from how we may expect them to do on the basis of market research. Embracing their needs can lead not only to successfully developing BoP markets, but also to new ideas and business innovations.

Credit and Sales

BoP customers often do not have enough money to buy what they want or need. This is not unique to this group; otherwise, credit cards would not exist. The main difference is that for those living at the BoP, it is almost impossible to obtain a credit card and hence to delink earnings from consumption. They often rely on money lenders, who charge much higher rates of interest than banks—a perfect example of market inefficiency reproducing poverty and of prices at the BoP not necessarily being low or lower than in other market segments. Lack of access to credit reduces not only consumption but also entrepreneurship. For example, if a woman wants to buy a juice-making machine to start selling juice in a street market, the higher the interest rate she gets charged on a credit purchase, the less willing she will be to start the business.

The idea that providing the poor with credit could be a key pillar for reducing poverty was first experimented and diffused by NGOs and donors. Institutions providing microcredit, such as the Grameen Bank, have illustrated that in spite of the absence of collateral, the poor tend to comply with their obligations, especially when credit is distributed using existing networks, such as community-level organizations. Danone distributes a BoP product in South Africa through a network of women entrepreneurs. It provides the first batch of the product for free. When the women return, they pay for the second batch with the money earned from selling the first batch and keep the profit. Any of the participants could run away with the first batch of free products; however, most realize through making a profit on the first sale, there is an incentive in returning and building a sustainable business. Danone has found that there is a very low incidence of participants fleeing with the free products (Hawarden and Barnard, 2010). It is interesting to note that most of the projects that provide credit at the BoP focus on women, with the idea that providing them with extra earnings generates sufficient incentive for compliance. This is perhaps the most risky and yet more vibrant aspect of business at the BoP, with much experimentation being carried out by different types of organizations.

Building BoP Business Models, Not Just Products

The two risks to assess when targeting the BoP are scalability and social proof. The first reason why many projects targeting the BoP have failed is scalability. Selling items at very low prices and earning minimal marginal profits on each unit is okay as long as volumes are high. The economics of this can be tricky because the whole idea of targeting the BoP is new and therefore entails high investment in R&D, distribution, credit, and products. It may therefore take several years before a BoP project becomes profitable. To do so, it has to achieve a high market penetration. Notably, several firms that were successful at the BoP, such as Unilever is in India, already had a high market share in their fields and well-known brands to exploit. Emulating their success with a much lower initial market penetration rate and less developed logistical infrastructure can be very difficult. The BoP contains within it an extremely diverse range of people with different customs and ways of living. In order to achieve high market penetration, a product and its uses have to be accepted; it has to be admired, desired, and considered to be acceptable within local customs. This is known as "social proof," and to achieve it is particularly difficult for products that are not currently consumed in the BoP market that a firm is targeting. Avoiding adversely touching on consumers' cultural and religious beliefs as well as assessing the potentially negative impact of the perception that the product is from "the top" or from abroad are also important areas of risk that are important to bear in mind. BoP products have to become local products to be accepted. This means becoming part of the way of living of a given community and exploiting the most powerful marketing tool at the BoP—word of mouth. Central to ensuring that targeting the BoP is a profitable venture and not just an exercise in creative management is the importance of building a BoP business model behind the products launched. The critical point is getting to grips with what sort of volume is necessary to sell at minimum profit per unit in ways that reach BoP consumers and still make a venture profitable. Can such volumes be achieved? If they cannot, then it may be necessary to further reduce costs and assess again whether the product is still too costly for the target consumers. Are we trying to sell a product people at the BoP really need, or is it a product we have and cannot sell to anyone else? Through frugal innovation, we can reengineer our products and services in ways that actually suit the needs of those at the BoP. The business model also needs to be sustainable. It is not enough just to reduce the size of our packaging—we may also need to consider if we have the necessary logistical arrangements to deliver the smaller packets and the marketing needed to inform customers. Are there incentives for the corner shop to sell the product in its new reduced-size packs? Or would they be better off buying the product in larger quantities and making smaller units themselves to sell to the final customer? Taking the latter consideration, we need to ensure that the business model is profitable not only for us, but also for the other actors involved in the sale and distribution. In terms of quality and functionality, we must not compromise the basic features consumers look for, even if aiming for large volume and the minimization of costs of production per unit.

Keeping these principles in mind, we can develop business models and strategies suited to targeting the BoP market, and by doing so expand our operations in ways that can contribute to poverty reduction in emerging markets.

References

Adkins, S. (2011). Ambient Insight Comprehensive Report: The Worldwide Market for Mobile Learning Products and Services: 2010–2015 Forecast and Analysis. Retrieved from http://www.ambientinsight.com/Resources/Documents/Ambient-Insight-2010-2015-Worldwide-Mobile-Learning-Market-Forecast-Executive-Overview.pdf.

Akula, V. (2008). Business Basics at the Base of the Pyramid. *Harvard Business Review*, *86*(6), p. 53.

APICCAPS (2012). *World Footwear 2012 Yearbook*. APICCAPS.

Bain & Co. (2012). *Luxury Goods Worldwide Market Study*. Bain & Company, Inc.

Bearden, W. and Etzel, M. (1982). Reference group influence on product and brand purchase decisions. *Journal of Consumer Research, 9* (2), pp. 183–194.

BID (2009). *Poder a través de inversiones*. Retrieved from http://idbdocs.iadb.org/wsdocs/getdocument.aspx?docnum=1904581.

Capgemini & RBC Wealth Management (2012). *World Wealth Report*. Capgemini & RBC Wealth Management.

CEMEX (2013a). *¿Qué es el Programa Patrimonio Hoy?*. Retrieved from http://www.cemexcostarica.com/su/su_so_ph_ph.html.

CEMEX (2013b). *Centros Productivos de Autoempleo*. Retrieved from http://www.cemexmexico.com/DesarrolloSustentables/CentrosProductivos.aspx.

CEMEX (2013c). *Mejora tu calle*. Retrieved from http://www.cemexmexico.com/DesarrolloSustentables/ids2011/MejoraTuCalle.html.

ClickZ (2000). *Web Pages by Language.* Retrieved from http://www.clickz.com/clickz/news/1697080/web-pages-language.

Doyle, P. (1990). Building Successful Brands: The Strategic Options. *Journal of Consumer Marketing, 7*(2), pp. 5–20.

Farrell, D., Gersch, U. A., and Stephenson, E. (2006). The value of China's emerging middle class. *McKinsey Quarterly, 2*(I), p. 60.

Ferrari (2012). *Ferrari Challenge.* Retrieved from http://www.ferrari.com/english/scuderia/corse_clienti/Pages/ferrari_challenge.aspx.

Global Banking and Finance Review (2012). African telecom investment opportunities attract global interest. *Global Banking and Finance Review.* Retrieved from http://www.globalbankingandfinance.com/Global-Markets/African-telecom-investment-opportunities-attract-global-interest.html.

Gold, S., Hahn, R., and Seuring, S. (2013). Sustainable supply chain management in "Base of the Pyramid" food projects—A path to triple bottom line approaches for multinationals?, *International Business Review.*

Hawarden, V. and Barnard, H. (2010). Danimal in South Africa: Management Innovation at the Bottom of the Pyramid. Richard Ivey School of Business Foundation Case Studies. Prod. #:910M99-PDF-ENG.

Hindustan Unilever Limited (2013). Project Shakti. Retrieved from http://www.hul.co.in/sustainable-living/casestudies/Casecategory/Project-Shakti.aspx.

Internet World Stats (2012). *World Internet Usage* [Data File]. Retrieved from http://www.internetworldstats.com/stats.htm.

Jack, W. and Suri, T. (2010). The economics of M-PESA. Retrieved from http://www.mit.edu/~tavneet/M-PESA.pdf.

Kanbur, R. and Sumner, A. (2012). Poor countries or poor people? Development assistance and the new geography of global poverty. *Journal of International Development,* 24 (6), August 2012, pp. 686–695.

Kanter, R.M. and Bird, M. (2008). Procter & Gamble Brazil (A): 2 1/2 Turnarounds. Harvard Business School Case Studies. Prod. #:308081-PDF-ENG.

Khanna, T. and Palepu, K. G. (2010). *Winning in Emerging Markets: A Road Map for Strategy and Execution.* Harvard Business Press.

London, T. and Hart, S. L. (2010). *Next Generation Business Strategies for the Base of the Pyramid: New Approaches for Building Mutual Value.* FT Press.

London, T., Anupindi, R., and Sheth, S. (2010). Creating mutual value: Lessons learned from ventures serving base of the pyramid producers. *Journal of Business Research, 63*(6), pp. 582–594.

Mas, I. and Morawczynski, O. (2009). Designing Mobile Money Transfer Services: Lessons from M-PESA. *Innovations*, Spring 2009, pp. 77–91.

Monopoly [Def.1]. *Oxford Dictionary Online*. Retrieved from http://oxforddictionaries.com.

Monopsony [Def.1]. *Oxford Dictionary Online*. Retrieved from http://oxforddictionaries.com.

Oligopoly [Def.1]. *Oxford Dictionary Online*. Retrieved from http://oxforddictionaries.com.

Prahalad, C. K. (2006). *The Fortune at the Bottom of the Pyramid: Eradicating Poverty Through Profits*. New Jersey: Wharton School Publishing, Pearson Education.

Prahalad, C. K. (2010). *The Fortune at the Bottom of the Pyramid: Eradicating Poverty Through Profits*. Wharton.

Radjou, N. and Prabhu, J. (2013) Frugal Innovation: A New Business Paradigm. INSEAD Knowledge, January 10, 2013. http://knowledge.insead.edu/innovation/frugal-innovation-a-new-business-paradigm-2375. Accessed on 3/15/2013.

Rangan, V. K., Chu, M., and Petkoski, D. (2011). Segmenting the Base of the Pyramid. *Harvard Business Review, 89*(6), pp. 113–117.

Ravallion, M. (2010). The developing world's bulging (but vulnerable) middle class. *World Development, 38*(4), pp. 445–454.

Safaricom (2012). Celebrating 5 years of changing lives. Retrieved from http://www.safaricom.co.ke/mpesa_timeline/timeline.html.

Schrader, C., Freimann, J., and Seuring, S. (2012). Business Strategy at the Base of the Pyramid. *Business Strategy and the Environment*.

Shepherd, J. and Perez, F. (2007). Kerosene Lamps and Cookstoves—the Hazards of Gasoline Contamination. Retrieved from http://www2.galcit.caltech.edu/EDL/publications/reprints/KeroseneLampCookstove.pdf.

Simandis, E. (2012). Reality Check at the Bottom of the Pyramid. *Harvard Business Review*. Retrieved from http://hbr.org/2012/06/reality-check-at-the-bottom-of-the-pyramid/ar/1.

Simanis, E. (2009). At the Base of the Pyramid. *Wall Street Journal*. Retrieved from http://online.wsj.com/article/SB10001424052970203946904574301802684947732.html.

Steenkamp, J., Batra, R., and Alden, D. (2003). How Perceived Brand Globalness Creates Brand Value. *Journal of International Business Studies, 34* (1), pp. 53–65

Subrahmanyan, S., and Gomez-Arias, J. T. (2008). Integrated approach to understanding consumer behavior at bottom of pyramid. *Journal of Consumer Marketing, 25*(7), pp. 402–412.

Sumner, A. (2010). Global Poverty and the New Bottom Billion: What If Three-Quarters of the World's Poor Live in Middle-Income Countries? IDS Working Paper, November 2010.

Swaminathan, V. (2011). *The Pyramid Within the Pyramid: Segmenting the BoP Affordable Housing Market*. Next Billion, Development Through Enterprise. Retrieved from http://www.nextbillion.net/blogpost.aspx?blogid=2523.

The Economist (2010). First break all of the rules. Available at http://www.economist.com/node/15879359. Accessed on 3/15/2013.

The Economist (2006). Lighting up the world. Retrieved from http://www.economist.com/node/7904248.

W3Tech (2013). Usage of content languages for websites [Data File]. Retrieved from http://w3techs.com/technologies/overview/content_language/all.

Wealth X (2011). *World Ultra Wealth Report*. Wealth X.

Williams, D. (2012). International Development and Global Politics: History, Theory and Practice. Oxon, UK, Routledge.

World Bank (2007). GEF SE Lighting the Bottom of the Pyramid (formerly LED Off-Grid Lighting Initiative). IFC: Summary of Proposed Investment. Retrieved from http://www.ifc.org/ifcext/spiwebsite1.nsf/ProjectDisplay/SPI_DP521198.

World Bank (2011). Global Development Horizons 2011—Multipolarity: The New Global Economy. Washington, D.C. World Bank.

World Bank Group (2013). World Development Indicators [Data File]. Retrieved from http://databank.worldbank.org/data/databases.aspx.

Yeoman, I. and McMahon-Beattie, U. (2005). Luxury markets and premium pricing. *Journal of Revenue and Pricing Management, 4*(4), pp. 319–328.

Yunus, M., Moingeon, B., and Lehmann-Ortega, L. (2010). Building social business models: Lessons from the Grameen experience. *Long Range Planning, 43*(2), pp. 308–325.

PART III

The Emergence of Emerging Market Multinationals—Implications for Managers and Scholars

Multinational companies—firms that operate across multiple locations—are key pillars of the global economy. They contribute to a large share of the world's investment flows. As we have illustrated in Chapter 1, "What Are Emerging Markets?," and Chapter 3, "A Historical Perspective," they built most of the world's infrastructure, including the railways, ports, and roads needed for integrating local and international markets. Leading multinationals, such as Apple, Walmart, Toyota, Shell, Siemens, and Nestlé, have more assets than the majority of the world's governments. They contribute the lion's share of the world's spending in research and development, pushing technological and scientific innovation forward.

Multinationals not only invest in multiple countries, they also contribute to a large share of the world's trade in goods and services. They have unique capabilities to manage cutting-edge technological projects such as deep-water oil extraction. They also develop and run incredibly sophisticated distribution, logistics, and production networks that span the entire globe. They shape consumption patterns through advances in marketing and sales techniques, and they own the most recognized and valuable brands in the world—household names as Nivea, Coca-Cola, and Toyota.

Most management textbooks continue to explain the multinational corporation as a type of organization, based in developed economies, that has expanded to emerging markets to search for locations where production is cheaper, to extract natural resources, or simply to find new markets for its products. Certainly the most recognized companies in the world keep on being firms based in developed economies, partly because they have been around for longer (see Table III.1). The idea that multinationals are based in developed economies, however, is already obsolete. Since the 2000s, a growing array of emerging-market multinationals have conquered leading positions in most industries, forcing management practitioners and scholars to come to terms with this new phenomenon. Given that emerging markets have been defined and labeled in different ways (see Chapter 1 and the Appendix), it is not surprising that scholars have done much the same with multinational enterprises from developing countries. For example, Wells (1983) referred to MNEs from developing countries as "Third-World MNEs," and Mathews (2002) named them "latecomer firms." However, the most frequently used name is "emerging MNEs" (EMNEs), coined by Goldstein (2007). This part of the book discusses the international expansion of multinational corporations based in emerging markets, using the definition of Luo and Tung (2007), whereby EMNEs are multinational enterprises from emerging markets actively involved in value-adding investment in more than one country. Chapter 8, "Multinationals Based in Emerging Markets: Features and Strategies," illustrates how they differ from their competitors based in the Triad, explaining their competitive strengths and weaknesses, whereas Chapter 9, "The Internationalization of Emerging Market MNEs: A Critical Examination of International Business Theories," discusses the internationalization of emerging-market multinationals by looking at their implications for international business theory.

Table III.1   Most Valuable Brands 2012

Rank	Company	Country	Brand Value (US$ Millions)
1	Apple	USA	70,605
2	Google	USA	47,463
3	Microsoft	USA	45,812
4	IBM	USA	39,135
5	Walmart	USA	38,320
6	Samsung Group	Japan	38,197
7	GE	USA	33,214
8	Coca-Cola	USA	31,082
9	Vodafone	United Kingdom	30,044
10	Amazon.com	USA	28,665

Data Source: BrandFinance, Brand Valuation Report 2012 (http://brandirectory.com)

References

Goldstein, A. (2007). Multinational Companies from Emerging Economies. New York: Palgrave Macmillan.

Luo, Y. and Tung, R. L. (2007). International expansion of emerging market enterprises: A springboard perspective. Journal of International Business Studies, 38. pp. 481–498.

Mathews, J. A. (2002). Dragon multinationals: a new model of global growth. New York: Oxford University Press.

Wells, L. T. (1983). Third World Multinationals: The Rise of Foreign Investment from Developing Countries. Cambridge, Massachusetts: The MIT Press.

8

Multinationals Based in Emerging Markets: Features and Strategies

---

Introduction

By 2010, over one fifth of the Fortune 500—the 500 largest companies in the world by capitalization—were multinationals based in emerging markets, or emerging multinational enterprises (EMNEs). Over 20 percent of the world's flows of foreign investment now originate from emerging markets, mainly as a result of the internationalization of EMNEs. As of 2012, EMNEs are no longer a marginal category that can be discussed as a footnote; they have become an essential element of the global economy. Since 2005, EMNEs have invested an average of over US$120 billion per year, employed over five million people, and spent more than US$10 billion per year on research and development (Guillén and García-Canal, 2009; Aybar and Ficici, 2009). They are a manifestation simultaneously of the rise of emerging markets and a factor that contributes to their growing economic and geopolitical power in the world. This chapter discusses the nature of these emerging-market multinationals, explaining how their importance has increased dramatically during the last 20 years.

The emergence of emerging markets was not sudden. It occurred gradually and was by and large ignored in the rich world until the 2008–2009 crisis. EMNEs followed a similar growth path to the markets in which they are based—since the 1980s they developed gradually and perhaps even more under the radar than the economies where they are based. Their first phase of expansion was domestic. When they internationalized, it was often first at a regional level, targeting neighboring countries and other emerging markets. To acquire technology and managerial skills they invested heavily in R&D, purchased companies based in the Triad, and established different types of alliances with global leaders, local distribution, and production agreements, for example (Athreye and Sandeep, 2009). They started as cost leaders, exploiting lower costs and gradually became more sophisticated in terms of the products and services they could offer. Many EMNEs started out by providing rich-world multinationals with outsourced services, ranging from manufacturing to software development (Aulakh, 2007). Both Infosys and Tata Consulting Systems initially focused on offering the cheapest elements in the information technology services value chain. These EMNEs learned how to perform more complex tasks and develop their own brands instead of remaining subcontractors. Eventually, they became ever more global and began investing in multiple regions and all types of economies, joining the ranks of the largest companies in the world in many industries (see Table 8.1).

Table 8.1   The World's Largest Companies

Oil and Gas						
Company	Sales (US$ Billions)	Profits	Assets	Market Value	Employees	Country
Exxon Mobil	433.5	41.1	331.1	407.4	82,100	USA
Royal Dutch Shell	470.2	30.9	340.5	227.6	90,000	Netherlands
PetroChina	310.1	20.6	304.7	294.7	552,698	China
Petrobras	145.9	20.1	319.4	180.0	81,918	Brazil
BP	375.5	25.7	292.5	147.4	83,400	United Kingdom
Beverages						
Company	Sales (US$ Billions)	Profits	Assets	Market Value	Employees	Country
Coca-Cola	46.5	8.6	80.0	158.8	146,200	USA
PepsiCo	66.5	6.4	72.9	101.3	297,000	USA
Anheuser-Busch InBev	39.0	5.9	112.4	115.3	116,278	Belgium/Brazil/U.S.
SABMiller	15.1	2.5	38.7	65.7	69,212	South Africa/United Kingdom
Diageo	15.9	3.0	30.9	60.4	23,786	United Kingdom
Metals and Mining						
Company	Sales (US$ Billions)	Profits	Assets	Market Value	Employees	Country
Codelco	15.8	3.8	31.6	N/A	18,247	Chile
BHP Billiton	71.7	23.6	102.9	187.5	40,757	Australia
Vale	55.4	20.3	127.6	126.8	79,646	Brazil
Rio Tinto	60.5	5.8	119.5	110.2	67,930	United Kingdom
Glencore International	179.6	3.9	85.2	45.9	54,800	Switzerland
China Shenhua Energy	33.1	7.3	63.6	84.2	65,154	China

Data Source: Company websites

When the world noticed, they had already displaced many of their older and better known competitors from the U.S., Europe, and Japan. Now we find EMNEs among the global leaders in the production of personal computers (Lenovo from China), bread (Bimbo from Mexico), oil (CNPC from China, Gazprom from Russia), cement (CNBM from China, Cemex from Mexico), steel (Mittal-Arcelor from India, Baosteel from China), information technology services (Infosys and Wypro, both from India), wine (Concha y Toro from Chile), meat (JBS from Brazil), midrange commercial aircraft (Embraer from Brazil), and many other goods and services, ranging from port operators (PSA from Singapore, DP World from Dubai, and Cosco from China) to telecommunication networks (China Mobile from China and America Movil from Mexico). Their ascent has been rapid, but not anymore rapid than Toyota's ascent from an unknown small producer to a global leader between the 1960s and the 1980s. It seemed more dramatic because of the continuing rich-world-centric focus of management scholars, management schools, and the books used to prepare the world's future leaders. The next section explores the nature of EMNEs, illustrating the features that they share.

What Are EMNEs?

Emerging market multinationals include thousands of companies operating in a broad range of sectors. Among them we find state-owned corporations such as China National Petroleum Corporation, one of the largest oil companies in the world, diversified private conglomerates such as the Tata Group, which operates in cars, telecoms, steel, and many other sectors, and family businesses specializing in one product or niche, such as Arcor, a sweets producer based in Argentina. They are indeed a very mixed group of firms. In spite of their heterogeneity, they also share some key features:

- Home country advantage
- Entrepreneurial aggressiveness
- Flexibility

Home Country Advantage

Industrialization, mechanization, mass production, and investments in technology and education allowed the Triad to become extremely wealthy (Abramovitz, 1986). The economic stagnation of first Japan and now the U.S. and Europe illustrate that the benefits of having been the first industrializers have now run out of steam and have become insufficient to push growth further in rich economies. Markets are saturated in developed economies, costs are high, and productivity increases very slowly. Macroeconomic imbalances, decrepit aging infrastructure, debt and aging populations make a sudden restart of growth in the Triad very unlikely. Emerging markets, on the other hand, are now benefitting from the same dynamics that pushed growth in the Triad—infrastructure development, the diffusion of durable consumer goods, industrialization, urbanization, investments in education and health, and the development of new physical and virtual markets. All of these factors combined contribute to explaining the rise of emerging-market multinationals. If we look more carefully, most EMNEs come from the largest emerging markets—China, Brazil, India, Russia, Turkey, South Africa, and Mexico—precisely because being based in a large domestic market provides them with *home country advantage.*

British multinationals developed when the British Empire was the largest, fastest-growing, and most innovative economy in the world. British leadership in steam-powered manufacturing and banking and finance generated immense wealth, which fueled the domestic markets and financed the expansion of the Empire. The protagonists of this expansion were British multinationals. They were also some of the main beneficiaries: the capital and expertise accumulated at home served as a basis to expand abroad. American multinationals developed as the U.S. moved from being a sparsely populated agricultural colony to an emerging industrial power. Many of today's leading multinationals, such as Ford, McDonald's, and Coca-Cola, expanded thanks to a large and fast-growing domestic economy that provided unprecedented business opportunities. Many of them (for example, Ford and Standard Oil) reaped the benefits of periods of quasi-monopolistic positions in their fast-growing domestic markets. Chandler (1990) argued that it is precisely because they made very high or, in economic terms, "abnormal" profits that these corporations could invest highly in research and development and push forward the technological frontier. A similar process is now taking place in emerging markets—several emerging markets, notably the BRICS, already rank among the largest economies in the world. Perhaps even more importantly, emerging economies are *growing* fast; some of them, such as China and Vietnam, have achieved growth rates above 5 percent for several subsequent years. They provide the same home country advantages that Europe, the U.S., and Japan provided their multinational corporations with in other historical periods. So, how does the growth of the domestic economy support the development of EMNEs? Through consumption and investment.

First, let's discuss consumption. As domestic economies expand, the purchasing power of consumers increases. This means that consumption of existing products expands while simultaneously the market for more expensive goods opens up. Companies that have a good understanding of the local market in terms of consumer taste are better placed to exploit this expansion than new players. They have a better grasp of the differences in local taste and consumption patterns that characterize different regions of large countries, such as China and Mexico. Well-known local brands can scale up and exploit their brand equity to offer better-quality products to their existing consumers. Domestic firms also have an advantage in terms of distribution and logistics: they already have agreements with retailers and distributors, they have warehouses, and they manage supply chains.

Next comes investment. The growth of emerging markets provides local firms and governments with extra revenues. Increasing wealth and consumption also generate demand for more energy, water, shelter, and better transport infrastructure. In times of economic growth, governments tend to invest more, even if this is contrary to the idea that government investment should be anti-cyclical. They build more roads, housing for the poor, power plants, and airports. This generates a high demand for construction services, construction material (cement, steel, sand, gravel), and equipment. China has been the largest investor in infrastructure for several years and as a result it has also been the largest consumer of construction materials and machinery in the world. This has provided demand for leading global companies, such as Caterpillar, but also for an array of local players, which were able to exploit their knowledge of the local market to expand at breakneck speed. By 2013, strong domestic demand allowed Chinese firms to climb the global rankings in all sectors related to construction, ranging from cement and steel to construction equipment. In 2013, the China State Construction & Engineering Corporation and China Railway Corporation rank among the top five providers of construction projects, and Sany and Zoomlion among the top ten construction equipment and heavy machinery producers. Accelerated domestic expansion has generated the revenue and scale that allow these firms to pursue aggressive internationalization. The EMNEs that are now global players are the firms that exploited the fortunes made through domestic market growth by investing in new facilities, new products, new machinery, and research and development, and by acquiring other companies to expand their reach to other markets.

EMNEs have learned to exploit the characteristics of their home markets to their advantage not just by selling goods and services to a growing number of new consumers; many EMNEs became competitive by building their production base in their home market and exploiting the existence of lower cost structures in specific niches. Acer, a PC and consumer electronics manufacturer based in Taiwan, exploited lower production costs to become a successful subcontractor for several American companies. It produced a broad array of components for PCs and electronic consumer goods. As a subcontractor, its sales were to the original equipment manufacturer (OEM) who designed the products, engineered them, branded them, and took care of distributing them. Acer expanded its operations and grew to become one of the leading global producers in its industry. During the 1980s, it established links with multiple Triad OEMs and developed alliances with local firms operating in different niches of the PC manufacturing business, such as batteries, interfaces, and different types of memory. It exploited its growing revenues to invest in R&D and gradually acquired the know-how to become an OEM itself. It only then launched its brand, and began to compete head to head with the Triad OEMs that used to be, and in some cases remained, its main clients in the subcontracting business. Between the mid 1990s, when the first Acer branded PC went on sale, and 2012, Acer captured 10 percent of the world's market for personal computers. In the 1980s, when Acer became a large player in the industry, and up to the late 1990s, Taiwan was generally considered an emerging economy, and it still often classified as such (EMGP, 2013). As Taiwan developed, its labor costs increased. Acer responded by emulating Triad multinationals—it offshored production to China, while moving toward selling higher value-added goods and services.

Acer's success story was possible because of home country advantage, though in this case not in terms of market, but in terms of the competitive advantage that Taiwan developed as a location for electronics manufacturing. HTC, another Taiwanese producer of consumer electronics, one of the five global market leaders in the fast-growing smartphones market, grew following a similar strategy—it moved from being a no-brand manufacturing subcontractor for Triad OEMs, to designing and developing products for OEMs, to launching its own brand products and competing with the likes of Apple, Samsung, and Nokia. Both Acer and HTC exploited their geographic and cultural proximity to China—when labor costs increased in Taiwan, they offshored production to China while maintaining their product development and engineering in the highly sophisticated Taiwanese electronics cluster. The Indian companies Infosys, Wipro, and Tata Consulting Services (part of the Tata Group) exploited the Indian home country advantage in software engineering—India turns out some of the best engineers in the world in large numbers. As the Taiwanese firms brought some of the manufacturing processes needed to make PCs to Taiwan, the Indian firms brought some of the program development processes needed to provide information technology and business services to India by working closely with Triad corporate clients. They also began by specializing on low-cost, simple services and moved up the value chain into the more profitable, more sophisticated niches. Albeit a different strategy than growing first in the domestic market, the strategy relies on the same idea—exploiting features of the home market to grow organically and accumulate resources, then to leverage these resources to become global competitors.

Entrepreneurial Aggressiveness

EMNEs are more aggressive, more creative, and often more entrepreneurial than companies based in developed economies, and especially those based in the Triad. There are several reasons for this—they are younger, more insulated from shareholders, and often continue to be led by charismatic business leaders.

The vast majority of multinational corporations based in developed economies are old. A few of them, such as the British insurance firm Lloyds and the scandal-ridden Italian bank Monte dei Paschi di Siena, are several hundreds of years old. A larger number are the American firms that emerged between the 1920s and the 1960s, driving the diffusion of mass manufacturing and mass consumerism. These firms shaped the global economy and continue to play an important leadership role in several fields, notably information technology, media, fast food, and fast-moving consumer goods. Even firms such as Microsoft, Apple, and Intel, which many management textbooks discuss as "young," are by now decades old. By contrast, most firms based in emerging markets are relatively young players in the global economy. Many were state-owned corporations run as arms of the state that have been privatized and now compete in the global economy. Some, such as Tata Consulting Systems, are innovative parts of older diversified conglomerates. Others, such as Arcelik, operated domestically for several years before internationalizing. And many more, such as Acer, HTC, and Lenovo, have been internationalized for years but and have progressed over time from being subcontractors to designing their own products and developing their own brands.

EMNEs are still expanding, learning, and experimenting. They are at a different developmental stage than multinationals based in developed economies, and especially those based in North America, Europe, and Japan. To give a historical comparison, when Toyota was experimenting with different production techniques in the 1960s, GM and Ford were already well established and had little reason to question their business models, which were generating healthy sales and profits. Toyota's experiments and its attempts to deal with a domestic market characterized by raw material and space scarcity led to the development of lean manufacturing. EMNEs are now at a comparable stage to Toyota during the 1950s to 1960s: they are growing thanks to booming domestic markets, they are becoming larger and investing in different fields, and they are testing their capabilities and their organizational models. This is simultaneously their weakness and one of their strongest competitive advantages. It is a weakness because they still lack the accumulated experience and know-how of older companies. In most cases, they still fail to compete for premium market niches, though this is gradually changing. EMNEs are trying to develop their brand quicker, without necessarily going through the learning process that allowed Toyota and Samsung to build their respective business empires. EMNE experimentations could lead to costly mistakes. However, being less bound by tradition and corporate custom, they are bolder, more entrepreneurial, and less risk averse than Triad multinationals.

EMNEs are targeting niches that may appear to be unprofitable, gaining market share from larger and older firms. Haier, for example, was initially able to enter the U.S. market by focusing only on small fridges aimed at university students, a niche deemed irrelevant by its competitors (Guillén and García-Canal, 2009). They are venturing into markets perceived to be too risky or unstable by Triad firms, ranging from North Korea to Sudan and Myanmar. In this they differ from the Japanese multinational companies, which internationalized aggressively but initially targeted mainly the U.S. market. EMNEs are experimenting with radical innovations and are entering markets dominated by old and well-established firms—think of Tata, which attempted to break into the automotive market by launching the first "no frills" car, the Tata Nano, before global leaders such as Volkswagen, GM, and Toyota. And they spend lavishly on acquisitions in both emerging and developed markets (Curevo-Cazurra, 2007). EMNEs are often bolder and therefore more creative in their management style than older multinational corporations. Confident that they will maintain profitability thanks to their home market advantage, they take risks experimenting.

There are two other reasons why EMNEs are more entrepreneurial: leaders and insulation from shareholders. The fact that most EMNEs are relatively new in their current form means that the leading managers, founders, or entrepreneurs who transformed them are usually still around. In the case of family businesses, founders continue to play a key role in providing their firms with a clear strategic vision as well as inspiring the workforce (Musacchio and Lazzarini, 2012). These leaders—people such as Carlos Slim, founder of Telmex and Telefonica, and Ratan Tata, chairman of the Tata Group for two decades—have acquired a global standing through their managerial success. They are often interviewed and quoted in management books—they are gurus. They are revered by their managers, and this provides a strong incentive to follow their bold strategy style. Their contacts with political elites and other businesses continue to provide ideas and opportunities for their businesses even after they formally step down from their positions.

The entrepreneurial aggressiveness of EMNEs can be partly attributed to visionary leaders who did not fear investing a large share of the corporate resources to pursue ambitious objectives and who took these firms onto an evolutionary path that differed from that of Triad multinationals. The importance of leaders not only applies to family-owned groups. The top managers that led emerging-market state-owned corporations through their transformation from loss-making inefficient behemoths to internationally respected enterprises acquired credibility both with their governments and with the private sector. The influence of their management style often continues after they have changed positions or is carried over when they move to other corporations. The recent outstanding success of Apple under the direction of Steve Jobs illustrates the importance of entrepreneurial leadership even for sophisticated corporations focusing on high technology. Even putting aside the exception of Apple, EMNEs tend to be run in a more entrepreneurial way than multinationals based in developed economies. Again, as for many of the characteristics of EMNEs, this can be a double-edged sword—visionary managers are a hard act to follow, and when they retire, it can be difficult to find a replacement to fill their boots or to continue their vision coherently.

The second reason why EMNEs can be led in a more entrepreneurial and aggressive way is that they are more shielded from the obligation to generate quarterly returns for shareholders. Some of them, such as the Argentinean firm Bunge, largest processor of oilseed in the world, are still controlled by members of their founding families who hold important managerial positions. Others, such as Baosteel, a Chinese firm that ranks as the third largest producer of steel in the world, are state-owned corporations. Both family-owned and state-owned EMNEs are more insulated from shareholder pressures than Triad multinationals. They can engage in long-term strategies and risky investments, betting that these will be profitable in the very long run, even if costly in the initial years (Athreye et al., 2009).

Several EMNEs have exploited their recent successes to go through an international public offering (IPO) in order to acquire further resources to finance their expansion. Most EMNEs have not, however, moved toward the "dispersed ownership" structure that characterizes most Triad multinationals, favoring structures that allow for power centralization instead. An example of this might be limiting the issue of shares with preferential voting rights to family members or state agencies (Musacchio and Lazzarini, 2012). Other arrangements include shares that exclude holders from voting on certain issues, and multi-firm structures where cross-ownership and hierarchical ladders of companies facilitate the concentration of managerial control by a few companies or actors who do not necessarily own the majority of shares (Buckley et al., 2007). These structures have been criticized because they separate ownership from control, which can endanger shareholder interests. They may also facilitate nontransparent practices, ranging from cross-subsidization to tax evasion. However, they also allow companies to develop long-term strategies without suffering from the scrutiny of shareholders who may be more interested in their immediate returns than in the future of the company.

Flexibility

The fact that EMNEs have become global players shows that they are far more flexible and adaptable than Triad firms. Part of this stems from their entrepreneurial management and the bold steps these managers take. But a more important reason for their flexibility is that they are based in emerging markets, in home contexts that are characterized by institutional voids, infrastructural deficiencies, often political and economic uncertainty, and in some cases, armed violence and conflict (Khanna and Palepu, 2010). The very fact that they have survived and thrived in these environments illustrates their flexibility and ability to adjust. The ability to deal with unpredictable environments is one of the most important competitive advantages of EMNEs; it makes them formidable competitors in emerging economies, but also in the increasingly volatile macroeconomic environment of the U.S. and Europe.

In previous chapters of this book, we outlined the features that distinguish emerging markets from developed economies, and we emphasized how business risks can be generated in emerging markets. One of the most talked about, though not necessarily the most important, is macroeconomic instability. Up to 2008, macroeconomic imbalances, such as debt and sudden currency or banking crises, were associated mainly with emerging markets—the Tequila crisis, the Asian crisis, the Russian crisis, the Argentinean crisis. A large number of emerging markets, most Latin American countries, with the notable exceptions of Argentina and Venezuela, have become more stable, reducing their internal and external debt and succeeding in containing inflation. But many emerging markets continue to experience high inflation, debt, and violent macroeconomic fluctuations.

EMNEs are founded and developed in environments that have historically been much more unstable than those of Triad economies. Russia, Brazil, Mexico, and Thailand, among others, experienced some major financial, debt, and currency crises during the 1990s to 2000s. EMNEs that are able to operate successfully in these sorts of circumstances develop the managerial skills and experience needed to be profitable in spite of ever-changing exchange rates, escalating prices, and different forms of control over the use of foreign currency. This equips them well, not only to operate in other emerging markets, but also to operate in the increasingly unpredictable macro environment of Triad economies where certainty about country ratings and currencies is all but lost.

nvironmental challenge for businesses based in an emerging market is that
ome regulatory structures and red tape. The vast majority of emerging mar-
pecially the BRICS (Brazil, Russia, India, China, and South Africa) have very
complex regulations and inefficient, slow bureaucracies. For example, it takes almost 90
days to establish a firm in Cambodia or Angola, compared to only five days in Canada.
A common task, such as paying tax, becomes daunting in most emerging markets. Vietnam, a country ruled by a communist regime, is no exception. According to the World
Bank, it takes a company operating in Vietnam an average of 872 hours per year to comply with its corporate income, value-added, and labor and social security regulations. In
Nigeria, it takes around 956 hours, and in Brazil, one of the much praised BRICS, up to
2,600 hours. Even in France, a Triad country often criticized for having a large public
sector and cumbersome regulations, complying with the same regulations requires only
132 hours per year. These factors generate extra costs for any company—costs of paying accountants and lawyers and ensuring compliance with the rules. Firms based in
emerging markets have worked within this sort of regulatory environment from their
foundation—they may not like it, but they will have developed the capability to manage complex bureaucracy and red tape in ways that do not impede strategy execution.
By contrast, firms based in the Triad frequently struggle to understand the complexity
of emerging-market bureaucracy, to factor in the extra cost generated by this and to
develop suitable strategies to manage it.

Institutional voids exponentially multiply the cost of operating in highly regulated environments. The director of a German engineering company operating in Nigeria told us,
"The problem is not the rules. We are used to complying with many rules. The problem
is understanding how they implement them here." Slow and corrupt bureaucracies can
mean that rules are enforced selectively and as a means of favoring special interests. It
is difficult to discern which rules are effectively implemented and which exist only at
the formal level. The inefficiency and slowness of judicial systems, which tend to be
overloaded and under-resourced in emerging markets, can prolong legal battles, often
making them a very costly way of settling disputes. In this context, having obscure and
frequently changing regulations benefits the enforcer—the more difficult it is to comply,
the easier to extract bribes or favors. By contrast, the simpler the rules and the higher the
compliance, the fewer opportunities there are to extract personal or group benefits. This
explains why emerging markets tend to have complex regulatory frameworks, even when
they may lack the resources to enforce them.

EMNEs have developed in environments where institutional voids are the rule and have
learned how to navigate these environments by exploiting personal and political connections, as well as ensuring that they operate according to local customs (Khanna and

Palepu, 2010). This has proved to be a competitive advantage when internationalizing to other emerging markets. Triad multinationals that are currently expanding in emerging markets, ranging from McDonald's to Ferrero, face a harder challenge; these companies have to adopt an entirely different business environment.

The third challenge is the policy uncertainty and unpredictability that characterizes emerging markets. A large number of emerging markets are governed by systems that are less democratic and less accountable to their citizens than the Triad democracies, despite the flaws of the latter. A few of them, such as China, Cuba, Saudi Arabia, and North Korea, continue to have authoritarian regimes and unelected leaders. Many, such as Russia and Angola, moved from authoritarianism to electoral democracies that were captured by one dominating party. Others, such as Argentina and Zimbabwe, are ruled by strong leaders and their families who have managed to stay in power for decades by meddling with electoral rules and through control of natural resources and state agencies. The concentration of economic and political power that often characterizes emerging markets can negatively affect the business environment by generating unpredictable outcomes and sudden changes—think, for example, of the abrupt expulsion of ethnic Indians from Uganda enacted by the then-dictator Idi Amin, or the failure to inform the public of the health conditions of the president Hugo Chavez, who was treated in secrecy in Cuba, before his death in 2013. Many emerging markets are ruled by tightly networked groups of people who exploit their control of state resources in order to acquire wealth and expand their personal power and whose political styles are often characterized by secrecy and unpredictability. The absence of democratic dialogue and of a healthy political opposition mean that economic policies are at times implemented without consultation and may favor businesses linked to the government and may potentially affect all others negatively. Examples of unpredictable changes in policies vary: they include sudden devaluations, tax rises on specific sectors, nationalizations, import duties, and different types of regulations. EMNEs have had to deal with such unpredictable policy changes since they were founded.

Many emerging markets are also affected by political instability, ethnic or religious tensions, and armed violence. Think of the border between India and Pakistan or between North and South Korea, civil unrest in Kenya after the 2007 elections, guerrilla groups in the Philippines, the ongoing civil war in Syria, and the heavily armed drug lords of Central America. EMNEs operate production plans, mines, oil wells, and distribution networks in areas where different forms of violence often manifest themselves. They have developed strategies to manage in spite of such environmental challenges. In a similar fashion, they are used to managing infrastructural deficiencies, ranging from perilous mud roads to lack of reliable power and water supplies. In short, EMNEs differ from

Triad multinationals because they have developed and grown in environments affected by several types of risk and barriers to business. This process equips them with the competitive advantage of flexibility and adaptability, which only a few of the oldest Triad multinationals, such as Nestlé, have acquired through decades of experience outside of their home markets and costly "learning by doing" experiments.

State-Owned Enterprises, Conglomerates, and Specialized Players

EMNEs can be categorized according to their three most common organizational forms: state-owned enterprises (SOEs), conglomerates, and specialized firms. State-owned enterprises are very common in industries that require very high initial capital and that are considered to be strategic by governments: extractive industries, steel, energy, and defense. Diversified conglomerates are the dominating organizational structure in Asia, including in Japan and South Korea. They encompass firms operating in all types of industries. Finally, specialized players are the emerging-market multinationals most similar to Triad businesses, as we illustrate in the following sections.

State-Owned Enterprises

SOEs have existed for a long time and are by no means exclusive to emerging markets. SOEs played an important role in the industrialization of Germany, Japan, France, and Italy. Both Volkswagen and Renault, two leading European car makers, were partly owned by the state for prolonged periods. Many European multinational corporations, such as the French EDF and Thales, or the Italian ENI, TIM, and Finmeccanica, continue to be partly owned by the state. State ownership of productive assets fell out of fashion and decreased dramatically during the 1990s. Ideologically, the fall of the Soviet Union seemed to prove that state control over the economy was inefficient and anachronistic. From an economic perspective, many countries in the Triad and the emerging world were affected by unsustainable levels of public debt. Privatizing state assets allowed them to reduce the debt burden. In many cases, SOEs were managed as arms of the state: to generate employment and distribute favors. Highly paid managerial positions were often appointed according to political affiliation. As a result, emerging market SOEs were often found to be draining as opposed to generating extra resources for the state. They were overly staffed, inefficient, corrupt organizations, which differentiated them strongly from private enterprises. Operating under heavy tariff protection or with monopolistic concessions, they were shielded from competition and thus had few incentives to become more productive or change their practices (Bulmer-Thomas, 2003).

Between the 1990s and the 2000s, a large number of these firms were privatized and others were "professionalized," introducing more meritocratic and technical career systems. Emerging markets opened fields such as telecoms and energy to competition. The SOEs that were not fully privatized, such as Petrobras, the Brazilian petroleum company, had to restructure, become leaner, acquire new technology and skills, and compete to retain their share of the domestic market. Most of the SOEs of today are very different from the SOEs of the 1970s—most are now profitable, run more like private multinational corporations than like arms of the state, and generate healthy tax returns. They continue to play a key role in their domestic markets and, increasingly, in the global economy. The vast majority of oil reserves are, for example, held by SOEs from emerging markets. SOEs rank among the top producers of steel, oil, gas, and carbon in the world. They are particularly mighty forces in the largest emerging economies, such as China, Brazil, and Russia. SOEs represent about 80 percent of the value of the Chinese stock market, over 60 percent of the Russian stock market, and almost 40 percent of the Brazilian stock market. From year to year, three to five SOEs rank among the top companies in the world in terms of revenue. Twenty percent of the largest EMNEs are SOEs, with a particularly strong concentration in oil and energy. Remarkably, although the state as a whole has become smaller in most emerging markets, SOEs have been growing, acquiring new assets both at home and abroad. All of the largest SOEs recently went through IPOs in order to increase their access to funds and accelerate their professionalization. The state has retained different measures of control through partial or full ownership.

There are two forms of SOEs—companies that continue to be owned and controlled mainly by the state, and firms where the state remains a minority owner. Majority-owned SOEs are the most common organizational structure of EMNEs in China, Vietnam, Russia, and all of the ex–Soviet Republics. Minority-owned EMNEs are more common in other economies, such as Brazil and Mexico (Musacchio and Lazzarini, 2012). In the case of China, even though the state remains the majority owner, SOEs have been reformed through the last 20 years to introduce more checks and balances, and to professionalize the management and provide incentives linked to economic performance and profitability, as opposed to incentives linked to employment or quantity of output produced (Luo et al., 2010). Another key difference between these new breed of SOEs and the older-style SOEs is the competitive environment and internationalization. Old-style SOEs were conceptualized as domestic monopolies; the new breed is generally operating in a competitive environment, often vis-à-vis other SOEs. The state pushes them to compete, to be competitive, and also to internationalize (Ralston et al., 2006; Luo and Tung, 2007). The idea is not to substitute the capitalist economy at home but rather to become competitive pillars of the economy that venture abroad, and by doing so become an expression of national competitiveness and geopolitical power. Minority-owned SOEs, such as the

Brazilian Vale, the largest iron producer in the world, operate as private firms, competing both at home and abroad. In theory, the state does not influence their strategies or management. In practice, it can do so by exploiting their large exposure in the domestic market. In 2011, the Brazilian government, for example, hinted several times that it may force Vale to use domestic contractors for its new equipment purchases even if this may result in higher costs, a tactic that allegedly caused the resignation of its CEO.

Not all SOEs are efficient and managed in modern ways—the national coal and electricity companies of India are examples of old-style, inefficient SOEs, which fail to perform the function for which they were created (i.e., generating and distributing energy). They have the benefits of a large and booming market, and, in the case of coal, of natural resource abundance and low labor costs. In spite of this, they work more like two of the many arms of an inefficient, highly bureaucratic state than as globally competitive multinational corporations. PDVSA, the Venezuelan national oil company, was used as an instrument of patronage by the government of Hugo Chavez for about 15 years. Although the idea of using oil riches to finance social progress is certainly admirable, Chavez pursued this by meddling with PDVSA management, firing a high share of its management when the latter disagreed with his views, and depriving the company of the needed investment to maintain its competitive edge. As a result, PDVSA moved from being one of the most admired SOEs in Latin America to being an ailing giant that fails to keep up production in spite of the high prices oil commands. A large number of the senior managers, engineers, and technical personnel of PDVSA fled to other oil companies, notably in neighboring Colombia, whose oil sector has been growing strongly since the 2000s.

A large number of EMNEs are SOEs and have become formidable competitors to Triad companies. SOEs benefit from the support of the state, and more explicitly so in the case of majority-owned SOEs. State support can benefit SOEs in different ways. It can allow them to gain quasi-monopolistic positions in the domestic market by protecting them from foreign competitors. It can provide subsidies for R&D. It can incentivize internationalization through tax exemptions and export credits. And it can provide diplomatic support in the countries where they operate. Clearly, this can come at a cost—following the priorities of the government. The Chinese, Russian, and Brazilian governments have shown themselves to be very interested in having competitive SOEs. India, Venezuela, and Argentina, on the other hand, have subdued the business interests of their SOEs in order to achieve political objectives, such as providing employment or subsidizing public sector projects.

Diversified Conglomerates

A large share of private business in emerging markets is organized in diversified conglomerates—groups of firms that are formally or informally linked and where ownership and managerial control cross organizational barriers. Some of the most famous EMNEs, such as the Tata Group, include businesses ranging from food to automotives, steel to information technology. Their success has long puzzled management scholars because it challenges the idea that strategic focus allows firms to be more competitive (Khanna and Palepu, 1997). There are several reasons why diversified conglomerates exist and why they tend to be more common in emerging markets than in the Triad. The first is that diversification is a good survival strategy in unpredictable and risky environments. If, for example, regulation suddenly makes a business completely unprofitable, the group can cross-subsidize for a certain period and assess whether conditions may change. This would be much more difficult for a specialized firm, unless the latter operated in several markets simultaneously. Emerging market conglomerates are diversified because they started from a difficult domestic base and diversifying helped them grow in their home market. In many cases, such as that of Tata, internationalization corresponded to an increased focus on a few industries and activities.

Another reason for diversifying is access to credit and foreign exchange. Most emerging markets experienced or continue to experience inferior access to credit and unsophisticated financial institutions. As a result, it is much more costly for companies to obtain credit in an emerging market than in the Triad. Diversifying also allows groups to finance new operations with the profits made by older companies in the group and hence rely less on external finance. Brazil, Mexico, India, Argentina, Malaysia, Venezuela, Turkey, China, and Vietnam all had (or continue to have) regulations that limit and make access to foreign exchange extremely costly. Any business involved in importing or exporting faces extra costs and lengthy bureaucratic practices. Having a diversified structure with foreign operations can facilitate access to credit.

Emerging market firms dealt with inferior access to specialized inputs during their first decades of operations and many still manage such challenges. A steel producer may have suffered from unreliable power supply or from untimely deliveries of carbon and iron from local providers. A company producing cars may struggle to find local producers of steel that comply with its quality requirements. Diversifying provides a means to compensate for the absence of reliable local suppliers. Not only has it shielded companies from policy changes that have made certain sectors and businesses unprofitable in different periods, it has helped them acquire access to high-quality inputs when these were not available locally. This sort of vertical diversification (i.e., diversifying in activities that are part of the value chain for a given type of product or service) is typical also of the Japanese and Korean conglomerates, and it allows for important synergies.

Diversified conglomerates can also benefit from other advantages—they can build a global brand name, as Tata did, exploiting its cross-industry diffusion, and they can pool together resources to support strategic operations with a long-term perspective. The main weakness of conglomerates is that it could become difficult to pursue the strategic objectives of each firm that is part of the group while simultaneously forwarding group-level objectives. Conglomerates can lack strategic focus and loose competitiveness. However, if there are links between their business divisions, they can also build up a set of cross-supportive units, as the chip, LCD, and telephone divisions of Samsung have done.

Specialized Players

Not all of the EMNEs from emerging markets are diversified groups. There are also specialized niche players that share some of the features of EMNEs while adopting an organizational structure more common in North America and Europe. The Mexican firm Bimbo, the largest bread producer in the world, and the Chinese firm Haier, the largest producer of white goods. These companies expanded both domestically and globally while focusing on one main business. Some, such as Embraer, a Brazilian producer of mid-range commercial jets, are partly owned by the state. The majority, however, are private entrepreneurial companies run mainly by their founders and their extended families. Most of these firms share a similar evolutionary path, which followed these steps:

1. Domestic market growth

2. Consolidation in the domestic market through investments in technology, infrastructure, and skills

3. Internationalization

Following their foundation, these companies successfully captured a growing share of their domestic market, exploiting strong growth dynamics. They out-competed local firms using the same techniques as global multinationals—aggressive investment, brand building, and agreements with buyers, suppliers, and distributors. Their understanding of local customers, local taste, and also of the local institutional voids allowed them to position themselves as market leaders, out-competing even foreign multinationals in spite of having inferior resources and know-how. Haier, for example, benefitted from the booming Chinese demand for cheap-but-reliable consumer durables, which Triad firms could not always provide. When foreign competitors began betting more on the Chinese market, Haier had already built a reputation and an impressive distribution network.

Specialized EMNEs are skilled at playing institutional voids and to their advantage. The Argentinean candy and sweet producer A exploited to its benefit the abrupt and unpredictable changes in econom characterized its domestic economy. During periods of high protectionism and consumption growth, such as the 1950s and 1960s, it invested at home, developing product lines and vertically integrating its production to sugar and other inputs. When the Argentinean government reduced import taxes on capital goods and maintained a strong exchange rate, such as during the 1990s, it invested massively in new machinery, importing state-of-the-art equipment. In periods of devaluation, such as the 2000s, it used its domestic production capacity to export. Arcor became a leading global producer of sweets thanks to its ability to turn the instability of its domestic market environment to its advantage.

Before internationalizing, specialized EMNEs expanded in their home markets, achieving dominant (in some cases, quasi-monopolistic) positions through very aggressive and focused investments. They invested in lobbying governments to look away from their monopolistic practices or to allow them to benefit from special treatment during privatizations. They invested in a capacity to reach unique economies of scale in the domestic market, in product development to fit first local and then regional tastes, and in distribution networks, technology, and brands to consolidate their positions. By 1991, Haier, for example, was the largest Chinese producer of refrigerators. Until 1998, it sold over 98 percent of its products in the home market. Only then did it begin to invest aggressively in internationalization.

The second expansion phase of these firms resembles that of American multinationals such as Ford, GM, Coca-Cola, and McDonald's. Their position in the domestic market meant they became large players in terms of revenues, employment, and production capacity *before* they internationalized. Another Latin American multinational, the Mexican firm Bimbo, expanded domestically by developing strategies aimed at overcoming market failures and institutional voids. Bimbo, a producer of bread and other bakery products, conquered the Mexican market by reaching directly to lower-income consumers. It developed small-batch packaging to suit the frequent cash purchase model of the consumers at the Base of the Pyramid. Realizing its consumers live too far from large supermarkets, it invested in a broad distribution network in order to reach corner stores and cut the cost of relying on multiple intermediaries. By doing so, it became the dominant player in Mexico. The resources it developed in its domestic market helped it internationalize and become a top player in the US and subsequently global bread industry.

Among EMNEs, the Indian firms providing outsourced services are an exception. From their inception, they targeted the American market. The reason that they did not first

two factors. First, the nature of the industry in which
nce of firms specialized in providing outsourced infor-
ss services depends on the technological and organiza-
ed in Silicon Valley by leading American firms. Second,
nd professional ethnic-based networks. As Saxenian (2006)
ounded by entrepreneurs with business links to U.S. compa-
ping the outsourced services business model on which they
a large diaspora of Indian professionals working in Silicon Val-
and business opportunities back home.

Specia.. .ave internationalized following different strategies according to
their industry. 1.. have relied on acquisitions to enter new markets and subsequently
attempted to build their brands internationally. All of them maintain an important
domestic base—the domestic market provides them with revenues, profits, and often
with the production capacity to penetrate new markets. Brazilian agro-industrial firms
continue to generate a high share of their meat and soy output in Brazil, exploiting its
abundance in fertile land. Indian outsourced services companies, such as Wypro, built
their competitiveness using the low cost and high skills of Indian engineers. In this sense,
however, the internationalization of EMNEs is not different from that of other types of
EMNEs, which we discuss in the next section.

Internationalization

Emerging market firms entered into an accelerated internationalization phase between
the 1990s and the 2000s. By the end of the 2000s, many operated across several countries and continents. Previously unknown company names, such as Haier and Bimbo, are
gradually becoming known to Triad consumers. There are several reasons why EMNEs
internationalized in this specific period. First, their home markets expanded strongly
after the 1990s, providing the necessary resource base to venture into new markets. Second, the 1990s were characterized by a dramatic fall in barriers to trade in goods and
services. As a result, EMNE found themselves threatened in their domestic markets.
To maintain their profitability in the face of higher competition, they had to become
more efficient, invest in technology, and modernize. By doing so, they also became more
suited to penetrating other markets. Internationalizing was also pursued as a defensive
strategy—gaining market share abroad could compensate for the loss of profitability
that could occur in the domestic market if the latter were to become more competitive due to foreign entrants. Market liberalization also provided important opportunities to purchase new imported technology and export to new markets. The 1990s were

also characterized by a large wave of privatizations. EMNEs acquired distressed public companies and in some cases obtained monopolistic concessions that were functional in providing them with the needed funds to internationalize.

To understand what motivated the internationalization of EMNEs, let's look at EMNEs operating in extractive industries, which are the simplest case to examine: they internationalized to gain access to natural resources. The Chinese SOEs, for example, have invested aggressively in Africa and Latin America to secure access to oil, gas, and minerals. This is not dissimilar to the internationalization of the large American and European oil and gas companies during the 1950s and 1960s. Like Exxon and BP, the Chinese SOEs exploited diplomatic support and the growing geopolitical power of China to seal the deal with specific regimes. They have acted opportunistically, exploiting the dissatisfaction of emerging-world regimes with the Triad's use of business as a geopolitical tool. For example, since the late 1990s, the U.S. and Europe have banned emerging-market firms from operating in Sudan as a way of pushing that regime to solve the humanitarian crisis in Darfur. Chinese firms responded by scaling up their investments in Sudan, exploiting the gap between the potential business opportunities that emerged and the supply of investment and technical expertise from abroad. In 2013, they dominate the Sudanese oil and gas industry.

Companies specializing in different industries internationalized with other objectives, such as gaining new markets and acquiring strategic assets. Firms such as Bimbo, Arcor, Haier, and the Tata Group internationalized in order to decrease their reliance on the domestic market for their revenues and profits. Although the latter allowed them to become the resourceful firms that they are, their management explicitly pushed them abroad in order to be less dependent on the often volatile fluctuations of their domestic economy. After having learned how to manage one of the world's largest bakery production and distribution networks in Mexico, Bimbo ventured into the U.S., then also entering Brazil and China. Penetrating developed markets also has a "brand image" function. Triad markets are typically more sophisticated and competitive. Consumers have had a high purchasing power for longer, even though it is not growing much anymore. Consumers in the Triad look for increasing quality and product diversification while being unwilling to spend more year on year. They often develop marked brand loyalties, which makes it difficult to establish the credibility of new brands. Capturing a share of Triad markets as Bimbo, Haier, and Lenovo have done, signals that emerging market firms can outcompete Triad multinationals on their home turf. Notably, several EMNEs, especially those operating in consumer goods manufacturing and information technology services, exploited inward FDI to their home economies to forge links with leading multinationals. American investments in India, Taiwan, and China were an essential vehicle for the technological learning of EMNEs in those countries. Through licensing, subcontracting agreements, and other forms of alliances, they generated the channels to "learn"—to acquire and absorb the technology and skills of leading companies.

EMNEs internationalized not only to capture markets and gain access to natural resources; as Luo and Tung (2007) explain, EMNEs internationalized as part of their growth strategy:

> "Emerging Market Multinationals use outward investments as a springboard to acquire strategic assets needed to compete more effectively against global rivals and to avoid the institutional and market constraints they face at home. Their 'springboard' behaviors are often characterized by overcoming their latecomer disadvantage in the global stage via a series of aggressive, risk-taking measures by proactively acquiring or buying critical assets from mature MNEs to compensate for their competitive weaknesses" (p. 482).

To compete with Triad multinationals, EMNEs needed resources, technology, expertise, and brand equity. They acquired growing financial resources by expanding in their domestic markets. In order to gain the missing factors, they first established different types of cooperation agreements with Triad firms, such as working as subcontractors for lead firms and learning how a good is engineered and manufactured. Next, they went on a spending spree and acquired large numbers of distressed Triad firms. Haier, for example, worked with German and Italian companies in order to improve its technical capabilities during the 1990s, after which it acquired several smaller firms with high technological expertise in specific product niches. Arcelik, a Turkish white goods manufacturer, followed a similar path to that of Haier. To acquire the technical skills needed to design and engineer white goods, it produced goods designed by Triad companies using license agreements. Lenovo, a Chinese PC producer, was also IBM's main subcontractor for a long time; it then acquired IBM's manufacturing operations and gradually developed its own brand. The Tata Group achieved the leap when it purchased Land Rover; it invested in Land Rover and revived its fortunes, exploiting the fact that it already had a powerful brand.

The internationalization of EMNEs varies depending on the industry. However, in all cases, it is possible to note that it was not through simple market expansion, but rather through the development of a two-way relationship, which Luo calls "springboard perspective," whereby foreign ventures are often financed using profits made at home, and they provide the home base with new technology, products, ideas, and brands. In 2010, Geely, a Chinese car producer, acquired Volvo for 1.8 billion dollars. It is now using Volvo's engineering know-how, design, and brand to expand back into the Chinese market while having also gained a foothold in the European market. In this sense, the internationalization of EMNEs differs strongly from that of Triad firms, which developed their managerial and technological base at home and internationalized mainly to acquire markets and resources. Firms such as the Japanese car maker Toyota, the German engineering giant Siemens, and the American aerospace company Boeing continue to develop most of their new products and technologies at their headquarters. Their competitive advantage stems from their know-how, which flows mainly from their home base to their subsidiaries. Their internationalization occurred after they had consolidated their managerial and technical skills. As the next chapter illustrates, EMNEs internationalized differently, often at an earlier phase of their evolutionary trajectory, as part of their search for the assets and resources they needed to be globally competitive.

EMNEs are a true representation of the increasing global weight of emerging markets. They illustrate that managerial and technological capabilities are not a prerogative of Triad firms and developed economies anymore. They show that the industrial policies implemented at great costs by countries such as Brazil and China can generate globally competitive national champions. And they project national economic power and prestige abroad, providing investment, jobs, and revenues in a growing array of markets. In some well-known cases, it is EMNEs that have saved ailing Triad firms, avoiding the social costs of closure and the loss of long prestigious brands. Through its set of acquisitions, the Tata Group, for example, has now become one of the largest employers in the UK, the former colonial power that dominated the Indian market for centuries. The next chapter discusses more in detail the internationalization of EMNEs, examining them from the perspective of international business theory.

References

Athreye, Suma and Kapur, Sandeep (2009). Introduction: The Internationalization of Chinese and Indian Firms—Trends, Motivations and Strategy." *Industrial and Corporate Change, 18*(2): pp. 209–221.

Aulakh, Preet S. (2007). Special issue on emerging multinationals from developing economies: motivations, paths and performance. *Journal of International Management, 13* (No. 3): pp. 235–402.

Aybar, B. and Ficici, A. (2009). Cross-border acquisitions and firm value: An analysis of emerging-market multinationals. *Journal of International Business Studies, 40*(8), pp. 1317–1338.

Bonaglia, F., Goldstein, A., and Mathews, J. A. (2007). Accelerated internationalization by emerging markets' multinationals: The case of the white goods sector. *Journal of World Business, 42*(4), pp. 369–383.

Brand Finance (2012). *Brand Valuation Report 2012.* Retrieved from http://brandirectory.com.

Bremmer, I. (2009). State capitalism comes of age. *Foreign Affairs, 88*(3), pp. 40–55.

Buckley, Peter J., Clegg, Jeremy, Cross, Adam R., Liu, Xin, Voss, Hinrich, and Zheng, Ping. (2007). The Determinants of Chinese Outward Foreign Direct Investment. *Journal of International Business Studies, 38*: pp. 499–518.

Bulmer-Thomas, V. (2003). The economic history of Latin America since independence (Vol. 77). Cambridge University Press.

Chandler, A. D. (1969). *Strategy and Structure: Chapters in the History of the American Industrial Enterprise* (Vol. 120). MIT Press.

Chandler, A. D. (1990). *Scale and Scope.* Belknap Press of Harvard University Press.

Cuervo-Cazurra, A. (2007). Sequence of Value-added Activities in the Multinationalization of Developing Country Firms. *Journal of International Management, 13*(3): pp. 258–277.

EMGP (2013) Emerging Market Global Players. Retrieved on 4/24/2013 from http://www.vcc.columbia.edu/content/emerging-market-global-players-project.

Forbes Magazine (2012). *Global 2000.* Retrieved from http://www.forbes.com/global2000/list/.

Fortune Magazine (2012). *Global 500: Annual ranking of the world's largest corporations.* Retrieved from http://money.cnn.com/magazines/fortune/global500/2012/full_list/.

Girma, S. and Gong, Y. (2008). FDI, linkages and the efficiency of state-owned enterprises in China. *The Journal of Development Studies, 44*(5), pp. 728–749.

Goldstein, A. (2008). *The internationalization of Indian companies: The Case of Tata.* OECD: CASI Working Paper Series. No. 08-02.

Guillén, M. F. and García-Canal, E. (2009). The American model of the multinational firm and the "new" multinationals from emerging economies. *The Academy of Management Perspectives, 23*(2), pp. 23–35.

Hoskisson, R. E., Eden, L., Lau, C. M., and Wright, M. (2000). Strategy in emerging economies. *Academy of Management Journal*, pp. 249–267.

Khanna, T. and Palepu, K. (1997). Why focused strategies may be wrong for emerging markets. *Harvard Business Review, 75*(4), pp. 41–48.

Landes, D. S. (2003). *The Unbound Prometheus: Technological Change and Industrial Development in Western Europe from 1750 to the Present.* Cambridge University Press.

Luo, Y. and Tung, R. L. (2007). International expansion of emerging market enterprises: A springboard perspective. *Journal of International Business Studies, 38*(4), pp. 481–498.

Luo, Y., Xue, Q., and Han, B. (2010). How emerging market governments promote outward FDI: Experience from China. *Journal of World Business, 45*(1), pp. 68–79.

Musacchio, A. and Lazzarini, S. (2012). Leviathan in Business: Varieties of State Capitalism and Their Implications for Economic Performance. Available at SSRN 2070942.

Ralston, D. A., Terpstra-Tong, J., Terpstra, R. H., Wang, X., and Egri, C. (2006). Today's state-owned enterprises of China: Are they dying dinosaurs or dynamic dynamos? *Strategic Management Journal*, *27*(9), pp. 825–843.

Ramamurti, R. and Singh, J. V. (Eds.) (2009). *Emerging multinationals in emerging markets* (Vol. 1). Cambridge: Cambridge University Press.

Wright, M., Filatotchev, I., Hoskisson, R. E., and Peng, M. W. (2005). Strategy Research in Emerging Economies: Challenging the Conventional Wisdom. *Journal of Management Studies*, *42*(1), pp. 1–33.

9

The Internationalization of Emerging Market MNEs: A Critical Examination of International Business Theories

Chapter co-authored with Ying Liu[1]

Introduction

Since the beginning of the 2000s, the increased popularity of emerging markets together with the international expansion of EMNEs have led scholars to question the conventional view that EMNEs have weak competitive advantages (Buckley, et al., 2007). According to UNCTAD (2012), in 2010, more than half of FDI went to emerging markets; in 2011, the two major players in emerging markets, China and India, received increased inward FDI of nearly 8 percent and 31 percent, respectively (see Figure 9.1). In terms of outward FDI from emerging markets, it fell slightly in 2011, but it still "remained important, reaching the second highest level recorded" (UNCTAD, 2012, p. 4; see Figure 9.2). In addition, the involvement of emerging markets as well as the role played by EMNEs are increasingly important in global sustainable development to solve the challenging issues of global climate change, food security, and poverty alleviation (UNCTAD, 2012).

---

[1] Ying Liu (MBA, University of Connecticut) is a doctoral candidate in Management and International Business at Business School, Florida International University. She has an MBA degree in Operations and Information Management from University of Connecticut. Her current research interests include global strategy and international business of firms in emerging economies, inter-firm cooperation and competition, and corporate governance.

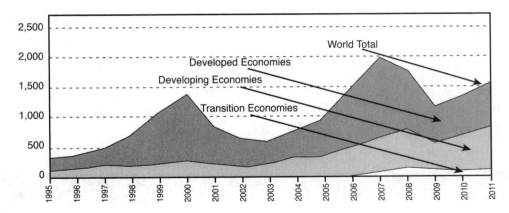

Figure 9.1 FDI inflows, global, and by group of economies (billions of dollars), 1995–2011.

Data Source: UNCTAD, 2012.

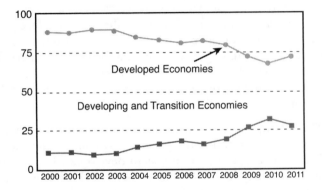

Figure 9.2 FDI outflow shares by major economic groups (percent), 2000–2011.

Data Source: UNCTAD, 2012.

Foreign investment flowing from developed countries to emerging economies has triggered the birth of a series of International Business (IB) theories—for example, product life cycle theory by Vernon (1966), the financial type theory by Lessard (1976, 1977, 1979; Aliber, 1970), and the OLI framework by Dunning (1977). In response to contemporary MNE internationalization activities, some scholars updated their initial theories to strengthen their predictive power. For example, Dunning and Lundan (2008, 2010) updated their OLI framework to include Oi, institutional advantages (see Box 9.1). Yet, other scholars put forward new theories; for example, Oviatt and McDougall (1994) proposed the theory of international new ventures. More scholars are involved in intensive conversations on whether new IB theories are needed, whether existing IB theories still have explanatory power to predict the internationalization activities of firms effectively, and whether the extension of existing IB theories is sufficient. In 2012, Cuervo-Cazurra (2012) provided an analysis of this scholarly debate, known as the "goldilocks" debate; his finding being that current theory is neither "too hot" nor "too cold" but "just right"—that is, it can be used to extend theory.

Box 9.1: The Eclectic Paradigm or OLI Paradigm

The **Eclectic paradigm** or **OLI paradigm** was developed by John Dunning, a British scholar, to answer three different questions about the internationalization activities of firms. Namely, *why* firms go abroad, which is answered by a firm's possession of ownership advantages such as managerial or technological skills over competitors (O advantages); *where* firms go, which is answered by a firm's possession of location advantages such as favorable government policies toward foreign direct investment (FDI) or natural resources in host countries (L advantages); and *how* firms go abroad, which is answered by firms obtaining benefits by internalizing foreign activities (I advantages). The OLI paradigm has been modified and extended over the years since its first publication in 1973 in response to criticisms and the changing business environment.

Dunning (1973) attempted to answer the question *why* firms invest overseas by examining factors that determine the pattern and composition of firms' foreign investment. Thus, his initial intention was to develop an International Business (IB) theory at the country level: "My main focus of interest is in explaining the international production of all firms from a particular country or group countries" (Dunning, 2002, p. 40). However, the focus of his later analysis was mainly at the firm level and we therefore categorize the OLI paradigm as a firm-level IB theory in this chapter.

Building upon internalization theory (Buckley and Casson, 1976; Rugman, 1981) and acknowledging Hymer's (1960, 1976) argument of firms' possession of proprietary advantages, Dunning (1977) introduced location factors into the determinants of a firm's FDI, arguing that all the three types of advantages are needed for firms to invest abroad. In a later publication, Dunning (1980) explained that firms may create O advantages internally or absorb them externally, depending on home-country-specific advantages (CSAs), and assumed firms can transfer these ownership advantages to host countries to generate rents easily. In his earlier work, Dunning organized ownership advantages into asset advantages, or Oa ("exclusive possession and use of certain kinds of income-generating assets," Dunning, 1988b, p. 25), and transaction-based advantages, or Ot ("their ability to coordinate separate value-added activities across national boundaries, and their capacity to reduce environmental and foreign exchange risks," Dunning, 1988b, p. 25). Ownership advantages were later expanded to include institutional advantages (Oi), which are capabilities dealing with formal and informal institutions at the firm level that govern a firm's daily operations (Dunning and Lundan, 2008, 2010).

Dunning (1988a, p. 13) outlined three types of motivations for the internationalization of firms: namely "market seeking," "resource seeking," and "efficiency seeking." Later, he (1991) added a fourth one: "strategic asset seeking." In 1993, Dunning emphasized the interaction of O, L, and I advantages and the dynamic feature of a particular configuration of OLI at time t, which influences a firm's strategy in time t+1.

When applying the OLI paradigm to the internationalization of EMNEs, scholars have found some deficiencies that needed improving: Cuervo-Cazzurra (2012) points out the dual purposes of EMNEs going abroad: exploiting O advantages that are developed in the home country while simultaneously complementing O disadvantages at home to better compete with rivals in the home market. Second, with respect to L advantages, Cuervo-Cazzurra (2012) asserts that EMNEs go abroad to minimize home country L disadvantages. Luo and Tung (2007) emphasize both L advantages (e.g., favorable FDI policies) and L disadvantages (e.g., weak institutional environment) in the home country. Hennart (2012) observes that the OLI paradigm assumes L advantages in the host country to be equally and freely accessed by EMNEs, but in reality firms need to have certain FSAs (e.g., capabilities of networking with resource controllers in the host country) to access host country L advantages. The studies on the internationalization of EMNEs suggest that scholars expand the scope of O and L advantages to consider both home and host country factors, and O advantages should include not only firm-level ownership advantages, such as tangible assets and financial resources, but also individual- or group-level ownership advantages, such as the personal networks of top managers and advanced technologies. L advantages should include both home and host country L advantages and disadvantages.

Case Study: Haier

To illustrate the application of the OLI paradigm, we take the example of Haier, a Chinese MNE in consumer electronics and home appliances. We map out the OLI advantages and disadvantages in Haier's international expansion. First, Haier succeeded as one of several companies that survived competition from more than 300 refrigerator manufacturers in 1984. Domestically, Haier focused on developing Oa advantages through brand building using self-enhanced quality criteria, being sensitive and innovative to customer requirements and niche market needs, and establishing distribution channels (China's retail infrastructure was underdeveloped at the time). Haier faced domestic institutional disadvantages (Oi disadvantages) such as lack of financial, quality control, and human resource intermediaries. These Oi disadvantages propelled Haier to build its own Oa advantages (for example, its self-enhanced quality criteria to boost its brand reputation) and simultaneously propelled the firm to go to developed countries such as U.S. in the early stages to learn from global competitors, build relationships with powerful distributors such as Walmart, and show commitment to building international quality standards, which contributed to its brand building (an asset-based ownership advantage).

Haier initially set up its overseas manufacturing facilities mainly in Southeast Asia (largely in India) before its expansion to the U.S. Thereafter, Haier simultaneously entered developed countries, such as Japan and the United Kingdom, and developing countries, such as the Philippines and Pakistan. Haier's entry into developed countries allowed it to better compete in its home market of China against competition from DMNEs. Thus, Haier's internationalization process highlights the attractiveness of developed countries (L advantages), which contribute to Haier's accumulation of Oa advantages at home. The L disadvantage in the U.S. is due to Haier's lesser familiarity with the business environment, and the necessity of finding local personnel to mitigate the difficulties of operating in foreign countries. However, the potential disadvantage of recruiting local managers is that of less integration between foreign facilities and headquarters.

The interaction of O, L, and I advantages suggested by Dunning (1993) and Dunning and Lundan (2010) is applicable to all EMNEs, including Haier, to enhance their performance. Haier has benefited from its internationalization into the U.S. because of its asset-based ownership advantages. Haier's I advantages can be partially attributed to its Oa advantages. The joint impact of O advantages and L advantages enable managers of MNEs such as Haier to choose the optimal entry mode (internalization) into a foreign market. Additionally, scholars and managers need to notice that L advantages, such as low-cost labor, in emerging markets are diminishing; therefore, governments of developing countries are making efforts to strengthen their institutions to improve their business environment.

In this chapter, we focus on examining the applicability of existing IB theories to explain the internationalization activities of EMNEs, illustrating how these theories developed through time (see Figure 9.3). We expect our contribution to help readers grasp the theoretical implications of the global expansion of EMNEs, which is of interest for scholars, students, and managers alike, given that, as we showed in Chapter 8, "Multinationals Based in Emerging Markets: Features and Strategies," EMNEs are an increasingly important type of player in both emerging and developed economies. The rest of this chapter is organized as follows: we first introduce the roots of IB research field. We then analyze mainstream International Business (IB) theories sequentially from country level to industry level to firm level, followed by a look at the challenges and opportunities faced by the internationalization of EMNEs. Finally, we discuss the inconsistencies of extant IB theories, followed by our suggestion for future IB theory development and empirical studies.

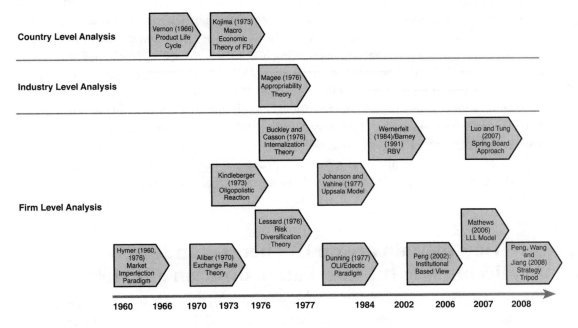

Figure 9.3 A timeline of IB theories.

The Roots of the IB Research

Many scholars (Dunning, 2009; Guillen and Garcia-Canal, 2009) attribute the first comprehensive analysis of MNEs to Hymer's (1960, 1976) dissertation. Hymer based his work on industrial organization economics, and particularly the studies of Bain (1956), who explored firms' attempts to seek competitive advantage by building entry barriers. Industrial organization economics primarily examines the structure of the market and the boundaries between firms and markets. Industrial organization adds elements of real-world friction, such as limited information, transaction costs, and barriers to entry of new firms to the perfect competition model (namely, the economics model of price theory).

Conner (1991) summarizes five theories of the firm that demonstrate industrial organization economics. First is "neoclassical perfect competition theory: firms as combiners of inputs" (p. 123). This theory assumes firms work as containers of resources, such as labor and capital, to provide final products that are simply the joint outputs of multiple resources. Second is "Bain-type industrial organization: firms as output-constrainers" (p. 124). In this theory, firms either ally with other firms or exercise monopolistic power to constrain outputs. In so doing, firms are able to artificially increase the price and then secure above-normal profits with the sacrifice of consumer benefits. Third is "Schumpeter's response: a focus on dynamics, with firms as seekers of new ways of competing" (p. 127). This theory posits that a firm's seeking of consistently new technologies or innovations is more effective than simply lowering the price of existing products to outperform competitors (Schumpeter, 1950). Fourth is "Chicago's response: a renaissance of price theory, with firms as seekers of production and distribution efficiencies" (p. 128). The fifth and final theory is "Coase/Williamson transaction cost economics: firms as avoiders of the costs of market exchange" (p. 130). Based on the work of Coase (1937) and Simon (1957), Williamson (1975, 1989) proposes that firms exist to minimize the costs of market exchange (for more details about industrial organization economics, see Conner, 1991).

A Review of Mainstream IB Theories and Their Applicability to the Internationalization of EMNEs

IB theories can be classified into three categories in terms of unit of analysis: country level, industry level, and firm level. We next identify and discuss the main theories at these different levels in exploring the internationalization of EMNEs.

IB Theories: Country Level

The first set of theories we examine includes the Product Life Cycle framework and macroeconomic theories of FDI.

Product Life Cycle

Vernon's (1966) product life cycle framework asserted that new products are invented, designed, and manufactured in developed countries. When these products are mature, mass-manufacturing technologies are developed and demands from other developed countries increase. The manufacturing is then shifted to the other developed countries where there are consumers with similar purchasing habits. When the products are standardized, the manufacturing is moved to developing countries to take advantage of the low-cost labor there. Finally, the developed countries import such products from the developing countries. The essential argument here is that firms' internationalization activities or patterns are associated with product life cycle, meaning that technologies are transferred from the U.S. to other developed countries and finally to developing countries.]

Many empirical studies supported the prediction of the product life cycle (Wells, 1972; Hirsch, 1967). Giddy (1978) found that the explanatory power the product life cycle theory declines only when the differences between developed countries have decreased. The theory gradually lost its predictive power when scholars began to examine a much broader range of countries, especially when emerging markets were included in the studies] Cantwell (1995) argued that the two main hypotheses of the product life cycle theory—namely, that innovations originated in the home country of MNEs and that technological leaders led the international diffusions of technological and managerial practices—are only historically valid.]

Cuervo-Cazurra (2012) argued that there are confounded assumptions in the product life cycle model—namely, the high income status of consumers and the similarity of consumer needs. In the context of EMNEs' internationalization practices, he argued that EMNEs may sell their innovations to developing countries where there are consumers with similar needs and also to developed countries where there are consumers who are willing to pay the premium of the innovations. Because EMNEs are already in developing countries with low operation costs, they may be less inclined to move their manufacturing to other developing economies (Mudambi, 2008; Cuervo-Cazurra, 2012). Take, for example, the Chinese MNE Haier's "three-thirds" strategy: "Haier's revenue derives in equal parts from sales of goods in three categories: one third from goods produced and sold in China, one third produced in China and sold overseas, and one third produced and sold overseas" (Palepu, Khanna and Vargas, 2006, p. 10). The strategy indicates Haier sells its products domestically and in other nations, including developing and developed countries. Haier builds its innovation centers, which act as "eyes and ears" in host countries to contribute to its overall innovative capabilities (Williamson and Zeng, 2009). Besides building its manufacturing facilities in other developing countries, as predicted by the product life cycle theory, Haier established a manufacturing facility in United States in 2000 without closing its domestic manufacturing facility. Thus, the explanatory power of the theory is limited with regard to the internationalization of EMNEs because these firms may not follow the trajectory of foreign expansion espoused by Vernon (1966), and may, as Haier did, invest aggressively in developed economies. The motivation for the internationalization of EMNEs can be attributed to a combination of technology exploitation vis-à-vis exploration.

Macroeconomic Theory of FDI

Two Japanese economists—namely, Kojima (1973, 1978, 1982, 1990) and Kojima and Ozawa (1984)—extended the factor endowments of countries (comparative advantages) theory to explain the patterns of FDI in intermediate products (i.e., technology and managerial skills). They claimed that production of intermediate goods should be conducted in countries that have comparative advantages in resources and capabilities related to the preceding. Influenced by Hymer (1960), Kojima and Ozawa emphasized structural market imperfections and ignored transactional market failure. Their contention is that it is market forces and not firms' hierarchical structure that determine a firm's internationalization of intermediate products. Macroeconomic theory posits that inward FDI stimulates the economic development of the host country and considers outward FDI a response to the accumulated national competitiveness. Empirical studies by Ginzburg and Simonazzi (2005) and Dowling and Cheang (2000) found supportive evidence for this trend. The recent World Investment Report of UNCTAD (2012) indicates EMNEs from emerging markets generally follow this trend at a macro level: "For example, 65 percent of FDI projects by value (comprising cross-border mergers and acquisitions and greenfield investments) from the BRIC countries (Brazil, Russian, India, and China) were invested in developing and transition economies" (UNCTAD, 2012, p. 5). However, as Arndt (1974) observed, Kojima and Ozawa's theory ignored micro-level factors of FDI. For example, firms may internationalize to achieve higher economies of scale, which is not necessarily related to countries' factor endowments. Gray and Dunning (1993, p. 92) stated that the "Kojima/Ozawa theoretical model is an inadequate explanation of the behavior of multinational enterprises, Western or Japanese." This statement, in our opinion, is also valid with regard to outward investment of EMNEs from Brazil, Russia, India, and China.

IB Theories: Industry Level

In this section, we discuss IB theories that focus on the industry level.

Appropriability Theory

Johnson (1970) found that firms invest abroad to maximize the returns on their intangible assets, including new technologies, new products, and processes. Drawing on both Industrial Organization economics and the classical arguments of rent appropriation from investment in sophisticated technologies, Magee (1976, 1977, 1981) put forward the appropriability theory, incorporating both industrial-level and firm-level analysis. The main argument is that sophisticated technologies are less likely to be imitated, allowing for the successful appropriation of returns. Thus, firms have incentives to invest in creating additional sophisticated technologies. Magee (1976, 1977, 1981) posits his arguments at the industry level such that young industries generate new technologies faster than old industries, and as a consequence, firm size is linked to the internationalization of those new technologies. Industries that are mature have a limited capability to create new technologies, resulting in diminished firm size. In terms of firms' takeover activities, Magee (1976) explained that it's the natural consequence of pursuing optimum size or pursuing monopolistic advantages by "absorbing the most likely interlopers" (p. 333). Caves (1971, 1974) took a different perspective, stating that firms seek to maximize economic advantages by internalizing and controlling tangible and intangible advantages in subsidiaries.

According to Magee (1977), there is an industry cycle (namely, invention, innovation, and maturity or standardization) that is parallel to Vernon's (1966) product life cycle. Appropriability theory emphasizes firms' incentives to invent new technologies and pursue optimal size, which they do through acquisitions and international expansion. Thus, industry structure is a dynamic output of existing industry structure and R&D intensity. Theoretically, the proposition of appropriability can be supported, but empirical studies on the relationship between industry structure and firm size are scarce. The Indian software industry should provide some evidence of the initial positive relationship between the growth of industry and the increase of firm size: "The Indian software industry has been a remarkable success story. It has grown more than 30 percent annually for 20 years" (Bhatnagar, 2006, p. 95). Following the prediction of Magee (1977), Indian software companies such as Infosys, Satyam, and Tata Consultancy Services have been growing in size as the industry, which is far from mature, evolved. For example, the number of employees in Infosys increased from 90,000 in 2007 to 150,000 in 2011 (Infosys, 2013). Overall, more studies are needed to examine the applicability of appropriability theory in the contemporary globalization context by looking at the interaction among industrial structure, firms' innovative capabilities, and firms' size in the context of MNEs in BRICS and elsewhere.

IB Theories: Firm Level

The last set of theories we examine comprises firm level explanations of IB, which comprise, among others, the Resource Based View of internationalization as well as the Eclectic Paradigm.

Hymer's Market Imperfection Paradigm

Hymer (1960, 1976) is given credit for providing comprehensive analysis of the internationalization of firms (Guillen and Garcia-Canal, 2009). In his dissertation, Hymer (1960) questioned the assumption of market perfection, and for the first time, shifted the unit of analysis from the country level, which at the time dominated IB research, to the firm level. He cited Dunning (1958) and Penrose (1956) and explicitly pointed out that certain proprietary firm-specific advantages are required to offset liabilities of foreignness (Zaheer, 1995) when operating abroad. Strongly influenced by Bain type IO (Bain, 1950, 1956) advantages, Hymer asserted that firms seeking to control foreign activities needed to remove competition to fully appropriate economic rents. Thus, Hymer's study focused on the imperfection of final products markets and emphasized firms' incentives to exercise monopolistic power, a feature that we discussed in Chapter 3, "A Historical Perspective," when looking at the history of multinational enterprises. Dunning and Rugman (1985) argue that Hymer (1960) ignores firms' Williamson-type transaction costs by emphasizing their potential to use firm-specific advantages to manipulate structural market failures. Hymer perceives firms' attempts at becoming vertically integrated as a means to pursue monopolistic control of the market; yet this point of view conflicts with more contemporary assumptions regarding the efficiency of vertical integration.

Hymer's assertion of the possible liability of foreignness faced by firms when internationalizing can be easily extended to explain the difficulties faced by EMNEs when expanding abroad. However, Hymer's argument that firms need to have developed specific advantages before internationalizing has been challenged by different scholars. Rugman (2009, 2010), for example, suggested a new model of combining EMNEs' firm-specific advantages with their home countries' country specific advantages. Through this mechanism, EMNEs' firm-specific advantages would cease to be necessary if there are country-specific advantages.

Guillen and Garcia-Canal (2009) argue that EMNEs have no firm-specific advantages but strong political advantages. This is supported by the fact that a large number of EMNEs have relied on country-specific advantages rather than firm-specific advantages in order to operate abroad, which points to the limited explanatory power of Hymer's market imperfection argument when applied to the internationalization of EMNEs.

Oligopolistic Reaction

Knickerbocker (1973), Flowers (1976), and Graham (1975, 1978) have observed that the internationalization of multinational companies is not only determined by locational variables but also by the behavior of other firms, especially those of their competitors from similar economic environments. This school of thought emphasizes firms' behavioral interaction with other firms, such as following each other to new markets to secure their own interests. The purpose of following each other is to reduce the perceived risks or competitive threats from the rivals (Knickerbocker, 1973). They term this theory "oligopolistic reaction." Similar to the appropriability theory, but from the perspective of risk reduction, the oligopolistic reaction theory emphasizes the influence of industrial structure on firms' entry investment decisions. Knickerbocker (1973) found that the relationship between entry and industry concentration is positive to a point and then becomes negative. Flower's (1976) study of the entrance of MNEs from EU and Canada to the U.S. supports this finding. Graham (1975) explained this bilateral behavior between two countries as "exchange of threat" and found a nonlinear relationship between industry and entry investment concentration.

This was one of the dominant theories explaining the foreign investments of MNEs from developed countries. However, the theory was challenged by the emergence and internationalization of EMNEs. The entrance of EMNEs into developed and developing countries does not necessarily follow their industry leaders' behavior. As we described in Chapter 8, EMNEs may internationalize by adopting unique strategies based on their home-country-specific advantages and firm-specific advantages. Ramamurti (2009b) summarizes five unique strategies followed by EMNEs:

- Natural resource vertical integrator
- Low-cost partner
- Local optimizer
- Global consolidator
- Global first mover

Ramamurti (2012) argues that since EMNEs have different kinds of advantages compared to developed-country MNEs, they actually go abroad to exploit differences instead of similarities and complement their competitive disadvantages at home. EMNEs seek to pursue exploitation in developing countries and exploration in developed countries. His contribution illustrates the extent to which EMNEs differ from multinationals based in developed economies, highlighting the need for new theoretical developments to account for their strategies and competitive practices.

Internalization Theory

In mid 1970s and early 1980s, a group of scholars from the University of Reading—namely, Buckley and Casson (1976), Rugman (1981), and Hennart (1982)—contributed greatly to the advancement of internalization theory. Based on Coasian transaction cost economics (Coase, 1937), Buckley and Casson (1976) argued that the markets for knowledge such as expertise and R&D are embedded in intermediate products that are imperfect and difficult to organize. Thus, firms have incentives to internalize and maximize profits by bypassing intermediate markets, and cross-border internalization gives rise to MNEs. Buckley and Casson (1976) focus on the intermediate product markets and emphasize the reduction of transaction costs by replacing an inefficient transaction in the market with an internal transaction (Rugman, 1981).

Can the internationalization activities of EMNEs be explained by Internal Business theories? Different scholars observe the interesting phenomenon of simultaneous internalization and externalization through outsourcing and offshoring, occurring within MNEs, including EMNEs. In a recent publication in *Global Strategy Journal,* McDermott, Mudambi, and Parente (2013) focus on the global sourcing of talents. They state that the strategy of firms to increase globalization and competition is part of a "strategic modularity" through which MNEs segment activities along value chain, redesign, and package segments, and then allocate within their partner network. This strategy requires the strong capabilities of firms to modularize production, establish and manage networks, and learn to adjust its organizational structures continuously and acquire new technologies. Cuervo-Cazurra (2012) argues that EMNEs internationalize differently from firms based in developed economies because they face relatively high transaction costs in their home economies due to the weak institutional environment, a feature we discussed in Chapter 8. The work of Cuervo-Cazurra (2012) points out that to understand EMNEs, it is necessary to deal with contextual factors such as firms' country of origin as well as firm-level characteristics and strategy.

Financial Type Theory

Aliber (1970) observed the failure of financial markets and was concerned about why firms invest abroad using their home country currencies. He proposed the exchange rate theory, arguing that firms based in countries with strong currencies can gain or borrow capital with lower financial costs than those based in countries with weak currencies, and this enables them to capitalize on the different exchange rates and interest rates between home and host countries. The risk diversification theory, proposed by Lessard (1976, 1982) and Rugman (1976, 1977), considers MNE to be a better vehicle of diversifying investment portfolios than an international equity market. This is based on two assumptions: that equity markets are less efficient in evaluating risks and benefits of diversification than MNEs, and that certain nonfinancial advantages are available to MNEs, resulting in effective management of investment portfolios (Agmon and Lessard, 1977). The risk diversification theory also predicts the location of potential investment, which is a function of the geographic distribution of existing assets and the perceived uncertainties of potential investments. Some early empirical studies support the risk diversification theory (Rugman, 1979). However, Kim and Lyn (1986) find that the premium paid to shareholders by investing in MNEs is from advertising and R&D intensity as well as from its monopolistic power, but not related to a firm's risk diversification. Similarly, Morck and Yeung (1991) find a high correlation between R&D investment and multinationality but no explicit relationship between multinationality and a firm's market value. Broadly speaking, the multinationality-performance relationship remains a puzzle among IB scholars (Cardinal, Miller, and Palich, 2011; Wiersema and Bowen, 2011). Although a large volume of studies has been conducted, results were mixed. Aliber's theory connects a country's critical macroeconomic adjustment and control of a firm's investment behavior, and according to UNCTAD (2012), explains the timing of a firm's FDI and the pattern of a country's FDI in the long run. The theory is useful to explain bilateral investment from strong- to weak-currency countries as well as investment in strategic assets seeking. Currently, there continues to be insufficient empirical evidence to apply financial theories to explain the internationalization of EMNEs. Nonetheless, we believe that these theories can help in understanding EMNEs' behavior, and should be included in future research agendas on EMNEs.

Eclectic Paradigm or OLI Paradigm

Building upon internalization theories (Buckley and Casson, 1976; Rugman, 1981) and acknowledging Hymer's (1960, 1976) argument of firms possessing proprietary advantages prior to FDI, Dunning (1977) provided an integrated model, namely the OLI framework or eclectic paradigm. One of the key insights of the OLI framework is that ownership-based advantages of firms along with a country's location-specific advantages should be taken into consideration to explain internalization activities (Dunning, 1977). Ownership advantages include asset advantages (Oa), which are tangible and intangible assets such as managerial and technological skills, and transactional advantages (Ot), which are capabilities or strengths in coordinating among geographically distributed subunits. Dunning and Lundan (2008, 2010) added institutional advantages (Oi)—that is, formal and informal institutions at the firm level that govern a firm's daily operations. Location advantages indicate the attractive features of the target countries, such as rich natural resources, market size, government policies toward FDI, and cultural and institutional environment—features that we have discussed in the first and second parts of this book.

Internalization advantages refer to the benefits that firms obtain from internalizing intermediate production activities that otherwise would occur in the market. There are four types of motives for firms to invest abroad—namely, natural resource seeking, market seeking, efficiency seeking, and strategic asset seeking (Dunning, 1998). The purpose of internalizing intermediate production activities is to seek effectiveness and efficiency. Dunning (1993) and Dunning and Lundan (2008) emphasize that the O, L, and I advantages impact each other and a firm's strategic decisions. Thus, according to the OLI framework, there are interactions between country-level factors (L advantages) and firm-level factors (O and I advantages). In addition, O and I advantages are not independent and should be considered simultaneously when making decisions about foreign investment.

The OLI paradigm has been criticized mainly for the lack of rigorousness of O advantages. For example, Itaki (1991) argues that it is redundant to consider both O and I advantages because they cannot be separated, and they are not separable because O advantages are inevitably influenced by L advantages. Additionally, Itaki (1991) argued that the OLI paradigm's attempt to explain firms' decisions regarding internationalization and entry mode comprehensively leads to its lack of theoretical parsimony. When applying the OLI paradigm to the internationalization of EMNEs, scholars found some deficiencies. For example, Rugman (2010) emphasizes the inseparability of O and I advantages that are mentioned by Itaki (1991).

Cuervo-Cazzurra (2012) points out that EMNEs internationalize for dual purposes—namely, exploiting O advantages that are developed in the home country and at the same time complementing O disadvantages at home to better compete with competitors in the home market. With regard to L advantages, Cuervo-Cazurra (2012) asserts that EMNEs go abroad to minimize a home country's L disadvantages. Luo and Tung (2007) emphasize both L advantages (e.g., favorable FDI policies) and L disadvantages (e.g., weak institutional environment) in the home country. Hennart (2012) observes that the OLI paradigm assumes L advantages in the host country to be equally and freely accessed by EMNEs, but in reality firms need to have certain firm-specific advantages (e.g., networking capabilities with resource controllers in host country) to access host-country L advantages. The insight of these studies is that future research should expand the scope of O and L advantages to consider both home-country as well as host-country factors. For example, O advantages should include not only firm-level ownership advantages, such as tangible assets and financial resources, but also individual- or group-level ownership advantages such as top managers' personal networks and advanced technologies. Similarly, L advantages should include both home- and host-country L advantages and disadvantages. The dynamic view of the evolution and interaction of a firm's O, L, and I advantages suggested by Dunning (1993) and Dunning and Lundan (2008) also applies to EMNEs, but it still needs to be empirically verified.

Resource-Based View

The resource-based view (RBV) was developed as a complement to IO, arguing that it is a firm's possession of sustainable competitive advantages that makes certain firms outperform in relation to other firms in the same industry (Barney, 2002; Peteraf and Barney, 2003). Wernerfelt (1984) pioneered the research about firms' internal resources as the source of competitive advantages, followed by scholarly work from Rumelt (1984), Barney (1991), Conner (1991), Peteraf (1993), and many others. The central argument of RBV is that firms must possess valuable, rare, inimitable, and nonsubstitutable (VRIN) resources to develop sustainable competitive advantages (Barney, 1991).

Since its emergence, the RBV has been one of the most influential theories in the management research field (Barney and Arikan, 2006). In contrast to some early studies, such as Schmalansee (1985), which argued that industry factors are more critical than firm factors on a firm's performance, Rumelt (1991) provided evidence that firm effects are more important. The assumption of RBV is that firms need to have resources available before going abroad to compete with competitors in host countries (Cuervo-Cazurra, 2012). Studies of EMNEs' internationalization behavior have challenged this view. Cuervo-Cazurra (2012) suggested that the RBV should be complemented with the knowledge-based view (Grant, 1996) and the institutional-based view (Peng, 2002; Peng, Wang, and Jiang, 2008). The knowledge-based view argues that preexisting knowledge has effects on the other resources of the firm and enables their learning and the accumulation of new knowledge. The weak institutional environment of emerging markets forces EMNEs to develop more intangible resources, such as business process innovations, rather than relying on institutions (Cuervo-Cazurra, 2012) to deal with volatile government policies, and to be better prepared for operating in similar institutional environments abroad (Cuervo-Cazurra and Genc, 2008). Thus, EMNEs do not necessarily rely on existing resources or advantages before they go abroad but rely on their preexisting knowledge and the unique experiences of operating in weak institutional environments to advance their resources at the same time when they conduct international expansion.

Guillen and Garcia-Canal (2009) expressed a concern that EMNEs have to seek a balance between the exploitation of their existing capabilities and resources in other emerging economies and the exploration of sophisticated capabilities in developed countries. However, it is precisely this tension between exploitation and exploration of resources and capabilities that has supported the accelerated internationalization of EMNE. This point has been supported by the empirical evidence of the rapid expansion into developing economies in Asia as well as developed markets such as the U.S. and UK of Indian software companies and Chinese telecommunication MNEs.

Uppsala Model
Drawing on the learning perspective of both Penrose (1959) and Cyert and March (1963), Johanson and Vahlne (1977, 1990) provided a model of the internationalization process of firms—namely, the Uppsala model. Penrose's (1959) emphasized firms' experiential and nontransferrable information learning. Cyert and March's (1963) contended that the learning and accumulation of knowledge and capabilities of a firm facilitates decision-making processes by reducing the firm's efforts on information searches. Johanson and Vahlne contend that firms need to take into account the risks of operating in foreign countries when they make decisions on internationalization. Based on the empirical study in the context of Swedish MNEs, they proposed that firms increase the resource

commitment in their foreign investment depending on their experiential learning and knowledge accumulation about the foreign countries. The Uppsala model predicts that firms tend to invest initially in psychically proximate countries and then expand to distant locations. **Psychic distance,** the key concept used in the Uppsala model, is defined as "the factors preventing or disturbing firms learning about and understanding of a foreign environment" (Vahlne and Nordstrom, 1992, p. 3).

The early empirical studies of Vahlne and Wiedersheim (1973) and Nordstrom (1991) found supportive evidence of the Uppsala model. However, the Uppsala model is criticized for being "deterministic and rigid in light of the variety of different approaches adopted by firms as they internationalize" (Dunning and Lundan, 2008, p. 92). Kogut (1983) found that the prediction of Uppsala is more applicable to a firm's initial internationalization than its subsequent foreign investment activities. Lundan and Jones (2001) contended that the Uppsala model applies better to small firms from emerging economies with less internationalization experience. When applied to explain the internationalization of EMNEs, the Uppsala model can explain the gradual or incremental internationalization of firms based in BRIC nations. However, we have illustrated in Chapter 8 that many EMNEs conduct their outward FDI in an aggressive way in both emerging and developed countries, which is contrary to the deterministic prediction of the Uppsala model. Cuervo-Cazurra (2012) pointed out that the Uppsala model emphasizes the risks faced by EMNEs when they internationalize while ignoring the possible benefits and market attractiveness of accelerated internationalization. In order to explain the internationalization of EMNEs, it would be necessary to extend or modify the Uppsala model, complementing it with new elements such as market attractiveness and firm characteristics.

Contemporary EMNE Theory

During the 2000s, new theories were developed to explain the internationalization of EMNEs, including the institutional-based view of Peng (2002), the Strategy Tripod by Peng, Wang, and Jiang (2008), the LLL model by Mathews (2006), and the springboard perspective by Luo and Tung (2007). International Business scholars have long been discussing why firms from different countries have different strategies (Rumelt, Schendel, and Teece, 1994; Peng, 2004). Peng tried to answer this question from the perspective of the different institutions of various countries. He termed this perspective an institution-based view to parallel Porter's (1980) industry-based view and Barney's (1991) resource-based view. Porter (1980) argued that it is the differences in industrial conditions that make firms choose different strategies. Barney (1991) argued that firms' different resource endowments contribute to their different strategic decision making.

According to DiMaggio and Powell (1983), Meyer and Rowan (1977), Scott (1995), and North (1990), firms cannot avoid the influence of institutions that firms are embedded in. Therefore, both the industry-based view and resource-based view are criticized for ignoring the institutional settings in which firms are embedded (Kogut, 2003). By definition, institutions are "the rules of the game in a society or, more formally, are the humanly devised constraints that shape human interaction" (North, 1990, p. 3). Davis and North (1971, p. 6) defined institutional framework as "the set of fundamental political, social, and legal ground rules that establishes the basis for production, exchange, and distribution." Scott (1995, p. 33) defines institutions as "cognitive, normative, and regulative structures and activities that provide stability and meaning to social behavior." As we illustrated in Chapter 2, "Markets and Institutions," there are formal institutions (e.g., political rules, judicial decisions, and economic contracts) and informal institutions (e.g., socially sanctioned norms and behavior) that complement each other, so that when formal institutions are ineffective, informal institutions come to play to guide the behavior of firms (North, 1990).

North (1990) and Williamson (1985) viewed institutions from an economic perspective. Influenced by North and Williamson's economic view of institutions and drawing on previous institutional work in strategy (Peng and Heath, 1996; Oliver, 1997), Peng (2002) proposed that a firm's strategic choices are not only influenced by industry conditions and firm-specific advantages, but also by the formal and informal institutions (Scott, 1995; Oliver, 1997). Peng (2002) emphasized that the relationships among institutions, industry environment, and firms are dynamic and interactive. Subsequent research in the context of emerging economies, such as London and Hart (2004), Meyer (2004), and Ramamurti (2004), provides strong support for the institution-based view. In 2008, Peng, Wang, and Jiang put forward the concept of a "strategy tripod"—namely an industry-based view (Porter, 1980), a resource-based view (Barney, 1991), and an institutional-based view (Peng, 2002)—further emphasizing the role of institutions in firms' strategic choices and performance.

Mathews (2006) proposed another model, called the LLL (linkage, leverage and learning), which extended Dunning's (1993) OLI framework to explain EMNEs' accelerated internationalization. Mathews (2006) argued that EMNEs do not necessarily possess existing advantages/assets in order to internationalize, but have a high organizational learning ability. **Linkage,** the first L in the model, is the ability to connect with partners to acquire resources and "complementary asset" globally. **Leverage,** the second L in the model, involves using network and inter-firm linkages to access resources. The final L in the model, **learning,** means using linkage and leverage to more effectively perform the operations through which firms are able to accelerate their internationalization.

From a somewhat similar perspective, Luo and Tung (2007) proposed the springboard approach. They argued that EMNEs invest in foreign countries with the purpose of obtaining strategic assets to compensate for competitive disadvantages and to compete with DMNEs effectively. They observe that EMNEs invest abroad to avoid unfavorable institutional and market environments in their home countries, while at the same time taking advantage of the favorable policies from their home government. Thus, the mixed effects of a home country institutional environment (favorable and unfavorable) push EMNEs to invest abroad. According to Luo and Tung (2007), there are four types of "leapfrog trajectories"—namely, commissioned specialist, niche entrepreneur, transnational agent, and world-stage aspirant. The internationalization of Chinese MNEs, such as Haier, Huawei, and Lenovo, and Indian MNEs, such as Infosys, Wipro, and Bharti Airtel, can be explained using Luo and Tung's (2007) springboard perspective.

Conclusion

In this chapter, we discussed the theoretical implications of the emergence of EMNEs, examining how IB theories can explain this phenomenon. Our discussion illustrated a few important points that future research on EMNEs should take into account. First, both home-country factors (e.g., mixed effect of institutional environment) and host-country factors (e.g., location advantages such as advancement in technology) can contribute to explaining the international expansion of EMNEs and should thus be included in new theory development. Second, the relative distance between home country and host country continues to be an important factor for the internationalization and market selection process of multinationals, including EMNEs. As such, this factor should also be considered and empirically tested. Third, the link between the initial country-specific advantages and EMNEs' internal capabilities building should not be overlooked. Scholars have examined external factors (e.g., favorable policies given by EMNEs' home government). We argue that for the survival and growth of EMNEs in a long run, internal factors should not be ignored because EMNEs have to build their firm-specific advantages, embedding or transferring country-specific advantages into built-in firm-specific advantages through organizational learning. Fourth, new research needs to focus not only on firms but also on individuals, which, as we pointed in Chapter 8, continue to play an important role in the management of many of the most competitive EMNEs.

Fifth, given the complexity of EMNE internationalization, IB scholars need to use more qualitative studies to probe into the behavior and motives of EMNEs and take into consideration the multilevel context (namely, home-country context, industry context, and firm context). Last but not least, the accelerated internationalization of EMNEs has injected some new energy into the internationalization debate, making it necessary to answer the why-where-how questions regarding internationalization simultaneously, rather than considering them in a sequence, as conventional theory and the practice of developed economies MNEs suggests. In conclusion, through their different, often innovative and creative practices, EMNEs have changed the competitive scenario that most businesses operate in. This has forced managers and entrepreneurs to react, and scholars to reflect upon the applicability of existing management and business theories. We hope that this book provides a useful guide for business operating in emerging markets, and that this final part of the book contributes to explaining EMNEs through the strategic lenses of Chapter 8 and the theoretical lenses of this chapter.

References

Agmon, T. and Lessard, D. R. (1977). Investor recognition of corporate international diversification. *Journal of Finance*. 32. pp. 1049–55.

Aliber, R. Z. (1970). A Theory of Direct Foreign Investment. In Kindleberger, C. P. (Ed). *The International Firm*. Cambridge, Massachusetts: MIT Press.

Arndt, H. W. (1974). Professor Kojima on the macroeconomics of foreign direct investment. *Hitotsubashi Journal of Economics*. 14. pp. 26–35.

Bain, J. S. (1950). Workable competition in oligopoly: theoretical considerations and some empirical evidence. *American Economic Review*. 40. pp. 35–47.

Bain, J. S. (1956). *Barriers to New Competition*. Cambridge, Massachusetts: Harvard University Press.

Barney, J. B. (1991). Firm resources and sustained competitive advantage. *Journal of Management, 17*. pp. 99–120.

Barney, J. B. (2002). *Gaining and Sustaining Competitive Advantage*. Prentice Hall.

Barney, J. B. and Arikan, A. (2006). The Resource-Based View: Origins and Implications. Hitt, M., Freeman, E., and Harrison, J. (Eds.). *The Blackwell Handbook of Strategic Management*. Oxford: Blackwell.

Bhatnagar, S. (2006). India's software industry. Chandra, V. (Ed.). *Technology, Adaptation, and Exports: How Some Developing Countries Got It Right*. World Bank.

Buckley, P. J. and Casson, M. C. (1976). *The Future of the Multinational Enterprise*. London: Macmillan.

Buckley, P. J., Clegg, L. J., Cross, A. R., Liu, X., Voss, H., and Zheng, P. (2007). The determinants of Chinese outward foreign direct investment. *Journal of International Business Studies, 38*. pp. 499–518.

Cantwell, J. (1995). The globalization of technology: what remains of the product cycle model? *Cambridge Journal of Economics, 19*(1). pp. 155–174.

Cardinal, L. B., Miller, C. C., and Palich, L. (2011). Breaking the cycle of iteration: forensic failures of international diversification and firm performance research. *Global Strategy Journal, 1*. pp. 175–186.

Caves, R. E. (1971). International corporations: the industrial economics of foreign investment. *Economica (New Series), 38*. pp. 1–27.

Caves, R. E. (1974). Multinational firms, competition and productivity in host-country industries. *Economica* (May). 176–193.

Coase, R. H. (1937). The nature of the firm. *Economica, 4*. pp. 386–405.

Conner, K. R. (1991). A historical comparison of resource-based theory and five schools of thought within industrial organization economics: do we have a new theory of the firm? *Journal of Management, 17*(1). pp. 121–154.

Cuervo-Cazurra, A. (2012). Extending theory by analyzing developing country multi-national companies: solving the goldilocks debate. *Global Strategy Journal, 2*(3). pp. 153–167.

Cuervo-Cazurra, A. and Genc, M. (2008). Converting disadvantages into advantages: developing country MNEs in the least developed countries. *Journal of International Business Studies, 39* (6). pp. 957–979.

Cyert, R. M. and March, J. G. (1963). *A Behavioral Theory of the Firm. 2nd Edition.* Prentice Hall, Englewood Cliffs, New Jersey.

Davis, L. and North, D. C. (1971). *Institutional Change and American Economic Growth.* Cambridge: Cambridge University Press.

DiMaggio, P. and Powell, W. (1983). The iron cage revisited: institutional isomorphism and collective rationality in organizational fields. *American Sociological Review, 48*(2). pp. 147–160.

Dowling, M. and Cheang, C. T. (2000). Shifting comparative advantage in Asia: new tests of the "flying geese" model. *Journal of Asian Economics, 11*. p. 446–463.

Dunning, J. H. (1958). *American Investment in British Manufacturing Industry.* New York: Arno Press.

Dunning, J. H. (1973). The determinants of international production. *Oxford Economic Papers, 25* (November). pp. 289–325.

Dunning, J. H. (1977). Trade, Location of Economic Activity and the MNE: A Search for an Eclectic Approach. Ohlin, B., Hesselborn, P. O., and Wijkman, P. M. (Eds.). *The International Allocation of Economic Activity.* London: Macmillan.

Dunning, J. H. (1980). Trade, location of economic activity and the multinational enterprise: some empirical tests. *Journal of International Business Studies, 11*(1). pp. 9–31.

Dunning, J. H. (1988a). The eclectic paradigm of international production: a restatement and some possible extensions. *Journal of International Business Studies, 19*(1). pp. 1–31.

Dunning, J. H. (1988b). *Explaining International Production*. London: Unwin Hyman.

Dunning, J. H. (1991). The Eclectic Paradigm of International Production: A Personal Perspective. Pitelis, C. N. and Sugden, R. (Eds.). *The Nature of the Transnational Firm*. London and New York: Routledge.

Dunning, J. H. (1993). *Multinational Enterprises and the Global Economy*. Wokingham: Addison Wesley.

Dunning, J. H. (1993). The globalization of business: the challenge of the 1990s. London: Routledge.

Dunning, J. H. (1998). Location and the Multinational Enterprise: A Neglected Factor? *Journal of International Business Studies, 29*(1) pp. 45–66.

Dunning, J. H. (2002). *Theories and Paradigms of International Business Activity: The Selected Essays of John H. Dunning*, Vol. I and II. Cheltenham, UK: Edward Eglar.

Dunning, J. H. (2009). The Key Literature on IB Activities: 1960–2006. Rugman, A. M. (Ed.). *The Oxford Handbook of International Business*. Oxford University Press.

Dunning, J. H. and Lundan, S. (2008). Institutions and the OLI paradigm of the multinational enterprise. *Asia Pacific Journal of Management, 25.* pp. 573–593.

Dunning, J. H. and Lundan, S. (2010). The institutional origins of dynamic capabilities in multinational enterprises. *Industrial and Corporate Change, 19*(4). pp. 1225–1246.

Dunning, J. H. and Rugman, A. M. (1985). The influence of Hymer's dissertation on the theory of foreign direct investment. *American Economic Review, 75*(2). pp. 228–232.

Flowers, E. G. (1976). Oligopolistic reaction in European and Canadian direct investment in the U.S. *Journal of International Business Studies VII*, pp. 43–45.

Giddy, I. H. (1978). The demise of the product life cycle model in international business theory. *Columbia Journal of World Business, 13.* pp. 90–97.

Ginzburg, A. and Simonazzi, A. (2005). Patterns of industrialization and the flying geese model: the case of electronics in East Asia. *Journal of Asian Economics, 15*(6). pp. 1051–1078.

Goldstein, A. (2007). *Multinational Companies from Emerging Economies*. New York: Palgrave Macmillan.

Graham, E. M. (1975). *Oligopolistic Imitation and European Direct Investment*. Ph.D. dissertation. Harvard Graduate School of Business Administration.

Graham, E. M. (1978). Transatlantic investment by multinational firms: a rivalistic phenomenon? *Journal of Post-Keynesian Economics, 1.* (Fall). pp. 82–99.

Grant, R. M. (1996). Toward a knowledge-based theory of the firm. *Strategic Management Journal, 17* (Winter Special Issue). pp. 109–122.

Gray, H. P. and Dunning, J. H. (1993). *Transnational Corporations and International Trade and Payments, Volume 8.* Psychology Press.

Guillen, M. F. and Garcia-Canal, E. (2009). The American model of the multinational firm and the "new" multinationals from emerging economies. *Academy of Management Perspectives, 23* (2). pp. 23–35.

Hennart, J. F. (1982). *A Theory of Multinational Enterprise.* Ann Arbor: University of Michigan Press.

Hennart, J. F. (2012). Emerging market multinationals and the theory of the multinational enterprise. *Global Strategy Journal, 2*(3). pp. 168–187.

Hirsch, S. (1967). *Location of Industry and International Competitiveness.* Oxford: Oxford University Press.

Hymer, S. H. (1960). *The international operations of national firms: A study of direct foreign investment.* (Ph.D. thesis). Massachusetts Institute of Technology. Cambridge, Massachusetts: The MIT Press, 1976.

INFOSYS (2013). Employee data. Available from http://www.infosys.com/investors/financials/Pages/employee-data.aspx (accessed: 4/25/2013).

Itaki, M. (1991). A critical assessment of the eclectic theory of the multinational enterprise. *Journal of International Business Studies, 22*(3). pp. 445–460.

Johanson, J. and Vahlne, J. E. (1977). The internationalization process of the firm: a model of knowledge development and increasing foreign market commitments. *Journal of International Business Studies, 8*(1). pp. 23–32.

Johanson, J. and Vahlne, J. E. (1990). The mechanism of internationalization. *International Marketing Review, 7*(4). pp. 11–24.

Kim, S. W. and Lyn, E. O. (1986). Excess market value, the multinational corporation, and Tobin's q-ratio. *Journal of International Business Studies, 17*(1). pp. 119–25.

Kindleberger, C. P. (1969). *American Business Abroad.* New Haven, Connecticut: Yale University Press.

Knickerbocker, F. T. (1973). *Oligopolistic Reaction and Multinational Enterprise.* Cambridge, Massachusetts: Harvard University Press.

Kogut, B. (1983). Foreign Direct Investment as a Sequential Process. Kindleberger, C. P. and Audretsch, D. (Eds.). *The Multinational Corporation in the 1980s.* Cambridge: MIT Press.

Kogut, B. (2003). *Globalization and context.* Keynote address at the First Annual Conference on Emerging Research Frontiers in International Business, Duke University.

Kojima, K. (1973). A macroeconomic approach to foreign direct investment. *Hitotsubashi Journal of Economics, 14.* pp. 1–20.

Kojima, K. (1978). *Direct Foreign Investment.* London: Croom Helm.

Kojima, K. (1982). Macro-economic vs. international business approach to direct foreign investment. *Hitosubashi Journal of Economics, 23.* pp. 1–19.

Kojima, K. (1990). *Direct Foreign Investment Abroad.* Tokyo: International Christian University.

Kojima, K. and Ozawa, T. (1984). Micro- and macro-economic models of direct foreign investment: toward a synthesis. *Hitosubashi Journal of Economics, 25.* p. 1–20.

Lessard, D. R. (1976). World, country, and industry relationships in equity returns— implications for risk reduction through international diversification. *Financial Analysts Journal, 32* (1). pp. 32–38.

Lessard, D. R. (1977). International Diversification and Foreign Direct Investment. Eiteman, D. and Stonehill, A. (Eds.). *Multinational Business Finance, Fourth Edition.* Reading, Massachusetts: Addison-Wesley.

Lessard, D. R. (1979). Transfer Prices, Taxes, and Financial Markets: Implications of Internal Financial Transfers Within the Multinational Firm. Hawkins, R. B. (Ed.). *Economic Issues of Multinational Firms.* JAI Press.

Lessard, D. R. (1982). International Diversification and Direct Foreign Investment. Eiteman, D. K. and Stonehill, A. (Eds.). *Multinational Business Finance.* Reading, Massachusetts: Addison-Wesley.

London, T. and Hart, S. L. (2004). Reinventing strategies for emerging markets: beyond the transnational model. *Journal of International Business Studies, 35*(5). pp. 350–370.

Lundan, S. M. and Jones, G. (2001). The commonwealth effect and the process of internationalization. *The World Economy, 24*(1). pp. 99–118.

Luo, Y. and Tung, R. L. (2007). International expansion of emerging market enterprises: a springboard perspective. *Journal of International Business Studies, 38.* pp. 481–498.

Magee, S. P. (1976). Technology and the Appropriability Theory of the Multinational Corporation. In Bhagwati, J.N. (Ed.). *The New International Economic Order: The North-South Debate.* Cambridge, Massachusetts: MIT Press.

Magee, S. P. (1977). Information and the Multinational Corporation: An Appropriability Theory of Direct Foreign Investment. Bhagwati, J.N. (Ed.). *The New International Economic Order: the North-South Debate.* Cambridge, Massachusetts: MIT Press.

Magee, S. P. (1981). The appropriability theory of the multinational corporation. *Annals of the American Academy of Political and Social Science, 458.* pp. 123–135.

Mathews, J. A. (2002). *Dragon multinationals: a new model of global growth.* New York: Oxford University Press.

Mathews, J. A. (2006). Dragon Multinationals: New Players in 21st Century Globalization. *Asia Pacific Journal of Management, 23*(1). pp. 5–27.

McDermott, G., Mudambi, R., and Parente, R. (2013). Strategic modularity and the architecture of multinational firm. *Global Strategy Journal, 3.* pp. 1–7.

Meyer, J. W. and Rowan, B. (1977). Institutionalized organizations: formal structure as myth and ceremony. *American Journal of Sociology, 83*(2). pp. 340–363.

Meyer, K. E. (2004). Perspectives on multinational enterprises in emerging economies. *Journal of International Business Studies, 35*(4). pp. 259–276.

Morck, R. and Yeung, B. (1991). Why investors value multinationality. *The Journal of Business, 64*(2). pp. 165–87.

Mudambi, R. (2008). Location, control, and innovation in knowledge-intensive industries. *Journal of Economic Geography, 8.* pp. 699–725.

Nordstrom, K. A. (1991). *The Internationalization Process of the Firm—Searching for New Pattern and Explanations.* Stockholm: Stockholm School of Economics.

North, D. C. (1990). *Institutions, Institutional Change, and Economic Performance.* Cambridge, Massachusetts: Harvard University Press.

Oliver, C. (1997). Sustainable competitive advantage: combining institutional and resource-based views. *Strategic Management Journal, 18*(9). pp. 679–713.

Oviatt, B. M. and McDougall, P. P. (1994). Toward a theory of international new ventures. *Journal of International Business Studies, 25.* pp. 45–64.

Palepu, K. G., Tarun, K. and Ingrid, V. (2006). Haier: Taking a Chinese Company Global. *Harvard Business School Case 706-401,* August 2006. (Revised from original October 2005 version.)

Peng, M. W. (2002). Towards an Institution-Based View of Business Strategy. *Asia Pacific Journal of Management, 19*(2). pp. 251–67.

Peng, M. W. (2004). Identifying the big question in international business research. *Journal of International Business Studies, 35*(2). pp. 99–108.

Peng, M. W. and Heath, P. (1996). The growth of the firm in planned economies in transition: Institutions, organizations, and strategic choices. *Academy of Management Review, 21*(2). p. 492–528.

Peng, M. W., Wang, D., and Jiang, Y. (2008). An institution-based view of international business strategy: A focus on emerging economies. *Journal of International Business Studies, 39*(5). pp. 920–936.

Penrose, E. T. (1956). Foreign investment and the growth of the firm. *Economic Journal, 66.* pp. 220–235.

Penrose, E. T. (1959). *The Theory of the Growth of the Firm (1995 Edition).* New York: John Wiley and Sons.

Peteraf, M. A. and Barney, J. B. (2003). Unraveling the resource-based tangle. *Managerial and Decision Economics, 24.* pp. 309–323.

Peteraf, M. A. (1993). The cornerstones of competitive advantage: a resource-based view. *Strategic Management Journal*. 14. pp. 179–191.

Porter, M. (1980). *Competitive Strategy*. New York: Free Press.

Ramamurti, R. (2004). Developing countries and MNEs: extending and enriching the research agenda. *Journal of International Business Studies, 35*(4). pp. 277–283.

Ramamurti, R. (2009a). Why study emerging-market multinationals? Ramamurti, R. and Singh, J. (Eds.). *Emerging Multinationals in Emerging Markets*. Cambridge University Press.

Ramamurti, R. (2009b). What have we learned about emerging-market MNEs? Ramamurti, R. and Singh, J. (Eds.). *Emerging Multinationals in Emerging Markets*. Cambridge University Press.

Ramamurti, R. (2012). What is really different about emerging market multinationals? *Global Strategy Journal, 2*(1). pp. 41–47.

Rugman, A. M. (1976). Risk reduction by international diversification. *Journal of International Business Studies, 7*.

Rugman, A. M. (1977). *Risk, direct investment and International diversification*. Weltwirtschaftliches Archiv 113.

Rugman, A. M. (1979). *International Diversification and the Multinational Enterprise*. Lexington, Massachusetts: Lexington Books.

Rugman, A. M. (1981). *Inside the Multinationals: The Economics of Internal Markets*. London: Croom Helm.

Rugman, A. M. (2009). Theoretical aspects of MNEs from emerging economies. Ramamurti, R. and Singh, J. (Eds.). *Emerging Multinationals in Emerging Markets*. Cambridge University Press.

Rugman, A. M. (2010). Do we need a new theory to explain emerging market MNEs? Sauvant, K. P. Maschek, W. A., and McAllister, G. A. (Eds.). *Foreign Direct Investments from Emerging Markets: The Challenges Ahead*. Palgrave McMillan: New York.

Rumelt, R. P. (1984). Towards a Strategic Theory of the Firm. Lamb, R. (Ed.). *Competitive Strategic Management*. Englewood Cliffs, New Jersey: Prentice-Hall.

Rumelt, R. P. (1991). How much does industry matter? *Strategic Management Journal, 12*. pp. 167–185.

Rumelt, R. P., Schendel, D., and Teece, D. (1994). *Fundamental Issues in Strategy: A Research Agenda*. Boston: Harvard Business School Press.

Schmalensee, R. (1985). Do Market Differ Much? *The American Economic Review, 75*(3). pp. 341–351.

Schumpeter, J. A. (1950). *Capitalism, Socialism and Democracy (third edition)*. New York: Harper & Row.

Scott, W. R. (1995). *Institutions and Organizations.* Thousand Oaks, California: Sage.

Simon, M. A. (1957). *Models of Man, Social and Rational: Mathematical Essays on Rational Human Behavior in a Social Setting.* New York: John Wiley and Sons.

UNCTAD (United Nations Conference on Trade and Development). (2012). *World Investment Report 2012.* New York: United Nations.

Vahlne, J. E. and Nordstrom, K. A. (1992). *The Internationalisation Process—Impact of Competition and Experience.* Stockholm: Stockholm, School of Economics.

Vahlne, J. E. and Wiedersheim-Paul, F. (1973). Economic Distance. Model and Empirical Investigation. Hornell, E., Vahlne, J. E., and Wiedersheim-Paul, F. (Eds.). *Export and Foreign Establishments.* Stockholm: Almqvist and Wiksell.

Vernon, R. (1966). International investment and international trade in the product cycle. *Quarterly Journal of Economics.* 80. pp. 190–207.

Weigel, D. R., Neil, F. G., and Dileep, M. W. (1998). *Lessons of Experience No. 5: Foreign Direct Investment.* International Finance Corporation and World Bank.

Wells, L. T. (1972). *The Product Life Cycle and International Trade.* Cambridge, Massachusetts: Harvard University Press.

Wells, L. T. (1977). The Internationalization of Firms from Developing Countries. Agmon, T. and Kindleberger, C. P. (Eds.). *Multinationals from Small Countries.* Cambridge, Massachusetts: MIT Press.

Wells, L. T. (1983). *Third World Multinationals: The Rise of Foreign Investment from Developing Countries.* Cambridge, Massachusetts: The MIT Press.

Wernerfelt, B. (1984). A resource-based view of the firm. *Strategic Management Journal, 5.* pp. 171–180.

Wiersema, M. F. and Bowen, H. P. (2011). The relationship between international diversification and firm performance: why it remains a puzzle. *Global Strategy Journal, 1.* pp. 152–170.

Wilkins, M. (1974). *The Maturing of Multinational Enterprise: American Business Abroad from 1914 to 1970.* Cambridge, Massachusetts: Harvard University Press.

Wilkins, M. (2009). The History of the Multinational Enterprise. Rugman, A. M. (Ed.). *The Oxford Handbook of International Business.* Oxford University Press.

Williamson, O. E. (1975). *Markets and Hierarchies: Analysis and Antitrust Implications.* New York: Free Press.

Williamson, O. E. (1985). *The Economic Institutions of Capitalism.* New York: Free Press.

Williamson, O. E. (1989). Transaction cost economics. Schmalensee, R. and Willig, R. D. (Eds.). *Handbook of industrial organization.* Amsterdam: North Holland.

Williamson, P. J. and Zeng, M. (2009). Chinese multinationals: emerging through new global gateways. Ramamurti, R. and Singh, J. (Eds.). *Emerging Multinationals in Emerging Markets.* Cambridge University Press.

Zaheer, S. (1995). Overcoming the liability of foreignness. *Academy of Management Journal, 38* (2). pp. 341–363.

10

Conclusion

We decided to write this book to address the absence of accessible texts for business managers and management students addressing the significant structural changes in the global economy and the ever more important necessity of thinking about business strategies with an understanding of emerging markets. Since the mid 2000s, the world has been changing at a dramatic speed, with Europe precipitating a dramatic crisis, the U.S. struggling to recover from the effects of the recession started in 2008, and Japan continuing in its now decades-long stagnation. In spite of expansionary monetary policy and multiple government interventions to save ailing companies, notably banks, the old drivers of the world economy are in dire straits. Between 2009 and 2013, unemployment has risen to unprecedented levels in Europe. In 2013, it has reached a point where more than half of the young population of Spain, Italy, and Greece is out of work. Tax rises and job cuts have sparked mass mobilizations, and the rise of populist political parties is threatening the survival of the Euro and attacking the idea of European integration. Since 2009, the U.S. economy has been recovering at a very slow pace, amid political frictions and disagreements on how to reduce debt. Meanwhile, a broad array of emerging markets have achieved record growth year on year.

Remarkably, while the business world is adapting fast, creating emerging-market divisions and investing heavily in studying emerging-market consumers, academic theories have been evolving more slowly. In the management discipline, most of the work has been carried out by researchers with a finance background and addressing mainly a finance audience. More than 90 percent of the texts used in business schools and management departments are written with a Triad focus, with emerging markets being discussed, if at all, in separate, generally marginal sections—a metaphor of how these economies have been considered for many years by most scholars and managers. One of the main objectives of this book has been to address this gap with a fresh emerging-markets perspective on management. It differs from most work published up to 2013 because it is based on, and aimed at, nonfinancial businesses.

This book provides an essential guide to managers of international business or of businesses looking to move into the new areas of opportunity in this new international economic order. In the first part, we explained how the global economy has evolved from being centered on the U.S., Europe, and Japan—collectively known as the Triad—to being driven more and more by the growth of emerging markets. A historical event in this evolutionary process was achieved in 2008–2009, when the economic recession that hit the U.S. and Europe failed to cripple emerging economies. It merely slowed down their growth and signaled to anyone who cared to notice that emerging markets had become more interlinked with each other rather than to the now-ailing U.S. and European economies and that they had developed their own growth drivers. Our key message throughout the book has been that emerging markets, though rich in business opportunities, are tough, and require careful, fresh strategic thinking, not just the adaptation of stale products and ideas. Selling decades-old car models, such as Volkswagen and Fiat, used to do in Latin America, but is not enough to win in many of today's emerging markets. We need new ideas, new strategies, and new products. Most importantly, we need business models that put the emerging market consumer and context at their center.

The analytical tools we presented in the second part of the book serve the purpose of helping business students think about emerging-markets strategies, and help managers and entrepreneurs develop or refine their own strategies. Having explained how and why doing business in emerging markets differs from operating in developed economies, we suggested a clear analytical process to follow. First, identify the Determinants of Attractiveness, or the factors that make some economies more attractive than others for specific businesses. Second, think about the context focusing on four key dimensions—geography, population, business environment, and economic performance. Third, examine the risks that each of the four dimensions may generate in general and for the business activities we intend to operate. Fourth, develop suitable strategies to manage risk and target clients successfully in these environments.

The first tool we proposed, to identify the Determinants of Attractiveness, draws from the principles of international management—companies expand in new markets for specific reasons, which in turn determine the nature of their investments and operations (for example, the scale of their investments and their time horizons). Emerging economies, just like developed economies, can be attractive for multiple reasons, ranging from their natural resources, to their skilled labor and their expanding markets. We presented a set of exercises we have developed to help readers analyze the Determinants of Attractiveness and compare them across countries, distinguishing the factors that are strictly *necessary* for our business, from those that are *highly desirable, desirable,* or *not needed.* Our objective was not to proclaim which markets to invest in or which market is best to set up a jeans manufacturing plant. We trust that the managers and entrepreneurs who read our book will know better than us, and the last of our intentions is to teach them how to do their job. But we believe that our tools can help organize information and data in a structured way, thus facilitating strategic decisions.

The second step in our model is examining the four dimensions, which together explain the overall context of a given economy. Geography, population, business environment, and economic performance determine why a country may be an attractive location for extracting oil, while simultaneously giving us information about the potential risks of doing so. Combining the Determinants of Attractiveness with the four dimensions can generate encompassing country profiles, which is again a useful exercise for business students and a practical tool for managers and entrepreneurs of companies that are internationalizing to emerging markets. Looking at the four dimensions naturally leads to the following step in the model—the analysis of risk. We believe that this is an essential point in our book, and a point that distinguishes it strongly from most existing texts on the topic because of its practical and operational perspective.

To examine risk, we distinguish risks that can be expected, which companies can prepare for, from those that are unpredictable. We have pointed out a very encompassing range of risks, from natural hazards to criminal violence and social unrest, arguing that it is important to reflect upon the extent to which they can be classified as expected or unexpected. We then distinguished two further categories of risk—location and targeted—both of which can be either expected or unexpected. We called location risk the set of risks that can generally be associated with a country, which should provide us with a background of the environment for which we will develop strategies. Identifying targeted risk is the next, much more complex step. It involves examining the risks that are specific to our actual or intended business. This means focusing first geographically, on the region, city, and even neighborhood where our activities will take place—not just where the headquarters will be, but where the warehouses, factories, and delivery routes will be.

To assess and manage risk, it is paramount to know exactly how a business operates and where, and distinguish the more critical activities from those that can be temporarily interrupted in extreme circumstances. Throughout the second part of the book, we emphasize the need to examine the process through which risk management strategies are formulated and implemented, rather than treating these matters as last-minute details to be dealt with by field managers. We discuss the protection of the workforce and facilities, which is an important investment in ensuring the sustainability of emerging market strategies. To do so, it is necessary to have day-to-day strategies to manage the expected risks associated with running a specific type of business in a particular geographic area and also to have contingency plans for unexpected risks that may manifest themselves. Again, the objective of our discussion of risk was not to create another list of which countries are risky, why, and for what kinds of business. Risk changes on the ground every minute, so any list we may compile is bound to be obsolete by the time it is read, and there is no shortage of private companies offering risk analysis services. We have provided a structure to help in evaluating risk, leaving the specific judgment to the reader—an exercise for students, a guide for practitioners. Our most important message here was that risk evaluation is not an exact science; it is an exercise in subjective judgment. Do you remember Saddam Hussein's minister of information, who famously broadcast live claiming that the situation was calm and stable in Iraq while it was possible to hear explosions in the background? Official sources are not always as reliable as they should be. When examining risk, it is best to rely on multiple sources, and, if possible, to gather direct information from workers, neighbors, taxi drivers, and cleaners, rather than relying only on official corporate or government sources or reports processed by third parties.

The last step in our model, a step that applies only to companies that sell or plan to sell in emerging markets, is developing strategies to target emerging-market clients. Given the saturation that affects the markets of developed economies, understanding how to target clients in emerging markets is becoming essential for global companies. Smaller companies are also joining the ranks, and internationalizing aggressively to emerging markets, attracted by their dynamism and growing sophistication. We explain that not only do emerging markets differ from each other, they also include a diverse set of market segments. There isn't an emerging market consumer, or, for that matter, an Indonesian or Colombian consumer. There are different groups of potential consumers that companies can target, and they differ to such a great extent that they may require different products, processes, and strategies.

Emerging markets are more inequitable than developed economies. As a result, the income gaps between the rich and the poor are much more extreme. We have developed a set of strategies to segment and target emerging-market clients by their income group—the global rich, the upper-middle class, the new middle class, and the poor. The rich of emerging markets, which are growing in number and wealth every year, are well educated and well traveled and, for now at least, emulate the luxury consumption patterns of the rich from the Triad. They are the easiest group of emerging-market clients to target, which contributes to explaining why the luxury industry has been performing particularly well in spite of the 2008 crisis. The upper-middle classes are also highly attracted to Triad luxury products but are generally more influenced by local trends. They require more investment to detect and understand consumption patterns, building brands at the local level, and proposing innovative and creative solutions that go beyond what is currently on offer in the Triad. The new middle classes are the most dynamic group. They include the large number of people who, thanks to economic growth, have escaped from poverty and experienced a gradual increase in their average incomes. The new middle classes are far less exposed to international trends, and hence much more difficult to target. Their consumption may, but often does not, converge with that observed in the Triad during the expansion of mass consumerism. Their purchasing power is expanding fast, giving them access to a broad range of consumer durables, housing, and consumption products. As a result, competition between firms from the Triad and from emerging markets is becoming particularly heated in this specific market segment. We provide some ideas and hints about how to target these clients successfully.

We then thoroughly discuss strategies for targeting poor consumers, who make up most of the world's population, and yet who continue, by and large, to be marginalized from the world market. Drawing on the work of the scholars of the Base of the Pyramid, we argue that there are specific economic, institutional, social, and infrastructural barriers insulating the poor from the market. Large businesses have the resources and capabilities to overcome these barriers, especially if teaming up with the public sector and civil society organizations. Bringing the poor closer to the market can provide them with access to a broader range of higher quality goods and services, and more opportunities to find employment. It can also create new markets for low-price, high-volume repeat purchases. Though it is not easy to achieve the scale necessary to make these initiatives profitable, there are good economic, social, and ethical reasons for doing so.

We argue that targeting clients at the "base of the pyramid" means primarily understanding how they live, which is a million miles away from how the managers of multinational corporations, business students, and most entrepreneurs live, even if they are from emerging markets themselves. Improving access to information about the livelihood of the poor is a key prerequisite for developing Base of the Pyramid strategies, and it has an educational side effect—making the poor more visible. It can also spark innovations that can be applied outside of their context. Think, for example, of cell phone banking, which has diffused swiftly throughout Africa precisely because it helps consumers without a formal bank account to transfer money to their relatives living in other regions. We hope that our discussion inspires students and managers to think outside of the box and develop ideas, products, and strategies for the Base of the Pyramid, and to venture into the territory that the vast majority of Triad companies have shunned for many years, forsaking an opportunity to develop inclusionary, socially responsible business models.

Moving on from discussing how to develop emerging market strategies, the final part of the book focuses the empirical and theoretical implications that emerging markets have had on management, one of the most important of which is the rise of multinational companies based in emerging markets. We argue that these firms leverage the competitive advantage of being based in fast-expanding markets, which provides them with growing resources and healthy profits. In this sense, they are no different from the American companies that developed during the 1900–1929 and 1940–1960s periods, or the Japanese and German manufacturers that grew during the post–World War II years. The main difference between Triad multinationals and emerging-market multinationals is that the latter had to face much harder challenges to expand domestically, precisely because of the idiosyncrasies that affect their home countries. Being used to functioning in highly unpredictable business environments and dealing with malfunctioning infrastructure, crime, corruption, and often conflict, they have however developed an organizational flexibility that Triad firms tend to lack. They are more adaptable, more agile, and hence more suited to operating in other emerging markets, a feature that contributes to explaining the expansion of intra-emerging-market trade and investment flows. We also note that most emerging-market firms benefit from being more insulated from shareholder pressures, because most of them are either controlled by families or by the state. This gives them more flexibility to deploy long-term strategies, even if these fail to produce immediate returns.

States have supported the development of emerging-market multinationals in different forms. In its more evidenced form, the state is the owner and controller of a large share of these new multinationals, especially firms based in China, Russia, and the ex–Soviet Republics. Two of the largest Brazilian firms, Vale and Petrobras, are also partially state controlled. In other cases, the state has simply tolerated the monopolistic positions that some of these firms have acquired in their domestic market, which has allowed them to be particularly profitable. In exchange, they have expanded aggressively abroad, generating export revenues, gaining access to natural resources, and finding new markets for products made in their home countries. Again, this is by no means a feature unique to emerging markets. Some of the largest European companies, including the German car maker Volkswagen, the French energy company EDF, and the Italian oil and gas firm ENI, had been partly owned and controlled by the state at different stages of their corporate life. The hand of the state has become more visible in the case of emerging-market multinationals because of the sheer number of companies supported and their aggressive growth in domestic and international markets.

When discussing emerging-market multinationals, we note that their internationalization differs in form, timing, and objectives from that of American, European, and Japanese companies. Since the 2000s, these firms have expanded internationally much faster than either textbooks or competitors predicted. They have purchased competitors based in both emerging and developed economies, invested in new facilities, and diversified into new industries. Many of them, such as Lenovo, the Chinese company that acquired the personal computer manufacturing division of IBM and thus becoming the largest PC producer in the world, moved from being subcontractors to being original equipment manufacturers, capable of designing, engineering, and distributing world-class goods. Defeating the expectations of their Triad competitors, they have developed global brands at breathtaking speed.

In extractive industries, internationalization was driven primarily by companies attempting to secure access to resources located in other economies. Chinese companies have become omnipresent throughout Africa, building oil wells, mines, and export-supporting infrastructure. They have responded to the booming demand for energy and minerals that the Chinese infrastructural developments and real estate growth generated since the late 1990s. In other industries, however, emerging-market multinationals have internationalized to acquire skills, knowledge, and brands, instead of first developing their capabilities at home, then regionally, and only after that going global, as the American, European, and Japanese did in other historical periods. These firms have often become global *while* they were still growing in their home market. Their internationalization was functional to their overall corporate growth strategy—it helped them build their brands, improve their processes, and acquire the knowledge to operate at a larger geographical and business scale. They have now become formidable competitors for Triad firms and sparked the development of a whole new range of international business and management theories. The diverse organizational shapes and evolutionary paths of emerging-markets multinationals, together with their continuous change, make it difficult to draw conclusive remarks about them. What is certain is that, as we have argued throughout the book, they have become a key pillar of the global economy, which reflects the larger structural shift of the global economy toward emerging markets.

This book, though certainly not covering in a comprehensive way all of the topics related to emerging markets, provides a solid starting point for approaching internationalization in emerging economies. Its three parts explain the characteristics of these markets, discuss how to identify and manage risks, and explain how to target different groups of consumers. We believe that these are important objectives because emerging markets are here to stay. In the first part of the book, we provide a thorough multidisciplinary discussion, drawing from economics, economic history, industrial sociology, and management, of the steady and yet inexorable rise of emerging markets in the global economic and geo-political arena and explain why we think emerging markets will continue to matter in the future. One of our core arguments is that many of the factors behind the rise of emerging markets are structural—that is, the shift in the axis of the global economy is not temporary. Emerging markets are now in an accelerated catching-up phase—they are growing because they are converging, at last, with their richer counterparts. In the majority of cases, they still have a long way to go before reaching the levels of wealth per capita of developed economies, and this is a good first reason why their role in the world economy is likely to continue rising.

Breaking down this idea of catching up, we can find several driving trends that are sustaining economic growth in emerging markets. We can start with the most important factor—demography. Emerging markets are home to about 80 percent of the world's population, and the share is rising. Their population is also, on average, much younger than that of Triad economies. In developed economies, a shrinking number of workers generate the wealth needed to maintain a rising number of pensioners. In most emerging markets the opposite is true. Emerging markets have reached, or are in the process of reaching, the phase where the majority of their population forms part of the workforce—the demographic phenomenon that contributed to sustaining economic growth in Japan, Western Europe, and the U.S. during the 1950–1980s period. It is unlikely that birth rates in developed economies will revert. We are likely to see a scenario where emerging markets grow faster thanks to demographic reasons, and, having a larger population, come to account for a yet larger share of the world economy. By contrast, most of the Triad, and especially fast-aging countries such as Japan and Italy, are likely to move from being some of the leading world economies to being mid-sized economies. China has already surpassed all Triad economies, but the U.S., Brazil, Russia, and India have displaced old Western European powers in the list of the top ten largest economies in the world.

Emerging economies are not only more populous. Because they have been poorer for many decades, their markets are not saturated and are rich in business opportunities. While in the Triad it is unlikely that there will be much growth from consumers buying more cars, fridges, or other consumer durables, a very large number of emerging market consumers have never even driven a car. The expansion of consumer durable industries has been an important pillar for the industrialization of the Triad. Now it is fueling the economic growth and industrialization of emerging economies, while also providing their citizens with access to goods that can improve their quality of life.

Emerging markets are, unfortunately, still home to billions of poor people. The good news is that poverty has been declining throughout the last decades, which illustrates the extent to which economic growth can contribute to improving social outcomes. As the poor become less poor and join the ranks of the new middle classes, the markets for all goods, not only consumer durables, expand fast and become more sophisticated. Fast-moving consumer goods, entertainment, food, and beverages are many of the industries expanding at record speeds, benefitting from the rise of the average incomes of the emerging market poor. Nonetheless, there is still much scope to develop businesses that help to integrate the poor in the market and improve their living conditions, as we argued in the section on targeting the Base of the Pyramid. Though we cannot predict to what extent business will succeed in reaching a higher percentage of the poor in inclusive ways, we can suggest that this is yet another aspect that could generate future growth in emerging markets.

There are many other reasons why we think that the current shift in the world economy is not a temporary one. Think, for example, of basic infrastructure, such as roads and housing. In most of Africa and Latin America, rural populations often live in areas that are in theory not far from the nearest urban center, but which in practice require days of travel because of bad roads, road blocks, or bridges that get submerged in the rainy season. The urban poor live in precarious accommodation built with recycled materials, exposed to landslides, floods, and diseases. In the past, these conditions were explained by referring to dismal economic growth and lack of jobs and government revenues, which prevented public and private sectors from engaging in infrastructure developments. Now emerging markets are growing fast, in many cases reaching full employment. Wages are rising, and so are government revenues. There is an unprecedented opportunity for the private, public, and nonprofit sectors to engage in projects that improve infrastructure, hopefully aiming to improve the livelihoods of the poor and not just building new housing for the rich. Many emerging markets are already doing this, laying down new sewage systems and water pipes, extending electrical grids and roads, and building schools for the poor. Besides pursuing a social and ethical objective, these projects generate further employment and sustain economic growth.

Emerging markets are also home to most of the world's resources, ranging from oil and minerals to fertile land. The infrastructure developments we have discussed, together with global population growth, will ensure that demand for their natural resources will continue to expand in the future, providing another important growth driver. Brazil, for example, other than being a large market and having a diversified industrial structure and a highly competitive agribusiness industry, also has ample reserves of underwater oil. Depending on technological progress and oil prices, at some point in the future, Brazil is also likely to become a large energy producer. Angola and Sudan, two of the important oil exporters in Africa, are also rich in fertile land, and in the past have been highly productive agricultural exporters. Rebuilding their agricultural industry, which has suffered from years of internal conflicts, could transform them into more diversified economies and generate different sources of employment and economic growth.

In sum, we believe that demography, unsaturated markets, lower average incomes, abundance of natural resources, and the scope for infrastructural developments will sustain the future performance of emerging markets vis-à-vis developed economies, making them yet more important players, as opposed to being a passing fad. This means that they will continue generating interesting business opportunities in most industries. However, as we illustrated in the second part of this book, doing business in emerging markets is likely to remain more risky, complex, and altogether different than in Triad economies, which is why Triad-focused management theories fall short of providing practical strategic guidelines. We have developed this argument at length throughout the book, building on our experience as market analysts as well as our fieldwork and academic background. We explain that emerging markets differ from developed economies in terms of their institutions, infrastructure, and political stability.

Emerging economies are, on average, more unstable, unpredictable, and often more dangerous than Triad economies. Virtually all of the armed conflicts and areas affected by highest violent crime are in emerging markets. Investing in the stock market of these locations from a comfortable office in Wall Street is one thing. Setting up a factory and managing a supply chain is another. It requires developing strategies to run a business successfully in contexts that lack many of the features that companies take for granted in the Triad, ranging from functioning courts to roads that do not wash away during the monsoon. It is precisely in these situations that companies, entrepreneurs, and managers develop innovative strategies and adjust, evolve, and defeat conventional wisdom. If they didn't, there wouldn't be a thriving private sector in most emerging markets. On the contrary, in spite of an often failing public sector, small and big businesses find creative ways of operating, working around institutional, infrastructural, and often political barriers. We hope to have provided a first glimpse of this, helping our readers prepare for the long and somewhat messy journey needed to do business in emerging markets.

Discussing management, international business, and strategy with an emerging market focus is a daunting task, one that by no means can be covered in a single book. This is not just an attempt to bridge a gap in this kind of literature, and hence practice what we preach in our marketing and strategy classes; it is also an attempt to contribute to the evolution of our own industry, academia, toward a stance that is less dominated by U.S.- and Europe-centric ideas and theories. It is a step to complement the existing range of textbooks and manuals with a book conceived entirely from an emerging-market perspective, and to provide students and managers with a set of exercises useful to improve their understanding of these economies. If you, the readers, find our analyses insufficient and head straight off to look for further material, then we have done our job right, opening a small fissure in the confusing, fast-growing, and multifaceted black box that is emerging markets.

Since 2008, emerging markets have been contributing to the lion's share of the world economy. The countries that concentrate most of the world's population, which had been relegated to the economic periphery for over 200 years, are changing fast, growing, becoming less poor, and hence are also exercising more geopolitical muscle. In our view, this shift is good news—emerging markets are driving the world economy in times when Europe, the U.S., and Japan are struggling. It is good news for the millions of people who are gradually coming out of poverty thanks to economic growth in their countries, and it is good news for the businesses that can spot and successfully target the numerous opportunities that this shift is generating. Up to 2008, a large number of companies, political leaders, and management scholars preferred to ignore this structural change. But the opportunity cost of doing this is rising. The firms that invested aggressively in emerging markets are thriving, while companies that have chosen the allegedly safer Triad markets are now struggling to remain profitable. The one field where this has not yet happened is our own industry—academia. The vast majority of publications continue to focus on the U.S., Europe, and Japan. It remains difficult to publish theory-building articles based on emerging markets research, especially when discussing countries other than the BRICS. We are confident that academia will slowly adapt and become more emerging markets focused, and we hope through this book to have laid a small stone in the long path to develop a more encompassing understanding of management theories in emerging markets. We also hope our work will be part of a broader movement toward actively embracing, not just tolerating, a world that is becoming increasingly multipolar in terms of its sources of economic, political, social, and cultural dynamism.

Appendix

From Third World to Emerging Markets: Definitions, Contexts, and Meanings

nderstanding emerging markets means understanding their role in the world economy and how they are perceived by companies and policy makers based in the Triad. In this appendix, we explain the definitions that have been used to identify emerging markets in light of the geopolitical and economic context in which they first appeared. We point out that perceptions, and with them definitions, change through time, as circumstances change—economies once rather disparagingly grouped as the "Third World" are now promisingly called "emerging." We then clarify the meaning of the growing number of acronyms used contemporarily to group emerging markets—BRICS, Civets, N11s—providing short descriptions for each group.

The idea of categorizing countries according to their economic, political, and social status has been around for a long time. Before the 1950s, economic theories did not explicitly refer to "development" as a concept in itself, but rather to economic growth and industrialization. There was a widespread belief that industrialization would automatically create economic growth, which in turn would lead to the development of society. Following on from this was the assumption that all societies could be located somewhere along the same linear spectrum of development and that, consequently, the same yardstick could be used to measure all countries.

Development, Underdevelopment, and Economic Theory—Development theory arose in the immediate post-war period, within the context of a Europe destroyed by WWII and in need of massive reconstruction. The International Bank for Reconstruction and Development, later known as the World Bank, was established in order to manage this process. The experience prompted academics and policymakers to begin theorizing about the difficulties that many "backward" countries also faced regarding infrastructure, economy, institutions, and public services. Suggestions were put forward as to how best to improve this state of affairs, largely through industrialization and increased economic growth (measured in GDP per capita), such as the *Linear Stages of Growth Development* models. These became known as *Modernization Theories*.

The term "underdeveloped" was first used to describe poorer countries in 1948 in the Fourth Session of the conference of the United Nations Food and Agriculture Organization (FAO). No definition was offered, however, of what exactly was understood by the term, nor even its main features. It was used in the brief account of the highlights of the conference to express concern at the unsustainable situation of global food production and demand:

> "In general only [North America] is rich in material goods; most of the rest of the world is poor, much of it desperately poor. For both the physical and the economic health of their people, the underdeveloped areas must greatly increase their food production" (Fourth Session Report, FAO, Washington D.C., 1948).

With the beginning of the Cold War—and given the shifts in geopolitics that resulted from it—international relations and foreign policy began to occupy a much more important place on the agenda of new U.S. President, Harry S. Truman. In his inaugural speech in January 1949, he presented his Point Four Program of aid to "developing" countries, citing national security as his motive:

> "We must embark on a bold new program for making the benefits of our scientific advances and industrial progress available for the improvement and growth of underdeveloped areas....Their poverty is a handicap and a threat both to them and more prosperous areas" (Rist, 1997).

Third World and Non-Aligned Countries—Both the terms "developing" and "underdeveloped" soon became widely adopted in the media and common usage. In 1952, we see the emergence of another very popular way of defining countries with lower average incomes: "Third World." French economic historian Alfred Sauvy coined the term in an article published in *L'Observateur* magazine. Originally, the term was meant as a political category rather than a social or economic one, referring to those countries that were not aligned with either of the two major power blocs during the Cold War. According to Sauvy's model, the "First World" was represented by the "West," or NATO countries, the "Second World" by the "East," or Communist Bloc countries and their allies. The "Third World" countries were all the others, which happened to be poorer countries. For this reason, the term "Third World" quickly became adopted in common discourse to indicate developing economies, regardless of the economic model and ideology they favored (*The Economist*, 2010).

It is worth remembering that throughout the 1950s and 60s, a large number of former colonies in Africa and Asia had just gained their independence, would soon gain it, or were in the process of doing so. Many of these countries wanted to establish new models of development that broke away from market economics, which tended to be associated with the former colonial powers. The main alternative was the Communist Bloc model with its centrally planned economies. Non-aligned and newly independent countries in the "Third World" that did not want to go down either route had to find a third way. Taking inspiration from the fascist corporative states, the European post-war welfare states, and the Latin American corporativism implemented by Peron in Argentina and by Vargas in Brazil, a large number of developing countries adopted economic models that combined capitalism and enterprises with a strong state that managed and directed the economy through a variety of mechanisms.

In 1954, Sir Arthur Lewis published an article, "Development with Unlimited Supplies of Labor," in which he explained his theory of a dual-sector model of development, also called the *Lewis Model*. This was a highly influential theory of economic development, in particular because it was designed with "developing countries" in mind. Consequently, Lewis is regarded as one of the founders of developmental economics. The Lewis Model describes the growth of a developing economy as a process of replacing one sector with another: the subsistence sector (rural agriculture) with a capitalist sector (manufacturing and industry).

Another key figure in development theory was the American economist W.W. Rostow. The book he published in 1960, *The Stages of Economic Growth: A Non-Communist Manifesto* (titled in reference to Karl Marx's *Das Kapital* and *Communist Manifesto*), caused a great deal of controversy at the time but has since become a classic of development economics. In it, Rostow identifies the five stages necessary for what he calls a "traditional society" to attain an advanced level of development, which he describes as "the age of high mass consumption." The main criticism that was raised against his model was that it assumes that the stages of economic growth development will be the same for all countries, which fails to explain the variety of outcomes found in the real world.

The decade of the 1960s brought many changes, including changes in the way "development" was thought of. Several scholars began pointing out that there are other dimensions to development than just economic growth and industrialization, such as poverty and income distribution—an acknowledgement that, as Martin Mowforth writes in the first chapter of his forthcoming book, *The Violence of Development*, "there is more to development than can be counted in currency" (Mowforth, 2013).

Less Developed Countries—Perhaps born of this growing awareness and the increasingly stereotypical and pejorative associations of the term "Third World," during the 1960s, the UN came up with a more politically correct alternative, adopted by geography textbooks in the UK: less economically developed countries (LEDCs). The counterparts to the LEDCs were the MEDCs, or "more economically developed countries." The poorest countries in the world started to be referred to as "least developed countries," or LDCs. In 1971, the UN identified LDCs in its resolution 2768 (XXVI) according to the following criteria: 1) Low-income or poverty, based on the World Bank Atlas method (under $905 as three-year average GNI per capita); 2) The Human Assets Index (nutrition, health, education, literacy); and 3) The Economic Vulnerability Index (population, remoteness, export concentration and instability, liability to natural disasters, etc.). Most of Africa and some countries in Asia are considered LDCs.

Core and Periphery—During the 1950s and 1960s, a number of academics developed new economic perspectives called *Dependency Theory*. Linked to this theory are the concepts of "core" (or "center") and "periphery." Initially professor Paul Krugman of MIT, as well as Sean Shepley and Jonathan Wilmot (1995), described the core and periphery as a phenomenon created when firms and workers in a particular industry are concentrated in a specific geographical area because it is advantageous to them to cluster together, and "this results in densely populated industrial cores surrounded by relatively poor, sparsely populated, rural peripheries" (Shepley and Wilmot, 1995, p. 51). Over time, the Core and Periphery Model came to be used to describe, respectively, developed economies, mainly the Triad, and less developed economies.

Fourth World—In the 1970s, we see the rise of environmentalism and the emergence of the term "Fourth World." This was used to describe, on the one hand, tribal peoples and peoples without a corresponding nation-state (such as the Kurds, for example, and indigenous or nomadic populations) and, on the other hand, very poor sections of society in First World countries. In both cases, they are seen as "sub-populations" and are excluded or marginalized from mainstream global society.

The South—As of 1980, we also see the emergence of the terms "Global North" and "Global South," initially in response to the Brandt Report. This report was drawn up by an independent commission that had Willy Brandt (former German Chancellor) at its head. The aim of the Brandt Report was to assess the international development situation at that time and paint a clear picture of the enormous discrepancy that existed—and continues to exist—between "North" and "South." The Brandt Line, similar to Peter's Map, draws a line around the world at about 30° N latitude that passes between North and Central America, runs north of Africa and India, and swoops down under Australia and New Zealand, including them in the "North." In reality, any country that experiences sufficient economic growth and development can become part of the "Global North," irrespective of where they are located geographically.

The word "global" started being attached to the terms "North" and "South" routinely in the 1990s. "Global North" countries are usually those that have an HDI rating of 0.8 or more according to the latest UNDP reports. In 2005, this included 57 countries, the majority of which were located in the northern hemisphere. The "Global South" includes countries with medium-level HDI results (>0.8 but <0.5) and those with low HDI results (>0.5)

Most of the world's countries and population live in the "Global South," even though it has a much smaller proportion of the world's income. The majority of the countries in the "Global South" are located in Africa, Asia, and South and Central America.

The Triad—This term was coined by the Japanese writer Kenichi Ohmae to describe the concentration of economic activity in the three centers, the U.S., Western Europe, and Japan, during the 1980s. By the year 1980, the Triad generated over 70 percent of the world's manufacturing and more than 80 percent of its foreign investment. Since then, the Triad has declined in terms of its contribution to the world economy, though by 2013 it still contained many of the world's largest economies, such as the U.S., Japan, and Germany.

Newly Industrialized Countries, Asian Tigers, Asian Dragons—Four countries in Southeast Asia attracted international attention during the 1970s and 80s due to their exponential economic growth: Hong Kong, Singapore, South Korea, and Taiwan. Their rapid success was based on export-oriented manufacturing and strong public investments in education, infrastructure, and science and technology. They became known as the "Four Asian Tigers" or "Asian Dragons," which later gave rise to the name "Tiger Cub Economies" (used to describe other Asian economies following in their footsteps—namely, Indonesia, Malaysia, the Philippines, and Thailand). The original Four Asian Tigers were the first newly industrialized countries (or NICs), although they have now attained Human Development Index ratings equal to or greater than much of Europe and are seen as high-income economies by the World Bank and the IMF. Their model contrasted strongly with that of Latin American and African countries, which relied on state intervention with the objective to protect domestic industries as opposed to becoming competitive global exporters. Notably, in the 1950s the Asian Tigers had similar development indicators (e.g., literacy, life expectancy, GDP per capita) to those of an average Latin American country, such as Brazil and Mexico. By the late 1980s, the Tiger economies were catching up with the Triad in terms of educational attainments, while Latin American and African economies were falling behind. Their example illustrates the shortcomings of development models relying on closed economies, and also the importance of long-term investments in education, science and technology, and infrastructure that can support export-oriented industries.

Emerging Markets, Emerging Economies—In the 1980s, the terms "emerging market" and "emerging economy" began to circulate following the success of the early NICs. The former was coined in 1981 by Antoine van Agtmael, an economist then working for the World Bank. Emerging economies are economies that are growing rapidly in terms of size of the economy, wealth per capita, and population, and are starting to attract international investment.

Frontier Markets—Many other definitions have been used to qualify and distinguish groups of emerging markets. Several of them (ranging from BRICs to frontier markets) were developed by economists working in finance for a target audience of investors. As a result, their main focus was not the political system or level of development of a given country or market, but the potential returns and risks for investment. For instance, in 1992, Farida Khambata of International Finance Corporation coined the term "frontier markets" (Fowler, 2010). This refers to countries that have fast-growing economies but as yet very undeveloped markets, which represent both a high risk and high future potential for long-term investment. They usually have lower liquidity and market capitalization than other, more established emerging markets, such as the BRIC countries.

Standard & Poor's (S&P's) 2011 list of frontier markets includes Argentina, Croatia, Cyprus, Jordan, Kazakhstan, Kuwait, Nigeria, Oman, Pakistan, Panama, Qatar, U.A.E., and Ukraine, among others (S&P Select Frontier Factsheet, January 10, 2011, www.standardandpoors.com). Other countries that are often considered frontier markets are Botswana, Cote d'Ivoire, Ecuador, Estonia, Ghana, Jamaica, Kenya, Latvia, Lebanon, Lithuania, Mauritius, and Namibia. Regarding country classification, S&P's writes: "Country classification depends on a range of factors covering macroeconomic conditions, political stability, legal property rights and procedures, and trading and settlement processes and conditions. Further, the opinions and experiences of institutional investors matter" (S&P, 2011).

Transition Economies—As of 1991, after the collapse of the Soviet Union, most of the former Eastern bloc countries began a process of transition to change from their centrally planned economies to ones ruled by the so-called "free market" or "open market." In a market economy, prices are set according to demand, state-owned businesses are privatized, non-governmental financial institutions are established, a financial sector is created, private property rights are promoted, barriers to trade are reduced or removed, and the state is generally "rolled back." Those economies that were, have been, or are still going through this process of economic transition are called "transition economies."

At the start of the 1990s and in response to the collapse of the Soviet Union, the European Bank for Reconstruction and Development (EBRD) was founded in order to "help build a new, post–Cold War era in Central and Eastern Europe... [by fostering] market-oriented economies and the promotion of private and entrepreneurial initiative" (EBRD, 2013). The idea for the bank was first put forward by then French President François Mitterrand, in October 1989, and it officially opened its main office, in London, in April 1991. Today the bank is owned by 64 countries, as well as European Union and the European Investment Bank, and operates in more than 30 countries throughout Central Europe, Central Asia, and the Southern and Eastern Mediterranean. The bank's area of operation now includes Mongolia (entered in 2006) and Turkey (2009) as well as Egypt, Jordan, Kosovo, Morocco, and Tunisia (in 2012). The only country that no longer receives assistance from the EBRD because it is considered to no longer need it is the Czech Republic.

The EBRD is considered an expert body in managing and overseeing transitions from centrally planned economies to open-market economies. It has helped reform banking systems, liberalize prices, promote privatization, and create legal frameworks supporting private property rights. In addition, the bank provides loans for large-scale investments in both public and private sectors, such as modern infrastructure projects, normally financing up to 35 percent of total project cost. In this way, during the 1990s, the EBRD boosted many of the former Eastern bloc countries whose domestic capital alone would not have been sufficient to reconstruct and develop their economies as they have over the space of just a few decades.

All transition economies are also emerging economies. The transition economies of Central and Eastern Europe and Russia share a highly educated workforce, inherited from the investments in education made by former communist regimes. There are also notable differences among transition economies. Eastern and Central European countries—the majority of which are now members of the European Union—have achieved a better performance than other transition economies in terms of economic growth and improvement in living standards since the end of communism, largely thanks to better government policies.

Many of the ex–Soviet Republics, including Russia, have another factor in common: they have abundant natural resources, which they now export to the rest of the world. In terms of political systems, only China, Cuba, and Vietnam maintain a one-party political system, whereas the others are electoral democracies. Upon closer observation, some transition economies are ruled by "strong men," many with a Soviet past, who govern through long periods without much democratic alternation. This is only one of the symptoms of the fact that their economic and political institutions are still adapting to a different geopolitical context and economic model. For this reason, even if now they are fully capitalist and nominally democratic, most transition economies continue to be dubbed transition economies.

This also has important implications for the managers of Triad-based companies—the business environment of transition economies differs greatly from that of developed economies. As with all emerging markets, and a few developed economies, transition economies suffer from problems of accountability and transparency. The business environment can, in certain cases, be difficult for foreign companies. In theory, transition economies fully respect property rights and abide by the rules of capitalism. In practice, however, it is not uncommon for international firms to suffer from predatory practices, such as ad hoc regulations, or threats of expulsion and expropriation, in some transition economies.

G 20—In 1999, an international group was created called the Group of 33, made up of the world's 33 biggest national economies. This replaced the previous G22 and was in turn replaced by the current Group of 20 later the same year. The G20 was suggested by Canadian Prime Minister Paul Martin as a forum for economic and political cooperation and for promoting the stability of the international financial system. The G20's first meeting took place in December 1999. It is formed by the 19 leading world economies plus the European Union and collectively represents approximately 85 percent of the global economy (Thomas and Werdigier, 2009). The G20 gained importance after the 2008 Washington Summit and in 2009 declared that it was going to overtake the G8 as the world's principal economic council for industrialized nations.

The BRICS—Originally BRIC, this acronym BRICS was coined in 2001 by Goldman Sachs' chief economist Jim O'Neill to group together Brazil, Russia, India, and China. In 2010, the letter *S* was added to the acronym to include South Africa in the group. In 2006, the Dow Jones introduced the BRIC 50 Index, "a basket of 50 of the biggest companies listed on the stock markets of Brazil, Russia, India, and China. Initial market capitalization: US$446 billion." In 2006, the BRIC leaders held their first informal meeting on the sides of the 61st UN General Assembly, and in 2009, their first formal summit institutionalizing their forum, in Russia. Also in 2009, the BRIC countries marked a significant milestone when they successfully lobbied developed countries to "redistribute quotas and vote shares" within the World Bank and the IMF, giving them more of a voice in decision-making processes. BRIC leaders declared the G20 the world's number-one economic forum, overtaking the G8 (Hounshell, 2011).

The *Financial Times* writes: "O'Neill speculated that by 2041 (later revised to 2032) the BRIC economies would be richer than the six largest western economic powers" (Tett, 2010). His intuition about the future of the BRIC proved to be correct: China quickly surpassed Italy, France, the UK, Germany, and Japan, becoming the second economy in the world, while Brazil overtook both the UK and Italy in terms of total GDP. As of 2013, the BRICS account for about 20 percent of the world economy, more than a third of total GDP growth, and over 40 percent of its population. According to Goldman Sachs, the BRICS economies will overtake the U.S. economy in 2018. China is projected to replace the U.S. as the world's largest economy by 2020 and to be replaced, in turn, by India by 2050. According to GS Global ECS Research, 250 million people in the BRICS countries could join the "high income" class by 2025 (Goldman Sachs, 2008).

All its members qualify as "middle income" countries, with GNI per capita (measured at PPP) ranging from US$3,280 (India) to US$18,330 (Russia). Global GDP in 2011 was

US$69.97 trillion and the total GDP of the BRICS countries combined in the same year was US$13.9 trillion (World Bank, 2013). All of the BRICS but Russia have younger populations than the U.S., Europe, and Japan. They also have much lower GDP per capita, and less saturated consumer markets. The BRICS are well endowed with natural resources, especially in the case of Russia and Brazil. The BRICS are also home to some of the world's largest multinational corporations, as we explore in Chapter 8, "Multinationals Based in Emerging Markets: Features and Strategies." In 2012, China had 73 firms on the Fortune Global 500 list, compared with eight from India, eight from Brazil, seven from Russia, and none from South Africa (CNN Money Fortune 500, 2013). All the BRICS members have significant influence on global and regional economic and political affairs.

Beyond the convenience of grouping these countries together under one pithy acronym, the BRICS have in many ways more differences than similarities. For example, Russia and China share a past as command economies, where most resources were allocated by the state and private enterprises forbidden from operating in most sectors. Although the state played, and continues to play, an important role in the economies of Brazil and India as well, they have always been capitalist economies, which combine state-controlled economic assets with a diverse range of private businesses. In terms of demography, India and South Africa have the youngest populations in the group. Brazil and China are now reaping the benefits of having most of their population in its working age. China's low birth rates mean that soon it may change from being a country with a "young" population to one with an aging problem. Russia has very low birth rates, which mean that its population is likely to shrink between 2013 and 2030. The BRICS' industrialization, infrastructure, and institutions differ quite dramatically, as well as their overall levels of development. O'Neill pointed out that Brazil and Russia are both "natural resources-based economies" while China and India are rather "labor resource-based economies." Brazil is often seen as the future of agriculture, endowed with vast traits of fertile land, and globally competitive agribusinesses. Russia is seen as the future of the extractive industries and natural resource suppliers. India is often considered as the world's future intellectual workshop and new Silicon Valley, and China the world's manufacturing center. South Africa, Africa's largest economy, wields a great deal of regional influence, abundant natural resources, and has leading companies in mining and agribusiness. These generalizations, however, conceal a much more complex picture. Other than having one of the most competitive agriculture sectors in the world, Brazil is also rich in underwater oil, minerals, and has a strong manufacturing base. Russia is not only an exporter of oil and gas, it also has the most educated of the BRICS' populations and a still strong defense sector. China is not only a manufacturing powerhouse. It also has some natural resources, such as strategic rare minerals and coal, and a fast-growing software industry. India is also rich in coal, and has potential in many labor-intensive industries other than information technology services (for example, in jewelry).

The BRICS also share some characteristics, which justify the idea of grouping them together. Taking into account demography, GDP per head, natural resources, and the skills of their largest firms, the BRICS have the potential to continue growing and thus generate a yet higher share of the world economy.

N11—The "Next Eleven"—In 2005, Jim O'Neill again coined an acronym, this time the "Next Eleven" or N11 group. This comprised 11 countries that he believed had a strong potential of becoming the world's biggest economies, together with the BRICS, during the course of the twenty-first century. They are Bangladesh, Egypt, Indonesia, Iran, Mexico, Nigeria, Pakistan, Philippines, Turkey, South Korea, and Vietnam. This list was drawn up in a paper following on from O'Neill's 2003 report about the BRICS economies (O'Neill, 2011a). Both Mexico and South Korea are expected to outstrip many European countries by 2050 in terms of GDP per capita. In addition, the MIKT or MIST countries comprise a subset of the N11 that was created in 2011, also by Jim O'Neill (2011a). This grouping represents the four largest economies of the N11: Mexico, Indonesia, South Korea, and Turkey. (The *K* or *S* in the acronym stands for either "South" or "Korea.") Again, as for the BRICS, the N11 includes very different economies, ranging from South Korea, a developed economy in terms of income per capita, literacy achievements, life expectancy, and poverty, to Bangladesh, one of the poorest countries of the world. The N11 include resource-rich economies such as Nigeria and Iran, and resource-poor economies, such as Bangladesh. The idea behind the N11 is that they have a strong potential for growth given their demographics, past performance, and economic structure.

The diversity of this grouping has made the N11 a popular option for investors, as investing across a wide spectrum of countries mitigates risk and creates an attractive "basket." At one end of the spectrum, there is South Korea, which by most metrics, such as GDP per capita and the Human Development Index, is a developed economy. At the other end, there are economies as Pakistan and Bangladesh, which have incomes per capita more than ten times lower than South Korea. South Korea's peculiar feature is that, in spite of having already caught up with the Triad in terms of incomes and the sophistication of its economy, it continues to grow, driven by innovative manufacturing and engineering companies as Samsung, LG, and Hyundai. Whether and how far it is feasible that South Korea continues to sustain its growth, especially in light of potential tensions with North Korea, is an important question mark. Unlike the other members of the N11, South Korea has already "caught up"—it has already exhausted the easiest part of the cycle of economic growth, industrialization, urbanization, labor force education, and development. In fact, in many fields, such as education, it already scores higher than the

U.S. and most European economies. Its growth has made it similar to other rich economies also in terms of demographics—South Koreans live longer and have fewer children than they used to. As a result, South Korea has already exploited its "demographic dividend"—the period when most of the population forms part of the workforce. It is currently approaching the situation in the U.S., Europe, and Japan by having an increasingly large number of old people who depend on a shrinking workforce. Only if North Korea were integrated with the South could South Korea solve its demographic problem by incorporating over 20 million citizens that are, on average, younger. The dynamic economy of South Korea could easily accommodate the extra labor force, which would push low-skilled wages down, making its industries yet more competitive, while increasing the market for low-price products, ranging from food to basic consumer items such as toothpaste and beauty products. It seems unlikely at this point in time, however, that the political elite of North Korea is willing to accept economic reforms and become integrated in the world economy as China, Vietnam, and Myanmar have already done.

Turkey and Mexico are middle-income countries, with average GDP per capita of about ten times those of Bangladesh and Pakistan. They have diversified economic structures, a vibrant tourist industry, and a strong export-oriented manufacturing industry, especially in the car and textile sectors. They benefit from having free-trade agreements with some of the largest and richest economies in the world—the U.S. in the case of Mexico, and the European Union in the case of Turkey. They both export apparel, cars, and food to their richer neighbors.

Bangladesh and Pakistan have some of the lowest GDP per capita in the world, and rely mainly on labor-intensive manufacturing (for example, apparel and clothing production). Pakistan also has a very competitive export-oriented surgical instrument industry. Bangladesh is densely populated and often struck by natural disasters, whereas Pakistan is affected by political risk, particularly tensions across the border with India and Afghanistan, and armed attacks by insurgent groups.

Indonesia, Vietnam, and the Philippines are lower-middle-income economies with large populations and a strong growth record. Indonesia and Vietnam are strong exporters of agricultural products, the Philippines is a net exporter of outsourced business services, such as contact centers and information technology services. Vietnam is still ruled by the Communist party, and, like China, its economy is still dominated by a large number of state-owned corporations. Indonesia and the Philippines are democratic capitalist countries, the former being the most populous Muslim country, the latter the fourth most populous Catholic country. Indonesia and the Philippines have also suffered from violent attacks by armed groups, though to a much lesser extent than Pakistan.

Finally, Egypt, Nigeria, and Iran are middle-income countries, though in terms of economic structure, there is more divergence. Nigeria and Iran are energy exporters, with abundant oil and gas reserves. Egypt has a sophisticated economy, a large educated population, but a poor growth record. Iran has a relatively closed economy, which attracts very little foreign investment and exports—much less than it potentially could. Nigeria has a more open economy than Iran, and has been growing faster than Egypt, though it is very dependent on the performance of its extractive industries, which in turn depend on commodity prices. Nigeria also has a vibrant music and film industry, mainly concentrated in Lagos. In terms of risk, Iran is internally peaceful but the aggressive anti-Israel and anti-U.S. position of its government could eventually cause an international conflict. Nigeria has been strongly affected by armed violence by the Islamist group Boko Haram, among others. Frictions between the Muslim and Christian population of Nigeria could escalate and make it more unstable. Armed violence has also been sparked by the environmental contamination and consequent impoverishment of local populations caused by the oil industry. Egypt has gone through a democratic transition during the Arab Spring, deposing the despotic leader Mubarak. It is currently affected by political instability, protests, and potential frictions between its diverse religious groups.

Because the N11 countries have relatively young populations, they have an enormous potential for growth, especially among their burgeoning (and previously nonexistent) middle class. This is important because a large, young, and growing middle class will increase demand for consumer goods, creating strong consumer-driven economic growth at national, regional, and global levels. Indeed, potential for growth is the main reason behind the grouping N11. The combined GDP of the N11 countries for 2011 (measured at PPP) is US$5.36 trillion, thus contributing around 7.7 percent to global GDP (World Bank, 2013).

Jim O'Neill himself argues that it is time to find new names and economic groupings to effectively describe the world's changing reality and remain consistent in this dynamic setting. In an article published in Spring 2011, titled "Why we must stop talking about 'emerging markets,'" O'Neill writes: "It is my contention that most of the positive momentum behind the world economy is being driven from these 15 countries [N11 + BRIC], or at least by the majority of them. This is in turn affecting the lives of all of the world's 6.5bn citizens, not just those of their own people.... As a consequence, to describe many of these countries as "emerging markets" seems not only a bit inappropriate but quite possibly insulting." He suggests the term "Growth Economies," which has been used by Goldman Sachs since early 2010 "to describe... many of the world's most dynamic economies" (O'Neill, 2011b).

CIVETS—Colombia, Indonesia, Vietnam, Egypt, Turkey, and South Africa—The acronym was coined in 2008 by Robert Ward, Global Forecasting Director at the Economist Intelligence Unit. These are six emerging markets of particular interest to investors and international business due to their diverse, dynamic economies and their young and rapidly growing populations. Their aggregate population for 2011 is around 585.7 million, about 8 percent of the world's current population (Population Reference Bureau, 2013).

Current global GDP, according to the World Bank, stands at US$69.98 trillion and the combined GDP of the CIVETS countries is approximately US$2,827 billon. This means that the CIVETS together contribute around 4.04 percent of global GDP. Their national GDP ranges from US$846.83 billion to US$123.60 billion, with the order being as follows: Indonesia, Turkey, South Africa, Colombia, Egypt, and Vietnam. Turkey has the highest GNI per capita in the group, followed by South Africa, Colombia, Egypt, Indonesia, and Vietnam. The GNI per capita (PPP current international $) ranges from US$16,940 (Turkey) to US$3,250 (Vietnam). Significantly, Turkey's GNI per capita for 2011 was higher than that of either Brazil (US$11,420) or Mexico (US$15,390) (World Bank, 2013).

Again, the countries included are quite diverse, though the differences are less marked than within the N11 because the grouping does not include South Korea, which is an already emerged economy. South Africa, Indonesia, and Colombia are exporters of natural resource products, and have very dynamic extractive industries. Turkey, Vietnam, and South Africa are also manufacturing exporters, producing motorbikes, cars, and mechanical parts. There are many other differences across these economies. Indonesia, for example, has a much larger population than any other country in the group. Turkey has an economy closely integrated with that of the European Union, whereas South Africa is more integrated with African economies and Vietnam has strong trade and investment links with China. Vietnam, Turkey, Colombia, and Indonesia have all been growing fast during the last decades, while Egypt has not. In Vietnam, the state continues to control large shares of the economy through state-owned corporations. South Africa and Colombia have some of the highest income inequalities in the world, and high rates of armed criminal violence, especially when compared to other CIVETS. In short, the CIVETS are different in terms of not only their average incomes and economic structure—they also have different competitive strengths and structural weaknesses.

3G—In the year 2011, Willem Buiter and Ebrahim Rahbari of Citigroup coined the phrase "Global Growth Generators," or "3Gs," and claimed that BRICS, N11, and other economic groupings have now become obsolete. Their 3G index identified 11 economies as having a high potential for future profit and growth. In their paper "Global growth generators: Moving beyond emerging markets and BRICs," Buiter and Rahbari scorn the fashion for creating acronyms and go back to considering the fundamentals. They write:

> "We don't want 3G to join the list of patronizing acronyms or even the list of cute but uninformative and pointless ones (BRIC, Next Eleven, Seven Percent Club), although at one point we flirted with an intriguing/confusing label like the Magnificent Seven, the Nine Nazgûl, or The 39 Steps. Instead we view it as a question. What are the generators of global growth and profitable investment opportunities or the next 40 years?" (Buiter and Rahbari, 2011).

To attempt to answer this question, they have created their 3G index, using the following information: gross fixed domestic capital formation and gross domestic saving (both as a share of GDP), a measure of human capital (aggregating demographic, health, and educational achievement indexes), a measure of institutional quality, a measure of trade openness, and the initial level of per-capita income.

MIKT/MIST—Mexico, Indonesia, South Korea, Turkey—The acronym MIKT was again coined by Jim O'Neill of Goldman Sachs, in 2011, though it is sometimes referred to as MIST—the difference being that the former takes the *K* of "Korea" while the latter takes the *S* of "South." This group represents the four largest economies of the N11 and essentially constitutes a subset of the N11.

The combined GDP of these four countries comes to US$3,891.40 billion (or around US$3.9 trillion), which represents 5.56 percent of global GDP. Of the group, Mexico has the highest GDP at US$1,153.34 billion, followed by South Korea with US$1,116.25 billion, then Indonesia and Turkey last. Turkey has the lowest GDP of the four, with "only" US$774.98 billion, though it has the second highest GNI per capita (at current international $ PPP), at US$16,940. The country with the highest GNI per capita in the group is South Korea, at US$30,370. Mexico comes in third with US$15,390 and Indonesia last with just US$4,500 GNI per capita (World Bank, 2013).

The total population of the MIKT countries is 480.54 million, with each of them having quite different sizes. Indonesia is by far the largest, with 242.33 million, followed by Mexico with 114.79 million. Turkey comes next, with 73.64 million and South Korea last, with only 49.78 million. Together, the MIKT countries represent 6.89 percent of the total world population (World Bank, 2013). As with other groupings, there are notable differences among the four economies. South Korea has the average income per capita of a developed economy, and ranks better than all of the large developed economies in terms of education. South Korea has a population similar to that of Italy and Spain, which, furthermore, has ceased to grow fast. This factor limits the extent to which South Korea can become a much larger economy, unless the future brings some form of unification with the younger North Korea. Turkey and Mexico are mid-income economies, with younger populations than that of South Korea, much lower incomes per capita (about half of that of South Korea), and educational attainments that still lag behind those of the Triad. Their demographics and the fact that they are still poorer than South Korea, together with their larger populations, mean that they have the potential to become much larger economies than they currently are. Both Turkey and Mexico are strong manufacturing exporters, have a competitive tourist sector, and are well-integrated with the Triad (the former with the EU, the latter with the U.S.). Indonesia differs from all of the other countries. It is much poorer, with average incomes per capita that are about a third of those of Mexico and Turkey. It is much more populous than any of the other three, and its population is young and fast growing. It is also less integrated with the Triad, and its economy is more based on natural resource exports and manufacturing than any of the other three countries in this group. It also lags behind in terms of education, poverty, literacy, and life expectancy, which is consistent with the fact that it is a poorer economy.

Low Income, Mid Income—The World Bank classifies countries and geographic regions in income groups according to GNI per capita, using the World Bank Atlas method of calculation. The groups are low income, $1,025 or less; lower-middle income, $1,026–$4,035; upper-middle income, $4,036–$12,475; and high income, $12,476 or more (World Bank, 2013). These are sometimes referred to by their acronyms: LICs and MICs (low income countries and middle income countries, respectively). However, a number of development economists, such as Andy Sumner from the Institute of Development Studies, suggest that a more nuanced approach to global economic classification would paint a truer picture. In his working paper "Global Poverty and the New Bottom Billion: What if Three-quarters of the World's Poor Live in Middle-income Countries?," Sumner argues that the global poverty problem has changed because most of the world's poor—approximately 1.3 billon people—now live in MICs (Sumner, 2010). Sumner (2010) estimates that in 1990, some 93 percent of the world's poor lived in LICs, but by 2007–8 three-quarters were living in MICs and most of the remaining quarter in LICs, especially sub-Saharan Africa (World Bank, 2011). Poverty was traditionally assumed to be an LIC issue, but that is no longer the case.

This raises a number of important questions. In particular, Sumner and others ask whether it is still relevant and valid to use average national GNI per capita (at PPP) to measure countries' wealth, given that this can lead to simplistic classifications. In highly unequal societies, averaging out income per capita can be very misleading. Perhaps, they argue, it would be more advisable for economists to develop a new composite index, similar to the HDI, taking into account some of the different facets of a country's economy, institutional structures, political system, and wealth distribution, as well as its overall wealth. This would more accurately reflect the real complexity of the situation on the ground and the level of a country's "development." It would create less disparate groupings of countries under umbrella classifications that are often so broad as to be meaningless.

If, then, average per-capita income is no longer an acceptable measure of a country's wealth (or development) and if MICs can no longer really be considered middle income or LICs because the boundary between the two has become blurred by the "new bottom billion," this also has significant implications for business. Rather than being merely characterized by their poverty, "developing countries" or "emerging economies" are now rather characterized by their highly unequal societies. This extreme inequality in wealth distribution creates social tensions, violence, crime, insecurity, and even war, none of which is conducive to business, building good governance practice, or encouraging foreign investment.

Furthermore, if economic inequality were to be factored in when calculating a country's level of development and income bracket, this could lead to significant changes in how many countries are classified. For example, a country such as the USA, which has high social and economic inequality, would probably no longer rank highly among "developed" countries. This idea challenges our assumptions about what it means to be a "developed" or "developing" country or an NIC, transition economy, "emerging" or "frontier" market, LIC, MIC, or HIC.

As emerging economies grow and create an increasingly multipolar world, there is likely to be a shift in geopolitics and financial and economic power toward the "developing" world. This will have significant future implications for business, investment, corporate financing, and cross-border mergers and acquisitions. In addition, South-South foreign direct investment will rise, reducing the dependency of developing countries on developed for financing (World Bank, 2011).

It is clear that there is a need to alter economic labels and groupings as countries' situations change and in order to keep up with the dynamic nature of today's global economy. It will be interesting to see how, and if, some of the more successful groupings come together in the future to form a political force in keeping with their economic power, as the BRICS have done. Doing so may help these nations to achieve greater development by cooperating and acting together than they could have done alone. It will probably make emerging markets and companies from the "Global South" much less dependent than they currently are on the "Global North," its markets, and its financial institutions. And it will undoubtedly alter the face of international business, economics, and geopolitics, presenting us with the choice and the challenge to adapt to this changing world order.

Bibliography

Agtmael, van A. (2007). *The Emerging Markets Century: How a New Breed of World-Class Companies Is Overtaking the World.* New York: Scribner.

Arrighi, G. (2002). Global Capitalism and the Persistence of the North-South Divide. *Science & Society,* Vol. 65, No. 4.

Bozyk, P. (2006). Newly Industrialized Countries. *Globalization and the Transformation of Foreign Economic Policy.* Aldershot, UK: Ashgate Publishing.

Brandt Commission (1983). *Common crisis. North-South: Co-operation for world recovery.* Cambridge, Mass: MIT Press.

Brandt, W. (1980). North-South: A programme for survival. Report of the Independent on International Development Issues. London: Pan Books.

Brundtland, G. H. (1987). *Our Common Future: The World Commission on Environment and Development.* Oxford: Oxford University Press.

Buiter, W. and Rahbari, E. (2011). Global growth generators: Moving beyond emerging markets and BRICS. Centre for Economic Policy Research, Policy Insight No. 55 (April).

Castells, M. (2000). *End of Millennium, Vol. III—The Information Age: Economy, Society and Culture, Second Edition.* Oxford, UK: Wiley-Blackwell.

CNN Money Fortune 500, 2013. Accessed 4/30/2013 at http://money.cnn.com/magazines/fortune/global500/2012/full_list/.

EBRD 2013. History of the EBRD. Accessed 4/25/2013 at http://www.ebrd.com/pages/about/history.shtml.

Elliott, J. (2002). Development as improving human welfare and human rights. V. Desai and R. Potter (Eds.). The Companion to Development Studies. London: Arnold.

Esteva, G. (2009). Màs allà del desarrollo: la buena vida. *América Latina en movimiento,* Latin American Information Agency, Quito, Ecuador, No. 445 (June).

Fowler, H. (2010). Frontier Markets, the changing face of risk. Emerging Markets. Accessed 5/1/2013 at http://www.emergingmarkets.org/Article/2690705/FRONTIER-MARKETS-The-changing-face-of-risk.html.

Ghatak, S. (2003). *Introduction to Development Economics, Fourth Edition.* London: Routledge.

Goldman Sachs (2008). The expanding middle: the exploding world middle class and falling global inequality. Global Economics Paper 170. Accessed 4/25/2013 at GS Global ECS Research, Global Economics Paper 170 (July 7).

Havrylyshyn, O. and Wolf, T. (1999). Determinants of Growth in Transition Countries. *Finance & Development Magazine*, Vol. 36, No. 2. (June). International Monetary Fund.

Hettne, B. (1995). *Development Theory and the Three Worlds: Towards an International Political Economy of Development*. Harlow, UK: Longman.

Hounshell, B. (2011). BRICS—a short history. *Foreign Policy,* March–April 2011. Accessed 4/25/2013 at www.foreignpolicy.com/articles/2011/02/22/brics_a_short_history.

Kanbur, R. and Sumner, A. (2012). Poor countries or poor people? Development assistance and the new geography of global poverty. *Journal of International Development,* 24(6). pp. 686–695.

Knutsson, B. (2009). The Intellectual History of Development: Towards a Widening Potential Repertoire. *Perspectives*, No. 13, University of Göthenburg School of Global Studies (April).

Lacoste, Y. (1965). Géographie du sous-développement. Paris: Presses universitaires de France.

Mankiw, N. G. (2011). *Principles of Economics, Sixth Edition*. Cincinnati, Ohio, U.S.: South-Western.

Meadows, D. H., Meadows, D., Randers, J., and Behrens, W. W. (1972). The limits to growth: a report for The Club of Rome's project on the predicament of mankind. New York: Universe Books.

Mowforth, M. (2013). *The Violence of Development*. London: Pluto Press.

Mowforth, M. and Munt, I. (2009). Tourism and Sustainability: *Development, Globalisation and New Tourism in the Third World, Third Edition*. London: Routledge.

Myant, M. and Drahokoupil, J. (2010). *Transition Economies: Political Economy in Russia, Eastern Europe, and Central Asia*. New Jersey: Wiley-Blackwell.

Myrdal, G. (1957). *Economic Theory and Underdeveloped Regions*. London: Harper & Row.

Nederveen Pieterse, J. (2010). *Development Theory, Second Edition*. London: Sage.

Ohmae, K. (1985). *Triad Power: The Coming Shape of Global Competition*. Free Press.

O'Neill, J. (2011a). *The Growth Map. Economic Opportunity in the BRICs and Beyond.* London: Penguin Books.

O'Neill, J. (2011b). Why we must stop talking about emerging markets. Europe's World. Spring 2011. Accessed 5/01/2013 at www.europesworld.org/NewEnglish/Home_old/Article/tabid/191/ArticleType/articleview/ArticleID/21780/language/en-US/Default.aspx.

Perkins, J. (2006). *Confessions of an Economic Hitman*. London: Ebury Press.

Population Reference Bureau, 2013. Accessed 4/25/2013 at www.prb.org.

Ranis, G. (2004). Arthur Lewis' contribution to development thinking and policy. Center discussion paper No. 891 (August), Economic Growth Center, Yale University.

Rapley, J. (2004). *Globalization and Inequality.* Boulder, Colorado: Lynne Rienner.

Rapley, J. (2007). *Understanding Development: Theory and Practice in the Third World, Third Edition.* Boulder, Colorado: Lynne Rienner.

Rist, G. (1997). *The History of Development: From Western Origins to Global Faith.* London: Zed.

Rostow, W. W. (1990). *The Stages of Economic Growth: A Non-Communist Manifesto, Third Edition.* Cambridge, UK: Cambridge University Press.

S&P (2012). S&P Dow Jones Indices—Frontier Indices Methodology. Accessed 5/1/2013 at https://www.sp-indexdata.com/idpfiles/emdb/prc/active/methodology/methodology-sp-frontier.pdf.

Sachs, W. (2007). Upfront Reflections on 50 Years of Development. *Development, 50*(5).

Samir, A. (1976). Unequal Development: An Essay on the Social Formations of Peripheral Capitalism. *Monthly Review Press.* New York.

Sen, Amartya K. (1999). *Development as Freedom.* Oxford: Oxford University Press.

Shepley, S. and Wilmot, J. (1995). *Core vs. Periphery, in Behind the Myth of European Union: Prospects for Cohesion.* Amin and Tomaney (Eds.). London: Routledge.

Stiglitz, J. (2002). *Globalization and Its Discontents.* London: Penguin.

Sumner, A. (2010). Global Poverty and the New Bottom Billion: What if Three-quarters of the World's Poor Live in Middle-income Countries? IDS working paper (November).

Tanzi, V. (1999). Transition and the Changing Role of Government. *Finance & Development Magazine* (June), Vol. 36, No. 2. International Monetary Fund.

Tett, G. (2010). The story of the BRICS. *The Financial Times,* January 10. Accessed 4/25/2013 at http://www.ft.com/cms/s/0/112ca932-00ab-11df-ae8d-00144feabdc0.html#axzz2NQaySCdI.

The Economist (2010). Seeing the World Differently, June 10. Accessed 4/25/2013 at http://www.economist.com/node/16329442.

Thomas, L. Jr. and J. Werdigier (2009). No clear accord on stimulus by top industrial nations. *The New York Times,* March 14. Accessed 5/2/2013 at www.nytimes.com/2009/03/15/business/15global.html?pagewanted=all&_r=0.

Tomlinson, B. R. (2003). What Was the Third World. *Journal of Contemporary History, 38*(2). pp. 307–321.

UN (1948). Report of the Conference of FAO, Fourth Session. Washington D.C., November 15–29.

UN (1961). United Nations Development Decade: A programme for international economic cooperation. General Assembly Resolution 1710 (XVI). Retrieved from: http://www.un.org/documents/ga/res/16/ares16.htm.

UN (1970). International Strategy for the Second United Nations Development Decade. General Assembly Resolution 2626 (XXV). Retrieved from: http://www.un.org/documents/ga/res/25/ares25.htm.

UN (1974). Declaration on the Establishment of a New International Economic Order. General Assembly Resolution during its sixth special session 3201 (S-VI). Retrieved from http://www.un.org/ga/search/view_doc.asp?symbol=A/9559&Lang=E.

Waugh, D. (2000). "Manufacturing industries" and "World development." *Geography, An Integrated Approach, Third Edition.* Cheltenham, UK: Nelson Thornes.

World Bank (2002). Transition—The First Ten Years. Washington D.C.: World Bank.

World Bank (2011). Global Development Horizons 2011—Multipolarity: The New Global Economy. Washington D.C.: World Bank.

World Bank (2013). Country Profiles. Accessed 4/25/2013 at http://data.worldbank.org/data-catalog/country-profiles

Index

climate
geography, 135
location risk, 162
clothing, new middle class, 208
Coase/Williamson transaction cost
economics, 272
Coca-Cola, 17, 89, 245
Colombia, 38
call centers, 122
commodities, economic performance, 20
communal organization, 54
communication
disconnected markets, 200
infrastructure, 41
Communist bloc, 87
capitalism, Global Economy II (1948-1980),
90-91
Communist Party, China (one-child
policy), 33
Companhia de Mocambique, 84
Companhia Siderurgica Mannesmann, 90
comparative advantage, 57
competition, managing risk, 179
competitions, exports, 142
conflict zones, risk, 173
conglomerates, 254
diversified conglomerates, 257-258
Congo, 82
sovereignty versus property, 96
connectedness, 199
connections, World Wide Web, 201
Conrad, Joseph, 79
consumers
educating, 194
linking to, 190
Triad consumers, 8
consumption, 204
car ownership, 35
first-time buyers, 34-36
home country advantage, EMNEs (emerging
multinational enterprises), 246
imports, 142
replacement consumption, 204
contemporary EMNE theory, 282-271
core, 308

Core and Periphery Model, 308
corruption, 43
Corruption Perception Index, 43
Costa Rica, 25, 38
eco-tourism, 126
export platforms, 122
Global Economy I (1850-1914), 80-81
Intel, 137
Cote D'Ivoire, 45
country classification, 310
country level, International Business (IB)
theories (product life cycle), 272-273
country risk, 150-152
International Business theories, macroeconomic theory of FDI, 274
creative destruction, 3
creative economic policy making, 20
printing money, 22
credit
BoP (Base of the Pyramid), 233-234
diversified conglomerates, 257
crime, risk, 170-171
crimes against indigenous people, Africa,
83-84
CSAs (country-specific advantages), 269
Cuba
Global Economy I (1850-1914), 80
taxation levels, 39
currency
China, 21
Venezuela, 23
customer needs, embracing, 233
customers, targeting BoP, 223-224
cutting intermediaries, 225-226

D

Danone, 225
micro credit, 233
D'Arcy, William Knox, 86
Darfur, 261
De Beers Company, 84
debt crises, 23, 158
decreasing living standards, 63
DEI (Dutch East Indies), 77
Deli-Maatschappij, 78

internationalization, 260-263
- Arcelik, 262
- Bimbo, 261
- EMNEs, 262-263, 300
  - *China, 261*
- Geely, 262
- Haier, 262
- Lenovo, 262
- multinational companies, 262

internationalization theory, 277-278

Internet, 197-199

investment, home country advantage, 246

IPO (international public offering), 250

Iran, 316
- Global Economy II (1948-1980), 94

Italy, 16
- birth rates, 33
- corruption, 43
- country risk, 151

ITT, 94

J

Japan, 7, 16. *See also* Triad
- birth rates, 33
- Black Swans, 156
- education, 26
- electricity, 37
- lean production, 162
- stagnation, 8
- tsunami 2012, 162
  - *Toyota, 162*

Jardine Matheson, 74

Jersey Standard, 90, 93

Jobs, Steve, 250

J.P. Morgan, 80

jurisdiction, 53

K

Kaiser Aluminum, 96

Kazakhstan, 127

Keith, Minor Cooper, 80

Kennecott Copper Corporation, 165

Kennecott Mines Corporation, 80

key inputs, business, 172-174

Khambata, Farida, 310

Khanna, Tarun, 43

Khaw Soo Cheang, 78

Khrushchev, Nikita, 91

KickStart MoneyMaker Pressure Pump, 28

Kirzner, Israel, 69

Klein, Naomi, 185

Kojima/Ozawa theoretical model, 274

Kosygin, Alexei, 91

Krugman, Paul, 308

L

labor costs, export platforms, 119-120

land, geography, 133-136

languages
- disconnected markets, 200
- web pages, 199

Latin America
- Costa Rica, 80-81
- economic performance, 19
- electricity, 81
- Global Economy I (1850-1914), 78-82
- Guatemala, 80
- Peru, 79

lean production, Japan, 162

LEDCs (less economically developed countries), 308

legislation, market institutions, 42-45

Lenovo, internationalization, 262

Leopold II, 82

less economically developed countries (LEDCs), 308

Lewis, Sir Arthur, 307

Lewis Model, 307

Libya
- geography, 134
- Global Economy II (1948-1980), 93
- income inequality, 30
- unexpected risk, 157

LICs (low income countries), 319

life expectancy versus birth rates, 33

Likert Scale, 131

linking
- demand and supply. *See* demand and supply, linking
- to exclusive consumers, 190
- markets, 41-42

S

S. Pearson and Son, 86
sales, door-to-door sales, 226
Sany, 246
Sao Paulo Tramway, Light and Power Company, 82
Sao Tome, 84
Saudi Arabia, religion, 139
Sauvy, Alfred, 306
saving resources, 232-233
S.C. Johnson, 89
Schumpeter's response, 272
Schweppes, 92
Second World, 306
Second World War, 87
security, for businesses in risky areas, 172
sewage systems, 38
Shakti Women, 227
Shell, 85, 90
Shepley, Sean, 308
shelter, risk, 175
Shih, Stan, 240
shipping, 61
Siemens, 262
skilled labor, 137
Slim, Carlos, 249
smiling curve, 240
social proof, 234
Societe Generale de Belgique, 96
Societe Generale des Chemins, 82
Socony Vacuum, 93
SOEs (state-owned enterprises), 254-256
    China, 255
    EMNEs, 256
    India, 256
    minority-owned SOEs, 256
    Soviet Union, 254
    Venezuela, 256
solar panels, 232
Solow-Swan model, 26
sophisticated economies, 45-47
South, 308-309

South Korea, 314-315, 318-319
    economic performance, 19
    education, 26
sovereignty versus property, Global Economy II (1948-1980), 94-96
Soviet Union
    capitalism, 91
    fall of, 164
    SOEs, 254
Spain
    Americas, 78
    country risk, 151
specialization, 51, 53
specialized players, 254, 258-260
speed of change, markets, 124
sports, disconnected markets, 201
Standard Oil of California, 93
Starck, Phillip, 187
state-owned enterprises. *See* SOEs (state-owned enterprises)
statistics, risk, 170-171
stock market capitalization, 24
Stockholms Allmana Telefon (SAT), 82
strategic asset seeking, 269
strategic assets, 126-127
subsidies, 114
Sudan, 261
    natural resources, 302
Suez Canal, 25, 95
Sultan of Brunei, 77
Sumner, Andy, 319
super rich, 185
suppliers, targeting BoP, 223-224
supply and demand, linking
    cutting intermediaries, 225-226
    empowering the BoP, 226
    exploiting institutional voids, 226-229
    through infrastructure, 225
surplus, 51

T

Tabaksmaatschappij, 78
Taiwan, 63